Ethnicity and Violence

Routledge/Cañada Blanch Studies on Contemporary Spain

EDITED BY PAUL PRESTON AND SEBASTIAN BALFOUR
Cañada Blanch Centre for Contemporary Spanish Studies,
London School of Economics, U.K.

Also published in association with the
Cañada Blanch Centre:

Spain and the Great Powers
Edited by Sebastian Balfour and Paul
Preston

The Politics of Contemporary Spain
Edited by Sebastian Balfour

Ethnicity and Violence

The Case of Radical Basque Nationalism

Diego Muro

Routledge
Taylor & Francis Group
New York   London

Cañada Blanch Centre
for Contemporary
Spanish Studies

Routledge
Taylor & Francis Group
270 Madison Avenue
New York, NY 10016

Routledge
Taylor & Francis Group
2 Park Square
Milton Park, Abingdon
Oxon OX14 4RN

© 2008 by Diego Muro
Routledge is an imprint of Taylor & Francis Group, an Informa business

Printed in the United States of America on acid-free paper
10 9 8 7 6 5 4 3 2 1

International Standard Book Number-13: 978-0-415-39066-8 (Hardcover)

Library of Congress Cataloging-in-Publication Data

Ethnicity and violence : the case of radical Basque nationalism / Diego Muro.
    p. cm. -- (Routledge/Cañada Blanch studies on contemporary Spain ; 15)
    Includes bibliographical references and index.
    ISBN-13: 978-0-415-39066-8 (hardback : alk. paper)
    1. País Vasco (Spain)--History--Autonomy and independence movements. 2. Nationalism--Spain--País Vasco--History. 3. ETA (Organization)--History. I. Muro, Diego.

DP302.B55E84 2007
320.540946'6--dc22   2007010358

Visit the Taylor & Francis Web site at
http://www.taylorandfrancis.com

and the Routledge Web site at
http://www.routledge.com

To my parents

From the start, one discerns in it the (fruitful or calamitous) role taken, in the genesis of events, not by happiness but by the idea of happiness, an idea that explains — the Age of Iron being coextensive with history — why each epoch so eagerly invokes the Age of Gold. Suppose we put an end to such speculations: total stagnation would ensue. For we act only under the fascination of the impossible: which is to say that a society incapable of generating — and of dedicating itself to — a utopia is threatened with sclerosis and collapse.

Emile M. Cioran, *History and Utopia*

Blood and time are needed to make a nation.

Peixoto, ETA leader

Contents

Tables, Figures, Illustrations, and Map

ILLUSTRATIONS

MAP

Foreword

In a world afflicted by many different kinds of violent conflict, it is all the more important and urgent to analyse their forms and uncover, if possible, their causes. This is what Dr. Diego Muro's book seeks to do. By examining in depth one salient case of one all-important type of intractable conflict, he has illuminated some of the dark places of ethnic solidarities and nationalist ideologies. The originality of his analysis is revealed in the way in which a well-known and well-researched conflict, between the Basque military organisation, ETA, and the Spanish state both under dictatorship and democracy, is shown to be a development of mainstream Basque nationalism, and of the combination of its cultural and political components. For, although Dr. Muro's book gives us a firm chronological and political account of the development of Basque nationalism, it also analyses the basic elements from which not only Basque, but many nationalisms, have been forged; and it is this comparative reference that is particularly valuable for an understanding of the dynamics of nationalism.

What are these elements? There is, first, the role of ethnicity. Dr. Muro here follows Barth in emphasising the importance for Basques, and especially for Sabino Arana and other Basque nationalists, of the boundary-marking dimension of ethnic ties. While the content of Basque conceptions of their ethnic solidarity changed over the course of the twentieth century, the existence of a sharp boundary between Basques and foreigners, including immigrants, persisted throughout. Dr. Muro here gives an especially lucid account of the reasons for these changes, and the political advantages of these reinterpretations of ethnic difference. At the same time, he shows us why the belief in a deep continuity of the Basque nation, at once pure and chosen, and secluded from past invaders, has been the cornerstone of all kinds of Basque nationalist ideologies, including the most radical, and accounting for the strong strain of separatism. This belief is linked to a second element, the myth of a Golden Age. Developed by various Basque intellectuals from the sixteenth century onwards, this myth painted a glorious past age of splendour when the Basque nation was free and independent, preserving its own customs and institutions and its mountainous settlements and way of life. For Dr. Muro, it is not so much the content as the function of the myth that is crucial: he shows us that through this vision of the glorious past, Basque radical nationalists, in particular, have been able to inspire and mobilise their compatriots to self-sacrifice. This is because the vision contains a kernel of truth that resonates among the Basque population, constituting another element which radical Basque nationalism shares with many other nationalist movements.

At this point Dr. Muro introduces a third element, nostalgia. Again, this is a common feature of nationalisms, arising at the moment when the nation is felt to be in jeopardy or decline. In the Basque case, industrialisation and urbanisation brought many immigrants to the Basque provinces at the end of the nineteenth century, intruding into the formerly secluded and agrarian Basque society. Under the impulse of the Carlist Wars and the Romantic 'foralist' literary movement, Sabino Arana and his followers came to yearn for a restoration of the distant past, and evolved a radical nationalism that would return to the Basques their purity and independence and exclude Spaniards and foreigners. Nostalgia, therefore, far from being a sign of passivity and resignation, is essential to the sentiment and imagination of the nation and the visualisation of its heroic past and its restored future. Nostalgia, in turn, feeds, together with the myth of the Golden Age, a radical variety of nationalism. A novel feature of Dr. Muro's book is its insistence on the lineage of ETA in a long tradition of radical Basque nationalism. Radicals emerged early in the course of Basque nationalism, in opposition to mainstream moderate nationalism. This helps us to understand how and why violence was incorporated in the ideology of ETA, and how ultimately it became an end in itself.

Finally, there is the fact of violence itself. The key question here is why some nationalisms are predominantly peaceful, as occurred among the Czechs and Catalans, and others tend to resort to violence, as has been the case with the Irish and the Basques. While political and economic factors like Francoist repression are obviously significant, they are clearly inadequate; after all, the Catalans suffered the same degree of repression under Franco. We need also to consider the ways in which myths, memories, symbols and values of the respective ethnic communities are used to mobilise and direct their populations into radical solutions to perceived injustices. It is not just that a tradition of violence begets further violence, nor even that radical nationalisms are prone to violent conflict. Rather, the radical kind of nationalism must combine with an intense ethnic nostalgia for a Golden Age, in circumstances of decline and danger to the nation, if it is to precipitate violent actions. This, Diego Muro argues, is the lesson of radical Basque nationalism.

This is a powerful argument, one that is supported by a wealth of evidence and a clarity of exposition that will ensure a wide readership for Dr. Muro's book. Not only has his work opened up new avenues of research, it has revealed the benefits of marrying a modernist framework for the study of nationalism with an ethno-symbolist explanation of its character and appeal. Dr. Muro has provided a penetrating and balanced analysis of the political character of Basque radical nationalism and its various parties and organisations, but even more, a fertile and suggestive approach to the study of radical and violent nationalisms.

Anthony D. Smith
Professor Emeritus of Nationalism and Ethnicity
London School of Economics

Acknowledgements

This book is the result of five years of research, from 1999 to 2004, at the Department of Government at the London School of Economics and Political Science (LSE). As an intellectual journey, this work has not been done in solitude but in the company of many friends and colleagues which I gratefully acknowledge. Above all, I am indebted to both my supervisors, Anthony D. Smith and Mary Kaldor, for their constant guidance, sense of humour and wise counselling. I take pride in having had such prominent scholars as my mentors. I should also like to express my gratitude to colleagues that read chapters of this book and made valuable comments. In alphabetical order: Gregorio Alonso, Sebastian Balfour, Kerman Calvo, Daniele Conversi, José Luis de la Granja, William Douglass, Montserrat Guibernau, John Hutchinson, Gurútz Jáuregui, David Lowenthal, Josep Llobera, Ludger Mees, Alejandro Quiroga, John Sullivan, Kristina Zorita and the editors and anonymous reviewers for Routledge. I thank them all for their expert comments and apologise for the omissions and errors of this book which are, of course, my full responsibility.

This project has been made possible by the financial assistance provided by generous funding from the LSE and the Central Research Fund of the University of London. The Centre for Basque Studies of the University of Nevada and the Grice Hutchinson Bequest of King's College London also provided generous funding to do fieldwork. In the Basque Country, I received academic and personal support from individuals who made my research much more enjoyable. I am particularly grateful to Alfonso Pérez-Agote, José Manuel Mata, and Pedro Ibarra who helped me find my way in the University of the Basque Country and to the Flores-Chinchetru family, particularly Iratxe and Paco, who taught me much about Basque culture and society. In terms of sources, I am particularly thankful to Juan Jose Agirre from the Benedictine Convent of Lazkao who, at his own risk, has tirelessly collected material related to Radical Basque Nationalism for over forty years.

During my time at the LSE, I had the chance to be part of the most dynamic student-run organisation at the university: the Association for the

Study of Ethnicity and Nationalism (ASEN). I shared countless memorable moments with the other 'asenites' and contributed to making the LSE a research centre for nationalism studies. I must also thank the Cañada Blanch Centre for Hispanic Studies and its director, Paul Preston, for letting me use their library and attend the seminar on Spanish history and politics where I met leading Hispanists whom I can now count as my friends. Special thanks are due to Jerry Blaney, Helen Graham, Pilar Ortuño, Cristina Palomares, Isabelle Rohr, Francisco Romero, and Sandra Souto-Kustrin. I am also grateful to other LSE friends who made my life so much easier. Above all Sotiria Thedoropolou and Simon Usherwood with whom I have shared so many good moments. Finally, I thank the Archivo del Nacionalismo – Sabino Arana Fundación and Euskal Telebista (ETB) for their permission to reproduce the pictures and Hagai Katz from Ben-Gurion University for the map of the Basque Provinces.

I must also acknowledge the dedication of both my parents. I could not have completed this project without their continuous encouragement and support. To them, and to my brother Luis, I dedicate this work. Last but not least, I thank Esther, *la compañera de mi vida*, for making this long journey with me.

Diego Muro
King's College London

Diego Muro is Lecturer in European Studies at King's College London. He is an expert on nationalism and Spanish politics.

List of Political Terms and Organisations

Aberri Eguna   The day of the Basque fatherland celebrated on Easter Sunday.

Abertzale (Patriot)   The term is also used to refer to radical Basque nationalists.

Acción Nacionalista Vasca (ANV) (Basque Nationalist Action)   A political party founded in 1930 that combined nationalism with secular and socialist ideas. In 1978, it became one of the founding organisations of Herri Batasuna.

Alianza Popular (AP) (Popular Alliance)   Conservative party founded in 1976 by moderate Francoists. In 1989 José María Aznar became the leader of the party and renamed it to Partido Popular (PP).

Alternativa KAS   A five-point programme elaborated by ETA during the democratic transition as a basis to negotiate an end to violence between ETA and the Spanish government.

Batasuna (Unity)   A radical nationalist party which inherited the structure and support from Euskal Herritarrok and, previously, Herri Batasuna. It was banned by the Spanish Supreme Court in 2003.

Batua   A standardised and unified variety of the Basque language currently taught in schools.

Batzokia   Basque Nationalist Party's social centres. The *batzoki* usually hosts a bar or meeting place for members and sympathisers of the party. The first of these, the Euzkaldun Batzokija, was opened in 1894 in Bilbao.

Cipayo   Pejorative for the one who cooperates with a foreign ruler. It is mainly used against the Basque Autonomous Police (*Ertzaintza*).

Comisiones Obreras (CCOO) (Workers' Commissions)   A trade union created in the 1960s which had a crucial role in the democratic opposition against the Franco regime. Its main rival was the Unión General de Trabajadores (UGT).

Comunidad Autónoma Vasca (CAV) (Basque Autonomous Community)   One of seventeen autonomous communities created by the 1978 Constitution which covers the provinces of Bizkaia, Gipuzkoa and Araba.

Ekin (To do) A clandestine study group created in 1952 that became the embryo of ETA. Ekin is also the name KAS adopted in the late 1990s.

Elkarri (Among all of us) A Basque peace organisation born in 1992. Most of its members had been involved in the 1980s ecologist and *abertzale* protests against the Leitzaran Highway.

Ertzaintza A Basque police force of the Basque Autonomous Community revived in 1982. Basque police officers (*Ertzainas*) had already existed during the Second Republic (1930-1936).

Españolista A person who is in favor of centralism; derogatory term for Basques who do not support Basque nationalism or are not nationalist enough.

Etarra A member of ETA.

Euskadi (Basque Country) The name used for the Autonomous Basque Community which comprises the provinces of Araba, Bizkaia, and Gipuzkoa.

Euskadi Buru Batzar (EBB) National Executive Committee of the Basque Nationalist Party (PNV) made up of representatives of the seven Basque Provinces.

Euskadi Ta Askatasuna (ETA) (Basque Homeland and Freedom) An armed separatist group founded in 1959 which seeks an independent socialist state for the Basque homeland.

Euskara The Basque language, also known as Euskera.

Euskadiko Ezkerra (EE) (Basque Left) A coalition of parties which participated in the first Spanish elections in 1977 and dissolved in 1993 when they joined the PSOE. The main element of the coalition was Euskal Iraultzarako Alderdia (EIA), a party which had a prominent role in the disbanding of ETApm in 1982.

Euskaldun A Basque-speaker.

Euskal Herria (Basque Provinces) A cultural entity comprising all the Basque people. Euskal Herria has never existed as a political entity but it is often used to refer to the territory comprised by Euskadi, the Foral Community of Navarre and the French Basque Country.

Euskal Herritarrok (Basque Citizens) A radical nationalist party created in 1998 and successor to Herri Batasuna (HB), which had disappeared the previous year.

Eusko Alkartasuna (EA) (Basque Solidarity) A Basque nationalist party of social-democrat tendencies created after a split with the PNV in 1986.

Eusko Gudariak (Basque Soldiers) Anthem of the Basque army during the Spanish Civil War, currently adopted by ETA's sympathisers.

Eusko Jaurlaritza (Basque Government) Government of the Basque Autonomous Community (a.k.a. Euskadi or País Vasco).

Eusko Langileen Alkartasuna - Solidaridad de Obreros Vascos (ELA-STV) (Solidarity of Basque Workers) A Basque nationalist trade union created by the PNV in 1911. Since the 1980s it has been the dominant trade union in the Basque Country.

Euzkadi Neologism invented by Sabino Arana in 1896 to designate the seven Basque Provinces (also known as Euskal Herria).

Fuerismo (foralism) A movement in defence of the *fueros*, local charters and laws of medieval origin.

Gesto por la Paz (Gesture for Peace) A pioneer Basque peace organisation. Founded in 1987, its main demand was the disbandment of ETA.

Gora Ta Gora Official Basque anthem.

Grupos Antiterroristas de Liberacion (GAL) (Anti-Terrorist Liberation Groups) A secret paramilitary group funded by the Spanish state between 1983 and 1987 to carry out the 'dirty war' against ETA, which claimed a total of 27 deaths.

Grupos Y Youth groups made up of members of Jarrai which carried out street violence during the 1990s.

Gudari (Basque soldier) Name used for the soldiers who fought for the Basque government during the Spanish Civil War (1936-1939). ETA members also refer to themselves as *gudaris*.

Hegoalde (Southern Euskal Herria) The four Basque Provinces in Spanish territory (Bizkaia, Gipuzkoa, Araba and Navarre).

Herri Batasuna (HB) (Popular Unity) A radical nationalist party founded in 1978 and the political arm of ETA. HB changed its name to Euskal Herritarrok (those from Euskal Herria) in 1998 and to Batasuna in 2001.

Herriko Taberna Herri Batasuna's social centres, which usually hosted a bar or meeting place for members and sympathisers of the party.

Ikastola A school where all education is given in Euskara by *andereños* (women school teachers). Originally this was done on the margins of the Spanish education system but this has changed since the 1980s.

Ikurriña The Basque flag. It was designed by Luis and Sabino Arana in 1894 and modelled on the Union Jack.

Iparralde (Northern Euskal Herria) A name which applies to three Basque Provinces in southern France: Lapurdi, Zuberoa and Basse Navarre. Together with the territories south of the Pyrenees, also known as Hegoalde, Euskal Herria or the Basque Country is complete.

Izquierda Abertzale/Ezker Abertzalea (Nationalist Left) A term commonly used to designate radical Basque nationalism. It started to be used after ETA's Fifth Assembly in 1966-67.

Jaingoikoa Eta Lege-Zarra (JEL) (God and Fueros) The PNV's motto, created by Sabino Arana. The members of the PNV are known as *jelkides/jeltzales* or sympathisers of the JEL motto.

Jarrai (To continue)   A radical youth organisation linked to ETA. Founded in 1979, it was banned in 1999. Afterwards, Jarrai and the French organisation Gazteriak founded Haika and Segi which were also banned.

Kale borroka (Street Violence)   Small acts of violence perpetrated since the early 1990s by youth organisations with connections to ETA.

Koordinadora Abertzale Sozialista (KAS) (Socialist Patriotic Coordinator)   The political and coordination organ of ETA. KAS elaborated the 'KAS alternative' in 1976, a five-point programme that would form the basis of hypothetical political negotiations between ETA and the Spanish government.

Langile Abertzaleen Batzordeak (LAB) (Patriotic Workers Committee)   A trade union founded in 1975 with established links with KAS and the wider network of nationalist organisations.

Lehendakari   President of the Basque Government. The office of the president is known as *Lehendekaritza.*

Movimiento de Liberación Nacional Vasco (MLNV) (Basque Movement of National Liberation)   A self-named network of radical nationalist organisations founded in 1974. The most important members were the trade union LAB (Langile Abertzaleen Batzordeak), the political party Batasuna (previously called Euskal Herritarrok and Herri Batasuna) and the terrorist organisation ETA (Euskadi Ta Askatasuna), the undisputed leader of the movement.

Pacto of Ajuria Enea   A pact signed on 12 January 1988 by all Basque political parties with electoral representation (with the single exception of Herri Batasuna) rejecting terrorism as a 'means to determining' the political future of the Basque region.

Pact of Estella/Lizarra   A pact signed by all Basque nationalist parties (PNV, EA and EH) and Izquierda Unida on 12 September 1998 in the Navarrese town of Estella (Lizarra in Basque), in which they agreed to intensify the nation-building process by peaceful means.

Partido Nacionalista Vasco – Eusko Alderdi Jeltzalea (PNV-EAJ) (Basque Nationalist Party)   Basque party founded by Sabino Arana in 1895. The PNV is the dominant nationalist party in the Basque Country and has been in power since 1980. Its current leader is Josu Jon Imaz.

Partido Socialista de Euzkadi (PSE) (Basque Socialist Party)   Basque branch of the Spanish socialist party, the PSOE.

Pueblo Trabajador Vasco (PTV) (Basque Working People)   A term adopted by ETA in its Fifth Assembly (1966-67) to refer to the Basque nation in socialist terms.

Pyréenées-Atlantiques   The French administrative Department that includes the three Basque Provinces of Zuberoa, Lapurdi, and Behe Nafarroa.

Statute of Gernika   Statute of Autonomy for the Basque Country signed in October 1979.

Txakurra   This literally means 'dog'; pejorative for police forces.

Unión de Centro Democrático (UCD) (Union of the Democratic Centre)   An electoral coalition of parties which governed Spain between 1977 and 1982 and which had a crucial role in the political transition to democracy. Its leader was Adolfo Suárez.

Zutabe (Column)   ETA's internal periodical, published from the 1980s.

Zutik (Standing up)   ETA's internal periodical, published from the 1960s.

Zuzen (Direct)   ETA's internal periodical, published from the early 1980s.

The Basque Provinces

Bay of Biscay

Bearn

Bayonne

LABOURD

SOULE

Guernica

San Sebastian

St. Jean de Luz

Bilbao

Mauleon

VIZCAYA

Hernani

BASSE
NAVARRE

Tolosa

GUIPUZCOA

ALAVA

Pamplona

Vitoria

Castilla-
Leon

Estella

NAVARRA

Tafalla

La Rioja

Aragon

Tudela

N

There are seven Basque Provinces:
Vizcaya (Bizkaia in Basque), Álava
(Araba), Guipúzcoa (Gipuzkoa),
Navarra (Nafarroa), Labourd
(Lapurdi), Basse Navarre (Nafarroa
Behera) and Soule (Zuberoa). The
first four are in Spain and are divided
between the Basque Autonomous
Community (Euskadi) and the Foral
Community of Navarre. The three
French Basque provinces from the Pays
Basque comprise half of the depart-
ment of the Pyrénées-Atlantiques.
The seven Basque Provinces are also
known by the traditional national-
ist term Euzkadi or the cultural term
Euskal Herria, meaning country of
Basque speakers.

The Basque
Provinces

France

Portugal

Madrid

Spain

Lisbon

(c) 2006, Hagai Katz, ICTR

Map of the Basque Provinces

Introduction

It has been a long time now since Giovanni Sartori first warned about the proliferation of 'cat-dogs'. Talking about objects of study that do not exist, not some genetically engineered abnormality, the Italian political scientist pointed out how many scholars base their entire research agenda on imaginary creatures. In Sartori's story, the role of the archetypical scholar was performed by Mr Doe who, we were told, spent three years of research (and considerable funding) on studying the sound emitted by cat-dogs. One cannot be original, nowadays just with cats or just with dogs. After a good deal of fieldwork, Mr Doe consecutively rejected all his hypotheses on the sound they emitted (from 'bow wow' to 'meow meow') and brought to a stop his futile endeavour when he was told the simple truth, that cat-dogs do not exist.

The cat-dog stands as a clear metaphor for the kind of research a discipline will produce when it does not follow its own method. Unfortunately, and as if the laws of nature could be applied to the rest of the social sciences, these two-headed monsters have dangerously reproduced under the noses of scholars who, sometimes unknowingly, have allowed their own scientific errors to father even more cat-dogs. This epidemic of cat-dogs (or, worse, dog-bats) has created an uncanny fauna but also serious problems for most disciplines which are in serious need of mechanisms for control and prevention. One of the common errors is that of 'misclassification' which consisted in mislabelling the research object or ignoring established categories within the discipline and inventing self-tailored terminology. The other three fathers of cat-dogs are parochialism, degreeism and conceptual stretching (Sartori 1991: 247–249). The only way to prevent the birth of a new cat-dog, Sartori argued, was for scholars to follow the scientific method, accurately define their objects of study, establish clear classificatory orderings and observe methodological and linguistic discipline.

The field of nationalism is also prone to misclassification and, therefore, not immune to cat-dogs. As Walker Connor has pointed out, in this Alice-in-Wonderland world there is an inconsistent usage of key terms and nation usually means state, nation-state usually means multinational state, nationalism usually means loyalty to the state and ethnicity, regionalism and sub-nationalism among others usually mean loyalty to the nation (Connor 1994: 91, 111). The most persistent error of all is misusing the term 'nation' to refer to a state. And to avoid further confusion, I will follow Weber's classic definition of the state as 'a human community that (successfully) claims the monopoly of the legitimate use of physical force within a given territory' (Weber 1991: 78). Another well-known misclassification consists in equating nationalism with loyalty to the state rather than with loyalty to the nation. In an attempt to curb the procreation of even more cat-dogs, the following paragraphs will provide working definitions for nationalism and nation.

In recent decades, there has emerged a 'modernist' consensus on the processes that caused nationalism. According to this view, nationalism first appeared as a movement of political change in the aftermath of the French and American Revolutions and its emergence was inextricably linked to modern processes such as industrial capitalism, urbanisation, centralisation, state militarism and secularisation. When defined as a doctrine, nationalism was conceived and developed by European intellectuals but the impact of concepts such as 'popular sovereignty' and 'national self-determination' could be felt throughout the world. In Europe, the doctrine gave birth to the first system of states which was consolidated in the period from the Napoleonic Wars to the First World War and later expanded globally. In spite of this general consensus about the ideological and socio-political expressions of nationalism, scholars have not been able to come up with a universally accepted characterisation for this collective frame of reference. Ernest Gellner famously defined nationalism as a 'political principle, which holds that the political and the national unit should be congruent' whereas John Breuilly, another modernist, provides the working definition for this monograph when he emphasises the power-seeking character of nationalism when arguing that it is 'a political movement seeking or exercising state power and justifying such action with nationalist arguments' (Gellner 1983: 1; Breuilly 1993: 2).

The definition of 'the nation' as a historically formed community of people presents an even more complex issue. The question 'what is a nation?' posed over a century ago by the French theologian Ernest Renan, still awaits a satisfactory answer. As pointed out by Eric J. Hobsbawm, there are at least two ways of defining the elusive nation; one based on subjective characteristics and another on objective elements (Hobsbawm 1990: 5–7). Scholars that favour 'subjective' elements include Walker Connor, who captures the psychological essence of the nation when defining it as 'a group of people who believe they are ancestrally related' (Connor 1994: xi) or Benedict Anderson who emphasises the cultural element of the nation as 'an imagined political community' (Anderson 1983: 6). Nations are 'imagined' because they are too large for all of their members to know each other. Other authors believe it is not enough for a group of people to feel they are a nation and argue there must be a tangible set of characteristics or 'signs' of nationhood, such as language, religion, tradition, and a homeland. Most definitions of the nation, however, are eclectic and incorporate both subjective and objective elements. For example, this book will follow Anthony D. Smith in defining the nation as 'a named human community occupying a homeland, and having common myths and a shared history, a common public culture, a single economy and common rights and duties for all members' (Smith 2001: 13).

There may not be a commonly accepted definition of the nation but no one can deny the impact of nationalism on the modern world. At the root of wars, revolutions and political movements, few political ideologies have managed to incite individuals to sacrifice as nationalism does. Examples of heroism can be found throughout history and nowhere is the sacrifice more willing than when the nation is at stake. Wolfgang von Goethe first observed the phenomenon at the battle of Valmy in 1792, when a French citizen-army made of conscripts rose up to the battle cry of 'Vive la Nation', and successfully confronted the better equipped Prussian infantry troops (Brubaker 1996: 1). Since the French Revolutionary Wars, the example has been replicated countless times as citizens have willingly sacrificed for their nation as never before. And I do mean nation here, not state.

WHAT IS THE BASQUE CONFLICT?

Scholars of ethnic conflict are aware of the need to identify the constituent parts of a problem as a prerequisite for its resolution. Unfortunately, there is no overall agreement on what the Basque conflict is (Corcuera 1984). Some scholars argue that this is a conflict with roots in the nineteenth century when the Basque people first made a vigorous defence of their political sovereignty against French and Spanish attempts to impose uniformity (Letamendia 1994; Nuñez Astrain 1997, Bruni 1995). According to this view, the Basque resistance to these state policies of integration was led by various political forces, including 'foralists' and cultural patriots but since the end of the nineteenth century it has been dominated by nationalists (Jáuregui 2006: 239). Others argue that the Basque problem is ETA's violence in itself whereas there are others who argue that the problem is the multiple divisions among Basques over what their long-term national project should be (Burgo 1994; Escudero 1978). Finally, there are those who conclude that one should be talking about the Basque problems triggering once again the debate over what these might be (Roca 2002). None of these definitions is completely mistaken and, in fact, they are all partially right, but they fail to distinguish the different levels of analysis at which the Basque problem operates.

This book will take the view that the Basque problem is a two-level nationalist conflict. The first level is military and involves the Spanish government and ETA, who both want to hold exclusive control over the Basque territory. The state officially holds the monopoly of violence and ETA has challenged that authority on a regular basis since the 1960s. ETA's sustained violence was at its highest during the political transition to democracy in the late 1970s and has, since then, experienced a downward trend. The second level of the conflict is of a socio-political nature and opposes two coherent ideas of national belonging and territorial demarcation. Thus, Basque society is sharply polarised between a hegemonic Basque nationalist half which would like to see increasing autonomy, and maybe independence, and a Basque non-nationalist half which may be happy with more autonomy but wants to remain firmly integrated within Spain. As already pointed out by the anthropologist Marianne Heiberg, each of these opposing camps possesses a distinct interpretation of Basque history used to justify their political attitudes and demands. The nationalist half has traditionally argued that Basques have always been a people apart with a unique language and culture, and that its history is best understood as a continual struggle of a people to maintain their political autonomy and cultural heritage against the 'Spanish and French states'. The non-nationalist half denies some of these Basque particularities and sustains that in the context of the slow emergence and development of Spain, the King of Castile normally granted privileges known as *fueros* to regions (the Basque one included) in order to protect their economic and political peculiarities (Heiberg 1989). Moreover, they complain about the fact that nationalists manufacture 'Basque grievances' and ignore the desire of the numerous Basques who wish to remain firmly integrated within existing political structures. Other scholars prefer to deconstruct the above mentioned opposing camps into Basque-Basque vs. Spanish-Basque (Mansvelt Beck 2005) or, more crudely, between Basque nationalists vs. Spanish nationalists (Letamendia 1994). The main issue of contention is whether the so-called Basque non-nationalists are really unpatriotic citizens of a liberal kind or whether they are all Spanish nationalists in disguise.

The social cleavages that cut across the Basque people also divide the Basque party system which is characterised by its polarised pluralism (*pluralismo polarizado*).[1] The autonomous Basque parliament is clearly divided by the separatism-centralism cleavage giving way to two well-defined spaces of competition. Within each of these relatively stable blocks, there is a plurality of relevant parliamentary forces divided, once more, by the left-right spectrum. The high level of fractionalisation within this duality has remained a constant feature of the party system to date. Since 1979 the Basque nationalist section of the electorate has had three parties they could vote for: the Partido Nacionalista Vasco (PNV), a conservative catch-all party founded in 1898, Eusko Alkartasuna (EA), a social democrat and pro-independence party that split from the PNV in 1986, and, finally, the left-wing and anti-systemic Herri Batasuna (1978–1998), later renamed Euskal Herritarrok (1998–2001) and Batasuna (2001–2002), which advocated secession and radical socioeconomic policies. Similarly, Basque non-nationalists are extremely plural and have had three political options to choose from, each of them branches of state-wide parties: the PSOE branch in the Basque Country, the social democrats of the Partido Socialista de Euskadi — Euskadiko Ezkerra (PSE-EE), the Basque branch of the conservative Partido Popular (PP) and the communist federalists of Ezker Batua, an affiliate of the Izquierda Unida coalition.

Between 1980 and 1994 there was a high level of polarisation but the fracture between the two political blocs sharpened after the 1998 regional elections. These elections were preceded by the kidnapping and cold-blooded execution of a PP town councillor in the town of Ermua (Gipuzkoa) in July 1997. The killing of Miguel Angel Blanco provoked an overwhelming social response of indignation and gave rise to a new collective mindset, the so-called spirit of Ermua, which vehemently opposed ETA's violence. The political division between the two camps crystallised even further when the Basque nationalist parties (PNV, EA and HB) signed the 1998 Lizarra Agreement which was followed by an ETA truce of 439 days. The Lizarra document emphasised the political character of the conflict and urged the Basque patriotic bloc to adopt a secessionist agenda. As a response to the pan-nationalist strategy, the state-wide political parties PSOE and PP signed a political agreement (*Acuerdo por las libertades y contra el terrorismo*) which confirmed that an effective policy against ETA would be agreed by the two political forces. By the time the regional elections of 2001 and 2005 were held, the hegemonic position of Basque nationalism in the devolved autonomic institutions remained firm.

The two levels of the Basque conflict — military and socio-political — are clearly interdependent. Some actors are present on both levels whereas others are only present on one. For example, the Spanish party in government can influence outcomes in both arenas through its control of the state apparatus and its seats in the Basque parliament. Other actors, such as ETA, are constrained to one level yet they are able to influence what happens on the socio-political one. Following the logic of the 'two-level game', clever players can make moves on one level that will trigger realignment on other levels, 'enabling them to achieve otherwise unattainable objectives' (Putnam 1988: 434). It is then reasonable to expect that an eventual resolution of the Basque problems will take a two-level form and that actors will try to influence negotiations on both levels (Clark 1990a). It is important to mention that one should be cautious in establishing direct correlations between the social and political cleavages such as being a Basque nationalist *and* supporting ETA or not being Basque nationalist *and* supporting the Spanish state. Political allegiances and social identities are established in much more intricate ways. It can be argued though, that the use of violence has been increasingly being applied by ETA as a boundary maker, dividing those who see ETA as an indicator of a political problem or the problem in itself.

WHY DOES ETA KILL?

As Hannah Arendt has pointed out, violence 'stands in need of guidance and justification through the end it pursues' (Arendt 1970: 51). The function of any justificatory discourse is to provide individuals with a reason — at best, a good reason — that elucidates their engagement in a violent campaign. And the key issue here is time, because long-term politically motivated violence requires justification in a way that immediate acts of aggression or force do not.[2] Violent criminals or hostile mental patients can be aggressive and live at ease without a rationalisation of their actions but this is hardly the case for well-organised insurgencies. Armed groups come to a point when they have to decide whether instrumental violence, which Arendt defined as goal-directed, deliberate and designed to multiply the natural strength of the group, is the most appropriate course of action or not (Arendt 1970: 46). A violent organisation needs to provide its membership with a meaningful explanation of the costs and benefits of such a risky strategy. When faced with several courses of action, members of a group will usually support 'what they believe is likely to have the best overall outcome' (Elster 1989: 22).

The first reason why a group like ETA will adopt political violence is because such a tactic is *perceived* to be a rational action.[3] In this context, violence is seen as the best way of realising the group's objectives or, as choice theorists would put it, the most efficient means of maximising the group's utility (or list of preferences). The scholarly literature on political violence and terrorism seems to be in agreement when arguing that collective violent action is a wilful choice which can be justified using a string of plausible arguments. There are, of course, exceptions to this rule — from cold-blooded murder to unpredictable mutinies, riots or rebellions — but, on the whole, rational choice theory seems to be prevalent when analysing group violence.[4] From this perspective, violence is not mechanically determined by social structures but deliberately used by actors willing to influence a specific process or state of affairs. It is a means of acquiring some sort of 'power' or the capacity to achieve desired outcomes which can be of an economic, political, social, cultural but also symbolic nature. Closely related to the issue of being able 'to act', there is the capability of individuals to 'make a difference'. Individuals are more likely to contribute to a group effort when, in spite of the constraints, it involves the sense of transforming social reality in a positive way. For example, contributing to the defence of one's nation from a foreign oppressor is usually seen as a more righteous cause than building an empire and exploiting foreign lands. Personal sacrifice will only come about if it is useful and has the power of personal and/or collective redemption. The need to see violence as a truthful and legitimate act is explained by the fact that, at the core of sacrifice, one can usually find the idea of progress. Unfortunately, any inspiring scheme is very soon corrupted by the everyday pursue of destruction. Whether it is an act of self-immolation or an act of defence, willing sacrifice is usually performed by individuals who see it as a legitimate response to dysfunctional social structures. According to the first generation of ETA members (*etarras*), violence was the only effective means left of fighting those in positions of power. Following the teachings of the founder of the Basque nationalist movement, Sabino Arana, ETA argued their homeland was suffering under the authoritarian regime of General Francisco Franco and needed to break free. As Gurutz Jáuregui (1981) has put it:

> The ETA phenomenon is the result of two factors: the nationalist ideology of Sabino Arana and Francoism. It needs to be pointed out that ETA cannot be understood without reference to these two aspects: the nationalism of Arana, whose key idea is to consider Euskadi an occupied country, and Francoism, which makes that occupation real. (460)

The second reason why ETA members are willing to sacrifice for their nation is because violence contributes to ascertaining Basque ethnicity. The actions of ETA (*ekintzak*) help achieve the necessary social and political context in which Basques can become independent (Ibarra 1989; Sánchez-Cuenca 2001). ETA has long abandoned the idea that the Spanish state will surrender and will grant independence to the Basque homeland. Instead, ETA has become a politicisation agent whose main goal is to create a *truly* nationalist community that works actively towards independence and violence is the very medium that will achieve such freedom or emancipation. Within this subculture, the use of disciplined violence provides an immediate cosmology, a socially constructed narrative that establishes who is a devout member of the ethnic group and who is a hostile opponent. However, the full destructive potential of ETA is rarely observed. As pointed out by Ignacio Sánchez-Cuenca, bombs are not usually used to destroy schools or hospitals and, by and large, ETA does not kill people randomly or indiscriminately. The reason for such self-restraint in the use of lethal power is the armed group's need to minimise the use of its limited resources (weaponry, funding, information, militants, etc.) while maintaining some degree of popular support (who may disapprove of indiscriminate attacks against civilians) (Sánchez-Cuenca 2004: 2 & 18). ETA's radical nation-building has been best summarised by one of its leaders, Peixoto, who argued that a nation can only be made with 'blood and time', not with a 'decree law'.[5] From this perspective, the right to self-determination is not a natural right of every national group, it is a right that needs to be acquired by circumventing the democratic political process. As one of the earliest syntheses of ETA's ideology explained, the independence of Ireland, Israel and Cyprus had not been achieved through the help of an external agent but through the sacrifice of their nationalist youth.[6] Or as Machiavelli put it: 'all armed prophets succeed whereas unarmed ones fail' (Machiavelli 1988: 21). In this framework of mind, ETA is the vanguard, the charismatic army of a stateless nation that aims to achieve what other European nations have done in the past: become a nation-state.

The third reason why ETA continues to use violence is because it reinforces the internal cohesion of the radical community. In the long run, violence creates committed activists with a sense of duty. And nowhere is that camaraderie and joint effort more intense than in the line of fire. As Anthony D. Smith has pointed out: 'in a crisis, in the heat of battle, old divisions are laid aside, and the nationalist dream of ethnic fraternity becomes a momentary reality' (Smith 2004: 158). Moreover, as the quote by Peixoto suggests, personal sacrifice inspires a joint effort in the members of the nation in an intoxicating cycle of strikes and acts of revenge. As the first ETA members found out during the 1960s their clandestine violent actions were often followed by indiscriminate state repression which would, in turn, be followed by another daring action by ETA. This came to be known as the spiral of action-repression-action.

To sum up what has been said above, ETA violence can be accounted for by three factors: (1) Political violence is seen by radical nationalists as a rational, legitimate and necessary course of action. The key point here is that in order to sustain a long-term campaign of political violence, the group needs to have a justifying discourse and to be able to convince its members that the tactic is contributing to achieving the desired results. As it is the case with any successful national narrative, individual experiences of violence need to be integrated in a wider communal story of national suffering and potential redemption. If there is a continuous disagreement between the individual and the collective, the group's discourse fails to be effective and needs to be revisited; (2) Political violence is useful in reinforcing Basque ethnicity. The current cycle of ETA violence is seen by radicals as the last stage in the long-term conflict opposing Basques and Spaniards. This understanding of history and the need to glorify past sacrifices makes the use of political violence a tactic, strategic and moral need. From the point of view of a radical nationalist there is a lineage of Basque soldiers that goes back to the alleged defeat of Charlemagne and who have always fought the foreign invader. Ethnicity and violence are almost interchangeable conflict markers as *real* Basqueness is defined by membership and active support of the radical community; and (3) Political violence increases the internal cohesion of the radical nationalist community. Once the spiral of violence has started there are great obstacles for the membership of an organisation to change their mind about the use of physical force. Some young Basques have willingly joined ETA for decades. Whether they join for patriotism, love of adventure, to prove one's manliness, for social advancement, or in search of camaraderie, their arrest or death is inserted in a grand narrative whereby the nation is energised and the hero is forever remembered for fulfilling his duty. Police actions and judicial initiatives are also perceived by radical nationalists as yet another sign of Spanish oppression. With such a cycle in motion, there are great obstacles for the members of the community to reconsider the use of violence and come to the conclusion that past sacrifices were worthless and ineffective.

WHAT IS RADICAL BASQUE NATIONALISM?

Scholars have often approached the Basque problem by providing exhaustive accounts of ETA.[7] This trend has produced an important and detailed historiography about the ideological and strategic evolution of the organisation through its internal debates and numerous splits. However, as David E. Apter has pointed out, 'people do not commit political violence without a discourse' (Apter 1997: 2). The ideology that provides the paramilitaries with such a discourse is radical Basque nationalism, a term which has been used to describe three different stages and factions in the history of Basque nationalism:

1. *Radical as ethnicist*. Basque nationalism emerged in Bilbao at the end of the nineteenth century within the context of rapid social and industrial transformation. Its first followers mostly came from the urban lower middle classes, who had been moved to the periphery of society by the emerging financial and industrial oligarchy, and witnessed how their world was being turned upside down by forces beyond their control. As new waves of immigrant workers settled and the social structure of the city changed, these traditionalist native elites became uneasy of the Castilian-speaking immigrants. The founder of Basque nationalism, Sabino Arana, echoed these petty bourgeoisie feelings of rejection and developed a nationalist discourse and a successful mobilisation strategy which yearned for the medieval local statutes or *fueros* and established a fundamental opposition between all things Basque and Spanish. He described immigration as the latest attempt to colonise the Basques and discussed at length the immoral nature of the newcomer. Following from this analysis, Arana articulated a secessionist political programme based on the expulsion of the 'occupier', the rejection of everything Spanish, and the maintenance of a mythical Basque racial purity. One of the key elements of this radical nationalism was the use of the Basque language as an ethnic boundary, not as a mechanism of integration, which reinforced the division between the Basque nationalist militants and the non-nationalist outsiders.
2. *Radical as separatist*. From the beginning of the twentieth century, a contradiction between ideological purity and strategic realism tore apart the Basque Nationalist Party (PNV). Between 1895 and 1936 there was a group of 'radicals' who opposed the 'moderates' in control

of Arana's party. The radicals were separatists and believed they were defending the 'doctrinal purity' of the party against the political pragmatism of the moderates which were bankrolled by the Basque financial-industrial bourgeoisie. The radical and moderate wings of the PNV developed their own political parties in the period between 1921 and 1930. By the Second Republic (1931–1936), however, a new organisation had come into being: Basque Nationalist Action (*Acción Nacionalista Vasca* — ANV) which presented a left-wing and nationalist alternative to the conservative PNV. The figure of Eli Gallastegi and the *aberrianos* were later celebrated by radical nationalists during Francoism as key historical precedents.

3. *Radical as violent.* The expression 'radical Basque nationalism' has also been used to describe the political ideology and movement developed by the first ETA members since the 1950s. More specifically, the Basque Movement of National Liberation (*Movimiento de Liberación Nacional Vasco* — MLNV), a self-named network of organisations founded in 1974. This complex system is informally known as the 'patriotic left' (*izquierda abertzale*) and it is made up of a number of interconnected political organisations, social agents and NGOs with interests in the fields of feminism, environmentalism, internationalism, Basque culture, youth, students and prisoner's rights. The most important members are the trade union LAB (Langile Abertzaleen Batzordeak), the political party Batasuna (previously called Euskal Herritarrok and Herri Batasuna) and the armed group ETA (Euskadi Ta Askatasuna), the undisputed leader of the movement. The key characteristic of all the satellite organisations is their ideological and strategic dependency on ETA, which they follow as the forerunner of the movement. ETA sets the violent means to achieve the final goal (an independent Basque socialist state) but, more importantly, it establishes a link between ethnicity and violence for the members of the radical community. According to ETA, Basqueness is derived pre-eminently from active participation in the liturgy of national struggle.[8]

The key point is that there has been an ideological and, sometimes, organisational continuity between these three radical conceptions of Basque nationalism. Each stage of radical Basque nationalism stands as unique and historically determined yet it provides an important guiding model for the next generation in the form of commonly agreed historical truths. The pivots on which every one of the radical Basque nationalisms were based evolved through time in accordance to changing social, economic and political contexts. In fact, it is not uncommon for the building blocks of political ideologies to evolve, as has been observed in relation to the changing core values of Basque nationalism. According to Daniele

Conversi, the early nationalism of Sabino Arana (1865–1903) was based on the key idea of race but later formulations gradually incorporated non-ascriptive criteria such as language because it provided better chances of incorporating Spanish immigrants into the national community (Conversi 1990: 63). Although each of the three radical Basque nationalisms were particular to a socio-political context they reinforced each other by providing a steady connection to the past. And that link stood as evidence for two things that were crucial for radical nationalists: (1) that there was a long genealogy of true patriots of which they are the latest example; and (2) that the Basque willingness to fight stands as authentication that a historical conflict with Spain exists.

The latest ideological adaptation of radical Basque nationalism is worth examining because of its symbiosis with a violent organisation, but also because it combines a nostalgic view of the past (typical of previous radical nationalisms) with a revolutionary programme of action that aims to restore the characteristics that make Basques ethnically unique: language, *fueros*, democratic credentials, millenarian independence and so on. The interdependency of both ETA and the MLNV can be seen as two sides of the same coin. On the one hand, the MLNV is the main source of support and legitimacy to ETA's violent campaign and provides the ideal entry point for new recruits to this radical nationalist community. As it will later be shown, the MLNV argues that all their struggles (same-sex unions, removal of nuclear plants, refusal to do military service, drug prevention, etc) are part of a wider problem: the lack of a Basque state that guarantees their individual liberties. ETA, on the other hand, provides all these organisations with leadership and examples of individual commitment and group mobilisation. This mutual interdependence is reinforced by the existence of a common goal: to promote a narrative of Spanish oppression and Basque suffering that generates mass nationalist action. And the role of ETA is to provide a heroic example of national struggle and sacrifice. Violence is not only a means to an end, it has also become an end in itself as it allows the movement to stay united and move forward.

SOURCES AND TERMINOLOGY

In terms of sources, this study has been made possible by the great number of primary sources collected at the *Archivo del Monasterio de los Benedictinos de Lazkao*, which holds internal documents, pamphlets and posters of various Basque nationalist forces during Francoism and democracy. This archive was particularly useful when researching ETA, Herri Batasuna, Jarrai and LAB. The archive has been painstakingly compiled single-handedly by the librarian Father Agirre who started collecting this compromising material during Francoism. A catalogue which will allow researchers to work much more comfortably in the future is currently being compiled. Further primary and secondary sources were found at the following institutions in Spain: the PNV's Archivo Histórico del Nacionalismo Vasco in Artea (Biscay), the Biblioteca y Hemeroteca de la Diputación de Vizcaya (Bilbao), the Koldo Mitxelena Kulturunea (San Sebastián), the Library of the Universidad del País Vasco (UPV) in Leioa (Biscay), the Arxiu del Pavelló de la República, the newspaper library at the Universitat Autònoma de Barcelona (UAB), the Hemeroteca Municipal de Madrid, the Centro de Estudios Avanzados en Ciencias Sociales (CEACS) and the Biblioteca Nacional, also in Madrid. In the United States, use was made of the excellent library of the Centre for Basque Studies at the University of Nevada, Reno. In Britain numerous visits were made to the British Library, the Public Record Office (PRO) and the libraries of the London School of Economics (LSE) and King's College, London.

In the absence of politically neutral terminologies it is also important to clarify that a variety of languages are used in this monograph. Three languages are spoken in the Basque Provinces: Spanish, French and the Basque. Hence, most names can be found in two different languages and sometimes even three. Choosing one of the languages and not another is widely understood as taking a political stance and I have chosen the English names where possible. Hence, I talk about Biscay, Navarre, the Basque Country, Spain and so on. Where this has not been possible, I have chosen the Basque name (Araba, Gipuzkoa, Gernika, etc.) and in a few cases I have chosen the more familiar or commonly used terms in Spanish. For example, I have preferred to talk about Pamplona (rather than Iruñea), Bilbao (rather than Bilbo) and San Sebastián (instead of Donostia). Although this might be interpreted as lack of consistency it shows yet another aspect of the complexity and fragmentation of the Basque Provinces.

Finding a name for the Basque nation is a very telling example of the aforementioned problem. The main reason for this being that there are conflicting views on *what* territories constitute the Basque homeland. Most people would consider the Basque Autonomous Community (BAC) as the main building block (if not the only one) of the Basque nation. Many others would also include the Foral Community of Navarre in that demarcation, and, finally, a few more would also include the French Pays Basque in their geopolitical vision. Here I use the term 'Basque Provinces' to refer to the geographical extent of Euskal Herria (a cultural term that can be roughly translated as 'Country of the Basque Speakers'). The more traditional Basque nationalists, on the other hand, would prefer to name the seven provinces with the term Euzkadi, a neologism invented by Sabino Arana to encapsulate the seven-in-one (*zazpiak bat*). When talking about the Basque Country (or Euskadi, with an 's'), I refer only to the three provinces of Araba, Biscay and Gipuzkoa, and not to the Foral Community of Navarre.

OUTLINE OF THE BOOK

This book is a genealogy of radical Basque nationalism and the means by which this complex, often violent, political movement has reinforced Basque ethnicity. The monograph deals with the origins of the Basque problem and the reasons why the conflict has been reproduced. The book will argue that the use of politically motivated violence has been justified by radical Basque nationalist elites with a narrative that combines the loss of an idealised past with the urgent need to regain the qualities that made that earlier period unique. Let me offer here a short summary of the organisation of the book.

All nationalist movements can identify a point in time when their nation was an example of virtue and goodness. These glorious pasts are usually remembered in state-led ceremonies or spontaneous popular celebrations in order to draw political conclusions from the ancestors. However, in no other nationalism does the yearning for the past take a more central stage than in the Basque case. Chapter 1 introduces the myth of the Basque Golden Age as one of the crucial elements of this nationalism and defines it as a body of literature characterised by an idealisation of Basque ethnicity. A mixture of historical facts and legendary elaboration, the constitutive elements of the cultural myth portray an epoch characterised by great prosperity and happiness where Basques were virtuous, pure and authentic. The myth was born and reproduced between the sixteenth and eighteenth centuries and was decisively taken up by Basque romantics and nationalists who enlarged it during the nineteenth century. The body of mythical narratives is highly significant as it became a pre-modern vehicle of ethnic identity for Basque reading elites. The core function of the myth was to contrast the contemporary situation (usually characterised by decline) with an epic time of splendour which took different forms: from a racially pure Arcadian past to a sanctimonious devotion to the Christian faith or national sovereignty defended by heroic sacrifices. In spite of its changing nature, and its combination of facts and fiction, the pre-nationalist myth powerfully resonated among some Basques who perceived its genuine and meaningful qualities. Fully aware of the resonance of the myth, Basque nationalists incorporated elements of the story into their tailored-made historical constructs in order to favour popular mobilisation. Crucially, the people and the nationalist elites themselves probably perceived the myth as authentic.

Chapter 2 examines how Sabino Arana provided a line of continuity with previous advocates of Basque ethnicity by integrating pre-existent foralist and Carlist ideas into his programme. His nationalism mixed well-known elements such as Catholicism, traditionalism and agrarian romanticism together with new elements such as a nationalist sense of history and the celebration of the unique character of the Basque 'race' and language. The resulting nationalism was both backward looking and nostalgic about a lost past but also politically active and forward looking and aimed at providing a new political identity among the previously unpoliticised. The petty bourgeoisie of Bilbao, which felt displaced by the modernisation process, soon identified with this isolationist programme which advocated the reinstating of the charters known as *fueros* together with the expulsion of all 'exotic' and 'anti-Basque' elements. The programme of national affirmation was suitably furnished by Arana with the necessary nationalist trappings such as the flag (ikurriña), the anthem (Gora ta Gora), a neologism for the homeland (Euzkadi), and national festivities. By the end of Arana's life, Basque nationalism had become so successful that his followers worshipped him as a sort of Messiah. His authority within the political religion he created was absolute and allowed him to maintain internal coherence by personally solving any internal disputes associated with the expansion of the national movement.

Chapter 3 describes the early decades of the twentieth century as years of steady organisational growth for the PNV. Basque nationalism first originated in Biscay and successfully spread to the provinces of Araba, Gipuzkoa and Navarre although with considerably less success on French-Basque soil. On top of its geographical growth, the movement also managed to expand vertically penetrating all areas of Basque society. The strategy of moving beyond party politics gave birth to a network of organisations covering all areas of culture and leisure including youth groups, women's organisations, traditional dance, theatre, and football groups. The most important of those was the trade union Eusko Langileen Alkartasuna — Solidaridad de Obreros Vascos (ELA-SOV) with which the nationalist movement reached the working-class. After the traumatic loss of the last Spanish colonies in 1898, the nationalist ideology attracted the interest and financial support of the middle and upper layers of Basque society who gradually abandoned the Spanish national project and started to see in the PNV a suitable mechanism to channel their interests. Consequently, the PNV had to strike a difficult balance between its separatist core and its newly adopted autonomist agenda. This calculated ambivalence was not always possible and led the party to defend both autonomy and independence, sometimes simultaneously. After the death of Arana in 1903, the PNV cadres founded it difficult to maintain an equilibrium between pragmatism and dogmatism and the party split into two branches. The moderates were backed by the local industrial oligarchy whereas the radicals were uncompromising followers of Arana who openly advocated the secession of the Basque Country from Spain. This trend evolved into different forms after 1921 and reunited with the PNV in 1930 after the proclamation of the Second Republic which provided the Basque Country with its first statute of autonomy in 1936. The autonomous community of Euskadi was short-lived and it fell to the hands of the rebel side during the Spanish Civil War. In the early years of Francoism the PNV entered a period of paralysis due to the Francoist campaign of repression and to the fact that most of its leaders were in exile.

The first three chapters establish that the origins of radical Basque nationalism are to be found within the Basque Nationalist Party (PNV) whereas chapter 4 describes how, in the absence of competitive pluralist politics that characterised Francoism, a new generation of nationalists created ETA. The first ETA was heavily influenced by Basque nationalist doctrine and the prophetic writings of Arana. In a later stage, Arana's nationalism was fused with socialist ideals in order to form an ideology which was quick to identify the new subject of the national struggle: the Basque working class. The ETA of the 1960s was constantly torn apart between a nationalist and a socialist pole which produced numerous splits. The more socialist individuals who argued the fight should be directed towards the capitalist forces regardless of nationality were invited (or forced) to leave and the organisation split in 1966, 1970 and 1974. For those who favoured nationalism as the dominant element of their ideology, the idea of a golden past was retained as a powerful mobilising factor. The idea of a paradise lost, this time an egalitarian and democratic one, justified embracing nationalism and made necessary the realisation of a patriotic heaven on earth. And the means chosen to realise that political programme was a campaign of political violence. The success of the spiral of action-repression-action can partially be explained by a war memory that placed violent conflicts in a historical continuum where Basques and Spaniards had always stood against each other. The memory of the Carlist Wars, the Spanish Civil War and 'ETA's war' were seen as examples of heroic sacrifices that made the use of political violence a moral need. The so-called 'Basque conflict' between ETA and the Spanish state became, in itself, a powerful mobilising agent. The need to readdress past injustices went hand in hand with the celebration of past battles and redemptive sacrifices, hence removing the need to reflect on the usefulness of the armed struggle.

Chapter 5 moves into the democratic period and explains how, after the death of General Franco in 1975, a political transition led to the approval of a Constitution (1978) and a Basque Statute of Autonomy (1979). Since the establishment of devolved regional autonomy, the politics of the Basque Country have been mostly dominated by one party, the PNV, which initially took control of the autonomous government and the administration (or *diputación*) of the three provinces of Araba, Gipuzkoa and Biscay. ETA sympathisers did not acknowledge the political transformation and actively rejected the Constitution arguing that the new democracy had not established a tabula rasa with Francoism and that Spain remained an authoritarian regime. The belief that the Spanish democracy was nothing but a 'cosmetic change' was further reinforced during the 1980s by the introduction of new anti-terrorist legislation, the numerous reports of torture and ill-treatment of ETA detainees in police custody and the emergence of the state-funded paramilitaries of the Anti-Terrorist Liberation Groups (Grupos Antiterroristas de Liberación — GAL) which fought a dirty war against ETA and killed 27 people between 1983 and 1987. Refusing to be integrated into the new democracy, ETA continued to develop an anti-system network of organisations known as the Basque Movement of National Liberation (*Movimiento de Liberacion Nacional Vasco* — MLNV). The chapter also describes how radical Basque nationalists developed their own version of the Golden Age and integrated this mythical element into a 'triadic structure of nationalist rhetoric' (Levinger & Franklin 2001). Following this construct, the discourse of radical Basque nationalism first presents an idealised past where Basques were politically independent and lived harmoniously. Secondly, radical nationalists defined a myth of decline, starting in the Carlist Wars in the nineteenth century and continuing to the present day. This myth of decline involved the loss of the qualities that made the Basques an independent people. Thirdly, after the two aforementioned myths, came the myth of regeneration or salvation. According to nationalists, the Basque homeland could only be authentic and pure when it regained the original political freedom of past times. Since nations cannot reach statehood by peaceful means, the Basques had no other option but to resort to violent means.

By the 1980s, there can be no doubt the Spanish political system had been democratised in both theory and practice (Linz & Stepan 1996). Some of the authoritarian tendencies still present during the transition had disappeared and the country diligently followed the path set by the European Economic Community (EEC). France recognised those changes and increasingly cooperated in police and intelligence matters under the framework of Schengen. Chapter 6 explains some of these political developments and describes how ETA's discourse about the need to fight an urban war became increasingly empty. During the early 1990s the range of legitimate targets was expanded to journalists, judges, lecturers and politicians of various ideologies but, in particular those who sympathised with the PP and PSOE. The so-called 'socialisation of pain' provoked a proactive civil society reaction against ETA and the *abertzale* left. The high point of this antipathy was the summer of 1997 when the ETA hostage Ortega Lara was released and the town councillor Blanco was killed. The changing climate and the massive anti-ETA mobilisations pushed the Basque paramilitaries into a tactical retreat. The post-Blanco situation also provoked a strategic realignment of the Basque party system which became even more polarised.

Chapter 7 describes how in August 1998, the PNV signed a secret political agreement with ETA as a precondition for a ceasefire. The terms of the agreement were that ETA would announce a truce if the PNV changed its political strategy and took more decisive steps towards the building of Euskal Herria. The agreement was partially made public in September 1998 and was presented to the press as the Lizarra Agreement to which other nationalist organisations gave their support. Two weeks later, ETA decided to call an 'indefinite and unilateral' ceasefire which led to talks with the conservative government of José María Aznar. The widespread hopes that ETA could follow the IRA in disbanding were shattered 14 months later when ETA announced its decision to resume the armed struggle. The breakdown of the ETA ceasefire in November 1999 plunged Basque society into a deep sense of crisis. Political elites felt the possibility of finding a peaceful accommodation for the Basque conflict had been postponed by another decade. The electoral strength of Prime Minister Aznar who renewed his mandate in 2000, and the continuing strategy of moderate nationalists who did not reverse the radical strategy adopted at Lizarra made the possibility of finding common ground very difficult. The situation radically changed in 2004 with the Madrid train bombings. The way in which the PP government dealt with the attacks on 11M provoked a change of government in the general elections three days later in which the PSOE regained control of the executive. Under the leadership of José Luis Rodriguez Zapatero a new process of devolution was launched and several regions and nationalities reformed their statutes of autonomy. In March 2006 ETA declared a 'permanent ceasefire' which started a nine-month peace process which ended abruptly on 31 December when a car bomb exploded at Madrid's international airport. The device brought down a section of the multi-storey car-park and killed two Ecuadorean men which increased the number of total ETA victims to 836.

To conclude, understanding radical Basque nationalism is essential to comprehend the contemporary political situation in Spain and the Basque country. The political system has not been successful in fully accommodating and channelling the anti-systemic demands of the social movement led by ETA. There can be no doubt that the refusal of radical nationalists to abandon the violent subculture and embrace democratic institutions is part of the problem as this movement continues to mobilise their supporters on fronts beyond the political one. The main reason why these supporters allow themselves to be mobilised is provided by radical Basque nationalism where both ethnicity and violence are intertwined in a nationalist recreation of the Basque past which combines a nostalgic gaze at the Golden Age and a quasi-religious imperative to restore that lost distant past. With an income *per capita* well above the Spanish average and increasing levels of self-government and economic development for all of Spain's regions, observers sometimes find it difficult to understand what some Basque really yearn for. However, the moral worth of these nationalist demands in the current socioeconomic and political opportunity structures are well beyond the scope of this book, which stresses the role of inherited myths, memories and cultural symbols to explain the ability of radical Basque nationalism to endure.

1   The Basque Golden Age

The relationship between the nation and its past first attracted the attention of the French historian and theologian Ernest Renan (1823–1892). In a famous lecture delivered at the Sorbonne, *Qu'est-ce qu'une nation?* (1882), he suggested that the nation's existence was founded upon the desire to live together or, in his famous phrase, 'a daily plebiscite'. He defined the nation as 'a soul, a spiritual principle' and at once linked this definition of the nation to the existence of shared memories:

> two things, which in truth are but one, constitute this soul or spiritual principle. One lies in the past, one in the present. One is the possession in common of a rich legacy of memories; the other is present-day consent, the desire to live together, the will to perpetuate the value of the heritage that one has received in an undivided form. (Renan 1990: 19)

For Renan, it was the existence of a shared history which he defined as 'a rich legacy of memories' that forged the national community. The large aggregate of individuals that made up the nation was bound together by these common memories. The cement of their identity was not the past itself (what actually happened) but by what the community told one another in the present (what they remembered). 'Getting history wrong', in Renan's words, was a precondition of nationalist history because it required both an act of collective remembering and collective amnesia. From this point of view, it was not the scientific history that bound together the national community. Rather, it was the myths and symbols, the legends, the ballads, the epics, and the songs that were perceived as 'original' and 'authentic'. The content of these might not be entirely true and, in fact, they might have fictitious elements, but they were important insofar as they 'resonated' among the masses.

The extent to which a 'legacy of memories' could be fabricated was examined by Eric J. Hobsbawm and Terence Ranger in *The Invention of Tradition* (1983). This collection of essays was concerned with the role played in modern societies by constructed versions of 'the past' and examined the 'mass-producing' rituals that emerged in the period between

1870 and the outbreak of the Great War in 1914. The contributors to the volume examined rituals such as the royal Christmas broadcast, the British coronation ceremony, or the Highland tradition in Scotland and argued that these 'invented traditions' were 'highly relevant' to the analysis of the nation. Hobsbawm and Ranger argued that 'invented tradition' was taken to mean 'a set of practices, normally governed by overtly or tacitly accepted rules and of a ritual or symbolic nature, which seek to inculcate certain values and norms of behaviour by repetition, which automatically implies continuity with the past. In fact, where possible, they normally attempt to establish continuity with a suitable historic past' (Hobsbawm & Ranger 1983: 1–2).

During the course of the nineteenth century most European states indulged in the fabrication of traditions and the recording of their 'national memory'. Nations began to worship themselves through the ritualisation of their pasts and the establishment of public commemorations. In spite of being a secular movement, nationalism gradually incorporated the sacredness of organised religion by adopting temples, holy sites, and national holidays. For example, the Third Republic adopted La Marseillaise as the national anthem in 1879 and a year later, in 1880, Bastille Day was invented. The building of this new ritual and commemorative agenda was not free of challenge. Many refused to participate in these newly created rituals which took time to be consolidated. In Philadelphia, the place where the American Declaration of Independence was signed in 1776, there was no consensus on how the anniversary should be honoured until the 1850s (Gillis 1994: 9).

Renan's most perceptive observation was that as *the* collective memory of the nation was constructed (and more stories were left behind) there would be a rise of counter-discourses. Marginalised memories, Renan warned, would become aware of their origins, their defeats and the injustices they had suffered. The dominant national history (and its chief architects) would be both contested and fragmented and repressed memories would surface. The twentieth century offers ample evidence for this pluralisation of narratives of resistance. Entire social groups first challenged and then gained admission to national memories: from women, Jews, homosexuals, workers, and exiles to indigenous communities and various ethnic groups. All these collectives had a common grievance: they did not appear in the so-called official histories, and they wanted their lost past to be restored and preserved. In fact, they all shared in common the interest in studying and learning the past in order to avoid being left out again. In order to prevent future exclusion, these groups celebrated their present successes but also remembered their losses and defeats in an attempt to internalise the collective suffering of the community.

According to ethno-symbolist authors,[1] the form and content of any rediscovered past depends on the political needs of the group but also on the availability of what they call 'raw materials'. Anthony D. Smith has argued that these raw materials are reliable written sources on which a robust national discourse can be built. If a nationalist project is to have a significant impact, he warns, elites have to be careful about neglecting existing ethnic resources. Eric J. Hobsbawm made a similar point when arguing that elites have to broadcast on the wavelength to which the public is ready to tune in. Throughout history, intellectuals and politicians have usually taken a middle course and have recreated popular beliefs and conducts while, at the same time, adding the elements dictated by the historical context in which they lived. Hence, a certain degree of fabrication is always present, as it is the case with any narrative, but this can vary significantly from case to case. The point the next section makes is that at the core of nationalist narratives there is often a mythical idea of a glorious past.

1.1 A NATION'S GOLDEN AGE: A NECESSARY MYTH

The first reference to the Golden Age can be found in Hesiod's *Works and Days*, a Greek poem about moral decay composed after 700 B.C. The poem was divided into three parts and it is written in a simple, moralising style which provides practical advice on farming and general husbandry. The work has been described as a poetic manual and an early example of didactic poetry, which is meant to be instructive rather than entertaining, but it is also the response of a troubled individual to changes that have occurred in his world. In the first part, Hesiod traces the history of the world through five stages: from the age of gold to silver, bronze, demigods, and, finally, his own age of iron. For Hesiod, the members of the Golden Age had been created by Cronus and 'lived like gods'. They were also free from 'toils and grief', never grew old, and 'delighted in festivities beyond all evils'. In short, 'they had all good things'. The poem continues describing the members of the other ages (which were not created by Cronus but his son, Zeus) and their relations with the gods in what is a clear narrative of humankind's degeneration which culminates in the present day Iron race, into which Hesiod wished he had never been born. The final age, the antithesis of the Golden Age, is the decadent Iron Age: 'for now the race is indeed of iron. Not ever during the day will men cease from labor and grief; not even at night will they cease from being oppressed' (Hesiod 1996: 67–73). As with other myths, it is difficult to know whether Hesiod's remarks about the past were in any way accurate or were just a nostalgic recollection of the 'good old days'. What is clear is that the world in which he lived was imperfect and he felt all was lost.

Neither fiction nor a chronicle, the Golden Age is a mixture of history and legend. According to Smith, the concept has been used to describe epochs of 'moral virtue and literary and artistic creativity' for any 'collective achievement from religious zeal to military expansion and economic success' (Smith 1997: 40). As an idealised construction of the past, the myth is usually constructed by those who need to bear the burden of a 'period of darkness'. Correspondingly, the emergence of a myth of the Golden Age becomes an almost infallible indicator for a historical time in which there is a perception of decline, as the case of Hesiod indicates. The Golden Age is usually born in historical twilights or times in which rapid social and economic changes take place. Very often it is a reaction to a definite political or military threat from outside the community (Smith 1999: 83). However, the myth is also the result of imagination while being in contradiction with reality. It can be considered an exercise in escapism, but reality also tends to manifest itself in it. That is the reason why myths have contradictory structures. Desires are always implied in myths, such as the lost relative who comes back from the 'other world' to give final instructions of revenge; or the warrior who being surrounded by enemies, becomes invisible and saves his own life and the community. It is the imagination that produces the desire to save the warrior and projects reality onto a mythical surrounding. But that imagination does not always remain constant in the life of a community. The community's needs may change and, as a consequence, the content of the myth also has to evolve in order to be functional.

Golden Ages have mushroomed and their presence can be traced in almost any academic discipline, from cinema and animation to radio, comic-books, literature, classical antiquity, astronomy, and even economic performance. Any society that has lost a world will have an idea of an age of gold, or as Schiller remarked, 'all peoples that have a history have a paradise, a state of innocence, a Golden Age' (Levin 1970: xv). The term has been used to describe splendid times such as ancient Athens, Medici Florence, the period of 1572–1648 in the Netherlands or seventeenth century Imperial Spain. The content of each of these golden ages may be radically different from country to country but also through time. In any case, they remain as examples of virtue, splendour, and great courage and constitute a revolt against a concrete historical time. In fact, due to its potential to project an attitude and inspire political action, a golden past has become a necessary myth for nationalism.

But before considering the functional importance of the Golden Age for nation-building processes it is important to clarify what a myth is. The word 'myth' derives from the Greek *mythos*, meaning a 'tale' or 'story' and according to the *Oxford English Dictionary* (OED) is 'a traditional narrative, usually involving supernatural or imaginary persons and embodying popular ideas on natural or social phenomena'. According to anthropological research, myths are a source of knowledge and a legacy from the ancestors. A mixture of historical facts and legendary elaboration, myths have authoritative symbolic value, and they reveal meaningful aspects of social reality. The myth should be seen as a cultural institution that relates the individual to the ritual, and plays a leading part in moral conduct and social organisation. In other words, its function is to inspire and give meaning to both individual and collective existence. Its importance would be similar to that of the scriptures for Christians or the social contract for Liberals. In the words of Bronislaw Malinowski, the myth:

> is a story which is told in order to establish a belief, to serve as a precedent in ceremony or ritual, or to rank as a pattern of moral or religious conduct. Mythology, therefore, or the sacred tradition of a society, is a body of narratives woven into their culture, dictating their belief, defining their ritual, acting as the chart of their social order and the pattern of their moral behaviour. Every myth has naturally a literary content, since it is always a narrative, but this narrative is not merely a piece of entertaining fiction or explanatory statement to the believer. It is a true account of sensational events which have shaped the constitution of the world, the essence of moral conduct, and determines the ritual contact between man and his maker, or other powers that be. (Malinowski 1963: 249–250)

Following the functionalist anthropology of Malinowski, one can argue that myths are key constitutive elements of collectivities. They shape social behaviour and dictate parameters within which individuals and national movements might operate. What will these parameters be for devotees of a Golden Age? Could it be that the remembrance of a forgotten Golden Age inevitably leads to a tormented nationalist mind and condemns it to sterile nostalgia? Could there be any other outcome for those utopians looking for heaven on earth? Indeed there is. Yearning for yesterday can become a trigger for vigorous political action to recover that lost age. Many nationalist movements link a myth of decline with one of regeneration (Levinger & Franklin 2001). In this respect, nationalism takes much from the Judeo-Christian tradition which 'moves from paradise lost to paradise regained, from Eden through the wilderness of Canaan, the land flowing with milk and honey, and hence from retrospection to prophecy' (Levin 1970: 5). This structure was similarly present in Hesiod's story or Milton's *Paradise Lost*—an idealised past, a narrative of decline, and a decadent present—which, since then, resonates in successive golden ages. The superior virtues of an idealised past have become part of almost every national movement because they identify the heroic essence of the nation and the characteristics that need to be emulated. Almost every nation has a time in history which is looked on with furtive admiration and, even, a certain degree of sentimental recollection. According to the quote from Emile M. Cioran which opened this book, myths and utopias are indispensable guiding lights. These ideas are needed in all societies to inspire and uplift their members in prosperous times but, more importantly, in difficult times. Myths help human beings transcend the limits of history and leave an imprint of progress during their brief time on earth by participating in the national endeavour. Or as Benedict Anderson has put it, the magic of nationalism is to provide a quasi-religious answer to the suffering and contingency of life by turning chance into destiny (Anderson 1991: 11–12).

Another point worth making is that the memory of the golden past cannot survive without repetition and mechanisms of social and cultural reproduction. Without them, the theme of the Fall of Man would be forgotten and would be lost in time. For its survival, the myth needs new generations to believe in it, and pass it onto the next one by ritually thinking, writing, and adapting it to new circumstances. For that to happen, the myth needs to encapsulate universal meaning which can be understood by peoples from all times. Members of a community need to identify with the allegory or parable. Only if the myth has metaphysical content will people see their reflection and that of their ancestors. That is the reason why the myth so often takes, imitates, and repeats an archetype, so people can observe what Mircea Eliade called 'a situation in the cosmos' (Eliade 1955: 3). The myth does not only survive, however, because members of the collective spontaneously recognise its symbolic and intrinsic value. The role of the elites also needs to be recognised in the choice of which myths may be reproduced, particularly if they can spur social change. Because the golden past does not have to be historically accurate to be accepted, it is unproblematic to argue that intelligentsias might use those myths to achieve their own goals. However, if the Golden Age is to be effective, parts of it need to be widely believed and perceived as 'authentic'. As the leading figure of ethno-symbolism has persuasively argued, the Golden Age has to be historically verifiable if it is to last:

> Nationalist fabrications may succeed for a moment, but their inevitable exposure is likely to divert energy and induce cynicism and apathy for the national cause. To inspire wonder and emulation, the Golden Age must be well attested and historically verifiable. *Pure* 'invention of tradition' is ineffective. (Smith 1997: 59)

Smith rightly states that a *pure* construction is ineffective, but does not say how much fabrication is possible. He is right to point out that it cannot be entirely false, but it does not need to be historically accurate either. The level of invention allowed fluctuates and its acceptance does not only depend on the resonance it has with the people, but on the power of elites to impose such discourse. What is sure is that the point of equilibrium where popular and elite demands intersect will coincide with a period of perceived decline. As the next section explains, the first steps taken to develop the Basque Golden Age coincided with the decline of the Spanish empire.

1.2 THE BASQUE GOLDEN AGE

By the end of the seventeenth century the long period of prosperity characterised by Spain's pre-eminence in both Europe and the Americas was
over. At the height of its power, the Spanish Empire was one of the rich-
est and most powerful actors of the sixteenth century with territories in
the West Indies, Cuba, Florida, Mexico, Central America, much of South
America, and the Philippines. The main hurdle for Spain had been to control all these widely scattered territories at a time when slow communica-
tions made long-distance government practically impossible. In a matter
of decades, Spain declined from being the most feared military power in
Europe to a loose conglomerate of territories that the monarchy could no
longer defend. The empire had made colossal exertions in order to control
its vast territories and an overstretched state was now taking its toll on the
country's resources and morale. Furthermore, it was precisely at the time
when resources were most needed that Spain's rulers needed to legitimately
extract and organise resources efficiently. Some regions of the Hispanic
Monarchy revolted while others, like the people of Biscay and Gipuzkoa,
developed a pre-modern body of literature which emphasised their ethnicity and argued that they should be exempt from taxation.

According to John H. Elliott, the decline of Spain was caused by the
exhaustion of a model and what one may call 'imperial overstretch'.[2] This
model had showed a few signs of fatigue by the end of the previous century.
Foreign enterprises to fight 'heresy' had gone tremendously wrong and, in
1588, the supposedly invincible Spanish Armada had suffered defeat in the
English Channel. Castile had severe economic and demographic problems
which, together with epidemics, rising taxes, and food shortages, led to a
wave of general dissatisfaction. On top of it all, the death in 1598 of the
king, Philip II, who had governed Spain for more than fifty years, marked
the end of a century characterised by a mixture of triumphs, disappoint-
ments, and miseries.

The beginning of the seventeenth century was no different and, in spite
of Spain still being the hegemonic power in Europe, was characterised by
a mood of introspection and bitter self-criticism. General disillusionment,
particularly from the 1620s, was felt by the popular classes and a sense of
insecurity and decay prevailed. Intellectuals and scholars turned to analyse
the social ills of Spain, also with great fatalism. The *arbitristas* (projectors),
for example, were writers who developed *arbítrios* or proposals for economic and political reform. According to Elliott the *arbitristas* proposed
that government expenditure should be slashed; that the tax system in Castile should be overhauled, and the other kingdoms of the Monarchy be
called upon to contribute more to the royal exchequer; that immigration
should be encouraged to repopulate Castile; that fields should be irrigated,
rivers be made navigable, and agriculture and industry be protected and

fostered (Elliott 1969: 295). Their projects for economic, social, and moral regeneration were not always feasible but they remain as important testimonies of the worries of the time. Their pessimistic writings focused on Castile, rather than Spain, and the political life of the capital, rather than the life of the provinces.[3] The distinction between Castile and Spain was noteworthy because Hapsburg Spain was not a unified state in the modern sense but a conglomerate of sovereign territories which enjoyed their own laws, institutions, and monetary systems. The main building blocks of Spain were the three Christian Crowns of Castile (which included Castile, the kingdom of Navarre, and the Basque Provinces); Portugal and Aragon (which comprised the regions of Aragon, Catalonia, Valencia, and the Balearic Islands). One could describe the Iberia of the time as a loose federation of territories united by religion and by a Hispanic monarchy based on a pact between the diverse realms. The organisational structure of the state was not unusual and, at the time, other European monarchies such as France, Britain, Denmark, Hungary, or the Holy Roman Empire were also ethnically and politically composite.

The Hispanic conglomerate started to show some cracks in the early seventeenth century when the Hapsburg monarchy attempted to take further the process of centralisation by unifying legal codes, taxes, and armies. The critical state of the royal finances led frustrated Castilian political elites to advocate tighter control of the different realms of Spain. Their view was that if the imperial dominions were to be maintained, the duty of other parts of the Monarchy was to come to the relief of an exhausted Castile. In other words, it was necessary to set up a unitary fiscal-military state that could extract substantial resources from society, centralise them and create permanent armed forces under direct control of the Monarch. The first calls to increase taxation and conscription fell on deaf ears, particularly in Catalonia. Up until that point, Castile and Portugal had reserved all trade with their colonies to their own 'nationals' and people from other kingdoms were excluded from exploring the New World. Unsurprisingly, non-Castilians did not rush to salvage a sinking empire that did not belong to them. Furthermore, the Castilian efforts to increase military co-operation and economic integration were seen as a rupture of the pact between realms that sustained the Hispanic Monarchy and, as a reaction, territorial identities came to the fore during the mid-seventeenth century. In 1640, revolts in Portugal and Catalonia represented major challenges to the composite monarchy and led to the eventual separation of the former and a temporary partial annexation of the latter to France. The rebellion in Catalonia was motivated by the taxes and military charges that the head of government, the Count-Duke of Olivares (1587–1645), attempted to impose on the region to finance the war against France. The Catalan Parliament refused to cooperate with the Hispanic Monarchy, arguing that the imposition of those taxes was against local laws. The Catalan and Portuguese revolts precipitated the fall of Olivares and indefinitely put a stop to his plans to frame a centralised monarchy based on Castilian laws while marking an end to Spanish hegemony in Europe. A few years later, Spain was compelled to acknowledge the independence of the Dutch (1648), and later that of the Portuguese (1668) and was forced to cede numerous territories to France, the new emerging European power. With the arrival of the Bourbons to the throne in 1714, both the Habsburg dynasty and the imperial grandeur collapsed dramatically.

Praise for the foral identity of the Basque provinces emerged in parallel to the growing sense of crisis and the gradual dismantlement of the Habsburg system of government in favour of a more centralised state. With the end of Spain's hegemonic empire the possibilities for many Basques to climb the social ladder disappeared. Biscayans and Gipuzkoanos had traditionally nurtured the imperial administration as scribes, functionaries, ecclesiastics, technicians, sailors and soldiers, and made their presence felt in Castile and the Indies. According to Gregorio Monreal, there can be no doubt that 'Basques of Alava, Guipúzcoa and Vizcaya manifested strong loyalty to the Castilian monarchy throughout the Middle Ages' and that there was 'clear gratitude' from Basques 'towards the Catholic Kings, who during the fifteenth and sixteenth centuries played a major role in the pacification and modernisation of the Basque Country' (Monreal 1985: 19–20). However, with the decline of the empire, the demise of the Habsburg dynasty and the arrival of the centralising Bourbons, some members of the Basque reading elites started to define an age of gold in contrast to Spain's decline.

According to the pioneering work of the anthropologist Juan Aranzadi, the Basque Golden Age was a body of literature characterized by an idealization of Basque ethnicity. A mixture of historical facts and legendary elaboration, the constitutive elements of the myth portrayed an epoch characterised by great prosperity and happiness where Basques were virtuous, pure, and authentic (Aranzadi 1979, 1994, 2000). The myth was born and reproduced between the sixteenth and eighteenth centuries and was decisively taken up by Basque romantics and nationalists who enlarged it during the nineteenth century. This body of mythical narratives was highly significant because it became a pre-modern vehicle of ethnic identity for Basque reading elites. As has already been suggested, the core function of the myth was to contrast the contemporary situation (usually characterised by degeneration) with an epic time of splendour, but this often took different forms: from a racially pure Arcadian past, to a sanctimonious devotion to the Christian faith, or a national sovereignty defended by heroic sacrifices.[4] The Golden Age cannot be considered as a unified and homogeneous set of practices and beliefs but, rather, an evolving narrative. As can be seen in Figure 1.1, the myth can be divided into three domains: religious, social, and political. The religious domain made reference to the idea that the Basques were a people chosen by God to set the moral standard in the world. Also in the religious domain we find the idea of Basque being a divine language. The second domain, the social, referred to concepts of

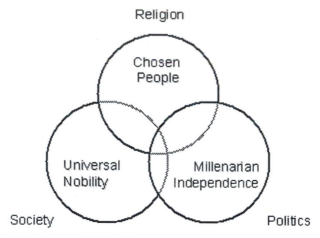

Figure 1.1 The Basque Golden Age

universal nobility and purity of blood, meaning free of Moorish or Jewish influence. Finally, the political sphere highlighted the *fueros*, or codes of ancient laws and privileges whose maintenance was sworn by the kings and queens of Castile down to the sixteenth century, as symbols of its millenarian independence.

It is difficult to pigeonhole the authors who contributed to the myth in one single sphere. Their interests went beyond these boundaries. However, the time in which they lived influenced the topics they chose. For example, the topics belonging to the first two domains, the religious and the social, were pre-eminent during the sixteenth and seventeenth centuries, in the works of authors such as Juan Martínez de Zaldivia, Esteban Garibay y Zamalloa, or Andrés de Poza. They expressed their political thought in historiographical works which, although not very influential at the time, became 'literary weapons' during the seventeenth century when Spain was trying to enforce its influence on the Basque Provinces. On the other hand, the political sphere was seen in the work of an eighteenth century priest, Manuel de Larramendi. His work stands on its own as a forerunner of Basque ethnic identity at a time of increasing centralisation. Overall, all these works stand as important ideological precursors of modern nationalism because they contributed to the formation of an early ethnic consciousness at an elite level in the provinces of Biscay, Gipuzkoa, and Araba based on ideas of racial purity, religious devotion, divine language, territorial nobility, and the existence of a covenant with God (Molina 2005: 65–87).

1.2.1 Religion

The religious aspect of the Basque Golden Age is epitomised by the idea of the chosen people. The concept was not originally Basque and it could be found in many other examples—from biblical Israel and the Roman Empire to twentieth century Germany, Japan, Iran, and the United States—where the sense of sacredness is a significant factor of national identity. The first nation to make use of the term 'chosen people' were the Israelites, who assumed they had been chosen by God to fulfil the mission of proclaiming his truth among all the nations of the world. The term is a free translation of the biblical terms 'am segullah* (treasured people) and 'am nahallah* (heritage people) and is a recurring theme in Jewish liturgy as expressed in many passages of Scripture. One example is the conversation between Moses and God: 'if you obey me fully and keep my covenant, then out of all nations you will be my treasured possession. Although the whole earth is mine you will be my kingdom of priests and a holy nation' (Exodus 19: 5–6). The idea of a chosen people is important because it gives a sense of collective mission, whereby the individual strengthens his or her links with the community.[5] The importance of the sacred idea is its functional character:

> Briefly, it sees a particular people as the vessel chosen by a deity for a special religious task or mission in the world's moral economy. By performing that mission, the elect will be set apart and sanctified, and their redemption, and that of the world, will be assured. The people in question may be felt to possess special qualities which justify the privilege bestowed upon them, and their destiny is defined in religious terms as redemption through correct and full performance of the sacred task with which they were entrusted. (Smith 1999: 335)

In the sixteenth century some Basques thought that, like the Israelites, they had been chosen by God because of their superior characteristics. The similarities with Israel are particularly fascinating because Basques did not feel like Israelites, but somehow 'knew' they were Israelites. As Parellada has argued in *El orígen de los Vascos* (1976) the attempts to establish a link with the Israelites included thorough comparisons of the Basque language and Hebrew in a desperate search for similarities (Parellada 1976: 217–218). Furthermore, during the sixteenth century authors from Gipuzkoa, like Juan Martínez de Zaldívia, considered the Basques to be one of the ten lost tribes of Israel. In his *Suma de cosas cantábricas y guipuzcoanas* (1564), Zaldivia traces the noble origins of the Basques to the biblical Flood and, more specifically to Noah himself:

> After that memorable Flood all human beings perished except the eight souls the Scriptures mention. Those involved in the construction of that tower of Babylon which is mentioned in chapter 11 of Genesis spoke one of the 71 languages. Tubal, son of Japheth, spoke one of those languages and when he came to Hispania, he brought it with him. But he stopped in the Pyrenees and the Basques and the Navarrese have his language, Euskera, which Tubal and his fellow travellers brought. (Azurmendi 2000: 28)

Oddly enough, the Basques of that time liked to compare themselves to the Israelites of the Book of Genesis but insisted they did not descend from the ancient Hebrews. Since 1492, when the Catholic Kings had expelled all the Moors and Jews from Spain, only 'second class subjects' were known to have Jewish blood. Pure ancestry and personal honour were equated in the popular mind and, by 1547 statutes of *limpieza de sangre*, or purity of blood, had spread throughout the country inducing the Spanish Inquisition to search for converted Jews—known as *conversos* or *marranos*. Since the Basques' pure ancestry could only be maintained by keeping Jewish blood at a distance, some authors draw a very peculiar moral lesson from their survival of the Flood. If they had lived to tell the cataclysmic event, then, they would have been a living example of what God considered an example of supreme moral behaviour and justice. According to the biblical timeline, God decided to chastise all men and women except the direct descendants of Noah, whose ark came to rest on the top of Mount Ararat after the Great Flood. After the miraculous landing, Noah's progeny immigrated to other lands and Tubal, who would be remembered as the 'original' Basque, repopulated Hispania (Parellada 1976: 93–95).

A direct consequence of being a chosen people concerned Euskara. If Basques were the first inhabitants of Spain and they spoke the language of their founding father, Tubal, then their language had to be of divine origin. The dominant myth of the origin of Euskara during the sixteenth and seventeenth centuries was that Basque was one of the seventy-one languages which came into being after the destruction of the Tower of Babel. The antiquity of the Basque language was mainly developed in the work of the Basque chronicler, Esteban de Garibay (1533–1599) whose main concern was Spanish history but also wrote accounts of the Basque Provinces and even became an authority on the history of Navarre (Caro Baroja 2002: 233). His work also underlined the leading role of Tubal in the history of Spain and emphasised things Basque as often as he could. Following Martínez de Zaldivia, Garibay emphasised the ancient origins of Euskara when asserting that: 'one thing is certain, that no author will come up with a language that predates it in Spain'.[6] By affirming that Euskara was a pre-Babel language spoken in God's Paradise, these authors could argue that those who spoke that language had not committed any sin. They were a people with holy characteristics and a divine language which had been saved from the cataclysmic flood by embarking on Noah's ark. God punished the rebel peoples during the destruction of the Tower of Babel by depriving them of their original language but 'chose' the Basques among a few others.

1.2.2 Society

The history of the Golden Age is a living example of how a successful narrative of ethnic distinctiveness is constructed. This section will analyse one of the most influential aspects of pre-modern Basque identity: the doctrine of 'universal nobility' (*hidalguía colectiva*), which conferred social prestige and important financial and legal advantages, most notably the exemption from payment of taxes to the Crown. The doctrine was made official in 1526, when the government of the province of Biscay approved the *Fuero Nuevo de el Señorío de Vizcaya* by which the status of nobility was applied to all native residents of the territory. The province of Gipuzkoa did the same in 1610 and universal nobility was transformed into a territorial phenomenon which had a positive effect on the inhabitants of the province. Basque 'universal nobility' was also an essential first step for achieving a military or administrative position in the opportunities offered by the exploration and exploitation of the Americas. The Basques of Biscay and Gipuzkoa, all of whom were equipped with noble status, staffed the Spanish state administration.

The argument that Basques were all noble was used as a defence against the attempts of the Count-Duke of Olivares to unify the separate kingdoms of the Iberian Peninsula and introduce a universal tax system. If the nobility of the Basque Provinces could be proven, 'special treatment' in the form of regional tax exemptions would have to be granted. On the other hand, the government in Madrid strongly opposed what it saw as an artificial creation purely designed to erode the state's power to impose its will. An example of that tension between the centre and the periphery was a debate held at the end of the sixteenth century between the Crown's prosecutor at the *Chancillería de Valladolid* (Royal Court of Justice) and the province of Biscay. In 1588, the Castilian prosecutor Juan García sent a letter to the authorities of Biscay questioning the common saying in the region that 'all Basques were nobles'. The basic contention of the prosecutor was that no noble ancestral estate existed without vassals attached to it. The Seignory of Biscay's immediate reaction was to hire prestigious writers to defend the doctrine of universal nobility and prepare a reply to the prosecutor.[7] The most important of them was Andrés de Poza, a lawyer who had written a book on the antiquity of the Basque language a few years earlier.

The dispute between Biscay and the Royal Court of Justice was of great importance to the public revenues. In the sixteenth century, rank and hierarchy dominated a highly stratified social structure. At the top end, a high aristocracy with strong links to the court shared power and status with a powerful elite which included the military, the church, and the bureaucratic elites. The remaining aristocracy was the lesser aristocracy, whose members, distinguished by the prefix *Don*, were known indifferently as knights (*caballeros*) or *hidalgos*. These noblemen or *hidalgos* possessed coats of arms and were distinguished from the rest of citizens because they enjoyed, among many other privileges, the exemption of paying taxes to the Crown. According to Elliott, the social reputation and practical advantages attached to the privilege of nobility (or *hidalguía*) made it an object of universal desire. This meant that vast quantities of time and financial resources were spent in the fabrication of genealogical tables which would prove the existence of aristocratic ascendancy. However, for all those who could not prove they were nobles by birth, but had the economic means, there was the possibility of social advancement through the acquisition of a privilege of nobility from the Crown (Elliott 1969: 101–105).

It soon became clear that if the Northern provinces were able to secure the right to territorial nobility, the Castilian Crown would suffer the consequences. Such a precedent of collective social mobility would endanger the economic and social foundations of a hierarchically-ordered society where the supreme aspiration was to find acceptance among the ranks of the aristocracy. On a more practical level, the exemption of taxes associated with personal distinction—*hidalguía*—would put the increasingly bureaucratic state under great financial strain at a time when the Empire's troops were struggling to keep the overseas dominions together. The Crown's *Chancilleria de Valladolid* argued that the only way to have nobles, or *hidalgos*, was to have tax-payers or bibs (*pecheros*). If this difference was not enforced they argued that people considered of 'inferior quality' such as Jews, blacks, and Muslims could easily become nobles and the distinction would not be valid anymore.

The correspondence between the Castilian Juan García and the Biscayan Andrés de Poza continued for several years and constitutes a fascinating example of how the would-be Basques defended the territorial doctrine of universal nobility.[8] To respond to the query of the prosecutor, Poza wrote *De nobilitate in proprietate. Ad Pragmaticas de Toro & Tordesillas*, a turgid compilation of legal quotations. His main argument was that the 'historical rights' of the Basques were 'sacred' and that their 'ancestral' condition was a consequence of their direct descent from Tubal, and not from the Goths, from whom the Spaniards draw their ancestry. The Basque claim to nobility derived from the mere state of being a native of the land. In a nutshell, Andrés de Poza put forward, as early as 1588, the idea of Basque sovereignty, namely that the relationship between Biscay and the Kingdom of Spain was one based on free association. If the King of Spain wished to change the relationship with the Basques, he argued, he needed to go to Biscay to renegotiate it, instead of ordering it from Madrid, because he had no authority over them. Poza first pioneered an argument about the Basques' historical rights, an example that would be later followed by numerous romantics and nationalists.[9]

The exchange of debates between Madrid and Biscay over the *fueros* was to continue for the next three centuries. Indeed, the search for the 'historical truth' that could legitimise Castile's configuration as the centre of Spain ran in parallel to Spanish state-building. The nineteenth century liberal project of centralisation produced a resurgence of debates between the Basque authorities and the Spanish state. This time, the exchange of views was between Don Juan Antonio Llorente, canonical lawyer and historian, and the Basques Francisco Aranguren and Domingo Lerín. Llorente's *opus magnum, Noticias Históricas de las tres provincias Vascongadas,* was published between 1806 and 1808. Llorente's main aim was to prove that the Basques never had an independent kingdom which could sign the *fueros* freely with the King of Castile and that the *fueros* were a concession of the monarch to those provinces. He did not see any particularity to the history of the Basque lands as they had been Romanised, invaded, and had historical links with Castile. According to his own words, he never opposed the defence of the *fueros* as such but he strongly opposed the defence of such rights based on pseudo-historical facts. Curiously, the Spanish government sympathised with his views but never helped him to finance his intellectual enterprise. His work, though, had the personal approval of the Prime Minister Godoy, who gave him full access to Ministry archives and documentation and promised him glory if he succeeded in the endeavour of discovering the 'historical truth' (Fernández Pardo 1990: 69–84).

The response of the Seignory of Biscay came from the pen of Francisco Aranguren in a short book with a long title: *Demostración del sentido verdadero de las autoridades de que se vale el Dr. D. Juan A. Llorente y de lo que en verdad resulta de los historiadores que cita con respecto al Muy Noble y Muy Leal Señorío de Vizcaya* (1807). In this book Aranguren attacked Llorente's work and argued that his sources were not reliable and the conclusions had no validity. The debate with Llorente, as he himself acknowledged, was about: 'the legitimacy of each of our sovereigns on Biscay' (Fernández Pardo 1990: 81). Despite the critique of Llorente's sources, Aranguren did not offer alternative sources from which different conclusions could be extrapolated. Instead he offered a different interpretation of Llorente's very own sources and concluded that Biscay was a sovereign land which had always enjoyed its own laws. The debate continued for some years while both Llorente and Aranguren started to receive extra support from both parties: the state and the *Señorío.* The historiographical debate was handled with great care by the Seignory of Biscay who saw with anxiety the legitimacy Llorente's theses could provide for the government's policies. But the debate was not to continue endlessly. Llorente had just finished the fifth volume of his *Noticias Históricas* when the French troops crossed the Pyrenees to invade Portugal. The invasion of Spain (1808) by Napoleon Bonaparte and the absolutist regime (1814–1833) of Ferdinand VII inhibited literary activity during the first three decades of the nineteenth century. As will be seen in chapter 2, Napoleon's attempt to change the dynasty and install his brother Joseph Bonaparte provoked a wave of anti-French sentiment among the Spanish people and set off the War of Independence (1808–1812). The revolt against the French boosted Spanish nationalism and initiated the liberal project which set aside, for a few decades at least, the debate over the *fueros.*

1.2.3 Politics

The political aspects of the Golden Age mainly refer to the *fueros* as symbols of ancient political independence and the principle of pre-modern egalitarianism (*igualitarismo*). Both elements were fully developed by Larramendi (1690–1766), a cleric born in Gipuzkoa at the end of the seventeenth century who dedicated himself to a tranquil life of study. Larramendi soon stood out as one of the brightest students and academics of the University of Salamanca and, according to José Ignacio Tellechea, he was a man who lived for philosophy and theology and 'never lost 15 minutes in useless conversations, gossiping, or trivialities' (Tellechea 1992: 31). The fame and wisdom of the Jesuit scholar spread to the Court and he was called to work for Queen Maria of Neuberg, widow of Charles II, as a personal confessor in 1730. However, he did not find pleasure in his comfortable position and three years later, he returned to his academic solitude (Larramendi 1882: 5–7). In spite of his unperturbed biography and the limited impact of his work during his lifetime, Father Larramendi then became an influential pre-modern thinker and his memory is still worshipped in nationalist circles for having sketched the main goals of political nationalism. His politically charged work earned him the title of forerunner of Basque nationalism by many scholars (De Otazu 1972: 216; Elorza 1992: 137; Arzalluz 1992: 75; Mansvelt Beck 2005: 127).

One of the most important of Larramendi's books, *Coreografía de Guipúzcoa* (1754), was written when Larramendi was 60 years old, and it was an attempt to build an ethnic marker between Basques and Spaniards.[10] The book was divided into two parts. The first half was a treatise of ethnography of the province of Gipuzkoa in which the author analysed the geographical, political, and religious character of 'this very noble and very loyal province' (*M.N. y M.L. província*). The other half explained the distinct character of the people from Gipuzkoa (*guipuzcoanos*) and their peculiar lifestyles, clothing, leisure and particular language, Euskara. In the introduction to the *Coreografía*, Larramendi argued that his objective was to define Gipuzkoa and all its inhabitants, because Spaniards often call the Basque people 'Biscayans' when this term only applies to people living in one of the Basque Provinces. However, his book did not attempt to distinguish Gipuzkoa from Biscay, but Gipuzkoa from Spain. If his intention was to inform Spaniards of the particularities of his province, he could have chosen to provide a description of Gipuzkoa's own culture, economy, or politics. Instead, he preferred to trace the biblical genealogy of the Basques and emphasised the 'well-known qualities' of *guipuzcoanos* who had 'a noble blood, free from the races of Jews, moors, blacks and mulattos' (Larramendi 1882: 123).[11] According to Larramendi all Basques descended directly from Tubal and were a pure and noble nation because their blood had never been corrupted.[12] As a matter of fact,

The Basque nation, and particularly the Gipuzkoa nation, has been looked after by God with special attention [because its] blood has never mixed with that of any other nation that came from abroad: Moors, Goths, Alans, Siling Vandals, Romans, Greeks, Carthaginians, Phoenicians or any other people. Proof of this truth is the Basque language, which distinguishes us from other nations. (Larramendi 1882: 128)

Larramendi argued that it was easier for Basques than for anybody else to recognise their noble origin. They did not need the help of documents or genealogies because they had never been invaded by any of the other peoples that had marched into Spain. And the indicator of that political independence was their unconquerable native language which had always been spoken in the Basque lands, whereas in the rest of Spain different languages and dialects had been used. One of the main contributions of the *Coreografía* was to update and modernise the doctrine of Basque egalitarianism (*igualitarismo vasco*). As explained by Alfonso de Otazu, Basque egalitarianism had its roots in the doctrine of universal nobility. The latter had been born in the middle of the sixteenth century and was developed during the seventeenth by some of the authors already mentioned. However, it was to be Father Larramendi who defended and clearly expounded the political implications of the doctrine in the *Coreografía de Gipuzcoa*. According to the Jesuit there were two ways of being noble—by 'origin' or by 'occupation'. Hence, one could organically inherit original nobility or one could acquire it through labour. Within this scheme, Basques enjoyed the original nobility which was common to all of them. Finally, Larramendi argued that Gipuzkoa was different to Rome because the inhabitants of the former could not be distinguished 'between patricians and plebeians' and were 'equal in all things' (Larramendi 1882: 142). Yet again, the importance of this doctrine is that it will be used during the nineteenth century by both Carlists and nationalists as a political weapon (Otazu 1973: 7, 101).

The second major book by Father Larramendi, *Conferencias sobre los Fueros* was written between 1756 and 1758 and is best understood in the light of the Bourbon centralising project of the early eighteenth century, which laid the foundations of the modern Spanish state. The Bourbon dynasty, which still rules Spain today, initiated a series of reforms in politics, imperial policy, finance, and the army which attempted to endow its domains with a sense of unity based on French enlightened despotism. Most of these reforms were implemented to pay for the War of Succession (1700–1714) which at the time was fought by the Bourbon and Austria dynasties to confirm their right to the Spanish throne. In 1705 the realm of Aragon showed some reluctance to financially help Castile and Philip V seized the opportunity to enforce his will and suppress the *fueros*, which stood in the way of the reorganisation of Spain. In an infamous 1707 decree, Philip V abolished the *fueros* of Aragon and Valencia and expressed his desire to 'reduce all the realms of Spain to the uniformity of the same laws, traditions and courts and govern them with the laws of Castile' (Kamen 2001: 65). Nine years later, in 1716, royal laws suppressed the parliaments and local charters of Catalonia and Majorca—with the exception of civil, penal, merchant, and administrative laws. Meanwhile, Galicia, Asturias, the Basque Provinces, and the Kingdom of Navarre, supporters of the Bourbon candidate and firmly within the Castilian kingdom were allowed to maintain their traditional institutions and laws.

The disastrous state of the Treasury (*Hacienda Pública*) after the War of Succession, forced Madrid to establish tighter control over one of the greatest sources of revenue, the customs system (Fernández Albaladejo 1977: 149). The fiscal imperative was one of the reasons why Madrid tried to remove the internal borders with the Basque Provinces, arguing that an internal border was offensive to the Kingdom, promoted contraband, and involved a great loss of public revenue. Thus, in 1717 a Royal Decree established that the Customs Office should move from the border with Castile to the maritime ports of the Basque Country. Many entrepreneurs protested against the decree but they were silenced by threats to use neighbouring ports to export Castilian goods. The move meant that Madrid was slowly eroding the Basque *fueros*. In the Prologue of his *Conferencias*, Larramendi hoped his work would help Basques, who seemed 'blind' and 'mute', and were oblivious to the wound the Spaniards were inflicting on them: 'the pain of seeing Gupúzcoa disregarded increases day after day and this torments me. Does it matter if I write in solitude, when fantasy makes the enemy present, as if I could see and hear them?' (Azurmendi 2000: 295).

Larramendi wrote his *Conferencias* hoping it could help redeem Basques for their historical ignorance and their lack of love for their nation and its 'glorious *fueros*'. He did so by establishing a clear ethnic divide and identifying a dichotomy which consisted of a millenarian people of divine origins and a threatening Castilian kingdom hungry for power. Hence, for Larramendi, the Northern Star was closer to Gipuzkoa than to Castile; the Basque territory was highly homogeneous, and the *fueros* of Gipuzkoa were Spain's oldest. Larramendi's conception of the Basque people continued the works of Zaldivia, Garibay, and Poza and contributed to the enlargement of the Golden Age tradition. Again, Noah's mythical grandson, Tubal, was presented as the founding father of the northern peoples and the origin of the noble blood of Gipuzkoa. However, the central intention of Larramendi's work was not to establish a myth of descent for Gipuzkoa but to define what Basques had lost. The decadent present was set in contradiction to the glorious past in order to mobilise Basques to emulate the achievements of their ancestors and initiate a project of national redemption: 'if we all get together, we would alarm the French in France and the Spanish in Spain. Where is that union? I would rather be silent. My greater pain is to see the harms that follow this situation. And it seems to be that we won't be able to see them until we lose the few good things we have left' (Azurmendi

2000: 238). This quote by Larramendi resembled the end of *Bizkaya por su Independencia* (1892), one of the most important texts ever written by Sabino Arana published shortly after the *fueros* had been forever lost: '[t]oday.—Bizkayans is a province of Spain, Tomorrow? Heed these words, Bizkayans of the nineteenth century, the future depends on what you do' (Arana Goiri 1980: 106–153). It is difficult to know whether Arana read the works of Larramendi because the former rarely cited other authors in his works. In any case, the *Corografía de Guipuzcoa* was one of the first coherent books about what Ortega y Gasset called 'Basque pride' or inner belief in the perfection and ethnic superiority of the 'Basque race' (Ortega y Gasset 1961: 115–116).

1.3 CONCLUSION

The Golden Age has been outlined as a body of literature characterised by the idealisation of Basque ethnicity and its cultural components. The myth was born in the sixteenth century and it was reproduced and enlarged between the seventeenth and eighteenth centuries by authors concerned with Basque tradition. A mixture of historical facts and legendary elaboration, the myth encapsulated perceptions, memories and commonly held beliefs about the origins and defining characteristics of the Basque people (chosen people, divine language, universal nobility, purity of blood, collective nobility, etc.). The components of the myth appeared well before the emergence of professional historiography and were not careful reconstructions of an earlier period but a passionate quest for collective identity. The constitutive elements of the myth portrayed an epoch characterised by great prosperity and happiness where Basques has been virtuous, pure, and authentic. As an evolving literary tradition, it was highly significant because it became a pre-modern vehicle of ethnic identity for Basque reading elites and a symbolic framework, albeit a malleable one, for the socialisation of successive generations. The core function of the myth was to contrast the contemporary situation (usually characterised by decline) with an epic past time of splendour which took different forms. The symbolic and cultural components of the Basque Golden Age contributed to three different domains—religious, social, and political—but they were all united in defining and shaping a culturally distinct group. As a literary tradition, the mythical age could be seen as an attempt to define the separate existence and character of the Basque people by tracing generational lineages with the presumed ancestors in accordance with European concerns (Poliakov 1971).

The Basque Golden Age is significant for its historical resilience and ability to resonate in successive generations. As chapter 2 will reveal, some of its cultural components were taken up by romantics and nationalists in order to create a wider group consciousness. In the nineteenth century, the self-affirmation and exaltation of the age of gold was venerated by those who perceived it as a reservoir of meaning and an original source of inspiration. By studying the lost past, they could find evidence of the ideals and qualities (language, ethnic purity, institutions, etc.) that made earlier times 'authentic' and recreated them in the present. Identifying the essential tenets of the heroic past went hand in hand with interpreting the—selected—evidence and designing blueprints for collective action. As the past came to legitimate present actions, and the Golden Age became increasingly autonomous, the Basque nationalists' fascination with their alleged biblical ancestry and 'loss of innocence' drove them to conceptualise an exclusive national community based on blood ties.

2   The Emergence of Basque Nationalism (1833–1903)

Basque nationalism emerged at the end of the nineteenth century within the context of rapid industrialisation, urban expansion, and massive immigration. The transition from the agrarian to the industrial stage uprooted local elites, eroded traditional forms of life, and produced a whole new socio-economic system. The epicentre of this rapid transformation was the prosperous city of Bilbao where the new financial and industrial bourgeoisie was based. The capital of Biscay was also the theatre where modern categories confronted each other: traditionalists vs. liberals, workers vs. bourgeoisie, socialists vs. Catholics, and Basques vs. Spaniards. Besides being the by-product of a city, nationalism was the act of protest of a Basque traditionalist class that had been gradually displaced from the centres of power. The urban lower middle classes of Bilbao, still in shock because of the loss of the *fueros* in 1876, felt under pressure from the process of modernisation, and, unable to benefit from industrial development, faced the prospect of proletarianisation. Artisans, small businessmen, and the professional middle classes witnessed how the population increased dramatically with many of the new inhabitants of Biscay coming from the impoverished areas of rural Spain. These immigrants brought with them new lifestyles, languages, and ideologies which were seen as a menace by the churchgoers of Bilbao. Some traditionalists consciously took refuge in the foralist literary works that praised a harmonious vision of a pre-industrial and rural Basque Country. Other dislocated traditionalists made obvious their discontent with the situation and were ready for a political movement that went beyond celebrating the pre-industrial Basque Arcadia.

Sabino Arana's nationalism effectively articulated these feelings of nostalgia for a vanishing order and advocated a project of regeneration based on achieving sovereign statehood. His political programme combined an empathy for pre-existing popular ideas such as the Carlist tradition, Catholicism, and agrarian romanticism with a critical rejection of industrialisation and its consequences: immigration, secularisation, and urban expansion. John Sullivan has noted that Arana 'transformed the Carlist desire for the restoration of the *fueros* into something quite new—the demand for complete separation of the Basque Country from Spain' (Sullivan 1988: 5).

To the eyes of Arana the evils of industrial society, such as the decline of Catholicism, the changing social structure, and the declining use of Euskara, coincided with the arrival of the newcomers. The Spanish immigrant was seen as the agent responsible for the moral and racial decline of the Basques but also as a symbol of Spain's oppression. Identifying the ultimate source of the problem was followed by the development of a plan of action which could contain the 'foreign' element. At first, the immigrant, pejoratively called *maketo*, was described as an 'outsider', both 'exotic' and 'dangerous', but soon came to be described in clinical and quasi-religious terms. According to Arana, the contaminating effects of the outsider were felt in the Basque body and soul. It did not take long before the immigrant was degraded to the category of a moral and viral infection. In Arana's view, segregation was the only way to purge, heal, and protect the Basque people from the 'anti-Basque' disease:

> It is evident that the salvation of Basque society, its current regeneration and hope in the future are all pinned on absolute isolation, on leaving aside all outside elements, on racial exclusion and on leaving out all that is not clearly Basque, inexorably rejecting everything that is exotic, immoral and harmful. (Arana 1980: 1761)

As time progressed and the non-Basque immigrant integrated into society it became more difficult for Basque traditionalists to identify foreign elements. The Basque language could have been used as a dividing line but Euskara was little spoken in the major towns where immigrants settled. As in Ernest Gellner's prototypical Ruritania, the urban elites of Bilbao and San Sebastián preferred to speak the language of Megalomania (Gellner 1983: 58). In the absence of visible differences, new markers were constructed and used to distinguish what was Basque from what was not. In fact, Arana's whole political work can be seen as an attempt to erect a clearly identifiable ethnic boundary between Basques and Spaniards so to avoid the mixing of the two groups.

Arana's contribution, however, can only be understood when framed in nineteenth century Spanish history. Several other regions in the Iberian Peninsula have a distinct identity: Andalusia, Aragon, Catalonia, and Galicia, to name just a few. Were we to explain the persistence of ethnic identity exclusively by the 'national character' of their peoples, whatever that might be, then Spain would be a country of fabulous regional characters. Rather, it seems that an effective explanation for the persistence of non-Castilian forms of identity needs to take in account the weakness of the Spanish state-building project. Paraphrasing George Mosse (1975), it is only in the early twentieth century that Spain came to possess a fully effective state apparatus capable of nationalising the masses. The lack of robust state structures in previous eras helps to explain the persistence of regional and local forms of identity at least until the aftermath of the French revolutionary wars. Although developments in Spain did not completely differ from general European trends, it is crucial to examine Spanish nationalism and its nation-building process in order to understand the resonance of Basque nationalism.

2.1 THE SPANISH NATION-BUILDING PROCESS

Every Hispanist has to come to terms with an observation of Juan Linz which is reproduced here: 'Spain is a state for all Spaniards, a nation-state for a large part of the population, but only a state and not a nation for important minorities' (Linz 1973: 36). Contemporary Spain has become a quasi-federal state where multiple national ideologies compete for the allegiance of its citizens. The Spanish nation continues to be the main source of identity but a majority of Spaniards have developed a form of 'dual patriotism' by which they are loyal to political and cultural communities other than the Spanish, such as the Basque, the Catalan, the Galician, the Canarian, the Andalusian. But how can we make sense of the central importance of the centre–periphery cleavage in contemporary Spain? Is it enough to examine the history of the twentieth century or is it necessary to go further back? How can it be explained that one of Europe's oldest polities, which started the unification of its land as early as the eight century and was territorially complete by 1513 with the annexation of the Kingdom of Navarre, was not able to create a united Spain?

Historians have often argued that the answer to all these questions needs to be found in the nineteenth century, and, predominantly in the weak nation-building process which never overcame regional identities. While the majority of scholars agree on the lack of synchronisation between state and nation-building processes in Spain, they tend to disagree on the level of resonance of Spanish nationalism vis-à-vis peripheral nationalisms.[1] But before examining the so-called 'problem of Spain', it is also worth pointing out that the question of whether liberal Spain failed or not to integrate its political, social, cultural, and territorial components very much depends on the countries Spain is compared to. When compared to the most accomplished case, the French Third Republic, the process of nationalisation of the masses in the nineteenth century seems weak.[2] If compared to the United Kingdom, Germany, or Italy where regional identities have proved durable, then the Spanish case is not so extraordinary. If the comparison considers multi-national and multi-lingual empires with uneven industrial developments and a multiplicity of ethnic groups within its borders, such as the Austro-Hungarian or Ottoman empires, then the conclusion would be that the Spanish case was quite successful (Quiroga 2004: 31).

Before the invasion of Napoleon's army in 1808, Spain was characterised by the strong presence of diverse traditions, political privileges, and legal codes. The Catholic faith and dynastic loyalty acted as unifying factors but, in spite of the efforts of the Bourbon monarchy to endow its domains with a sense of unity based on French enlightened despotism, the country remained stubbornly divided by internal borders and regional peculiarities. Throughout the eighteenth century a new sense of state based on the reinforcement of royal authority, state centralisation, and the unification of laws and monarchy emerged across the European continent. In Spain the Bourbons used the new state to intervene in the economy, create royal academies, improve the rudimentary transport network, reform the army, and defend monarchism. However, these early state-building attempts did not, and could not, create a homogeneous Spain. The social conditions needed to create a shared culture, which were usually provided by an industrial society—a growth-oriented economy, universal literacy, and a mobile division of labour, amongst others—were not yet in place (Gellner 1983). Moreover, the cultural richness and diversity of the country was a formidable obstacle to the enlightened reformism of the Bourbons as no less than ten languages were spoken in agrarian Spain. It is not surprising then that the majority of the population felt more attached to their local and regional identities than to a Spanish 'imagined community' (Álvarez Junco 1996: 89; 2001b: 75). Last but not least, there was the issue of the state-building project being quintessentially Castilian. The demographic dominance of Castile explained the political, cultural, and economic pre-eminence of the Kingdom in the Spanish Monarchy. Along these lines, between the sixteenth and eighteenth centuries, its elites became the main drivers of the state-building process and Castilian rose to be the cultured and official language of Spain and the Empire. The interests of Castile were not always in step with the rest of the territories that formed the Spanish monarchy as the revolts of 1640 and 1714 indicate. Not that they needed to be. Castile was the dominant ethnic group (*Staatsvolk*) in Spain and its hegemonic role was to provide the impetus for a unification project in the same way as England would do in Britain, Prussia in Germany, and Piedmont in Italy. And yet, this Castilian prevalence did not mean the disappearance of the other Spanish ethnies, but a rather high level of integration within the Spanish monarchy.[3]

The War of Independence (1808–1814) was the turning point in the history of Spanish nationalism. The invasion of Napoleonic troops mobilised an important sector of the population in the struggle against the French and triggered the liberal revolution, which resulted in the approval of a constitution which established the 'Spanish nation' as the ultimate sovereign (Muro & Quiroga 2005: 12). The liberal bourgeoisie further developed a modern idea of Spanish nationalism and decided that, in order to imbue the masses with a sense of patriotism a uniform state was needed, modelled on the French ideal. Following the 1833 division into provinces, the state-building project frantically continued during the mid-nineteenth century with the integration of the economy. After the creation of the Stock Exchange (1831), the unification of the tax system (1845), and the formation of the Bank of Spain (1856), came the imposition of the peseta as the national currency (1868). With regard to the monopoly of violence, the Civil Guard was created in 1844 and the Penal Code was drafted in 1848. A mass education system was introduced at the secondary and university levels between 1845 and 1857. Finally, the symbolic elements were introduced with the adoption of the national flag in 1843 and the national anthem in 1908. To employ a variant of Massimo d'Azeglio's observation, after establishing the Spanish state the reformist elite still had the pending issue of 'making Spaniards'.

The lack of financial resources meant that the liberal project of creating a single unified culture 'from above' through a programme of mass, standardised, compulsory, public education could not be realised. Spain had become chronically indebted with the war against the Napoleonic army, the American wars of independence in the first half of the nineteenth century, and the costly Carlist Wars (Alvarez Junco 1996, 2001a). Furthermore, the unevenness of the process of industrialisation meant that Asturias, Catalonia, and the Basque Country were modernised in the last decades of the nineteenth century whereas the rest of Spain remained anchored in the pre-industrial age.[4] The state institutions were not able to influence the economy or implement political reforms and were not being omnipresent in Spanish society. For example, the two most important agents of nationalisation, the army and education, were heavily under resourced and would contribute very little to the creation of a common identity. At a time when France and Great Britain were establishing vast colonial empires, Spain was incapable of projecting economic and military power over its Spanish American empire and was struggling to find a realistic project that could mobilise the national body. With the single exception of the successful war against Morocco (1859–1960), which resulted in the acquisition of the Ifni, Spaniards were not aroused by the foreign military undertakings of a state which was incapable of expanding its overseas territories. Only those who could not pay their way out of the system of *quintas* were conscripted into a demoralised army which devoted 60 per cent of its budget to officers' salaries instead of modernising its equipment and training. Unable to provide social mobility for its troops or imbue Spaniards with a strong sense of mission, the officers of both the army and the navy became sensitive to civilian politics and started to dictate public policies through military intervention. The praetorian character of the institution was confirmed by numerous *prounciamientos* or attempts to change the political system by the direct use of force. The military lobby came to believe that their interests, which were often dressed up in the guise of patriotism, were synonymous with those of the nation and made it their chief occupation to maintain order and intervene in politics when they saw fit. In the absence of a clearly defined foreign enemy, the Spanish army blurred the division between civilian and military spheres and turned its attention to the internal enemies of Spain which included Catalan and Basque regionalism as well as the latent anti-militarism of the working class. Its active role in the public administration (over 88 per cent of the Spanish civil servants were military or militarised personnel) meant that the military could interfere in the political process and stop unwanted reforms such as the much needed downsizing of the armed forces. According to one estimate, by mid-century the army and navy consumed 27 per cent of the state budget (Boyd 2000: 73–74).

The colossal public deficit also had financial consequences for the education system which was having little success in creating a uniform national culture. In theory, all Spanish children had been receiving free schooling up to the age of nine since 1857. In practice, the primary education of most Spaniards, particularly those belonging to the lower classes, had been left in the hands of various religious orders belonging to the Catholic Church. The Moyano Law of 1857 established the bases for a secular, enlightened education and allocated the responsibility for primary instruction to the often bankrupt local authorities. Secondary education was under the aegis of the individual province and the ten universities, which were reserved for social elites, were maintained at the state's expense. The liberal ambitions for a universal public educational system had to be balanced with the Concordat of 1851 which established religious supervision of schooling and gave the Church the right to review the moral and doctrinal content of teaching and textbooks at both the primary and secondary levels (Puelles 1991: 142–156). Moreover, the blueprint for a state education had to come to terms with the harsh socio-economic reality of rural and provincial Spain (*la España profunda*) where the majority of Spaniards lived on very modest means. When, in 1898, Spain lost all of its remaining colonies in the Caribbean and Asia-Pacific regions, the adult literacy rate was estimated at 40 to 45 per cent. Although analogous to other Southern European countries' rates, Spain could not compare itself to Germany, France, or Italy where the number of children attending school was much higher (Nuñez 1992: 292–293; Boyd 1997: 3–40).

The difficult historical development of Spanish nation-building allowed for the maintenance of regional cultures and languages but also for the reformulation of these deep-rooted historical traditions into regional-nationalist aspirations. Among the regions which had successfully retained distinct customary laws and legal codes were Catalonia and the Basque Country which developed political movements that were highly critical of the corrupt, inefficient yet stable political system of the Restoration monarchy. The political projects of these regions could not be absorbed or co-opted by the rigid structures of a system based on electoral fraud, patronage and fictitious political change. As pointed out by Francisco Romero, the fraudulent rotation of the dynastic parties and the widespread apathy of the masses provided nationalist elites with enough ammunition to question the legitimacy of the political system, condemn the centralist structure of the Spanish state, and put forward demands for the advancement of their own traditions and cultures (Romero 1996: 120–121).

2.2 BUILDING BLOCKS OF BASQUE NATIONALISM

Even though Basque ethnic identity has roots in pre-modern times, the movements that preceded, shaped, and deeply influenced modern nationalism are to be found in the nineteenth century. The two key building blocks of Basque nationalism, Carlism and foralism, greatly contributed to the formation of a cross-class political and ideological movement which advocated a pre-industrial idea of Basqueness. It is not the victory of these two movements but, rather, their defeat that breathed a nostalgic soul into Arana's nationalism. In effect, his work provided a radical version of the Carlist and foralist ideas and resentfully described the loss of the *fueros* in a typically modern fashion.

2.2.1 The Carlist wars

In the last decades of the eighteenth century, the French and American revolutions engendered a series of political convulsions that continued into the next century. The political systems these two revolutions had created were as much praised as despised in European courts, and 'tradition' and 'revolution' took leading roles in both dismantling the *ancien régime* and introducing a capitalist, secular, modern society. In Spain, the gradual transfer of power from the nobility and the clergy to the middle class set the liberals against the traditionalists, who came to be known as Carlists. Liberalism had come to power during the War of Independence (also known as the Peninsular War) and, in spite of initiating a set of reforms based on ideas of equality, active citizenship, and the rule of law, it did not constitute a coherent body of thought and action. With the introduction of the first liberal Constitution in 1812, popular sovereignty was introduced and the traditional interdependency of Church and state began to change in favour of secularism. In contrast to liberals who put forward rationalisation measures, absolutists were adamantly opposed to any reform that altered the status quo and demanded that the country be ruled by a responsive monarch who would be answerable to the *Cortes* and would uphold the central position of the Church (Burdiel 2000; MacClancy 2000).

Carlism first entered Spanish politics in 1833 to initiate the first of two Spanish civil wars in the nineteenth century, the Carlist Wars. At the time, Carlism gained the attention of Karl Marx, who proposed to study this combination of peasants, minor aristocracy, and clergy with an open mind. Dismissed by Raymond Carr as a 'revolution of inadaptables', the Carlists shared in common their difficulty in adapting to the penetration of capital in the rural world and, according to Gerald Brenan, 'had no policy but to return to the seventeenth century' where 'safety and tranquility' could be found (Carr 1992: 187; Brenan 1943: 204–205). A counter-revolutionary movement, Carlism did not have a political programme outside the intransigent defence of the Church and the absolutist monarchy against the liberal political, social, economic, and religious policies. With regard to its social basis, Carlism could draw on the support of the social classes tied to the pre-industrial economic structure: peasants, rural owners, clergy, and craftsmen. Although it is debatable whether Carlism is a truly Spanish phenomenon or not, it took deeper root in the Basque Country than anywhere else in Spain, with the sole exception of Catalonia (Coverdale 1984; Payne 1977).

The First Carlist War, from 1833 to 1839, was fought principally in the Basque Country, Navarre, Aragon, and Catalonia. Initially a dispute about dynastic rights, the war brought urban liberalism into confrontation with rural traditionalism. The triggering event was the so-called *cuestión dinástica* after the death of King Ferdinand VII in 1833. The King had been unsuccessful in producing a male heir and after his death his daughter Isabelle II was proclaimed monarch. The King's brother, Don Carlos, denied the validity of this promulgation through the Salic law of 1713, which decreed that only male offspring could succeed to the throne. The two opposing sides came to be known as *isabelinos* and *carlistas*, taking the names of the two contenders to the throne. Carlist strength was confined to the rural east (Aragon and Catalonia) and the north of Spain, especially Navarre and the Basque Country, where there was strong support for the traditional Roman Catholic order represented by the religiosity of Don Carlos and his circle. The Church hierarchy also rose up against the government's liberal centralism and mobilised the rural population and the lower classes of small urban centres, some of which had been directly displaced by the disentailing laws and forced to move to the industrialising cities.[5] The main Navarrese and Basque cities, Pamplona, San Sebastián, Vitoria, and especially Bilbao, remained liberal and Castilian-speaking.[6] Carlism did not appeal to the economically successful urban middle classes who were able to shape liberal legislation during the war. At the tactical level, the 'red berets' were a resilient rural force which skilfully used guerrilla tactics in the mountainous terrain of the north against the Queen's troops. The war in the Basque region ended with the Treaty of Vergara (1839), which recognised Isabelle as the legitimate sovereign and protected the autonomous character of the *fueros*. In a famous law approved in the Spanish Parliament in October 1839 the *fueros* of the Basque Country and Navarre were confirmed as long as they did not affect the constitutional unity of the Monarchy (*sin perjuicio de la unidad constitucional de la Monarquía*).[7]

Between 1847 and the 1860s there were intermittent violent outbreaks in Catalonia, Aragon, Navarre, and Gipuzkoa, but these events did not seriously threaten the ruling monarch. With the exception of the Catalan uprising of the *matiners* (1846–1849), Carlism languished well into the 1850s and Isabella's reign was never seriously in danger.[8] However, the Carlist movement reorganised itself in the 1860s, adapting its programme in the process—switching its central priority of 'king' to that of 'Church'—and actively preparing for a second civil war. When, in 1868, the Isabelline monarchy was deposed by the 'Glorious Revolution' of General Prim and replaced with a monarchy and then a republic, the Carlists felt their chance had come once again. In December 1872, the foral governing bodies sponsored a Carlist rebellion which grew into the Second Carlist War (1872–1876) where much of what had happened in the first offensive was re-enacted. Yet again, the hegemonic presence of the ultra-Catholics in the rural areas was counterbalanced by their fifth column, the Basque cities. As in the first war, the Carlists attempted to siege Bilbao where they were defeated for a second time.[9] In the 1830s the leader of the Carlist forces, Zumalacárregui, had died in the siege of the Biscayan capital, which was quickly becoming an important industrial centre of crucial strategic importance. This time, the most popular Carlist generals, Ollo and Rada, died and the Carlist cause was crushed. In 1876, after almost four years of fighting, Carlos VII was forced to follow the example of his grandfather and fled across the Pyrenean border. Shortly after the Carlist defeat, on 21 July 1876, the liberal government suppressed the Basque and Navarrese *fueros*.

The defeat of Carlism in the Second Carlist War was one of the most important political events in the development of a Basque ethnic identity in the nineteenth century (Molina 2005: 291). In the first Carlist war, the *fueros* had been a marginal issue but their defence became a prominent issue in the second one. Since the 1830s, Basque traditionalists had incorporated their own element into the Carlist motto: *Dios, Patria, Rey* (God, Fatherland, King), and turned it into *Dios, Patria, Fueros, Rey*. After king Alfonso XII decided to punish the 'rebel provinces' by cancelling their historical privileges in 1876, discontent and frustration spread throughout the Basque Country, and for the first time, the defence of the *fueros* was unanimous, regardless of political orientation (Solazabal 1975: 292). Even though not all the provinces were equally Carlist and many urban liberals were not against the *fueros*, the abolition produced an indignant body of citizens which mourned together and shared a common discontent with Spain. For the first time in their history, Basques received the abolishment as a collective affront. No direct link can be made between Carlism and nationalism since both political options co-existed for a long period. However, nationalism took over much of the political space the Carlists occupied and benefited from the anti-liberal discontent the foral abolition produced in the Basque psyche. According to Vicente Garmendia, Spain came to be synonymous with liberalism and Don Carlos' cause came to be remembered as the 'Basque cause' (Garmendia 1985: 140).

2.2.2 Foralism

The Basque Provinces and Navarre are historical anomalies inasmuch as they managed to retain the *fueros* until the modern age. These local charters had regulated Basque daily life since the Middle Ages and allowed the provinces to maintain economic concessions such as the province's exemption from military service, taxation, and internal tariffs that applied to the rest of Spain (Carr 1992: 74). At the political level, the provinces were allowed to have political institutions of their own, such as governing assemblies and collective territorial privileges. The governing bodies changed slightly from province to province, but they all had a general assembly with an executive branch, called a *diputación*. By the nineteenth century, the *fueros* were seen by liberals as an obstacle to the project of building a centralised nation-state. In 1833, the *fueros* were modified but they continued to be used after 1839. Liberal policies gradually eroded the *fueros* during the 1840s and, especially, after their victory in the second Carlist War. In 1876, the abolition decree wiped out the medieval charters in all areas except one, taxation. A system called *conciertos económicos* was established by which the Basque Provinces paid a tribute to Madrid to finance state expenditure (Villa 2004: 40–45).

The gradual erosion of the territorial privileges generated a movement that advocated the political and judicial system of the *fueros*. In its literary form, foralism had been present for as long as *fueros* existed. As chapter 1 explained, the foral system had been subject to attack from the Spanish Bourbon monarchies and authors from Biscay and Gipuzkoa (e.g., Garibay, Martínez de Isasti, Martínez de Zaldivia, Poza, Larramendi) had provided arguments and justifications for its maintenance. In the nineteenth century, the defence of the *fueros* would absorb the energies of many more authors who contributed and enlarged this cultural movement, which started at the turn of the century and was over by 1890.[10] The peak of this cultural movement was the period that followed the foral abolition.[11] During these years, foralism developed the literary tradition of romantic and epic undertones into a cultural movement (similar to the Catalan *Renaixença* and the Galician *Rexurdimiento*) that preceded the emergence of nationalism. The cultural movement had two clear foci—Navarre and Biscay—and mainly worked towards the rediscovery of Euskara but also of Basque history, traditions, and literature (Elorza 2001: 50). The Navarrese *Asociación Euskara* was created in 1878 by Juan Iturralde Suit, based on the ideas of Arturo Campión, a young lawyer. The members of the *Asociación Euskara* were involved in local politics, but their main activity would be the publication of the journal, *Revista Euskara*, where leading Basque intellectuals wrote about Basque identity (Elorza 2001: 49–50). The second organisation, *Euskal-Erria*, was created in Biscay in 1876 and was more concerned with the success of its businesses than with local history and religion. These two organisations preceded Basque nationalism and paved the way for its birth in the 1890s.

Foralism was the Basque version of a typically European process of romanticism and movements of cultural re-discovery preceding the emergence of political nationalisms. Originally, it was Johan Gottfried von

Herder who, at the end of the eighteenth century, gave a powerful impetus to the search for the linguistic and cultural origins of nations. His example was followed throughout Europe by historians, philologists, and archaeologists, who rushed towards the genesis of nations in their respective fields and recorded the native folklore, ballads, poetry, and music as well as previously ignored medieval and Renaissance works (Porter 1988). The romantic revolt against classicism and neo-classicism and its emphasis on the more picturesque, original, free, and imaginative styles chimed perfectly with a Basque traditionalist class which had lost everything it had stood for. Romanticism provided an opportunity to rediscover the essence of things and find examples of 'pure' and 'natural' things in the Basque past. Romantics such as Antonio Trueba, Juan Venancio de Araquistain, Francisco Navarro Villoslada, Vicente Arana, and Arturo Campión among others had readily available 'raw materials' in the Basque Golden Age. As shown in Table 2.1, Basque romantics could elaborate on the many contents and indicators of the Basque Golden Age.

The foralist literature praised the poetic virtues of the *fueros*, symbol of the Basque way of life, and depicted the northern provinces as an Arcadia. In this harmonious land, Basques had traditionally spoken their language and lived happily until they were forced to defend their rural paradise from invaders. The importance of these literary works was that, in spite of their mythical character, they were read and internalised as factual history. What were originally literary works, or romantic historiography at best, filled the vacuum of academic historical literature in the Basque Country. As Jon Juaristi (1987: 16) has pointed out, the historical novel, the legend, and the ballads and poems of an Ossianic nature became the Basque historiography of the nineteenth century. The works of the period, although aiming to be historically accurate, were often accused of being economical with the truth (Cirujano 1985). But as one of the romantic authors of this period, Juan Venancio de Araquistain, argued when replying to his critics: 'history will make erudite people, but not heroes, especially in the masses. Only traditions, songs, and stories [...] have the power to inflame the imagination of the peoples' (Elorza 2001: 47). Of course, not all Basque romantics were nationalists, but the search for origins led, for the most part, to an attempt to uncover a national past that could nurture the present. Romanticism, which found in the exotic and remote Middle Ages examples of virtuous and heroic life, provided the ideal for a renewal

Table 2.1 The Basque Golden Age

Domain	Content	Indicator
Religion	Chosen people	Language
Social	Universal nobility	Race/blood
Political	Millenarian independence	Fueros

that could awake the 'Sleeping Beauty' of the nation. As Mary Ann Perkins has rightly argued, romanticism was concerned with the resurrection of the past and the 'invention of tradition' (Perkins 1999: 52). Basque nationalists began to see their past as mythical, often involving glorious kingdoms, great empires, and indigenous political structures. When set in contrast to the past, the present time was seen as decadent and uninspiring, and often as though it were no more than the ruins of Antiquity. In short, the search for the elements that made the national past 'authentic' was also a search for the elements of decadence in the present.

2.3   SABINO ARANA GOIRI

The role of the intellectuals in the process of identity formation has been studied by a wide variety of scholars (Kedourie 1971; Nairn 1977; Breuilly 1982; Hroch 1985; Smith; 1991). Of them all, none has been more critical of dissatisfied intellectuals than Elie Kedourie, who described these self-proclaimed champions as 'marginal men' on the fringes of society (Kedourie 1960; 1971). As part of the elite, the role of the intellectuals was to provide a collective frame of reference which in some way represented the national population. This shared frame was necessarily selective as it simplified the main injustices endured by the dormant population and articulated a doctrine of national 'awakening' which, eventually would eliminate the unjust situation. From this point of view, the intellectual could be seen as a 'social

Illustration 1 Sabino Arana
Goiri, 1894

thermometer', an early warning system for a dysfunctional social structure, but also a cultural promoter of the language, culture, and history of the 'unconscious' nation. The articulation of the Basque frame of reference was the contribution of Sabino Policarpo de Arana Goiri (1865–1903), the person to whom Basque nationalism owes almost everything. The founder of the Basque nationalist movement endured, as did many of his contemporaries, the ideological, economic, and political upheavals of the time as the industrial revolution gathered steam. His political ideology was a reaction to the complete incorporation of the Basque Country into Spain and to the rapid industrialisation which violently transformed the *ancien régime* structures into a modern industrial society. His nationalism was the cry of a traditionalist reluctant to accept the newly arrived mechanised world; one so different to the harmonious agrarian world he had 'known' prior to the capitalist disruption (Corcuera 1979, 2001).

2.3.1 Industrialisation

The Basque industrialisation process was begun by a bourgeoisie with interests in minerals and backed by English capital. The metallurgical industry transformed the core of the Basque economy, which came to rely on banking and heavy industry, primarily steel and shipbuilding. The legal reforms which followed the abolition of the *fueros* in 1876 allowed for the entry of foreign capital and the establishment of low taxation, which facilitated the export of natural resources. The economic changes mainly occurred in Biscay, while Gipuzkoa and Araba went through a similar process later in the twentieth century. The main reason why industrialisation began in Biscay was the invention in 1855 of a new method of steel manufacture which made Basque iron essential. The Bessemer process required a low phosphorous iron, hematite, which was difficult to find in industrialised areas of Europe and was only widely available in Biscay and Sweden. Compared to its Scandinavian competitor, the Basque mines had three geographical advantages: they were open (which eliminated the need for expensive digging), were close to the coast, and enjoyed mild climate that allowed for exploitation all year round. In addition to all the foregoing, there was an abundance of cheap labour which acted as a strong economic incentive for foreign investors.

The province of Biscay became the most economically advanced area of Spain in a matter of decades. By the end of the nineteenth century cargo ships exported up to 60 per cent of the iron extracted to Britain and returned loaded with coal. The amount of exported iron increased from 55,000 tons in 1866 to 4,272,000 tons in 1890. And by 1885 until the end of the century, the mines of Biscay produced 77 per cent of Spain's cast iron, 87 per cent of its steel, and by 1900, 13.2 per cent of the world's iron ore (Fusi 1975: 17; Ortzi 1978: 112; Conversi 1997: 49; Kurlansky 1999: 155). Bilbao's shipping industry also experienced exceptional growth and it settled on the western bank of the Nervión River, changing the landscape with its shipyards, warehouses, and overcrowded houses for the proletariat. Around the heavy industries of mining, iron, and steel other minor factories mushroomed, providing the larger ones with all the necessary products they needed, from tubes and tools to all sorts of building materials. In terms of infrastructure, new roads were made and the first rail line was built to connect the mines to the port of Bilbao, which was modernised to cope with the increased traffic.

The extraction and export of minerals gave way to a rapid and intense growth of capital in Biscayan hands. The families that shaped the Basque economy during the twentieth century were then making their fortunes. The Ybarra family, but also the Chávarri, Sota, Echevarrieta, Martínez de las Rivas, Lezama Leguizamón, Allende, and Gandarias families controlled the heavy industries but also the banking system (Corcuera 2001: 54). The presence of these industrialists on the boards of directors boosted the Basque financial sector and made it one of the most advanced in Spain. According to Juan Pablo Fusi, in 1870 there was only one bank operating in the city, the *Banco de Bilbao*, founded in 1857, but thirty-seven years later, in 1907, there were five: *Bilbao, Comercio, Crédito de la Unión Minera, Vizcaya,* and a franchise of the Bank of Spain. The money in deposits in the local banking system experienced an increase of 914 per cent between 1870 and 1899 which opened up the possibilities for investment (Fusi 1975: 53). The deposited Basque capital was used to transform Bilbao and its surroundings from being an area purely for the extraction of minerals to a fully industrial region with a spread of investments.

Labour mobility to the Basque lands was negligible until the 1860s but industrialisation changed the situation dramatically. As can be seen in Figure 2.1, the population of Biscay almost doubled in forty years. In 1860 there were 168,205 inhabitants and by 1900 it had increased to 311,361, a difference of 143,156. The flourishing Biscayan metallurgical industry needed a workforce that neither the province nor the whole of the Basque Provinces could provide. Between 1860 and 1890, 60,000 immigrants would arrive in Biscay. The immigrants first came from neighbouring provinces such as Logroño, Araba, Navarre, and Santander, but the increasing demand attracted people from more distant places such as Galicia or the Castilian provinces of Burgos, León, and Palencia. The immigrants' main destination was the largest city in the Basque Country, Bilbao, which grew exponentially from 83,000 inhabitants at the beginning of the twentieth century to 162,000 in the 1930s. As already mentioned, the area of the city which saw the highest increase of newcomers was the left bank of the river Nervión, where the coal, iron, steel, and naval industries were based.

The newly arrived workers had little option but to live in overcrowded houses and barracks with appalling hygienic conditions. The barracks had no latrines and beds were often shared by two workers who only could have a bath in the river, the final destination of all the dirty water and detritus of

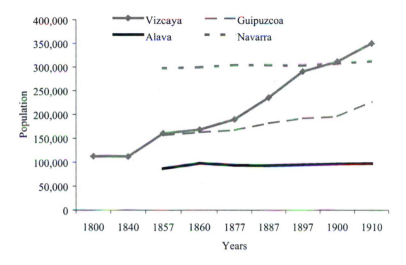

Figure 2.1 Population growth of the Basque Country and Navarre, 1800–1910.
Source: Corcuera 2001: 56

the city. Those who lived in houses had slightly better conditions, but they were all threatened by a very high mortality rate. Many of the social problems Biscay would have at the end of the nineteenth century were due to this uncontrolled growth in population. The first strike took place in 1903 and signalled the extreme polarisation between the deprived workers and the privileged industrialists who did not hesitate to show off their wealth by building palaces in the centre of the Biscayan capital. Bilbao, described by the conservative thinker Ramiro de Maeztu as the 'Socialist Mecca', was to be the stage where liberal monarchism, republicanism, and socialism battled each other to transcend ethnic lines and attract the support of both the newcomers and the old-timers (Fusi 1975: 501–504). The unfolding class struggle between the socialist proletariat and the industrial oligarchy was witnessed by an increasingly confused and worried traditionalist bourgeoisie that wanted to keep the Basque microcosm free from social unrest. After all, the process of industrialisation had turned their world upside down in a matter of years with the dismantlement of pre-industrial and agricultural modes of production, the dissolution of traditional social relations, and the decline of religious beliefs and the use of Euskara.

2.3.2 Biography and the nationalist project

The rise of modern Basque nationalism was tied to the life of Sabino Arana Goiri who was born in the suburb of Abando, now part of Bilbao, on 26

January 1865. As financial supporters of the traditionalists during the Second Carlist War, the Arana family had been forced to leave for France. From his exile in the French Pays Basque, an eleven-year-old Arana came to terms with the disappearance of the certainties that had made up his life and witnessed the decisive victory of the liberals, the abolition of the *fueros,* and the immediate seizure of his loved ones' possessions in Bilbao. His nationalism came to express his own loss and the frustrations of a Catholic traditionalist class whose members were fast becoming victims of the industrial development. Arana's own family's business, a small shipbuilding firm in Biscay, encountered financial difficulties when the traditional wooden ships they manufactured became obsolete in favour of larger vessels made of iron. At the age of twenty-eight Arana abandoned the family ideology, Carlism, and embraced the separatist national principles to which he dedicated the rest of his life. According to his own words, he 'converted' to nationalism after an epiphanic discussion about Biscayan history with his brother Luis de Arana, whose historical knowledge was much superior to his own. Sabino started frantically studying the history and the laws of Biscay, as he himself explained in his essay, *Bizkaya por su Independencia*: 'but after one year of transition, the shadows that hid my knowledge of the motherland disappeared, and offering my heart to God, eternal lord of Biscay, I offered all I am and all I have for the restoration of the motherland' (Arana 1980: 158). The new project absorbed all of Arana's energy. After the death of his father in 1883, he moved to Barcelona to study law, where he rarely attended class. Instead, he taught himself and researched the Basque language and history, finally dropping out of university. His time in Barcelona coincided with the emergence of Catalan nationalism. However, Catalanism became an antithetic model because, in spite of being a political project designed on the periphery, it was not only for the periphery. In *Errores catalanistas* (1894), Arana pointed out that the failure of Catalonia in reforming Spain was a lesson to be learned by the Basque Country, a nation that had 'never [been] dominated by Spain'. While 'the enemy of Catalonia was the central power', the political and administrative structures that made the Spanish state, the Basques' enemy was Spain in itself, the 'foreign nation that had subjugated them'.[12] After his mother's death in 1888, Sabino and his brother Luis returned to Bilbao as young adults, where both of them began their political careers.

The original ideology of Basque nationalism stems from Sabino Arana's pivotal work, *Bizkaya por su independencia: Cuatro glorias patrias* (1892). In this important text, he articulated the nationalist doctrine on the eternal independence of Biscay and how the Basques lost their ancient political freedoms. Previously published in *La Abeja* journal as a collection of essays, he referred to Biscay, not *Euzkadi*, hoping that other Basques would see the truth in his words and would follow his teachings. In the text, Biscay was depicted as an independent entity since time immemorial which had to fight to maintain its status in four mythical battles against Castile: at Arrigorriaga (888), Gordejuela (1355), Ochandiano (1355), and Munguía (1470). He also provided a contemporary explanation for the loss of such eternal independence: it was not the military victory of the Hispanic Monarchy over Basques but the increasing hispanicisation (*españolización*) of the latter. *Bizkaya por su independencia* was initially ignored, but in subsequent years it had an important influence. Seven months after the publication of *Bizkaya por su independencia* Arana had another opportunity to provide followers with a historical hallmark. On this occasion he presented his thesis to an audience of professionals—mainly foralists and liberals—at the Larrazábal Farmhouse (*Caserío de Larrazábal*). In what came to be known as the Larrazábal Speech, Arana defined the basic tenets of Basque nationalism. He described the humiliation of Biscay by Spain, that 'miserable nation', mentioning the need to rescue Biscay from 'infectious foreign molecules' and lamented the alleged Spanishness of all political parties. Near the end of the speech he apologised for using Spanish, 'a foreign language', and encouraged those present to cheer for the independence of Biscay (*¡Viva la independencia de Bizkaya!*). His radical theses were received by his fellow diners with cold silence and accusations of being 'mad and visionary' (Arana 1980: xxxv, 154–160). But the setback at Larrazábal did not discourage the young Sabino who shortly afterwards founded the newspaper *Bizkaitarra* and the club *Euzkeldun Batzokija* (which had already adopted the motto *Jaun-Goikua eta Lagi Zarra* meaning God and Old Laws). Arana wrote almost all the articles of *Bizkaitarra* and became president of the informal club. According to scholars who wrote the definitive history of the Basque Nationalist Party (PNV), the statutes of the latter 'incorporated some of the main elements of early Basque nationalism: its endogenous character, its religious fundamentalism and its interpretation of the foreign sovereignty in a dynamic and separatist tone' (De Pablo, Mees, & Rodríguez 1999: 33).

The foundation stone of Basque nationalism was laid on 31 July 1895, Saint Ignatius of Loyola day, when Arana set up the *Bizkai-Buru-Batzar* (BBB) which was to become the core of the PNV.[13] The BBB only covered the province of Biscay and was involved in the publication of the newspapers *Baserritarra*, *El Correo Vasco*, and *La Patria*. The activities of the first Basque nationalists soon attracted the eye of the government in Madrid and both the PNV's social centre and the *Bizkaitarra* were arbitrarily closed down in 1895 while Arana and his sympathisers were sentenced to months in prison for inciting rebellious acts (Corcuera 2001: 460). The repressive measures continued until 1900 but they could not stop Arana's activities because he had managed to cluster together a small number of collaborators and nationalist organisations. Among them were the newspaper *Bizkaitarra* (1893), the club *Euskaldun Batzokija* (1894), the political organisation *Bizkai Buru Batzar* (1895), the publishing house *Bizkaya'ren*

Edestija ta Izkerea Pizkundia (1896), the recreational club *Centro Vasco* (1899), the magazines *Euskadi* (1901), and *La Patria* (1901), and the language academy *Euskal Zaleen Biltzarra* (1902) (Arana 1980: xxxv–xiv).

2.3.3 Political doctrine

After Spain's embarrassing defeat in the short 1898 colonial war against the United States, some segments of the bourgeoisie and a large portion of the middle classes criticised the role played by an incompetent and corrupt state in the conflict and became interested in Basque nationalism as a political movement. The loss of the last remaining overseas colonies of Cuba, Puerto Rico, the Philippines, and Guam in the age of imperialism and colonial prestige brought about a deep cultural pessimism.[14] What came to be known as *El Desastre* was an early decolonisation crisis that produced a general feeling of shock, humiliation, and, eventually, a depreciation of the Liberal model of the nation-state. The imperial collapse also signalled the end of the image of Spain as a great European power; it was a 'dying nation' as Lord Salisbury put it, and strongly influenced a whole generation of intellectuals to cry out for national renewal (*regeneracionismo*).[15] But more importantly, the national crisis signalled a turning point in Spanish history and initiated a sequence of events that led to the decline of the political system known as the Restoration Monarchy (1874–1923). During the *Restauración*, political life was based on the untroubled alternation (*turno pacífico*) of the two dynastic parties, the liberals and the conservatives, and on the rigging of elections by *caciques* or local bosses. After 1898, however, Spain came to know the involvement of the masses in politics and the decline of the local *caciques*, which paved the way for the emergence of peripheral nationalist movements (Jacobson & Moreno 2000).

In May 1902, four years after *El Desastre*, Arana attempted to send a telegram of congratulation to President Roosevelt for having granted independence to Cuba. Not only did the message never make it to Washington, D.C., but the telegraph officer informed the appropriate authorities and Arana was imprisoned. Due to their leader's precarious health, a group of more than 8,000 followers signed a petition asking for his release. But the response of the head of the Spanish government, Segismundo Moret, was clear: 'the peace of Spain outweighs the life of one man' (Arana 1980: xliii). Aware that the prestige of the Spanish national project was at its lowest, the executive felt that the time had come to take measures against rival nationalist organisations. In its questioning of Arana, the judicial authority showed great interest in the PNV's organisation and membership, in accordance with the government's desire to crush the movement. After almost half a year of imprisonment, Arana left for Vichy in Southern France where he hoped to be safe from the authorities' harassment. Arana finally returned to the Basque Country where he died on 25 November 1903, at the age of thirty-eight. To the government's despair in Madrid, the

Illustration 2 Poster of the first Aberri Eguna, 1932

death of the young nationalist did not bring peace to Spain, as Moret had hoped, and his nationalist politics were continued by many others.

Sabino Arana created a movement that could stand on its feet long after he was gone. He had provided Basque nationalism with all the necessary elements: he invented a name for the 'land of the Basques', *Euzkadi*, a flag, the red, green, and white *ikurriña*, modelled on the Union Jack, and a patriotic anthem, *Gora ta Gora*, which replaced the popular foralist anthem, *Gerni-kao Arbola*. His contribution was widely acknowledged and the day of his political conversion, Easter Sunday 1882, became the Basque national holiday, *Aberri Eguna* (Day of the Fatherland). He also provided the motto for the new politics that extended the foralist 'God and *Fueros*' (*Jaungoi-kua eta Foruak*) to 'God and Old Laws' (*Jaungoikua eta Lagi Zarra*). Not only did he invent all of the nationalist paraphernalia, he also managed to construct a nationalist ideology which drew heavily on a romantic nostal-gia for the *fueros* as the emblem of country (Juaristi 1987; Corcuera 1991; Elorza 2001). Indeed, Arana's political message appropriated pre-existing myths and memories of an idealised rural and Catholic past and combined it with a new anti-capitalist, racist discourse with a nationalist understand-ing of history. In fact, his nationalism needed to be understood in *la longue durée* or as the conflation of three historical periods in a charismatic man: first, the long-term formation of Basque identity as depicted in the writings about the Golden Age, which had created the necessary identity structures; second, the gradual defeat of the 'Basque cause' in the Carlist Wars, which seriously affected a few generations of Basques; and third, the rapid indus-trialisation of Biscay, which affected Basque urban middle-class individu-als like Sabino Arana (Braudel 1993: xxiv). In the next sections, the main elements of his political doctrine—race, language, religion, and the use of history—are discussed in detail.

2.3.3.1 Race

Sabino Arana believed 'race' was the essential element of the nation. There were other elements that defined a nation—language, government, laws, traditions, and what he called 'historical character'—but Arana devoted most of his efforts to defining the Basque race and establishing mecha-nisms to preserve it.[16] His view that Basques were a 'pure race', an eth-nographically different people that should avoid mixing with foreigners, was instinctive rather than based on Social Darwinist ideas. There were elements of the nation, such as language, that could be recovered if they entered a period of decline, but race, the 'substance of the nation', was not one of them (Arana 1980: 404). As already pointed out, Arana saw the coming of the Spanish workforce as a threatening 'invasion'.[17] Since the process of industrialisation seemed unstoppable, Arana's despair led him to propose, as a last resort, ethnic separation between Basques and Spaniards. But first, he devised ways of identifying Spaniards. Basque workers were already doing so and referred to Spanish workers as Chinese, Manchuri-ans, or Koreans. However, Sabino's favourite expression was *maketo*:

> In this country, a maketo is the person who comes from Maketania and its neighbouring islands [...] And Maketania is the country that

shares its north border with France, the Basque lands and the Cantabrian sea; in the west, with Portugal, and the south, with Africa. (Corcuera 2001: 245)

For Arana, Spaniards were inferior and contact with the so-called 'stumpy ears' was polluting. Hence, when Arana said that 'the *maketos* are our Moors' he was drawing on pre-existing memories of what the foreign invader had been.[18] He was not only adding a powerful metaphor to his Manichean view of the world but he was resorting to historical memory and ideas of purity of blood and universal nobility which were so important to Spaniards. The infectious character of second-rate races, Arana would argue, could not be treated lightly and a pre-emptive policy of quarantine was needed:

> If a Spaniard ever begged you for money, move up your shoulders and reply to him in euskera: *Nik eztakit erderaz* (I do not speak Spanish). If a Spaniard that has just arrived to Biscay asks you where is this village or that street, reply *Nik eztakit erderaz*. If a Spaniard was, for example, drowning in the river and was asking for help, reply to him: *Nik eztakit erderaz*. (Corcuera 2001: 385)

Since his definition of Basqueness was based on myths of origin and blood descent, the only way to recognise a Basque was through the genealogy of their surnames. Following a rule of 'eight family names', ethnic belonging was an exclusive right to those who could prove that all four of their grandparents were Basques. At the same time, if married, true Basques should have spouses of similar purity. Arana himself refused to marry a middle-class *bilbaína* of 'Spanish descent' and chose instead a peasant girl of low social status, Nicolasa Achica-Allende, who fulfilled the Basque surnames criteria. Although his choice drew some opposition from his own followers, Arana was sure of the adequacy and authenticity of his choice. The girl, he concluded, represented Basqueness because 'all Basques descend from villagers'.[19] Arana's prejudice was closer to anti-Spanishness than to racism *per se*, which has led some scholars to make apologetic remarks for his use of race.[20] It is true that Arana did not single-handedly invent either anti-Spanishness or racial discrimination from scratch; however, he certainly contributed racist elements to the idea of an independent Basque state. In his article, *Efectos de la invasión* (1897), he explained how the worst grief for the Basques was not to lose their language, history, or institutions but to continue 'in contact with the children of the Spanish nation'. Speaking in the 'ethnographic sense', he referred to the 'physical and natural' category of the 'Spanish race' which was substantially different from the 'Basque race'.[21]

2.3.3.2 Language

For Arana, language was a key indicator of a distinct national identity. Writing about this sign of nationhood, he argued that Euskara 'was the language of a people that had never been dominated by Spain'.[22] His interest in the Basque language made him write a grammar and a treaty on etymology. In an article for the journal *Euskal-erria*, he referred to Euskara as 'an essential element of the Basque nation' and linked its disappearance to that of the nation: 'where Euskara ends, moral and religious degradation starts' (Arana 1980: xxxiii). Bilbao, where the use of Euskara was in clear decline, was the best example of this moral decline and Arana used to refer to the city as 'the infamous prostitute of Biscay', a place where Basques would chose to speak Spanish in order to be socially mobile. He was not the first one to have this opinion. Wilhelm F. von Humboldt had visited the Basque lands at the dawn of the century and marvelled at the romantic 'primitive simplicity' of Basques but could hardly find anything to say about the flourishing city of Bilbao 'because the continuous transit of foreigners has displaced the national traditions, which can only be found in the countryside and the mountains, and even the language is highly impure and mixed with Spanish' (Humboldt 1998: 164).

Having defined his nationalism in terms of race, Arana used language as a *de facto* ethnic boundary that would enhance Basque identity as opposed to Spanish identity. And the way for Basques to protect themselves from contact with Spaniards was to avoid teaching the Euskara, what Arana called the 'national language', to Spaniards. According to Sabino Arana, one of the errors being made in Catalonia was the attempt to integrate Spaniards by teaching them Catalan. Basques should learn from that example and should reject Spaniards who flocked to the Basque region for jobs in the industrial sector. And if Spaniards ever learnt Euskara, Basques should abandon it and speak something else because language:

> is the means to preserve ourselves from contagion from Spaniards and avoid the crossing of the two races. If our invaders learnt euskera, we should abandon it [...] and speak, instead, Russian, Norwegian or any other unknown language to them. (Arana 1980: 404)

The nationalist use of the language was crucial to Arana. All patriots needed to speak Basque but there could be nothing more dangerous than non-Basques speaking Basque:

> Speaking euskera is worth nothing if one does not feel a patriot. The most important thing is patriotism, even if one does not speak euskera. The Patria will not be saved by euskera, only by patriotism. Propagate patriotism, and with it euskera will also propagate. If you propagate euskera as a nationless language, the enemies of the Patria will multiply. (Arana 1980: 1307)

In Arana's eyes, Euskara was just another element that differentiated the two nations: 'there is more difference between Euskara and any of the Spanish languages than between the latter and the language spoken by the inhabitants of India'.[23] And if there was any doubt as to how different the languages were, Arana would make them different. As Daniele Conversi has pointed out, much of Arana's work aimed at purifying Euskara of Hispanicisms. Thus, *erdera* (foreign) elements of the language would be eliminated and replaced by Basque neologisms 'based on logic' (Corcuera 1997: 34, 64). Among his contributions to the language were the name for his country, *Euzkadi* (from *Euskal*, meaning 'Euskera speaking', and the suffix *di*, meaning 'together'), the name for fatherland, *aberri* (from *aba*, father, and *erri*, country) and its 'logical consequence', *abertzale*, or patriot. In the later stages of his life, Arana finally understood the peasant's dismissal of Euskara, because it was 'of no use for his son', and, abandoning his reactionary understanding of industrialisation, he proposed to create a 'high culture' for Euskara. From that moment, the solution for the decline of Euskara was to create 'industries and shipping companies' and 'nationalise all spheres of human life' so that it could be functional. Surprisingly, at the end of his life, Arana shared the views of his opponent Miguel de Unamuno and other Basque intellectuals such as Pío Baroja or Ramiro de Maeztu who used the language of Castilian and refused to write in 'the language of the stables' (Heiberg 1975).[24]

2.3.3.3 Religion

According to Antonio Elorza (2001: 181), Sabino Arana was aware at all times that he was founding a political religion. Although this might be a bit too daring, there is certainly no shortage of Catholic symbolism in Arana's work, the most important being the crusades. Religion was present during all stages of Arana's life and, not surprisingly, this also influenced his thought. The college he attended in Bilbao, the *Colegio Orduña*, was directed by Jesuits who taught in accordance to foralism and traditional Catholicism. The 'good practices' he acquired in the college accompanied him all his life. He remained a devoted believer and even spent the first stage of his honeymoon as a pilgrim at the Sanctuary of Lourdes. He openly admired the figure of Saint Ignatius of Loyola and the Society of Jesus he founded, the most 'colossal and sublime work of the saint'.[25] In homage, Arana created the Biscayan core of the PNV, the *Bizkai-Buru-Batzar*, on the festival of Saint Ignatius in 1895, with the religious and political motto *Jaungoikua eta Lagizarra* (God and old laws). Arana also believed in a covenant between God and his people and asserted the Basque nation was sacred. He saw his evolution from Carlist to nationalist in religious terms and talked about his 'political conversion'. The day he was 'illuminated' by his brother, Easter Sunday 1882, later became the Basque national day (*Aberri Eguna*). From 1888 onwards, Arana reconciled religion and politics and would sign most of his works with the acronym GETEJ (*Gu Euzka-direntazat Ta Euzkadi Jaungoikuarentzat*; We for Euskadi and Euskadi for God). Furthermore, nationalism was a way of doing good on earth, it was a way of reaching God:

> Ideologically speaking, God comes before the Patria [...] but in Biscay to love God it is necessary to be a patriot, and to be a patriot it is necessary to love God. (Arana 1980: 615)

Arana's nationalist project was eminently religious. In his view, the project of regeneration that nationalism embodied (the independence of *Euskadi*) brought the Basques closer to God: Even the ultimate sacrifice, 'dying for the nation' was not a mundane thing to do, but 'a death for God' (Arana 1980: 1272). In the current situation Basques were being 'infected' by contact with Spaniards, who had only brought 'weakness, corruption of the heart...and the end of human society'.[26] Hence, the nationalist project went beyond politics and it was 'about saving souls'. No other cause was more noble and saintly than this and it had a divine blessing: 'if the cause is just and necessary as a remedy for a grave moral damage, God orders us to carry it out. God wants us to carry it out, and what he orders is never useless or impossible'. Finally, it was clear that: 'Biscay, if dependent on Spain, cannot address itself to God, it cannot be Catholic in practice' (Arana 1980: 1331–1333).

2.3.3.4 History

The fourth pillar on which Arana's political doctrine was based was 'history', or rather, his 'use of history'. History added to the other three components—race, language, and religion —and, at the same time, permeated all of them.[27] His understanding of religion and the use of race and language as ethnic boundary markers was based on his understanding of the Basque past. His nationalism was, above everything else, a restoration of the lost Basque freedom, a historical quest which shared a lot in common with *regeneracionismo*. The aim of the nationalist project was to recover Basque 'historical consciousness' and invoke the glories but also the sacrifices of the ancestors.[28] For example, in 1899 Arana argued in an article titled 'Regeneración' that the renewal of the Basque nation could only happen if Basques understood why until very recently they had 'lived free and happy' but then had 'lost everything' (in reference to the medieval *fueros*). The way forward for Basques, according to him, was to learn their 'own history' and identify 'their enemies' (Arana 1980: 1673). Deeply influenced by the writers of the Golden Age and the ultra-right Carlist propaganda, Arana provided an ethnoscape or idyllic image of the Basque territory. For Arana, like others in the nineteenth century, the Basque Country appeared as a democratic, rural, and bucolic Arcadia seated at the top of the Pyrenees, 'an oasis of liberty, purity and peace, without vagrants, thieves, assassins or social problems' (Garmendia 1985: 138). Medieval Biscay, for example, was:

> a state and a confederation of republics [...] Absolutely free and independent, at the same time harmonious and fraternal among themselves, these little political entities, governed by laws born of their own womb and founded on religion and morality, enjoyed a perfectly happy existence. (Granja 1995: 67)

His ideology was also a continuation of the foralist tradition that talked about eternal independence, vindicated the excellence and invincibility of the Basques, and maintained the Carlists' identification between 'God and *Fueros*' (Corcuera 2001: 657). The influence of such literature has led several authors to identify the mythical and legendary elements in Arana's work (Aranzadi 2000; Juaristi 1987; Elorza 2001; Corcuera 2001; Unzueta 1988). An example of this foralist influence and the nostalgic attitude towards the pre-industrial past can be clearly seen in an article titled 'La Patria' that Arana published in *El Correo Vasco* in 1899. In that short article, Arana explained the reasons that would lead a Basque to love the fatherhood. This was not the fact that the nation was great and wealthy, he argued, but because it was 'rich in virtues and it deserved sacrifices' to return it to the state in which 'many literary works talked about her: bathed in sunlight and with the splendour of all her virtues' (Arana 1980: 1729).

Yet again, his approach to Basque history was epitomised in his key text *Bizkaya por su independencia*. Besides describing four crucial battles against Spaniards, Arana wanted to demonstrate how the pact that bound together Spain and Biscay never existed. Significantly, he started the essay with a Greek phrase inscribed before the Oracle at Delphi, *Gnothi Seauton*, 'know thyself' and continued by inflating the four confrontations into an epic struggle for Basque independence, the most important of them being the 888 AD Battle of Arrigorriaga, where Castile suffered defeat at the hands of the Biscayans. For Sabino, the battle of Arrigorriaga was the symbol of the eternal independence of Biscay, which dedicated itself to the defence of 'universal nobility'. Arana talked about 'Basques' as willing to talk to the Spaniards only as their equals. At the time, nobody questioned either the myth of universal nobility or the battle of Arrigorriaga being chosen as a symbol of the struggle of the Basques (Otazu 1986). The general acceptance of these myths supports the Weberian view that it did not really matter if myths were historically accurate or not but only if they resonated.

When juxtaposing his idealised vision of the past, almost a Golden Age, with the present, Arana saw nothing but decay. According to Arana, Basques were living in a damned apocalyptic century:

> One century of Spanish rule, of degradation, of misery and ruin; one
> century of aberrations and backwardness; one century of slavery!...this
> nineteenth century is the sum of all infamies, miseries and ignomies of
> past ages. (Arana 1980: 123)

The time in which Basques were living as proud people was long gone
because they no longer cared about their virtuous past. He would repeat-
edly warn his contemporaries, 'Blessed are the people who know their own
history' (Arana 1980: xxxii). Therefore, the solution could not just be institutional and political but needed to be also moral and religious, a complete
programme of regeneration. But for the Basques to voluntarily engage in
such a separatist project, they first needed to study 'the glory of their past
in order to understand their current degradation' (Kurlansky 1999: 162).
The teaching of the past was fundamental because history was not only a
succession of events, battles, and kingdoms but a narrative that established
the moral standard of the community. As Arana pointed out,

> What is national history...but a painting where a people is taught their
> past life, the ways to avoid evil and obtain good both for themselves
> and in their relations with other peoples, and a testimony of the rights
> it has enjoyed? (Arana 1980: 1327)

The political agenda for the future was implicitly set when national history was invoked. What the nation had or had not done in the past set the
parameters of legitimate change and could legitimise or subvert the existing political order (Boyd 1997: xi). Arana, who perfectly understood the
integrative function of myths of origin and destiny, could only expect that
future generations would be more informed about the Basque past and
would help restore the pre-industrial independence of the Basque nation.

2.4 CONCLUSION

Basque nationalism emerged in the 1890s when the advent of economic
modernisation turned the Basque Country into a powerful industrial centre. The sudden economic and social transformations, the eradication
of the foral regime in 1876, and low confidence in the Spanish national
project after the country lost Cuba, Puerto Rico, Philippines, and Guam,
provided the political opportunity structure in which Basque nationalism
could emerge. Sabino Arana initially proposed a programme of isolation,
a return to the past which could save the Basque people from the economic and social ills of the time. Conceived as a response to what he saw
as the moral and racial decline of his hometown, Bilbao, his programme
celebrated the unique character of the Basque language, history, and race

and demanded the restoration of the *fueros*. In reaction against the invasion of immigrants, Euzkadi was defined in ethnic terms (*jus sanguinis*) and Basques were described by Arana as a chosen people who had lived in a harmonious and racially pure Arcadia for millennia. He rejected all 'foreign' elements and emphasised that national regeneration was only possible if Basques lived in isolation from immigrants and the Spanish state. In the eyes of Arana, secession was the ultimate political goal but also the means of attaining retribution and religious salvation against an immoral and sinful Spain. Such a combination of secular and sacred elements was common in the early days as the motto of the PNV, God and Old Laws, indicated. Finally, Arana furnished his secular religion with the 'invention' of a symbolic universe which included a flag, anthem, ceremonies of remembrance, and so on.

Support for the Basque Nationalist Party (PNV) first came from the urban lower-middle class and an anti-capitalist rural segment who shared Arana's nostalgic view of the harmonious rural Basque past. By praising the virtues of the Basque *fueros*, the purity and nobility of the Basque people, and the divine character of Euskara, Arana could draw support from the Carlist and foralist sectors alike. The adoption of past cultural repertoires for nationalistic purposes was the PNV's recipe for success but also its own obstacle for future expansion. The financial and industrial oligarchy and the rest of the middle classes were not consumptive romantics in search of past comforts and were not in the least interested in an archaic, isolationist, and anti-capitalist political movement rooted in the Basque Golden Age. The turning point came in 1898 when a pragmatic bourgeoisie (ready to bankroll the party) gathered their energies, joined the PNV, and convinced Arana to incorporate proposals for regional autonomy to his racialist, intransigent, and separatist agenda. Although contradictory, both tendencies co-existed as long as Arana acted as referee, and allowed the party to grow into a nationalist movement that reached all spheres of life. By the time of Arana's death in 1903 a moderate and radical trend had been firmly established, and the ideology of the PNV was set to swing in a 'patriotic pendulum' between secession and autonomy.

3 Between Autonomy and Independence (1903–1939)

The argument so far can be summarised by resorting to Miroslav Hroch's three stages in the development of European nationalist movements (Hroch 2000: 22–24). According to Hroch it is possible to outline a structural pattern of nation formation by what he calls 'non-dominant ethnic groups'. Using the comparative method, he argues that these ethnic groups became aware of their own identity throughout the nineteenth century. During the initial stage, which he calls Phase A, some intellectuals used the disciplines of archaeology, history, and anthropology to identify the 'signs' of ethnicity, such as language, culture, and history. These intellectuals committed themselves to scholarly inquiry and did not attempt to mount a patriotic agitation in part because they were isolated and in part they did not believe it would serve any purpose. In the second stage, Phase B, a new generation of patriots influenced a growing number of members of the small nation. The actions of these nationalist intelligentsias were not very successful initially, but in time their efforts found growing acceptance. When the masses became aware of their cultural, linguistic, and ethnic individuality, a fully fledged modern nation was formed, which Hroch identifies as Phase C. When compared to other European cases, Hroch notes that the Basque 'period of scholastic interest' (Phase A) started relatively late. He observes that this period started very early in some cases, that is, around 1800 (the Greeks, Czechs, Norwegians, Irish), one generation later in others (the Finns, Croats, Slovenes, Flemish, Welsh), or even as late as the second half of the nineteenth century (Latvians, Estonians, Catalans, Basques) (Ozkirimli 2000: 157).

Between 1870 and 1890 a foralist literature provided a historicist mythology of the nation which fixed the elusive character of the homeland. The romantic quest for 'authenticity' led Basque artists, historians, and educators to set up cultural associations which could help prevent the disappearance of their language. In spite of these cultural initiatives, Euskara continued to be neglected by an intellectual elite—Araquistain, Villoslada, Arana, Baroja, Unamuno—who preferred to write their works in Spanish. Compared to its Catalan counterpart (*Renaixença*), the *fuerista* movement had limited success on the cultural front but it clearly paved the way for the subsequent formation of a national identity. Contrary to the thesis of Hroch, Basque ethnic identity was developed at the popular level prior to this process of cultural regeneration and in relation to the defeats of the Carlists and the abolition of the foral system. The traumatic loss of the *fueros* popularised a nostalgic idealisation of the medieval charters which was rooted in the pre-modern works of Martínez de Zaldivia, Garibay, Poza, and Larramendi (see chapter 1). The transition to the 'period of patriotic agitation', Phase B in Hroch's model, coincided with the contribution of Sabino Arana. As was argued in chapter 2, the rapid socio-economic transformation of the province of Biscay provided the impetus for the formation of an assertive Basque nationalist movement. Political activity was initially reduced to the city of Bilbao and, more specifically, to the activities of the PNV, a Catholic and socially conservative party founded by members of the urban petty bourgeoisie in 1895. However, the loss of the colonies in 1898 deprived the economy of its protected external markets and discredited the Spanish national project in favour of other nationalisms.

The current chapter focuses on the transformation from Phase B (the period of patriotic agitation) to Phase C (the rise of a mass national movement). Following the death of Arana in 1903, and for the next thirty years, the PNV transformed itself from an urban elite movement into a modern mass movement in Biscay, Gipuzkoa, and, to a lesser extent, in Araba and Navarre. The apogee of this process of transition was the integration of the pragmatist *euskalerríacos* in the PNV during the First World War (Mees 2003: 11). The growing electoral success of the party was frustrated by the 1923 bloodless military coup of Miguel Primo de Rivera who suspended parliamentary life for seven years. Forced to resign in 1930, Primo's dictatorship was followed by the Second Republic (1931–1936) where the PNV re-emerged as a nationalist and conservative catch-all party and as the heart of a social network of organisations with interests in workers, women, mountaineers, youth, children, sport, folklore, culture, and education. By 1936, the PNV had successfully evolved from an amateur urban club in the 1890s to a well-oiled political machine which was to become the hegemonic nationalist party in the Basque Country during the Second Republic but also after the restoration of democracy in the 1970s. In between these two democratic periods, moderate Basque nationalism was wiped out as an escalation from military coup to civil war brought General Francisco Franco to power (1939–1975).

3.1 THE BASQUE NATIONALIST PARTY: GROWTH AND FRAGMENTATION

The Basque Nationalist Party had traditionally been divided between moderates and radicals. Both groups were united in their respect of Arana, the undisputed leader, but his death in 1903 left Basque nationalism with no reference point or guiding light. The disappearance of the venerated *Maestro* triggered internal fights for control of the party and for the 'correct interpretation' of the prophet's words. Pragmatists and intransigents accused each other of misinterpreting Arana for years and claimed to be the legitimate followers. The dispute was long and irreconcilable because of the eclectic character of Arana's works. Arana had never managed to reconcile his two main convictions, separatism and moderation, in one single doctrine (Granja 1991: 101; Elorza 2001: 303). Once he was gone, the doctrinal confusion gave birth to two very different trends of Basque nationalism within the PNV: the moderate and the radical. During the first three decades of the twentieth century the PNV oscillated between these two poles. The first scholar to identify this pendular movement was Antonio Elorza, who described the period between 1903 and 1937 as one characterised by autonomy and independence. Years later, the historians Santiago de Pablo, Ludger Mees, and José Antonio Rodríguez Ranz (1999, 2001), extended that period and argued that the whole history of the PNV could be described as the swinging of a 'patriotic pendulum' between autonomy and independence.

3.1.1 Beyond party-politics

From 1903 to the start of Primo de Rivera's dictatorship in 1923, the PNV established itself as a major Basque nationalist force with a presence in all spheres of life. By the 1920s, the transition from a minor political party to a social movement could be observed in the social background of its supporters. The social composition of the party founded by Arana had grown to include members of the working class, members of well-to-do bourgeois families, and mostly members of the lower middle class: artisans, salaried workers, clerks, salesmen, and small-scale merchants (Díez Medrano 1995: 78). The electoral results during these two decades were the best of the first half of the twentieth century and the PNV had to wait until the 1980s to obtain similar results. This is not to say that the PNV had a hegemonic position in the Basque Country; it actually shared the political scene, on much inferior terms, with monarchic and socialist parties. Basque nationalism was geographically confined during the 1920s to the province of Biscay, and during the 1930s to Biscay and Gipuzkoa. In Araba, the PNV had a minor presence and in the elections of 1936 it almost disappeared from the political scene whereas in Navarre, the Carlists had commanding control over the political scene. To the delight of modernist scholars, the strength of Basque nationalism coincided geographically with the most industrialised areas. As the historian Juan Pablo Fusi has pointed out, industrialisation (and nationalism) was of an 'impressive intensity' in Biscay, but it was a lot milder in Gipuzkoa, and almost non-existent in Araba and Navarre (Fusi 1984: 12–22).

The PNV's first significant victory was the election of Sabino Arana as provincial deputy of Biscay in 1898. The following year the nationalists were elected to the council of Bilbao and by 1907 they had succeeded in making one of their men, Gregorio de Ibarreche, Mayor of the city. The PNV did not have much of a presence during the early part of the century because it was not perceived as a decisive force at a regional level. Much less in national, meaning Spanish, elections where the PNV first took part in 1918. Although the party had been founded almost two decades earlier, in 1894, participating in Spanish elections implicitly meant accepting Spanish sovereignty as elected deputies had to take the oath on the Spanish legal system to be allowed to sit in the *Cortes* (Parliament). However, in March 1917 the PNV obtained the majority in the administration of Biscay province (*Diputación de Vizcaya*) and in the 1918 elections to the Madrid *Cortes* the PNV got six out of the provinces's seven MPs and one out of five in Gipuzkoa (Fusi 2000: 231). By the 1930s, the PNV had made itself a space in the Basque political scene, gaining the respect, and the votes, of people from a wider spectrum. The PNV of these years cannot be strictly described as a catch-all party but it was able to attract voters from almost all sections of Basque society in the name of the nation.

The cross-class message was a key advantage in the early success of the PNV, but three other interrelated processes were also important in facilitating the organisational growth of the party: first, the increasing professionalism of the party; second, the use of the printed media as an agent of nation-building, and third, the expansion of Basque nationalism to other

Illustration 3 Members of the Euskadi Buru Batzar (EBB) at Gernika, 1932. From left to right: Enrique Orueta, Rafael Mendiguren, Baltasar Ametzola, Luis Arana Goiri, Angel Zabala, Eli Gallastegi and Amancio Urruiolabeitia.

spheres of social life (leisure, youth, and unions). As already mentioned, the nationalist ideology spread unevenly from its Biscayan epicentre to the neighbouring provinces. In organisational terms, the PNV followed a similar pattern and evolved from its first provincial organisation, the Bizkai Buru Batzar (BBB), to the Gipuzko Buru Batzar in 1908 and the Araba Buru Batzar and Napar Buru Batzar in 1911. All the Basque Provinces under Spanish jurisdiction, known in nationalist circles as Hegoaldes, had their own organisational structure and met in the executive body of the party, the Supreme Council of Euskadi or Euskadi Buru Batzar.[1] A similar story can be told of the nationalist press which also seemed to follow the blueprint of industrialisation. In the early twentieth century Biscay had two nationalist newspapers: the *Euskalduna*, controlled by the moderates, and *Aberri*, under the influence of the radicals. The PNV understood the importance of having a homogenous high culture and, after an initiative of Luis Arana, it was decided that each Hegoalde ought to have its own newspaper. What came to be known as the 'Trust of the four nationalist weeklies' originated in the founding of the newspaper *Gipuzkoarra* in 1907, followed by *Bizkaitarra* (1909), *Napartarra* (1911), and *Arabarra* (1912).[2] The newspapers were financed by the PNV and, paraphrasing Clausewitz, they were seen as a continuation of politics by other means. Sabino Arana himself, who had founded the original *Bizkaitarra* in 1894, saw in the press a way of socialising the masses in matters of national importance and a way of engaging in public affairs.

The party and the newspapers were the main pillars of the Basque nationalist movement. Around them a whole range of organisations mushroomed, each of them touching upon a different sphere of social life. Of all of them, the most effective in terms of political socialisation was the *batzoki* or bar-restaurant where political and cultural activities were organised. The first *batzoki* was opened in Bilbao in 1894 by Arana himself and, in the following years, other *batzokis* were opened in San Sebastian (1904), followed by Vitoria (1907) and Pamplona (1909). According to the anthropologist Marianne Heiberg, by 1910 all the important towns and cities of Biscay and Gipuzkoa had *batzokis*, while the presence 'in Navarre and Araba was negligible outside the capital cities' (Heiberg 1989: 70). The *batzoki* was open to every citizen and, due to its non-profit character, was a focal point for community life.[3] As a social space, the *batzoki* often hosted the PNV offices and provided the party with a subtle agent of national mobilisation. The non-political atmosphere of the bar provided Basque men with a first taste of nationalism in their daily visit. In the Basque Provinces, it is still common for a group of friends (*cuadrilla*) to ritually meet after work. The most frequent activity of the *cuadrilla* is a pub crawl (*txiquiteo* or *poteo*) of the local bars where every member of the *cuadrilla* has a small glass of wine or beer (Pérez-Agote 2006: 167–173).

In 1899, Arana wrote that the 'regeneration' of Euzkadi depended on the creation of 'Basque societies, Basque newspapers, Basque theatres, Basque schools and Basque charities' (Arana 1980: 1674). By the early twentieth century, his supporters were following his instructions to the letter and were expanding its influence to specific sectors of Basque society. In 1901, Basque Youth (*Euzko Gaztedia*) was created and soon became one the most active cultural promoters of Bilbao organising lectures, workshops, theatre, music, and Euskara classes. In 1912, the Association of Enthusiasts of God (*Jaungoiko-zale Bazkuna*) was founded to provide Christian education in Euskara. A year earlier, in 1911, the nationalist and Catholic trade union Solidarity of Basque Workers had been created (*Solidaridad de Obreros Vascos-Eusko Langileen Alkartasuna, SOV—ELA*) and in 1922 women were provided with their own organisation (*Emakume Abertzale Batza*, EAB). In short, the strategy of the PNV was designed to create a micro society or, as the Basque president during the Second Republic put it, 'a whole new civilisation on Basque soil'.[4]

3.1.2 Arana's Hispanophile evolution

The moderate and radical groups within of the PNV crystallised during the last decade of the 1800s and fought bitterly for control of the party. The event around which their antagonistic positions unfolded was Arana's so-called 'Hispanophile Evolution'. This evolution has been described by Conversi as a 'second conversion' from radical separatism to a more compromising regionalist line (Conversi 1997: 68). This alleged conversion meant that Arana put forward the idea that the PNV should choose to advocate Basque autonomy rather than a full separation from Spain. This move baffled some of Arana's original supporters for whom full independence from Spain was the ultimate goal. The debate on the evolution started in 1902, shortly after the weekly *La Patria* published a report about Arana's plans to accept Spanish sovereignty in order to obtain an advanced form of regional autonomy.[5] According to the newspaper Arana had asked his followers for

> a final vote of confidence to edit and expound the program of a new Basque party that is also Spanish, aspiring to the well being of the Basque Country under the Spanish state without infringing established legality, offering a general plan for the reconstitution of the Spanish state with special autonomy for the Basque Country [...] adjusted to the needs of modern times. (Payne 1975: 80; Corcuera 2001: 587)

To be more precise, Arana wanted to create a new political party, the League of Pro-Spanish Basques (*Liga de Vascos Españolistas*) which aimed at obtaining 'the most radical degree of autonomy possible within the unity of the Spanish state'.[6] The proposal would force the PNV to abandon its separatist programme in favour of a more moderate, even regionalist programme, which embraced Spanish sovereignty. His initiative produced a two-fold reaction from the PNV cadres. While the moderate *euskalerría-cos* endorsed his suggestion, the radicals remained sceptical and puzzled about the real extent of the so-called evolution. Among the sceptical were the most devoted followers of Arana who saw in the progression the tactical move of a genius, although they could not quite make sense of it. Among the radicals was Arana's own brother, Luis, who accused him of being 'insane'. Sabino begged his brother to trust him in a letter that carried a hint of his real intentions:

> We must become pro-Spanish (*españolistas*) and work with all our soul for a program of that character. The Fatherland demands it of us. This seems a contradiction, but if people trust me, it must be accepted. It is a colossal stroke, unknown in the annals of political parties. All my reputation is tarnished and the work of many years, carried out at the cost of many sacrifices, is undone, but you will understand me. (Arana 1980: 2174–2175)

Arana, however, did not have time to make himself understood. Suffering from Addison's disease, a disorder that causes weakness, low blood pressure, and a progressive pigmentation of the skin, Arana could not finish the new party's statutes, and he finally died on 25 November 1903 at the age of thirty-eight. His sudden disappearance meant that the only person who was respected by both moderates and radicals was gone at the precise historical moment the moderates were unexpectedly becoming hegemonic.

Before discussing the implications of Arana's death for the Basque nationalist movement and its split into radical and moderate parties, it is important to establish the meaning of the 'Hispanophile Evolution'. Was Arana serious about the evolution? Was he really considering integrating the PNV into mainstream Spanish politics or was it a calculated manoeuvre as suggested in the letter to his brother Luis? Scholars are still divided about the real significance of the event. Some authors have pointed out that in the later stages of his life the harassment of the Spanish authorities intensified[7] and Arana might have felt the need for a change of strategy (Solozábal 1975: 363; Payne 1975: 81; Conversi 1997: 68). However, other authors remain doubtful about the real extent of the evolution and see it as a 'tactical retreat', not an abandonment of separatism (Beltza 1978: 159; Corcuera 2001: 591–594; Pablo, Mees, & Rodríguez 1999: 52). There are two reasons to support the second view. Firstly, putting Arana's political experience in perspective, this later reformist evolution was not consistent with all his criticisms of the moderates in his own party and the regionalist attitude of the Lliga de Catalunya. Secondly, Arana nominated a successor, Angel Zabala (Kondaño), who opposed the evolution. Why would he have nominated someone who strongly opposed his later view if he wanted the evolution to prosper? The scholarly debate over the question is important because similar arguments were used, at the time, by the PNV cadres to disentangle the 'real meaning' of the evolution. The moderates, a group of male professionals of the middle and upper classes who favoured reform and compromise rather than transgression or revolution, totally supported Arana's evolution and proposed to follow the autonomist path. The radicals, also known as *jelkides* or *jeltzales* (followers of the JEL motto) and who saw themselves as the true heirs of Arana (*sabinianos*), believed that the evolution was just a tactical realignment to avoid the authorities' harassment, attract more supporters and re-emerge in better times (Gallastegi 1935: 88–89). The president of the PNV, Angel Zabala, finally solved the debate in 1907 by approving a Manifesto which was especially designed to reconcile the two factions. According to Javier Corcuera, Zabala managed to impose his view and the evolution was presented as a mysterious and inexplicable event, promptly abandoned by Arana before dying (Corcuera 2001: 641). Zabala avoided specifying the sort of relationship that the Basque Country and Spain should have and blocked any divisive debate about what was going to be the core policy of the PNV. The Manifesto had forced the moderates and the radicals to discuss the political and institutional future of the Basques within the party, although never putting it in explicit terms. By doing so, Zabala temporarily managed to keep the party united but in the following years it became clear that the debate on the 'Hispanophile Evolution' was nothing but a badly healed wound. However, not everything can be blamed on Zabala; Arana himself had problems in synthesising fundamentalism and realism in a sole coherent programme.

3.1.3 The split between moderates and radicals

In the years that followed the debate on the Hispanophile Evolution both trends grew stronger, autonomous from each other, and increasingly irreconcilable. Some older members of the party like Engracio de Aranzadi (Kizkitza) and Luis de Eleizalde (Iturrain) struggled, with little success, to maintain the ideological equilibrium between autonomy and separatism, but they were not able to replace Arana in the role of arbitrator. The radicals, also known as *aberrianos* for their involvement in the weekly newspaper *Aberri*, were separatists and believed they were defending the 'doctrinal purity' of the party. *Aberri* had been created by the Basque Youth in 1907 and was the backbone for radical nationalists. Moreover, it was the platform from which they criticised the ambitions of the moderates who then controlled the PNV. The following 1919 editorial of *Aberri* typifies their analysis of the situation:

> At the same time as the [Basque] Nationalist Party is in gaining quantity it is also losing in quality. The Aranist spirit is cooling down and that austerity of principles and patriotic intransigence the Master instilled into the first Jeltzales is being mystified. We are going from concession

to concession, from surrender to surrender, forgetting our primitive fierceness. (Camino 1991:87)

The *aberrianos* did not elaborate a concise social and economic programme and merely proposed that Basque nationalism should be based on radical intransigence (Jáuregui 1981: 39). The main representatives of the *aberrianos* were Eli Gallastegi, Luis de Arana Goiri, Manu Egilor, José de Arriandiaga (Joala), Friar Evengelista de Ibero, and Santiago de Meabe. The undisputed leader was Eli Gallastegi (Gudari), who regularly contributed to the pages of *Aberri*. His articles were later compiled in a book, *Por la libertad vasca* (1933), which summarised the ideology of the radicals. Gallastegi agreed with Arana that Euskadi was an occupied nation that needed to be independent from Spain and France. However, he did not merely replicate Arana, and incorporated a progressive social element into Basque nationalism (Ibarzabal 1978: 118). Gallastegi had deep sympathy for the living conditions of the working class and believed that the newly arrived Spanish proletariat should be integrated and respected. For Gallastegi, it was attitude that mattered, not ethnic origin. He preferred a well-integrated immigrant who was concerned with Basque issues to an ethnic Basque with Spanish tendencies. In this sense, Gallastegi strayed from Arana's emphasis on the purity of race and contradicted him by arguing that socialism and nationalism were not irreconcilable ideologies and that some sort of fusion was possible (Gallastegi 1993: 43–68,104–126). Part of his work was dedicated to the nationalist struggles of other nations from which the Basques could learn. He looked closely at the cases of Ireland, Morocco, Cuba, Haiti, Macedonia, and India. In the case of the latter, he was profoundly impressed by the way Gandhi had achieved the political emancipation of India through civil disobedience.[8] However, his main contribution to Basque nationalism was the need for the PNV to further 'nationalise' all social activities. For Gallastegi, the struggle for independence needed to be reproduced on all fronts. Basque nationalism had to permeate all social activities and 'nationalise' the masses in their struggle with Spain. Following this idea, two more organisations were founded: in 1912 the association of mountaineers, the *Mendigoizale Bazkuna* and ten years later, in 1922, the *Emakume-Abertzale Batza* (Association of Nationalist Women) which clearly mirrored the Irish *Cumann nan Ban*.[9]

At the other end of the spectrum, the moderates were confident of their contribution and disregarded the *aberrianos*. They had entered the PNV in 1898 and, after convincing Arana of the need to participate in elections, they had saved the party from disappearance (Corcuera 2001: 313–324). They were known as *euskalerríacos* because they had participated in the *Sociedad Euskalerria*, a foralist party in Bilbao which failed to attract significant popular support. Their leader was Ramón de la Sota y Llano, a powerful industrialist of Bilbao's *ría* with an influential network of contacts in the industrial and financial sectors who saw in nationalism a way to influence Spanish politics to his own benefit. Their pragmatism, together with money, prestige, and good candidates accounted for the transformation of the PNV into a modern political party (Heiberg 1989: 64). The *euskalerríacos* did not exclude the possibility of establishing alliances with Spanish political forces. Their view could not be more opposed to Arana's radicalism, but 'doctrinal purity' was temporarily abandoned in favour of the party's survival. The PNV's new strategy proved to be correct, and after the fusion with the *euskalerríacos*, the party obtained its first electoral results, Arana being elected in September 1898. The positive trend continued in the following years, in tandem with the adoption of more moderate postures and in the long run the positions of the *euskalerríacos* became dominant (Corcuera 2001: 331).

The two wings of the party finally came to an irreconcilable disagreement in 1916, when the moderates attempted to rename the PNV in order to show Basque society the changing nature of Basque nationalism and faced the fierce opposition of the radicals. The idea behind the change of name was to create a movement for all Basques, a truly national movement that did not represent any sector or class in particular. However, the renaming was more than that in the eyes of the radicals. The PNV theoretically continued the path signalled by Arana but its attitude and political praxis were too close to the theses advocated by the moderates. The PNV had slowly turned to 'autonomism' while neglecting the most radical aspects of Arana's doctrine. Independence was no longer a goal and the PNV only demanded a return to a pre-1839 situation, before the first abolition of the *fueros*. The reasons for that ideological change were mainly of an economic nature. During the First World War, Spain's economy had been blessed with neutrality and among all the areas in Spain, the Basque Country benefited the most. Realising the extraordinary gains made by industrialists and manufacturers, the state tried to introduce a new tax on the profits resulting from the war. The initiative faced the opposition of the Catalan regionalists and the moderate Basque nationalists who, at the time, had close links with the financial oligarchy. Basque entrepreneurs who were funding the nationalists realised that to maximise their gains they had to be integrated into the political and economic structure of Spain and pressured the PNV to defend their interests and adopt a political project based on political autonomy within a multinational Spain.

Thus, in 1916 the PNV abandoned its original name for that of Basque Nationalist Communion (*Comunión Nacionalista Vasca*; CNV) to indicate their ideological shift.[10] The first reaction of *aberrianos* came in the form of a 1917 editorial titled 'In defence of doctrinal purity. What is Basque nationalism?'[11] The newspaper leader argued that Basques had been an independent state before being invaded by France and Spain and that, in consequence, sovereignty could only be regained by returning to that original independence (Elorza 2001: 329). The rebranding continued to be a source of bitter antagonism and in 1921 the polemic broke out again. In June that year, the weekly *Aberri* published an article by Jesús de Gaztañaga, 'Sabino's flag. In defence of doctrinal purity', which attacked the moderates Aranzadi, Eleizalde, and Kizkitza (Camino 1991: 88). The *aberrianos* position was that the reformist proposals of the CNV were an act of treason to Arana's doctrine. The members of the CNV, whom they accused of being 'Phoenicians' and '*españolistas*', were ready to trade separatism and revolutionary nationalism in exchange for the financial support of the financial-industrial bourgeoisie. The critiques of the radicals grew and in 1921 they were finally expelled from the CNV. Their leaders, among others, Gallastegi, Errasti, Uribe-Echebarría, and Vitorica, were the first to go. The organisations that supported their views, especially the Basque Youth, also ceased to have the protection and support of the Communion. After their expulsion from CNV, the *aberrianos* decided to re-establish the Partido Nacionalista Vasco-Euzko Alderdi Jeltzalea (PNV-EAJ) later in the year in a clear attempt to recover the 'doctrinal purity' of the Master. The fear of a split, which had worried the cadres of the party after Arana's death, became a reality. The difficult equilibrium achieved in 1907 by the Zabala Manifesto had only silenced, not reconciled, the opposing moderate and radical trends. However, the reasons for the split were not only of an internal nature: the international context had a decisive influence. After World War I international recognition of the right of self-determination for small nations, epitomised in Wilson's fourteen points, had fuelled the emergence of more radical options in both Catalonia and the Basque Country.

With the control of a party of their own, the Basque Youth prepared itself to put into practice its radical view of politics. Their first step was taken in 1923 when, together with Galician and Catalan nationalists, they signed what came to be known as the *Triple Alianza* (Triple Alliance). The aim of the Alliance, according to the founding text, was to unite 'patriots of Catalonia, Euzkadi, and Galicia' in order to gain, collectively, 'the national freedom of all three peoples'. The pact was subscribed to by separatist organisations such as the PNV and *Estat Català* but also by more moderate groups like the Galician *Irmandade Nazionalista Galega* and the Catalan *Unió Catalanista*. In the end, the radicals managed to impose their tone on the text, which made the *Comunión Nacionalista Vasca* (CNV) and the Catalan host, *Acció Catalana*, withdraw their final signature. According to Xosé Estevez, the Triple Alliance was characterised by its radical separatism, utopianism, anti-Spanishness, doctrinal character, and lack of both pragmatism and infrastructure (Estévez 1991: 640–656). The political alliance was signed on 11 September, the Catalan national day, and was followed by a demonstration 'in which the Spanish flag was ostentatiously abused' (Ben Ami 1983: 54). The pact was immediately criticised by the Spanish government and the press and hastened the preparations for an already planned *coup* two days later. On 13 September 1923, the captain-general of Catalonia, Miguel Primo de Rivera, established a right-wing military dictatorship signalling the end of the period known as the Restoration Monarchy.

3.2 THE 'BASQUE PROBLEM': AUTHORITARIAN AND DEMOCRATIC RESPONSES

With the death of Arana, the intransigent camp grew in numbers and strength within the party. After 1916, the radicals officially represented a different form of nationalism. However, their role in the following two decades was going to be secondary as turbulent times were about to come: not only the dictatorship of Primo de Rivera, and the unstable democracy of the Second Republic, but a Civil War and harsh repression that changed radical Basque nationalism forever.

3.2.1 Primo de Rivera

Miguel Primo de Rivera's personal conviction was that the defining characteristics of the Restoration—corrupt politicians, electoral fraud, and patronage—were the causes of Spain's decadence. During the Restoration Monarchy (1874–1923) the two dominant parties, the moderates and progressives, had come to an agreement known as *turno pacífico*, in which they decided to alternate in power, and the civil governors and local bosses (*caciques*) rigged the elections accordingly. Primo detested these professional politicians for having destroyed the country and suggested his dictatorship was to be a merely transitional solution until 'capable men' were found to lead Spain towards a better future. Primo saw his role as that of a doctor who had to operate upon a sick nation and 'promised a short rule in which the treatment of the gravely ill nation would be one of 'amputating the gangrened limbs" (Ben-Ami 1983: 58). Since the Disaster of 1898, Spanish regenerationist intellectuals had demanded an 'iron surgeon' (*cirujano de hierro*) capable of healing and regenerating Spain.[12] Following Mussolini, who had come to power a year earlier, in 1922, Primo provided himself with the necessary scalpels which included a corporatist state, the *Patriotic Union*, and the *Somatén* militia which somewhat mirrored their Italian counterparts (the *Partito Nazionale Fascista* and the *squadristi*).

The coup d'etat in 1923 was a response to the grave economic and political situation, the failing military campaign in Morocco, the actions of organised labour, and the 'separatist threat' epitomised by the Triple Alliance.[13] Primo's coup had the backing of the Church, large sections of the army, conservative groups, and the king himself. They all saw in Primo a 'saviour of the fatherland' who could purge the country of the vices of its political elite, restore law and order, revive conservative values, and introduce a range of social and economic reforms. The Church acquired extensive powers in primary education and also had some influence at the university level (see chapter 2). The military, on the other hand, would be the right hand of Primo throughout the duration of the regime. Early in the dictatorship the Military Directorate, which consisted almost entirely of generals, admirals, captain generals, and high ranking officers, controlled the civil government, local administration, and civil courts.

As a soldier, Primo de Rivera was imbued with a strong sense of nationalism which defined his dictatorial regime. Uncompromisingly loyal to the country, the Church, and the Monarch, Primo established a regime based on the appeal to reform and restore *la patria*. The military nationalism of Primo de Rivera could be traced to his foreign policy, particularly in regard to North Africa, and his economic policy, which aimed to create an autarkic national market by means of state monopolies and regulatory bodies. His idea of Spain could be observed in his domestic policy which aimed at indoctrinating Spaniards in the cult of the nation and creating a unified nation-state country at the expense of peripheral nations such as Catalonia and the Basque Country. Nationalising the masses in National Catholic values became the top priority and the state agencies, mainly the educational system and the army, were mobilised to an unprecedented extent (Quiroga 2004: 290).

In Primo's eyes, one of the diseases that could be lethal to the Spanish nation was the claim of other 'regions' to nationhood and, as the 'iron surgeon', he was willing to extirpate them. Fearing the worst, Basque nationalists suspected they might be the 'gangrened limbs' Primo had referred to and were extremely cautious in their initial reactions to the coup. *Euzkadi*, the newspaper of the moderate CNV carefully argued that

> with respect to our opinion of events, our readers will understand that we are not able to give it. Freedom to write does not exist today, and, not existing, we renounce everything which is not strict information. (Watson 1992: 14)

At the other end of the spectrum, the radical *aberrianos* refused to be cautious and immediately opposed the new regime. The day after the coup, on 14 September 1923 the editorial of *Aberri* complained of the 'implacable censorship the newspapers were under' and pointed at the Spanish state's craziness (*desquiciamiento*). The editorial compared Spanish politics to a 'prostitute', described Spain as 'rotten and carcinogenic', and warned that Primo's regime would be a 'slaughterhouse' and a 'fountain of hate'.[14] The newspaper also argued that Basques could hardly die for a Spanish fatherland they did not love.[15] The reaction from Primo was immediate and devastating. Following the publication of the article, the editor of *Aberri*, Manuel de Egileor, was arrested and the contents of the newspaper were subjected to meticulous military censorship. The PNV was banned without warning and some of its leaders were forced into exile in Mexico. The article gave Primo an additional excuse to 'save' Spain and approve a centralist programme of measures that included a 'decree against separatism' that he had planned to approve anyway.[16] A month later, the authorities closed all the *batzokis* and left the non-political mountaineers' organisation, the *mendigoxales*, with the monumental task of organising opposition to Primo's rule.

The seven-year dictatorship was a period of cultural regeneration. Both nationalist parties, the CNV and the PNV, tactically withdrew from the political scene, partly due to the repressive measures but also due to the belief that the dictatorship was not going to last long. At the beginning of his rule, Primo had promised that he would return the sovereign power to Parliament after three months. However, in 1925, two years after the coup, he was reluctant to resign and explained that there remained 'a lot of work to do' (Ben-Ami 1983: 89). On the one hand, the moderate CNV had its newspapers constantly scrutinised by the censors and had to go through a depoliticisation process in order to avoid the censor's fines. Only the less partisan organisations of the CNV, such as the women's charities, were fully active during the 1920s (Ramos 1985, 1988). On the other hand, the radicals comfortably moved in secrecy and organised the Basque nationalist resistance against the dictatorship (Camino 1991: 101). The same would happen thirty years later when, under Francoism, the PNV would disappear and radical Basque nationalism would rise to the surface with the founding of ETA. However, unlike Franco, Primo showed some understanding of the ethnic differences within Spain and allowed the celebration of non-nationalist events. In this regard, argued Cameron Watson, traditional sports such as boat races and *pelota* games were encouraged. Other cultural events included the *aizkolari* or wood-chopping competitions, the *irrintzi* contests, in which the winner was the person who could yell in the shrillest voice, and the *bertsolari* contests which were improvised oral poetry contests between Basque troubadours or *bertsolariak*. For Primo, Basque culture was not a threat to Spain but a sign of Spanish cultural richness. Euskara, which would be fiercely prosecuted during Francoism, continued to be spoken in public and Primo admitted 'eight specialists to the Royal Spanish Academy as representatives of the distinct linguistic diversity of Spain' (Watson 1992: 74, 86).

Cultural activities of political significance had to be organised in the countryside, away from the eyes of the *upetistas*, or supporters of Primo. The nationalists started their 'symbolic fight' against the dictatorship away from urban areas: in the mountains. The Association of Basque Mountaineers (*Euzko Mendigoizale Batza*) organised excursions to the mountains where Basques nationalists could safely sing their patriotic songs, hand out pamphlets, and openly display Basque *ikurriñas*. Although it was forbidden, they also visited Arana's grave on the anniversary of his death (Jemein y Lambari 1935: 348–351). Eli Gallastegi, the leader of the *aberrianos*, was one of the protagonists of many of the incidents against the dictatorship. At Gallastegi's wedding reception, 400 guests turned the event into a celebration where nationalist songs were chanted and leaders of the party gave speeches against Primo's regime. The event ended when the police entered the restaurant, pistols in hand (Jemein y Lambari 1935: 346). The second, and more serious event, was Gallastegi's participation in a conspiracy against the dictatorial regime. Gallastegi had contacted other separatist leaders like the Catalan Francesc Macià about a plot to overthrow Primo (Elorza 2001: 360). However, in 1926 Gallastegi fled into exile where he continued his political activity. In Saint Jean de Luz he founded the Euskadi Independence Commission (*Euzkadi-Azkatasuna—Aldezko-Batzarra*) which worked for the international recognition of the right of self-determination, mainly in the Americas. In the United States, Argentina, and Mexico, the Commission attracted enough funding from the nationalist diaspora to allow the publication and distribution of the journal *Patria Vasca*, which established the political thought of the *aberrianos*. According to Elorza (2001: 362), the Commission argued that the 'rights', 'character', and 'national soul' of Basques were a consequence of racial specificity. From exile, Gallastegi continued to maintain contacts with other nationalist causes in an effort to 'internationalise' the Basque problem. His contacts were especially intense with Sinn Féin, a movement he particularly admired (Gallastegi 1993: 11–40).

On 27 January 1930, Primo de Rivera resigned as head of state. The dictator had ceased to have the support of the army, the Church, the industrial oligarchy (Basque included), and King Alfonso XIII and faced growing opposition from republican forces. With the disappearance of Primo, Basque nationalism ceased to appear as radical, romantic, and extravagant as in earlier years and, to many in the lower-middle classes, it even began to appear as the most effective means of defending their interests and way of life. As the foundations of the Spanish monarchy crumbled and civic institutions were threatened with collapse, Basque nationalism was able to provide a new means of identity. The *primorriverista* repression had been effective in forcing nationalist politics underground but, in the long run, it was counterproductive because many sectors of the Basque and Catalan population turned to nationalism. The abuses of the dictatorship (particularly in Catalonia) boosted the appeal of nationalism and unwillingly reinforced the image of Spain as the arch-enemy of peripheral nations. Moreover, in their common struggle against the dictator, Basque moderates and radicals temporarily forgot the differences that separated them and, after the demise of Primo in 1930, the two trends reunited in the Partido Nacionalista Vasco (PNV).

3.2.2 The Second Republic

The fall of the dictatorship dragged down the Crown, which Primo had used to support his regime, along with it. Spaniards had already experienced what the 'iron surgeon' and the monarchy were capable of and were ready for a new republic. Alfonso XIII melancholically recalled the change in public opinion when he meditated about the condition of the monarchy. 'We are not in fashion', he lamented (Carr 1992: 576). The process that brought about the demise of the monarchy started with a pact signed in the Basque coastal city of San Sebastián by republicans, socialists, and Catalan nationalists in August 1930 in which the PNV refused to take part. On 12 April 1931 the coalition of republicans and socialists triumphed in the municipal elections of the main Spanish cities, and two days later a Revolutionary Committee issued an ultimatum to the king asking him to resign. Alfonso XIII abdicated and the Committee, which acted as Provisional Government, peacefully declared the Second Republic on 14 April 1931 with Niceto Alcalá Zamora as its Prime Minister.[17]

One of the unintended results of Primo's dictatorship was the reunification, on April 1930, of the uncompromising PNV and the temperate CNV under the name of *Partido Nacionalista Vasco* (PNV). However, the *aberrianos* managed to keep their distinct identity within the party structures and, from 1932 the *aberrianos'* political activity was clearly structured around the publication of the nationalist weekly *Jagi-Jagi* (Arise, Arise) which devoted most of its pages to celebrating the figure, work, and doctrine of Sabino Arana. The newspaper also discussed current affairs, such as the 'Irish revolution', and tried to develop a social agenda. Most notably, the separatist weekly published accounts of nationalists in prison and organised sympathetic campaigns of support for those behind prison bars. The backbone of the group was Eli Gallastegi and, under his leadership, the radical *aberrianos* became, yet again, an active trend promoting and engaging in debate with the moderate wing of the party, the *euskalerríacos*.

The Republic saw the moderates' turn to engage in a debate with the Spanish government and achieve a statute of autonomy that ruled out the radical aspirations of the *aberrianos*. Under the leadership of Jose Antonio Aguirre, the PNV maintained a pragmatic policy with Madrid, marked by sporadic confrontation, which silenced any criticism from the radicals. In Madrid, politicians perceived the PNV, and Basque nationalism in general, as a 'right-wing, Catholic, and xenophobic movement' (Fusi 1984: 189). The self-fulfilling images of 'the other' of both Basques and Spaniards made the granting of a Basque statute of autonomy a problematic issue which was only solved in 1936. In contrast, Catalonia obtained her home-rule statute in September 1932.

The Second Republic also cleared the way for the creation of new parties and in 1930 Basque Nationalist Action (*Acción Nacionalista Vasca*; ANV) was born. Most of the founders of ANV came from the moderate

CNV and complained that nationalism was too often equated with Arana's doctrine. For them, the Republican regime was an opportunity to renew the core elements of nationalism by incorporating goals such as 'individual freedom', 'democracy', and 'social justice', and establish a new relationship with the other peoples of Spain, a relationship that was not based on the tiresome repetition of the 'historical rights' but on the views of a majority of Basques.[18] With regard to the issue of 'race', the ANV did not share the racialist view of the PNV and proposed a civic vision of integration for those born beyond the borders of the Basque Country. From the ANV's perspective, the PNV was in the throes of ideological stagnation and it did not take long before the two conceptions of nationalism confronted each other in the pages of the nationalist press.[19] The main disagreements between the parties revolved around the religious issue and the relationships with other non-nationalist parties, such as the monarchic right, the republicans, and the socialists (Granja 1987: 55). At a more fundamental level, the ANV did not fully accept the JEL motto of the PNV (God and Old Laws) but it could not be described as anti-Aranist either.[20] According to Stanley Payne, the party was not against Catholicism 'or even particularly anticlerical, but stood on the principles of non-confessionalism, republican democracy, and greater attention to social reform' (Payne 1975: 108). In political terms, the ANV wanted to challenge the hegemonic position that both the PNV and its trade union ELA-STV had, and aimed at providing an alternative nationalism that could represent the interests of the workers. As the pages of the official newspaper of the party, *Tierra Vasca*, suggested, the ANV could become the 'leftist nationalist party' that represented the interests of the 'nationalist workers', challenged the 'bourgeois', 'rightist', and 'confessional' Basque Nationalist Party, and brought Basque nationalism up to date.[21] Besides, the critique of the PNV also included the ethnic politics that it had been using in order to attract workers to its side. According to the ANV, the PNV had led workers to believe that the only enemy was the Spanish trade unions and made them forget that the Basque financial and industrial oligarchy, intimately linked to the PNV, had also exploited the working class, sometimes resorting to the patriotic ideal. By playing the ethnic card, the PNV had made Basque workers forget to be 'both nationalist and worker to become only nationalist'.[22]

In relation to the forces of the Republican political system, the ANV supported the status quo and in the first municipal elections of the Republic joined with the progressive republican and socialist forces. Their nationalism was irreproachable because they did not support any kind of Republic except one based on federal principles. The ANV presented Basque nationalism with an opportunity to modernise, incorporate liberal principles, and move away from the more bourgeois and traditionalist principles. In the end, the ANV remained an irrelevant party in electoral terms but had a deep impact on later generations of radical Basque nationalists. The historian José Luis de la Granja has superbly summarised in six points the main contributions of the ANV: (1) it was the first party to present both a leftist and nationalist alternative to the PNV; (2) it contributed to secularising Basque nationalism; (3) it opened the door for Basque nationalism to establish political alliances with the Left; (4) it fused liberalism, socialism, and nationalism; (5) it anticipated the PNV's move to support the democratic system; and (6) it established a historical precedent for radical Basque nationalism (Granja 1986: 612–613).

The hegemony of the PNV remained undisputed as it managed to galvanise the nationalists during the 1930s. The first parliamentary elections held in 1931 in order to ratify the new constitution provide an indicator of the state of Basque politics and its unique relation to Spain. In the rest of the country voters endorsed the new regime and the left-wing coalition swept the peninsula. In Navarre and the Basque Country the political spectrum was also divided into two blocks: right-wing and left-wing (Table 3.1). However, the political tone of the discussion was slightly different to that of Spain. In the Basque Country, the debate was centred on the Statute of Estella (1931). The regional charter allowed the Basque lands to establish a Concordat with the Vatican, which would put a stop to any anti-clerical legislation from the new republican government in Madrid. The right-wing coalition was made up of Carlists from Navarre, Catholic and republican parties, and the PNV and they obtained the absolute majority of 56 per cent of the votes in the Basque Country and 53.1 per cent in Navarre. The right-wing block, which was dominated by Navarrese Carlists and Basque nationalists, won a clear victory, gaining 15 of the 24 *Cortes* seats for both Navarre and the Basque Country.

The Left had its stronghold in the urban areas and obtained 44 per cent of the votes in the Basque Country. Most of the leftist votes came from the southern part of Araba, also known as Rioja Alavesa. The Basque Provinces continued to be largely conservative and were denounced by an angry socialist leader, Indalecio Prieto, as a 'Vaticanist Gibraltar' (Payne 1975: 122). The campaign of the Left had been based on an attack on the autonomy statute and the defence of the reformist Second Republic. The Basque Statute, points out Granja, had to be liberal or there would be no autonomy at all for Euskadi (Granja 1990: 108–109).

In the next two elections of the Second Republic, in 1933 and 1936, Basque politics were gradually synchronised with the issues and concerns of the rest of Spain. In November 1933, the left-wing government lost the

Table 3.1 General elections in the Basque Country and Navarre, 28 June 1931

	Participation (%)	Right (%)	Left (%)
Basque Country	82.2	56.0	44.0
Navarre	83.5	53.1	30.7

Source: Payne (1975: 122); Granja (1986: 625)

Table 3.2 PNV results in general elections, 1931-1936

	Araba (%)	Biscay (%)	Gipuzkoa (%)	Navarre (%)	TOTAL (%)
June 1931	4,615 (21.8)	31,209 (50.8)	35,901 (14.5)	46,419 (12.7)	211,456 (22.4)
November 1933	11,525 (29.0)	79,258 (57.4)	236,177 (46.1)	69,325 (9.2)	625,263 (31.3)
February 1936	8,958 (20.8)	72,026 (51.6)	72,026 (51.6)	14,799 (2.0)	465,205 (23.0)

Source: Pablo, Mees, & Rodríguez (1999: 278)

elections and the Spanish Confederation of Autonomous Rights (CEDA) rose to power for two years (1934–1935) in what came to be known as the *bienio negro*. In the 1936 elections, the victory of the left-wing coalition known as the Popular Front allowed Manuel Azaña to form a government until the beginning of the Civil War. As shown in Table 3.2, the voting pattern of Basques in both elections roughly coincided with that of the rest of Spain but continued to have unique characteristics such as the electoral growth of the PNV.

By the 1930s the PNV had ceased to be a minority force and appealed to roughly one quarter of the population of Navarre and the Basque Country. This was due to the PNV's evolution from being a right-wing, Catholic, and xenophobic movement into a social-Christian, moderate, and, of course, nationalist party. According to Fusi, the PNV, like Basque society in general, had been modernised and now included a new 'generation of militants of Christian and democratic background' which pushed with 'determination to see some form of political self-government' for the Basque Country (Fusi 1984: 186–189). In the rapidly changing political situation, many in the lower-middle classes began to see in nationalism a valuable source of identity and an ideology that could secure their interests, way of life, and traditional values. The geographical pattern of Basque nationalist activity during the Second Republic coincided with the pattern during democracy in the 1970s and 1980s and also with the division of the Basque Country at the start of the Civil War in 1936. The PNV's electoral support remained confined to Biscay, Gipuzkoa, and some bordering areas which would remain loyal to the Republic, whereas Araba and Navarre, which had voted for Catholic-traditionalist parties, sided with the Francoist side.

Unaware of the forthcoming events, Basque nationalism reorganised and drafted a statute of autonomy. Insufficient social support for the PNV's bill, essentially confined to Biscay and to a lesser extent Gipuzkoa, made Basque nationalists turn to the Carlists in order to gain the necessary votes to propose home rule, as the initial step towards independence. Although Carlists defended the *fueros* and a similar theocratic and ultramontane view of politics to that of the PNV, they refused to support Basque home rule. Basque nationalists then turned to the Spanish socialist party, PSOE, which had a stronghold in the industrial area of Biscay, and finally, a statute that covered Araba, Gipuzkoa, and Biscay was approved in the Spanish parliament on 6 October 1936. By then, the Spanish fratricidal struggle had been setting Republicans against Nationalists for over two months.

3.2.3 The Spanish Civil War

The Civil War was not a clash between Spanish nationalism and peripheral nationalisms, but there is little doubt that the rebels saw the development of home-rule statutes as a direct threat to the national unity of Spain. The fears of Spanish nationalists were clearly expressed by the leader of the Right, José Calvo Sotelo, whose priority was to maintain the territorial uniformity and preferred 'a Red Spain to a broken Spain' (*antes una España roja que una España rota*). It is true that the national, or regional, issue was not a deciding factor in the outbreak of the Civil War but it was later used as a justification by the rebels. Rather, the coup of July 1936 was an old instrument used to stop the democratic modernisation of Spain in four crucial aspects: State–Church relations, education, army reform, and the redistribution of land and economic power (Graham 2005: 1–19). The secularisation of the state figured prominently in the reforming agenda of the Second Republic which aimed at establishing non-religious primary education. The republicans hoped that a strict division between earthly and other-worldly issues and the creation of a state-funded education system would limit the disproportionate influence of the ecclesiastical hierarchy. Following the legalisation of divorce the position of Catholicism was further eroded by the decision to terminate its status as Spain's official religion, which led the President of the Republic, Manuel Azaña, to assert that Spain had ceased to be Catholic (*España ha dejado de ser católica*). The Republic also attempted to reform the armed forces by cutting the number of officer corps, at the time filled by foes of the Republic, and bring the institution under civilian and constitutional control. The logic behind the downsizing of the army and the navy was to cut the military budget and release funds for more important structural reforms. Lastly, the Republic launched an ambitious agrarian reform that planned to divide up the southern large estates (*latifundios*) and redistribute the property among the landless peasants, who had been demanding radical social change for some time. As could be expected, the ambitious programme of reform was met by the opposition of Spain's oligarchy. Whereas the restructuring of the army and the property of the land only alienated the conservative traditional elites (Church, landowners, army), the Church reforms were met by the hostility of a much wider spectrum who saw how a temporary majority imposed its anti-clerical values.

In the eyes of Franco, the Second Republic was the culmination of a long period of decadence which had started in the eighteenth century. His view and that of many Spanish career officers (*Africanistas*) was that the political destiny of the country had been determined by corrupt and unpatriotic politicians for far too long and that the redemption of the fatherland depended on the elimination of the anti-Spain of atheists, separatists, and Reds by revolutionary violence (Reig Tapia 1986: 13). In the months that preceded the war, rumours of a coup d'etat spread throughout Spain and were even discussed in the press. The government rushed to transfer the army officers who could lead an insurrection to destinations far from Madrid. General Francisco Franco, for example, was sent to the Canary Islands as military commander. After some hesitation, he flew to Morocco to command the rebels and start a military uprising against the Popular Front government. On the following day, on 18 July 1936, Franco led the Moroccan Army, the Spanish Foreign Legion, and the Assault and Civil Guards to an offensive against on the Iberian Peninsula. The Spanish Civil War had started.

In the first days of the war, the Second Republic's warships put in place a naval blockade at the strait of Gibraltar which stopped Franco's rebel colonial army from crossing into mainland Spain. However, Franco had other means of transportation: the Junkers and the Savoia-Marchetti transport planes Hitler and Mussolini had supplied him with. The role of both Germany and Italy was to be crucial at this stage and continued to be so as their military advisors instructed Franco and his officials on how modern warfare (based on a co-ordination of ground and air attacks) was to be conducted (Iturralde 1978: 69, 222; Preston 1994: 224–247). On the other hand, the Western democracies of Great Britain and France adopted a multilateral policy of non-intervention and refused to provide any significant support to the legitimate government of the Republic which had little option but to ask the USSR for military aid. The Soviet military assistance and the help of 35,000 members of the International Brigades, anti-fascist volunteers from all over the world, saved the Republic from almost certain military defeat in the winter of 1936 (Graham 2005: 41–42). Coordination of the war effort was centralised by a national unity government which was a 'direct representative of all the political forces and different fronts that [fought] for the survival of the democratic Republic and against the rebels' (Iturralde 1978: 174).

In a clear attempt to bring to its side the Basque steel-making plants and shipyards of the industrial north, the government swiftly granted a home-rule charter to the Basque Country and the nationalist Manuel de Irujo became minister without portfolio of the Largo Caballero war cabinet.[23] The first ever Basque statute of autonomy was passed in the Spanish parliament on 1 October 1936 and, mirroring the Catalan one, was very brief, containing only fourteen articles. Although the text did not mention the incorporation of Navarre into the Basque Country or the historical rights of the Basque nation, it allowed the Basques to keep the economic entities by which they were financially independent. Ignoring the resistance of the radicals led by Luis de Arana, the PNV accepted the offer and José Antonio de Aguirre, former striker of the Athletic de Bilbao football team and Mayor of Getxo, was elected first *lehendakari* (president) of the autonomous government. For the nationalists, the statute was not the end of their struggle for statehood but brought them a step closer to regaining their alleged pre-1839 political independence. It was too late; by the time Aguirre took charge of the Basque army, the provinces of Araba, Gipuzkoa, and Navarre were already in Francoist hands. In Navarre hardly a shot was fired because the people had supported the coup from the very beginning. The general in charge of the Northern front, Emilio Mola, was 'cheered in Pamplona, with Carlist militiamen lining the streets shouting "Long live Christ the King"' (Kurlansky 1999: 185). Navarre was a Carlist and traditionalist bastion, just as it had been the place where the idea of the Francoist insurrection had originated. At the end of the war, Franco would recompense the faithfulness of Navarre by allowing it to keep its *fueros*, in clear contrast to the provinces of Biscay and Gipuzkoa which were declared 'traitor provinces' (*provincias traidoras*) in 1937. Araba also supported the insurrection while Biscay would be the only Basque province that would fully maintain the Republican order. The case of Gipuzkoa is somewhat more complex; a late insurrection was combined with the fragmentation of republican power. Finally, the majority of the 40,000 *gudaris* (Basque soldiers) recruited to defend the autonomous government were from Biscay, from where they fought an overwhelmingly superior insurgent army of 60,000 men led by General Mola (Tuñón de Lara 1987: 23).

According to Paul Preston, Franco saw the eradication of Basque nationalism as the necessary solution to a 'political and historical problem' (Preston 1994: 224). The event that came to represent Franco's hatred was the bombing, on 26 April 1937, of the Biscayan town of Gernika, the ancient town of the Basques and the centre of their cultural and symbolic tradition. In only three hours, the combined efforts of the German Condor Legion and the Italian Aviazione Legionaria levelled 90 per cent of Gernika, left 1,645 corpses, and broke the Basque spirit of resistance in preparation for the advance of ground forces. The annihilation of the ancient Basque city inspired the famous painting by Pablo Picasso, horrified the international press, and became the first aerial raid in history that exclusively targeted civilians.[24] After Gernika, other European cities—Berlin, Dresden, Potsdam, Coventry, London—were terrorised by the use of dive bombing and saturation bombing techniques, but as Hermann Goering recognised during the Nuremberg trial, the Basque Provinces had been a first 'testing ground for the Luftwaffe' (Tuñón de Lara 1987: 31).

The effectiveness of the Italo-German aerial forces in demoralising the Basque population at Gernika allowed General Mola to mobilise his forces north to seize Bilbao. The Biscayan capital had twice been the graveyard of the Carlists in the nineteenth century and was preparing itself for another long siege by surrounding itself with an 'Iron Ring', a system of trenches which mirrored the Maginot Line. Conscious of the challenges ahead, General Mola ordered planes to drop propaganda in which he warned Biscayans that 'it is my objective to end rapidly the war in the North. If you surrender, nothing will happen to you. If submission is not immediate, I will raze all Biscay to the ground, beginning with the industries of war. I have the means to do so' (Iturralde 1978: 215). It was not necessary for Mola to fulfil his threats as the rebels easily pierced Bilbao's 'Iron Ring' after a deserter, Captain Goicoechea, gave away the plans of the fortifications. On 19 June 1937, Francoist troops entered Bilbao and started a fierce wave of repression. The Basque army, which had been founded by Aguirre a year earlier, retreated into the neighbouring province of Santander. Away from their homeland and with the superior Nationalist army moving westwards, the *gudaris* decided to surrender to the Italians in August 1937 in the notorious Capitulation of Santoña.[25] With the end of the Civil War in April 1939, the dream of the Republic was destroyed, and along with it, the aspirations of Basques who thought an accommodation of the Basque nation within Spain was possible. The strategy of the moderate PNV had, in the end, proved positive as Basque nationalists had obtained a statute of autonomy. However, the Francoist response confirmed to Basque nationalists, especially the radical wing, that Spain could never be trusted. The war came to be perceived by successive generations of nationalists as yet another aggression of Spain against the Basques and not as a fight between Fascism and democracy.

3.3 CONCLUSION

In the period from 1903 to 1939, Basque nationalism expanded from a petit-bourgeois association based in Bilbao to a nationalist movement capable of taking charge of the albeit brief Basque Autonomous Government in 1936. The backbone of the movement was the Catholic and conservative Basque Nationalist Party around which a variety of organisations with interests in the press, dance, theatre, women, youth, and trade unionism revolved. Control of the party was battled over by radical and moderate wings which reproduced both received and rival versions of Arana's nationalism. In 1903, Arana passed away and the moderates and the radicals turned the history of the PNV up to 1936 into an alternation between independence and autonomism (and a few schisms along the way). In principle, the PNV was reluctant to negotiate ideological principles but its ability to make tactical concessions depended directly on its ability to participate in the political system. When, in 1936, Basques were forced to choose between 'Catholicism' and 'order' on the one hand, and 'national identity' and 'home rule' on the other, many chose to join the rebel side. After some hesitation, the PNV opted to support the Republican war effort in exchange for a state of autonomy.

The importance of the Civil War for the continuous reproduction of Basque nationalism can hardly be over-emphasised. At the outbreak of the war only Biscay and a small part of Gipuzkoa remained faithful to the Republic, whereas Araba and Navarre sided with the rebels. Despite the ideological fragmentation of the Spanish Basque Provinces, both moderate and radical Basque nationalists domesticated the immediate past and chose to remember the conflict as another act of Spanish aggression against the Basque homeland (Aguilar 1998). The 'fratricidal' dimension of the war was removed by the politics of memory which chose to 'forget' certain facts and preferred to 'remember' the '1936 War' or the 'Third Carlist War'. The victimisation of the Basque lands continued to occupy a central space in the nationalist collective consciousness well after the end of the civil war on 1 April 1939. In the early years of Francoism, there was no need for commemorations and rituals which could celebrate the symbols, memories, and myths of an 'oppressed nation' as the military dictatorship constantly reminded the defeated of their condition. Moreover, in the absence of political liberties, young nationalists identified the fighting heritage of their predecessors as one of the defining characteristics of the Basque nation. As will be explained in the next chapter, by taking the name of the Basque soldiers who fought in the Civil War, the sacrifice of ETA members was placed, yet again, in a long list of sacrifices in their historical opposition to the Spanish state. Whether such continuity was historically accurate and whether ETA members could be considered as a new generation of *gudaris* is a question beside the point. The fact that this distinctive reading of history resonated meant that nationalism had finally entered the Basque mind.

4   Francoism and the Birth of ETA (1939–1975)

The Spanish Civil War came to an end on 1 April 1939. In the Basque Country, however, the fighting had concluded two years earlier, in the summer of 1937. Having destroyed the Basque morale at Gernika, the rebel troops had marched north to besiege Bilbao, a city they captured in June 1937. The fall of the Biscayan capital dealt the final blow to the short-lived autonomous government, seriously weakened the Republican army's positions in the north, and brought Franco much closer to victory. The collapse of the Second Republic was followed by the personal dictatorship of General Francisco Franco who governed Spain from 1939 to 1975. Francoism lasted for almost forty years and had devastating consequences for the Basque nationalists of the PNV. The Basque government's strategy during World War II had been to stake all their political prestige on the so-called 'diplomatic card'. From their offices in New York, the *Lehendakari* Aguirre and his aides coordinated the provision of intelligence to the Allies and hoped to link the fate of Franco to that of Hitler and Mussolini. After the United States decided to turn the Spanish dictator into a useful pawn in their cold war against the Soviet Union, the Basque president had no other option but to recognise he had been mistaken all along. The misapprehension provoked a confidence crisis which brought the nationalist activity of the PNV to a standstill. In the meantime, the Basque population suffered years of reprisals and persecution in both the political and cultural spheres. The publication or use of the Basque language in commercial and official arenas was prohibited, and its status was downgraded to that of a 'dialect', whereas Castilian became firmly established as the only true language. In post-war Spain, nationalists had little option but to endure harsh repression, flee into exile, or galvanise themselves into clandestine action. In this political context, a generation of young nationalists who had not participated in the civil war founded the armed group Euskadi ta Askatasuna (ETA).

4.1 THE NATIONALISTS' SILENCE

During the Spanish Civil War, *Lehendakari* Aguirre had notified the Republican Government that his *gudaris* would only fight on Basque soil and resisted all demands to move his troops to other fronts. When, in 1937, Araba, Gipuzkoa, and most of Biscay had fallen only Bilbao remained as the last bastion of Basque resistance. But with the fall of the city in June that year Basque combatants had to leave their homeland in order to avoid persecution from the incoming rebel forces. Having fled to the neighbouring province of Santander, Aguirre's demoralised troops lost interest in fighting for a territory they felt was not their own, and for a left-wing republic that did not correspond to their model of social and Catholic observance (Nuñez 2005). From the Republic's perspective, it was clear that the Basques had acted from self-interest and were more concerned with defending home rule than the Republic. In the words of Indalecio Prieto, Basque nationalists 'were not mistaken in their attitude during the war; they only participated to save the Statute [of Autonomy]' (Granja 1990: 185). For nationalists the seven months' experience of autonomy had been a negotiation success and a landmark in their relationship with Madrid. The only previous experience of political independence for the Basques was the quasi-mythical Kingdom of Navarre in the Middle Ages. The moderates of the PNV claimed they had achieved this important political concession by negotiating with the Republican government, whereas the radical faction never endorsed the statute, and one of its leaders, Luis de Arana, resigned from the PNV on the day the statute was approved (Payne 1975: 179). According to Sabino's brother, the war was a Spanish problem in which Basques should never get involved. For the Biscayan population, however, the statute was a historical milestone and many did not hesitate to support it. The regional charter was rapidly developed with a complete administration and autonomous system of government for the three provinces that today constitute the Basque Autonomous Community, but by the time it could be implemented it only ruled over the province of Biscay.

Franco's victory over the Republican loyalists forced between 100,000 and 150,000 Basques of all ideologies, including 20,000 children, to accompany the Basque government into exile (Anasagasti & San Sebastián 1985). The numbers of refugees are quite considerable if compared to the overall Basque population. In 1937, Araba, Gipuzkoa, and Biscay had 1,300,000 inhabitants and Biscay and Gipuzkoa, the most affected provinces, had 850,000 inhabitants (Gurrutxaga 1996: 102). This means that 11.5 per cent of the population of the three provinces fled to safer areas, mainly Europe and America. Their destinations included France, Britain, the United States, and some Latin American countries, such as Mexico, Venezuela, and Argentina, where they developed a considerable diaspora. However, the majority of Basques could not afford to flee and stayed in their homes waiting for Franco's troops to arrive. Two months after the rebel forces entered Bilbao on 19 June 1937, almost 1,000 men were dead and 16,000 suspected Basque nationalists had been arrested (Iturralde 1978: 295). In the words of the British consul in Bilbao: 'Estimates of the total shootings effected at Bilbao since its capture by General Franco vary between a minimum of 300 and a maximum of 1,000. Many prisoners, however, still await trial' (Payne 1975: 224). A similar fate awaited the Basque soldiers who surrendered in Santoña (Santander). The terms of the capitulation had been agreed with Italian forces but the Basque prisoners of war were finally handed over to Franco's troops who passed 'hundreds of death sentences' (Preston 1994: 285). The purge continued in all the Basque Provinces but was particularly severe in Gipuzkoa and Biscay, the strongholds of Basque nationalism.[1] In 1937, Franco declared both Biscay and Gipuzkoa 'traitor provinces' and maintained the designation for more than thirty years.[2] On the other hand, the provinces of Araba and Navarre were rewarded for having supported the *alzamiento nacional* and they maintained the Economic Concerts, a special tax regime of an autonomous character. Franco banned the use of Euskara from the educational system and the church and imposed the use of Spanish. Basque cultural expressions, such as theatre, literature, folklore, and the use of Basque names for baptism, were also forbidden by the *Nuevo Estado*.[3] In addition, Francoism imposed on the Basque Provinces up to twelve 'states of exception', a measure that allowed the authorities to detain citizens for up to seventy-two hours without notification to the family and without formal charges. Four of these states of exception were nation-wide and six of the eight others covered the Basque provinces of Gipuzkoa or Biscay, or both (Llera, Mata & Irvin 1993: 107).

The repression of the 1940s and 1950s was so vicious and discouraging that there was hardly any political resistance to challenge Francoism. The only events of significance during these years were the strikes of 1947, 1951, and 1956. As a result of the war effort, salaries receded to nineteenth century levels while inflation rose incessantly. It is in this context that the Basque general strike of 1947 took place. Called on May 1st, the act of protest started in Biscay and extended to the Western part of Gipuzkoa. Although it was planned as a one-day strike, the harsh reaction of the authorities (mass dismissal of those refusing to work) angered the employees and, in the end, it lasted nine more days until May 10th. Around 30 per cent of the Biscayan workforce, 20,000 people, stopped working and 396 companies were affected by the action, while several thousands lost their jobs (Gonzalez Portilla & Garmendia 1988: 194–198). The action was sympathetically reported by the international press and received messages of support from the British trade unions and the World Federation of Trade Unions (WFTU), but none from the governments of the UK, United States, or France.[4] The organisers of the strike were the representatives of the Basque Government in the interior, the Council of Resistance, and three trade unions: Confederación Nacional de Trabajadores (CNT), Sociedad de Trabajadores Vascos (STV), and Unión General de Trabajadores (UGT). *Lehendakari* Aguirre took over the organisation, assumed responsibility for the labour dispute, and capitalised on its gains by arguing that Basques had responded to his calls. The difficult post-war situation intensified and the class conflict produced two more general strikes in the 1950s. The first one, in 1951, was widely supported in Biscay and Gipuzkoa and mobilised up to 250,000 workers whereas the second one, in 1956, had a lower support with 30,000 Basque workers participating in it (Molinero and Ysas 1994: 79–80). These protests illustrated the changing social and economic structure of the 1950s, the difficult position of the popular classes, and the birth of an incipient resistance to Franco. However, they also showed that the Basque Government on its own could not precipitate the fall of the dictator.

The early years of Francoism have been described by Michael Richards as a *Time of Silence* (1998). Motivated by a fierce desire for vengeance, the Francoist state reinforced the division between victors and defeated and continued to execute its former opponents long after the cessation of hostilities on 1 April 1939. For those who had sided with the Republic, the Civil War would continue throughout the 1940s in the form of institutionalised repression and discrimination by means of which the Franco regime constructed its power base. Aside from mass executions, hundreds of thousands of people spent time in prisons, concentration camps, or forced labour battalions. Within this context Basque nationalists decided to use safe channels such as football to express their political dissatisfaction. When, in 1943, the Athletic de Bilbao won the Cup of the *Generalísimo* the team was welcomed by thousands of fans at the San Mamés Stadium. The public did not follow the lead of the speakers which shouted 'Franco, Franco, Franco' and shouted instead 'Zarra, Zarra, Zarra', in reference to Telmo Zarra, the well-known striker in the team (Pablo, Mees, & Rodríguez 2001: 198). Other symbolic acts of resistance were the placing of banned *ikurriñas* and minor acts of sabotage which had an almost negligible impact. Another consequence of the climate of collective psychological fear was the confinement of nationalism to the private sphere. The Basque home became a sanctuary where families could speak Euskara, talk about politics, and freely express their cultural distinctiveness. However, for a significant part of society home would not provide enough shelter. In a society characterised by mistrust, cultural revisionism, and constant repression, many Basques opted to abandon their ideology completely. Parents who had traditionally spoken Euskara proved their loyalty to the regime by teaching Spanish to their children and abstaining from talking about the recent past. Silence and guilt became the norm for those who thought that political action would only be possible with the death of the dictator and the restoration of democracy.

4.1.1 The diplomatic bet

With the disappearance of both Hitler and Mussolini, Basque nationalists had been confident that the Allies would pursue the liberation of Europe beyond the Pyrenees. In a 1945 Christmas message, broadcast from exile, *Lehendakari* Aguirre euphorically proclaimed: 'this year we will come back to our homeland' (Beltza 1977: 21). He further argued that borders had historically changed as a result of conflicts, and that in the same way that many small nations had regained their freedom as a result of the Great War, it was only a matter of time for history to repeat itself. In retrospect, his words seem naïve, but he had good reason to believe that the dictator's days were numbered. The Basque Government had actively helped Britain and America by establishing an espionage network throughout the war. Intelligence had been collected through the organisation directed by Pepe Mitxelena, the Basque Service of Information and Propaganda, also known as Servicios. From Spain, the Servicios had established an information network in Bilbao and Madrid. Abroad, it had helped the FBI and the predecessor of the CIA, the Office of Strategic Services (OSS), to establish a web of spies throughout South America. The network was made up of the delegations of the Basque Government and its main goals were to provide information about communist activities and to work against German interests. In return, the FBI financed the Servicios, the diaspora centres in Latin America and the activities of the *Lehendakari*'s office in New York.

In contrast, the neutrality of Spain in the war had been breached by Franco who made available intelligence reports to the Axis, provided them with wolfram, an essential metallic compound for the German war industry, allowed the refuelling of U-boats, and approved the deployment of the División Azul, a group of 47,000 volunteers that joined the Wehrmacht on the Eastern Front until 1944. This duplcitious position towards the war had been defended by Spanish diplomats to the Western powers with the theory of the two wars. In their eyes, World War II could be seen as a two-level conflict. The first was that of the Axis against the Western democracies, in which Spain was neutral. The second was that against communism, in which she was belligerent. Franco's calm ambivalence and detached diplomacy changed with the death of Mussolini in April 1945. It was at that point that the dictator started to feel anxious and told his brother, 'if things go badly I will end up like Mussolini because I will resist until I have shed my last drop of blood'. The pressure mounted during the period 1945 to 1950, when Franco was convinced that 'he and Spain were under deadly siege' (Preston 1994: 535). Everything was looking good for the Basques and the Republican exiles, who were carrying out a successful campaign to stop Franco's regime from being internationally recognised. At the founding conference of the United Nations in San Francisco Spain had been denied entry, and also in 1945, the United Nations endorsed a Mexican-led resolution that condemned Franco's regime and the General Assembly urged the withdrawal of all accredited ambassadors from Madrid. Finally, in 1947, at the Paris Conference on the Needs of Europe, Spain was not even considered, just as it was not considered for the Marshall Plan (Romero 1999: 126–136).

The Conference of Potsdam (1945) confirmed Spain's geo-strategic importance in the unfolding Cold War between the two former wartime allies. At Potsdam, the map of Europe was divided into areas of influence and Spain became a potential ally of the West in its fight against the Soviet bloc. Franco astutely expressed his deepest antipathy for the 'Communist disease' (and freemasonry), which he sincerely thought had brought great tragedies to Spain, and waited for the Truman administration to notice his crusading anti-communism. They did, and the first years of the military build-up brought a swift *rapprochement* between the United States and Spain. By 1950 diplomatic relations had been 'normalised' and Spain was given the green light to join the World Health Organisation (1951), UNESCO (1952), and, finally, the United Nations (1955). To the dismay of Republicans and Basque nationalists, in a matter of years the West had fully replaced its policy of non–interventionism by full collaboration. In 1953, the new policy towards Franco was given a boost with the signature of the Pacts of Madrid which allowed the United States Air Force to have five bases—Torrejón, Seville, Zaragoza, Morón de la Frontera, and Rota—on Spanish territory in exchange for $226 million in military and technological assistance. As Shlomo Ben Ami pointed out, thanks to President 'Eisenhower, Franco entered the international system and managed to portray himself as the "sentinel of the west" against the Bolshevik menace' (Ben Ami 1983: 179).

To many Basques the pacts of the 'free world' with the dictator were something beyond belief and they were shocked by the betrayal. Even the optimistic and pro-American Basque president, who had concentrated all his hopes on the diplomatic card had to admit that the West had forgotten the Basques for 'strategic reasons'.[5] The consequences for the PNV were disastrous.[6] The strategy of the Basque Government had been, since its birth on 7 October 1936, one that pursued the development of a network of international contacts to support their cause. After the signing of the Defence Pacts between the United States and Spain in 1953 not even the most ardent pro-American could make sense of the nationalists' policy. Despair and bitterness set in. Furthermore, when it seemed that the situation could not get any worse, the Roman Catholic Church signed the 1953 Concordat with Franco which gave his regime further legitimacy and allowed him to intervene personally in the process by which bishops were designated. In parallel to the gradual strengthening of the dictatorship, the PNV started to lose touch with Basque reality and, unable to make sense of the world around it, entered a serious period of crisis and introspection.

4.1.2 The origins of ETA

The debacle of the PNV's strategy for Western intervention, their political procrastination, and the growing strength of the dictatorship, epitomised by the Defence Pacts, contributed to reviving more radical aspirations. In the early 1950s a group of young nationalist men grew disillusioned with the post-war caution and acquiescence of the PNV which they saw as a 'passive collaborationist' Francoism because it was 'limiting itself to forms of action that ignored the contemporary situation in *Euskadi*' (Jáuregui 1981: 59; Wieviorka 1993: 150). In the words of Txillardegi: 'from the Basque point of view, the situation was really sad. People had lost all hope. After 1953 no one believed the Americans would help restore democracy. We thought we needed to do something without relying on anyone, and we started to work'.[7] In this context, eight students in their early twenties rolled up their sleeves and created a discussion group called Ekin (To Act) which was divided into two cells, one in Bilbao and another in San Sebastian.[8] Founded in 1952, Ekin had the limited aim of examining and expressing the radical youth's ideological ambitions and tactical dissent from the PNV's conformity.[9] Most of them had an urban, nationalist, and middle-class background and were young idealists and autodidacts. They were mostly concerned with the repression of Basque culture and language and wanted to know more about their national past. They started to circulate discussion papers about political history, philosophy, and contemporary affairs from member to member and published some of them in their internal bulletin. During the 1950s, Ekin came closer to the PNV's youth organisation, Euzko Gaztedi Indarra (EGI), and the two organisations merged in 1957. However, the idealists of Ekin were a clearly distinct group within EGI, and over the course of the next three years they became frustrated with the subordination to the PNV. They complained the party was too controlling and paternalistic and that Euzko Gaztedi needed more autonomy and resources. The dissent between Ekin and the PNV cadres grew to the point where an Ekin leader, Benito del Valle, was expelled (Clark 1984: 25). The disciplinary measure resulted in a split, and in 1959 Ekin leaders founded ETA, taking hundreds of EGI members with them. Interestingly, they decided to found the underground organisation on Saint Ignatius day (31 July), the day chosen by Sabino Arana to officially launch the PNV.

ETA stood for *Euskadi Ta Askatasuna* (Basque Homeland and Freedom) and became an outstanding branding choice.[10] In Euskara, the conjunction 'and' is 'eta' and, when reading Basque, as Mark Kurlansky has correctly pointed out, any text 'appears to be peppered with these initials' (Kurlansky 1999: 234).[11] The early years of ETA were dedicated to building an ideological corpus, and it was only on 18 July 1961 that it first used force to derail a train of Francoist ex-combatants travelling to San Sebastián to celebrate the regime's '25 years of peace'. The derailment had a symbolic element, since it aimed at dishonouring the dictatorship on the anniversary of the *alzamiento nacional*. The bomb was carefully placed on the tracks so as not to cause any casualties, a prudent and calculated use of explosives which would gradually be abandoned as the organisation increasingly favoured more indiscriminate acts. At that point, ETA did not present any real danger to the regime, which managed to disband the organisation in a matter of weeks. The leaders of ETA were soon imprisoned and the state exerted a disproportionate level of repression on the Basque population as a whole. According to Jáuregui (2000: 205), it was at this point that ETA debated what the best means of fighting the dictatorship were, and seriously considered adopting political violence. The internal tactical disputes took place in the pages of the clandestine publication *Zutik!* during the 1959 to 1968 period. Founded in 1961, the bulletin was the forum in which ideological debates and strategic contributions were published. At that time, being in control of *Zutik!* was the equivalent of being in control of ETA.

The ideological debates usually materialised in the form of Assemblies, at the end of which ETA approved a set of principles or tactical contributions which clarified the organisation's aims and strategies.[12] As can be seen in Table 4.1, during the 1960s, and in parallel to the expansion of its militant base, ETA held five of these gatherings, establishing the pillars on which the organisation stands today. In the First Assembly, held in 1962, ETA approved the Ideological Principles, defined itself as a 'Basque Revolutionary Movement of National Liberation' and, following the book *Vasconia* (1963), it suggested that 'the most appropriate tactics should be used in each historical circumstance'.[13] In the Second Assembly, ETA focused on organisational issues and adopted the Revolutionary War as its core strategy believing that a war supported by the native population would bring about the independence of Euzkadi. The building of a theoretical and ideological body continued with the publication of the official bulletin of the organisation, *Zutik!*, and the *Cuadernos de ETA* and, in 1964, the Third Assembly approved the spiral of action-repression. The renowned tactic would start a cycle in which every action was followed by state repression, which, in turn, would encourage a larger revolutionary action, starting the cycle all over again. In the Fourth Assembly held in 1965, socialism was adopted, and finally, in its Fifth Assembly, held in the mid-sixties, ETA defined itself as a Marxist-Leninist movement, adopted a North Vietnamese-style fighting strategy, and decided to work on different fronts: cultural, political, workers, and military.

To recapitulate, ETA was the result of a failed strategy of Ekin 'to act' within the PNV. At the root of the problem was the clash of two generations of nationalists over organisational issues, but also over what should be the priorities of a nationalist movement operating under a dictatorship. Besides, the young nationalists had not witnessed the Civil War and refused

Table 4.1 ETA Assemblies, 1962–1967

Assembly	Date	Outcome
First Assembly	1962	Ideological principles & Vasconia
Second Assembly	1963	Revolutionary War adopted
Third Assembly	1964	Insurrection & spiral repression-action-repression
Fourth Assembly	1965	Marxism adopted
Fifth Assembly	1966–1967	The term 'Pueblo Trabajador Vasco' is coined and four fronts are created: cultural, political, workers, and military

Source: Garmendia (1996); Elorza (2000); Mata (1993)

to accept the PNV's attempts to monopolise Basque nationalism (Txillardegi 1978: 368).

4. THE IDEOLOGY OF ETA

ETA's ideology combined a pre-existing separatist trend with brand-new elements. The most obvious continuity was provided by the radical ideal which could also be found within the Basque Nationalist party. Like many *jeltzales*, members of ETA demanded national self-determination and worked towards secession from Spain. However, an important difference with the members of the PNV was that ETA did not believe national self-rule could be achieved through participation in established political institutions. ETA argued that mass revolutionary violence was the only means to bring down an authoritarian regime like Francoism and advocated the practice of guerrilla warfare. The example to follow had been set by the Third World national liberation movements which forced the British, French, Dutch, and Portuguese empires to grant independence to their former dominions. Following the ideological currents of the 1960s, ETA departed from the PNV's gradualism in adopting a form of revolutionary socialism which argued that social and political change could only be brought about by the joint efforts of the country's population.

4.2.1 ETA's nationalism

ETA's ideas of the nation were taken directly from traditional Basque nationalism. For the first *etarras* (ETA members) finding books on patriotism was an extremely arduous and dangerous task. The *Nuevo Estado* was effective in promoting national-Catholicism and the censors tightly controlled the contents of books, magazines, newspapers, and news bulletins, making sure nothing that was published or broadcast contradicted the state's ideology. The first *etarras* only had family libraries in order to teach themselves. The first readings to which they had access were the works of pre-war Basque nationalists such as Father Estella, Engracio de Aranzadi, Luis de Eleizalde, *Lehendakari* Aguirre, Eli Gallastegi, and, of course, Sabino Arana (Zirakzadeh 1991: 150; Letamendia 1994: 250). Not surprisingly, the first ETA members saw their activities as continuing a regenerative task started by nationalists well before them. For example, with regard to the need to re-discover the national past, ETA shared the same concerns of the Basque romantics and the founders of the PNV. As ETA's *White Book* (1960) explained, a 'people that does not know their different characteristics can hardly create a nation because they are not aware of the benefit of forming one' (*Documentos Y* 1979–1981: 191).

The need to study and record past events had also been Sabino Arana's passion and he also wrote about the topical questions of his time. Most of Arana's work was of a general character and pursued the Basques' awakening of their love for 'the freedom of the fatherland' and 'hate to death [of] those who enslave it' (Arana 1980: 615). For that reason he wrote historical pieces about an ideal Basque past while putting forward the need for an articulated and organised Basque patriotism. For ETA members, Arana's words resonated effectively because the problems and obstacles he had faced were similar to their own. In the light of Francoism, the writings of Arana acquired a new, pertinent meaning and his pioneering work was well regarded.[14] According to Gurutz Jáuregui there are three ideas that were uncritically adopted by ETA: (1) that in the remote past all Basques were equal and noble (universal nobility); (2) that Basques had eternally been independent (and that the *fueros* were an expression of that political independence); and (3) that the Basque nation had been occupied by two different states, the Spanish and the French (Jáuregui 1981: 93; 2000: 191). The first ETA members could not prove the historical accuracy of the first two points but accepted them. In this regard the insurgent group followed Arana and the Basque romantics such as Joseph-Agustin Chaho in decoding the Carlist Wars of the nineteenth century as national liberation wars, not as dynastic disputes. As for the third point, the occupation of the Basque homeland, they did not need any scholar to tell them it was true because Franco had made the myth of oppression very real.

ETA's nationalism also diverged from the PNV's orthodoxy on several issues. First, ETA broke with the religious traditionalism in Basque politics and declared itself non-confessional. Contrary to what many Basques believed, ETA argued that there should be a strict division between Church and state. Second, ETA gradually incorporated leftist ideas into its political corpus in clear contradiction to Arana's writings (who had described socialist ideas as foreign). Third, ETA radically broke with a previous collectivistic-authoritarian custom when emphasising that the Basque language was the core element of the Basque nation. For Arana it was 'race' that mattered and distinguished Basques from rival *maketos* or outsiders. Arana's concept of Basqueness was based on the law of blood (*ius sanguinis*) whereas ETA's Basqueness was individualistic-libertarian and based on territorial jurisdiction (*ius solis*).[15] It was the 'will' to be Basque that mattered, not membership in an alleged community of descent, and the expression of that will was to speak the Basque language. As one of the first ETA documents stated, Euskara 'must be the vehicle of expression of the Basque nation' (*Documentos Y 1979–1981*: 105). Whereas for Arana the decline of the 'race' brought the decay of the 'nation', ETA members followed the German romantics in suggesting that it was the refusal to speak the national language that doomed the homeland. As an Ekin member argued: 'useful languages coincide with so-called 'national' languages, meaning languages with their own governmental apparatus. Languages of free peoples are useful and vigorous; languages of politically oppressed peoples are useless and then they eventually die' (*Documentos Y 1979–1981*). This Herderian view of the vernacular language as indicator of the nation's character or *Volksgeist* suggested a course of action. Having defined Euskara as an essential element of Basqueness, and judging that languages only survive when they take a national form, there followed a logical programme of recovery for both the language and the nation.

4.2.2 ETA's socialism

Socialism was added to the essential tenets of radical Basque nationalism as a means of incorporating the newly arrived working class. The main consequence of the new phase of industrial change in the 1960s (*desarrollismo*) was a new wave of immigration. As can be seen in Figure 4.1, the

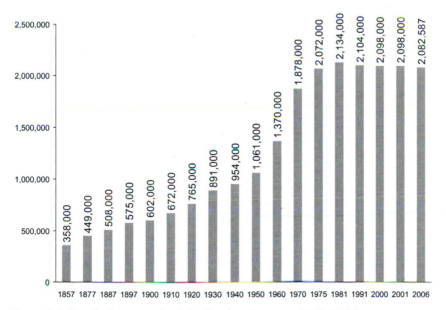

Figure 4.1 Population growth of the Basque Country, 1857–2006.
Source: Instituto Nacional de Estadística (www.ine.es)

population of the Basque Country grew rapidly from 1,370,000 inhabitants in 1960 to just over 2 million in 1975. The social structure changed with the addition of the newcomers but also with the increasing proletarianisation of the indigenous population. This new wave of settlers replicated the wave that Arana had witnessed at the end of the nineteenth century but was radically different in its reception by the Basque insurgents. Those who we might call 'new Basques', the offspring of the immigrants, would not support Basque nationalism unless they could identify with it. To include these new social sectors, ETA incorporated Marxist elements and recruited many of their first members—Txillardegi, Krutwig and Benito del Valle—from families that were not ethnically Basque (Jáuregui 1981: 135).

Before ETA, the difficult marriage between nationalism and socialism had only been tried twice in the Basque lands. The political party Acción Nacionalista Vasca (ANV) first established a delicate balance between the two elements in the 1930s and as a result became an important ideological precedent for radical Basque nationalists. The second precedent in combining the desire for political independence and the proletarian revolution was set by the radicals of the PNV, the *aberrianos*. Their leader, Eli Gallastegi, did not see any apparent contradiction between these two goals and developed a coherent theoretical work based on the two. Both the ANV and Gallastegi's *aberrianos* had an important impact on ETA. As the work of José Luis de la Granja has shown, the ANV was taken up as a useful model by ETA (Granja 1986). Emilio López Adán (Beltza) had also demonstrated that Gallastegi became a model of 'progressist and separatist nationalism' for ETA members and that the 'patriotic intransigence' of Aberri, the group Gallastegi commanded, was continued by this young generation of nationalists who felt the urge to fight for the independence of the Basque Country (Beltza 1977: 91–92).

ETA was successful in combining socialism and nationalism where the ANV and Gallastegi had failed because members of ETA were exposed to completely different political and ideological influences. First, the 1959 Stabilisation Plan and the successive Social and Economic Development Plans in 1964–1967, 1968–1971, and 1972–1975 had transformed Spain's post-war autarky in favour of a more open economy with liberalised foreign trade. The main consequence of this process for the Basque social structure was the expansion of the middle classes, a substantial increase of the working class, and the growing importance of the clandestine trade unions. By the mid-1960s ETA had made a decision to establish greater cooperation with the labour movement and incorporated the concerns of the proletariat into its political analysis by making reference to working conditions or endorsing strikes. References to the ethnic divide between native and immigrant wage-earners were toned down in order to facilitate socialist-based mobilisation. Secondly, ETA became well aware of the Third World struggles and the innovations of European New Left theorists. In the aftermath of the Second World War, a large-scale decolonisation backed by the United Nations ended in the creation of many new states which gained independence from the Western imperial powers. The first ETA members were sympathetic to the cases of India, Congo, Vietnam, Algeria, Cuba, Israel, Cyprus, and Ireland and saw them as possible models to follow. In the aftermath of May 1968, they saw parallels between the aspirations of the non-self-governing territories and their own, and saw themselves as romantic revolutionaries defending the rights of an oppressed nation in a world divided between colonies and colonisers. In their view, the Western powers exploited the primary resources of these nations and were draining their resources, jeopardising their future development. Thus, the first *etarras* read the writings of Che Guevara, Fidel Castro, Le Duan, Ho Chi Minh, Mao Tse Tung, and Frantz Fanon. Of all these, the most important were Fanon's *Wretched of the Earth* and Mao's *Red Book* where they learnt about the role of violent resistance in the decolonisation of Algeria and other French black African possessions (Unzueta 1988: 65)

4.2.3 ETA's violence

ETA's adoption of political violence as a legitimate tool was unprecedented in the history of Basque nationalism. Although several authors and organisations had considered the option, ETA was the first one to actually use it. Cameron Watson has consistently argued that a culture of symbolic warfare within Basque nationalist discourse paved the way for ETA's violence (Watson 1996). Although his argument is persuasive, it is unclear what the exact process was by which figurative violence came to be included in ETA's ideology. For example, no reference to violence can be found in ETA documents until 1961, when ETA adopted the 'Ideological Principles'.[16] Although Watson is right in pointing to the nature of Basque nationalism, the adoption of violence by ETA needs to be linked to the nature of Francoism. In a system that did not allow ETA members to express their grievances through institutional channels, violence synthesised their regenerative programme of secession and revolutionary warfare. ETA gradually adopted a discourse which justified the use of physical force during the first half of the 1960s. Two texts were extremely important in this respect: the first, *Vasconia* (1963), was written by Federico Krutwig, a Basque philologist of Italian and German descent, whereas the second, *La Insurrección en Euskadi* (1964), was written by José Luis Zalbide, one of the top dogs of ETA. In the pages of *Vasconia,* Krutwig attempted to adapt traditional Basque nationalism to the contemporary needs. For Krutwig, the Basques were a nation and, like any other nation, had the natural right to self-determination. In his own words:

> Achieving political independence by a people is internationally considered something *illegal* (according to the concept of legality of already existing states). That is why an oppressed people has no other means of

achieving national independence and sovereignty but by illegal means. [...] Sooner or later, the oppressed people [...] will have to use the force of arms, in other words violence, in order for its natural right [to self-determination] to be recognised. (Krutwig 1973: 328)

Krutwig proposed to set off a resistance movement by adopting the Algerian model of guerrilla warfare, a violent method used by irregular forces which lack the strength to oppose an occupying regular army. If the Algerian Front de Libération Nationale (FLN) had succeeded in expelling a powerful colonial power like the French Fourth Republic then the Basques could do the same with Spain. This is how the theory of action-repression-action was adopted. This doctrine, developed in the writings of Frantz Fanon, suggested that trained guerrillas could set a cycle in motion in which every action would generate an indiscriminate repressive reaction, which would in turn give rise to an even more revolutionary course of action, itself followed by even greater repression, and so on and so forth. Unaware of the identity of the guerrillas, the repressive forces would be forced to retaliate with indiscriminate repression affecting people who had not been involved in the original action. If the level of violence was well calculated, popular resentment would lead to greater militancy in the insurgency.[17] After creating such a spiral of violence and counter-violence, it could also be claimed that the measures taken by the security forces were 'repressive' and that the Basque Country was 'occupied' by foreign troops.

The second text that influenced ETA's decision on the use of violence was José Luis Zalbide's *La Insurrección en Euskadi*, published in 1964. The pamphlet built on Krutwig's proposals and developed some of his tactics in detail: how to attack the enemy, at which time of the day, how to retreat, etc. It also argued that ETA should adopt the kind of 'revolutionary war' that had been successful in Algeria, Cuba, and Indochina. But most importantly, the pamphlet glorified the guerrilla fighter as a sort of modern crusader. For Zalbide, destructive violence and death had a purpose beyond the elimination of human life. In the Basque case, the warrior's self-sacrifice would ritually accomplish the jubilant regeneration of the Basque nation. Following the work of Elie Kedourie, it may be argued that *Insurrección en Euskadi* was the most millenarian text ever written by ETA. Like some medieval Christian sects, who believed that the Second Coming of Jesus Christ and his saints would be followed by an apocalypse and a thousand-year period of peace on earth, radical Basque nationalists also had a 'millennial hope' which combined an idea of progress with the use of violence. As pointed out by Kedourie (1960), the doctrine of nationalism could be seen as a modern analogy of the millennial heresies of the Middle Ages—such as the revolutionary Anabaptists of Münster (1534)—because it promised that a global society of nation-states would put an end to all oppression and injustice. From this perspective, ETA dreamt of and looked for a nationalist paradise on earth in the same way as some of their medieval Christian predecessors had done. Zalbide's *Insurrección en Euskadi* had a remarkable impact on ETA which adopted it during its Third Assembly (1964). Tedious discussions about tactics were soon abandoned in favour of a contagious language which glorified the revolutionary struggle. This new mystical language was zealous, other-worldly, and managed to inspire many young nationalists to join ETA (Jáuregui 2000: 234; Sullivan 1986: 54–56).

4.3 ETA AND THE REVOLUTIONARY WAR

On 7 June 1968 two ETA members, Txabi Etxebarrieta and Iñaki Sarasketa, were driving in Villabona (Gipuzkoa) when they were stopped by a Civil Guard patrol. One of the agents, José Pardines Azcay, asked the driver for the car documents when Etxebarrieta opened fire on him. Pardines fell to the ground becoming the first victim of ETA. A few hours later, the two *etarras* were stopped at a control point near Tolosa, where Sarasketa was arrested and the 23-year-old Etxebarrieta was killed in retaliation for the murder of agent Pardines. The reaction of the Basque population to the death of Etxebarrieta was wide-ranging: demonstrations, funerals, and liturgies were organised in his honour throughout the Basque Provinces, from small hamlets to major cities like Bilbao, San Sebastián, Eibar, and Pamplona.[18]

4.3.1 ETA's actions

Two months later, on 2 August 1968, ETA responded to Etxebarrieta's killing by assassinating the police chief of Gipuzkoa, Melitón Manzanas González, who had a reputation for torturing Basques.[19] The reaction of the government to the premeditated killing of Manzanas was to declare a suspension of 'constitutional' guarantees known as 'state of exception' in the province of Gipuzkoa, a measure that was later extended to all of Spain. Within a month, the police had arrested numerous ETA members who were taken to court without further ado. Two years later, in December 1970, the next defining moment for ETA arrived. In the Burgos trial, sixteen ETA militants were accused of various acts of terrorism and banditry and six of them were accused of having murdered officer Manzanas.[20] The regime wanted to use the trial as a deterrent and decided to set up a military tribunal in Burgos which was the headquarters of the sixth military region (which had jurisdiction over the Basque Country).[21] The trial lasted twenty-five days and on 28 December 1970, the military court granted six death sentences and gave three of the accused double death sentences, thus increasing the penalty the prosecutor had asked for. The rest of the members were sentenced to twelve and thirty years in prison. Under domestic pressure and demands from the Vatican and the international community, two days later, on 30 December Franco commuted all death sentences to thirty years in prison.

The Burgos trial became an international *cause célèbre* 'of such pro-
portions that Spain was confronted with the most serious political crisis
since the Civil War'.[22] ETA militants were taken as a reference point by the
Spanish opposition and large sectors of international public opinion led
by Jean-Paul Sartre looked to ETA as the vanguard of anti-Francoist resistance. For the regime, the court trial was a political disaster because it fostered international support for clandestine political activity and magnified
the importance of an almost unknown armed group which was to receive
renewed support from the cadres of the PNV, the church, and elements of
the Spanish left, particularly the Communist Party (PCE). The legal process caused internal damage to the regime which saw how the most progressive Francoists (known as *aperturistas*) began to abandon 'what they
saw as a sinking ship' (Preston 1993: 754). The cycle of action-repression-
action doctrine had worked better than anyone could have ever imagined.
The sequence started by Etxebarrieta's death generated a spiral of violence
and counter-violence which was exploited by ETA to proclaim that the
security forces were 'repressive' and that the Basque Country was 'occupied'. Furthermore, the constitution of the Burgos military court could not
have come at a better time for the insurgency which was having trouble
launching guerrilla warfare attacks from their rural bases. In 1969, one
year before the legal proceedings, the insurgents' structures had been seriously weakened by police actions (Gurruchaga 2001: 67). After the court
trial ETA's message reached places that it had not reached before and many
Basque youngsters queued to join ETA.

In 1973, ETA carried out its most spectacular and daring action to date:
the killing of Franco's right-hand man and Prime Minister, Admiral Luis
Carrero Blanco.[23] ETA activists dug a T-shaped tunnel under a street Carrero used every day to attend Mass and filled it with 65 kilos of explosives. At 9:25 am, on 20 December 1973, the Prime Minister's car drove
over the secret tunnel and the ETA commando detonated the charge. The
car blew over a five-storey building, killing Carrero and the rest of the
occupants of the vehicle. The success of Operation Ogre (*Operación Ogro*)
demonstrated that ETA could carry out complex actions and boosted the
organisation's confidence that armed struggle was the single most effective weapon against the dictatorship. With the elimination of Carrero the
regime was left with no political heir and Prince Juan Carlos, who had
yet to show his democratic credentials, stood as the only contender who
could prolong 'Francoism after Franco'. The assassination endangered the
dictator's legacy by killing his alter ego and touched his feelings as no other
opposition group had done before. During the memorial service for Carrero on 22 December, a desolate Franco told one of his aides: 'They have
cut my last link with the world' (*Me han cortado el ultimo hilo que me unía
con la vida*).[24]

Comparatively speaking, the number of ETA actions (*ekintzak*) during
the 1968 to 1975 period was small. Born as a discussion group in 1959, ETA

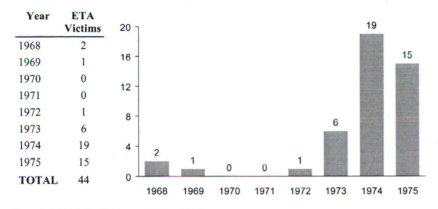

Year	ETA Victims
1968	2
1969	1
1970	0
1971	0
1972	1
1973	6
1974	19
1975	15
TOTAL	**44**

Figure 4.2 ETA victims, 1968–1975.
Source: Calleja & Sánchez-Cuenca 2006: 151

committed its first killing in 1968. As can be seen in Figure 4.2, over the next four years the number of attacks stayed low and were mainly carried out against policemen, army officers and regime politicians. By September 1974, indiscriminate attacks had become the norm as was shown by the bombing of the crowded Cafeteria Rolando in Madrid. In this dramatic act of violence alone, ETA killed twelve civilians and wounded another eighty. The dating of the attack was significant because between April and July 1974 the Portuguese and Greek military dictatorships had been deposed, Franco had fallen seriously ill and political change could finally be seen on the horizon. In 1975 ETA unleashed a violent campaign with the double objective of destabilising the regime and achieving a position of strength in future political negotiations with the democracy. In a desperate attempt to show firmness, the Franco regime executed two ETA members, Txiki and Otegi, and thereby outraged Basque public opinion which had long been appealing for clemency. Their death was to be added to the other two dozen ETA members who had been killed in shoot-outs, when detonating bombs, or were executed by the Franco regime.

4.3.2 Nationalism and violence as cohesive factors

The international press coverage of the Burgos trial generated a widespread movement of solidarity for Basque demands. The court-martial was supposed to serve as an example for underground groups but it backfired when it turned into a magnifying glass through which international public opinion could see the authoritarian nature of the regime and its brutality towards ETA members and sympathisers. The trial was of crucial importance to ETA, which was able to again recruit members and was able to unite the different competing trends within it. The repression had a centripetal effect on ETA, which learned the importance of 'action' in order to minimise internal controversies and splits. ETA's ideology rested on the two pillars of nationalism and socialism, which had not always been easy to reconcile and had been the source of three splits (Figure 4.3). In 1966 ETA underwent a split caused by the importance given to socialist elements. The split gave birth to ETA-Berri (or New ETA), later renamed Komunistak and incorporated into the Communist Movement, and ETA-Zarra (Old ETA), which later inherited the name ETA. The confrontation between nationalism and socialism was recreated and produced another split during the Fifth Assembly in 1970. That year, ETA split, for the second time, into two factions: ETA Fifth Assembly (ETA-V) and ETA Sixth Assembly (ETA-VI). ETA-V emphasised elements of ethnicity and was formed by the original members of ETA (*etnolingüístas*), whereas ETA-VI was formed by the new and more radical members who wanted a class-based struggle (*tercermundistas*). The members of ETA-VI wanted to establish alliances with other socialist movements and considered the Spanish *and* Basque 'oligarchy' as the enemy. Having defined their enemy in terms of class, ETA-VI established common interests, for example, with the working class of Andalusia. This allowed the nationalists of ETA-V to accuse them of being pro-Spanish and to argue for the emancipation of the working class, but only in the Basque lands. Finally, a third split between Marxists and nationalists occurred in 1974. The internal ideological conflict first related to the potential value and risks associated with increasing the armed struggle and making it autonomous. The second point concerned the relative merits of participating in a national or class front. This debate would culminate in 1974 with the division of ETA into ETA-Militar (ETA-M) and ETA-Politico Militar (ETA-PM). ETA-M continued with the use of violence and adopted the original name of ETA. On the other hand, ETA-PM followed a different evolution that ended in its dissolution in 1982.

The history of ETA splits during Francoism shows that nationalism and violence could act as powerful unifying factors. The 'socialist' splits of ETA resulted in ETA-Berria, ETA-VI, and ETA-PM. On the other hand, the use of violence kept united a nationalist trend within ETA until the restoration of democracy. Some scholars have argued that this dependency on these unifying factors have made successive generations of ETA more nationalistic and more violent (Elorza 2000). The truth is that the socialist element in ETA's ideology has been gradually marginalised as the traditional source of splits and, nowadays, it remains in ETA's discourse as empty rhetoric. Violence remains as the most important defining element of ETA, and arguably, the main reason for its existence.[25]

4.3.3 The support for ETA

Scholars of political violence and terrorism often point out that an armed group cannot carry out a long-term campaign of violence without social support. Ted Robert Gurr has argued that violent groups 'almost invariably emerge out of larger conflicts, and that they reflect, in however distorted

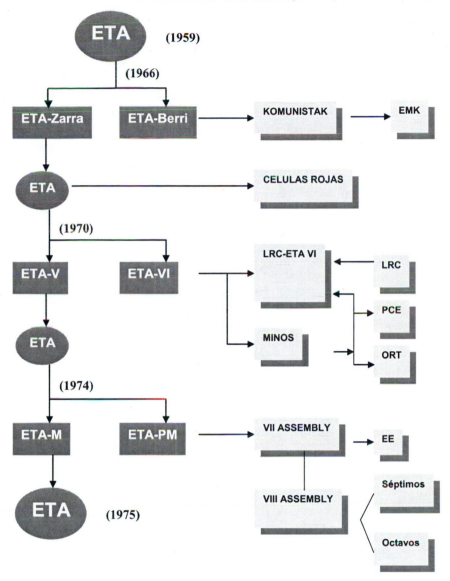

Figure 4.3 ETA splits during Francoism.
Sources: Based on Llera & Shabad 1990: 35; Vilar 1984: 409.

a form, the political beliefs and aspirations of a larger segment of society' (Gurr 1990: 86). When acts of violence are completely detached from group concerns, they are likely to be perceived as criminal acts. At the same time, a successful culture of violence allows for the individual experiences and memories to be interpreted and understood in a wider communal narrative. In the Basque conflict the government has tried, over and over, to depict ETA as a gang of distressed personalities. However, this was not the view of a significant section of the Basque population and the international left during Francoism. Needless to say, measuring the social support of an armed group under a dictatorship faces obvious empirical problems. In an authoritarian society where the Caudillo was worshipped and people had been disciplined to vote 'Yes' in every referendum, the general attitude of the public did not matter a great deal. There is no reliable data on public opinion for this period because Franco was not accountable to Spaniards and ruled 'for Spain, God and history'. However, what is known is that considerable support for ETA came from three groups: the wider Basque nationalist community, the Spanish opposition, and the Basque clergy.

First, the support from Basque nationalists is not difficult to explain if we bear in mind that the differences between the PNV and ETA were merely tactical. Basque nationalists strongly opposed the new centralist structure of the state, the abolition of the economic privileges of Biscay and Gipuzkoa, and the progressive loss of Basque identity. In the absence of democratic political institutions, ETA was the champion of Basque grievances. This tacit support should not be confused with active collaboration of the PNV with ETA. Xabier Arzalluz, president of the PNV from 1980 to 2004, explained that during Francoism there were three kinds of Basque nationalists. The first group retreated into culture, the second joined ETA and fought the dictatorship, and the third group, in which he included himself, did not 'read books' or 'set bombs', but helped those who set bombs to escape the police.[26] The first group of those who retreated into culture, was the largest. During the 1960s and 1970s a new generation of writers started using Euskara as their preferred language and a musical revival politicised the youth of the Basque Country (matched by the Catalan *Nova Cançó*). Others took refuge in sports and folklore, as they had previously done during Primo de Rivera's dictatorship. In the football stadium, the Athletic Bilbao provided Basques with an opportunity to wave their Basqueness. This shift from political to cultural nationalism is a common feature for nationalist movements which face rigid political structures. As Anthony D. Smith has pointed out, 'we often find the two kinds of nationalism alternating in strength and influence; as political nationalism falters and ebbs, cultural nationalists, as it were, pick up the torch and seek to rejuvenate a frustrated and oppressed community' (Smith 1998: 177).

Second, support for ETA came from the Spanish opposition, mainly from left-wing circles. ETA consistently used a Marxist language very similar to that of the communist party (PCE) from which they received support on several occasions. According to Sergio Vilar, between 1960 and 1973 the Spanish opposition, particularly the left, sympathised with the actions of ETA because they were all fighting a common enemy (Vilar 1984: 354). Patxo Unzueta, a journalist and former member of ETA, elaborated this latter point and added that support intensified after 1970 (Unzueta 1988: 80). The Burgos trial provided the Spanish opposition with a symbolic story of the struggle between heroic young activists and a ruthless regime. During the legal proceedings, Mario Onaindía defined himself as a 'prisoner of war' and denounced the Francoist regime for its treatment of the 'struggle of the Basque nation', and then began cheering, joined by the rest of the accused, for the freedom of Euskadi (*Gora Euskadi Askatuta*). Two members of the military tribunal responded by unsheathing their sabres and the security forces in the court drew their guns. This aura of romantic heroism increased even more after the elimination of Admiral Carrero Blanco, the official successor of General Franco, which confirmed the decisive usefulness of the armed struggle. The overall feeling was that, regardless of their ultimate objectives of creating a separate Basque state, the violent actions of ETA benefited the whole Spanish opposition.

Third, significant sectors of the Basque clergy provided support to ETA. On the one hand, the high echelons of the Basque hierarchy were directly nominated by Franco in accordance with the Vatican and unashamedly supported the regime. Under Francoism, the anticlerical legislation of the Second Republic had been abolished and the Church had been reinstated to its privileged position. In return for the support of the Church in his 'crusade' Franco re-established Catholicism as the official state religion, restored state subsidies to the church, outlawed divorce, and granted the clergy control of education. On the other hand, the lower Basque clergy provided ETA with churches and convents in which to conduct their assemblies and hide their weaponry. They also provided ETA with recruits and theoretical innovations such as Liberation Theology.[27] The reasons for their support were primarily two. First, the clergy had traditionally been the refuge of the Basque language and culture and had a fair amount of influence on Basque nationalism (Iturralde 1978; Gurruchaga 1985: 338–343). From Bernard Dechepare, author of the first book ever written in Euskara, to Father Larramendi in the eighteenth century, 90 per cent of the works in Euskara had been written by priests.[28] Second, many of the early ETA members had been educated in religious schools by priests who were *Euskaldun* (Basque speakers) from whom they learnt the 'nationalist faith' (*Documentos Y*, 1979–1981: 165). The sections of the Basque clergy that were nationalists also carried out their own campaigns throughout the period of Francoism.

The attitude of the lower Basque clergy to the violent conflict is often divided into two phases.[29] From 1940 to 1960, the lower clergy expressed their dissent through their daily preaching, collective letters (one of them sent to the Vatican), and the clandestine publication of the journal *Egiz* (Truly). The second phase lasted a decade and began in 1960, when 339 priests wrote a complaint about the prosecution of Basque signs of identity, and continued up until 1968 when a group of sixty priests called *Gogor* (Firmness) locked themselves inside the Seminary of Derio in Bilbao.[30] They demanded the resignation of their own Bishop, Pablo Gurpide, and protested against the Francoist repression by sending letters to the United Nations. The Bishop died during the protest and five of the priests were sentenced to ten or twelve years in jail (Salaberri 1971: 87). The rest of the group also served sentences in the specially created jail for priests in

Zamora (Unzueta 1988: 238–239). Also in 1968 the pulpits were used to launch highly political messages. In the Mass for Txabi Etxebarrieta, a prominent Jesuit, Father Pedro Arrupe, referred to violence, saying that 'it is a condemnable thing, but it is not so much so when there is a long and despotic tyranny that denies, in principle and in action, the rights of men' (Aulestia 1998: 34). Their support for ETA also came at a price for the clergy. Among the sixteen accused in the Burgos trial of 1970 two were priests and two had been educated in seminaries (Waldmann 1997: 64).

It is important to highlight some of the religious elements of Basque nationalism in order to make sense of the support of the Basque clergy for ETA. As the work of Izaskun Sáez has clearly shown, the founder of the PNV took great care to reconcile nationalism and religion in his motto *Jaun-Goikua eta Legi Zarra* (God and Old Laws). Sabino Arana incorporated some foralist and Carlist elements and turned nationalism into an instrument to better reach God. He argued that Basques could not be Catholic while attached to an amoral and atheist Spain and insisted that the real aim of this project was to save the Basque soul.[31] The subordination of the political to the religious could also be seen in Arana's design of the Basque flag (*ikurriña*). For Arana, the white cross, a religious symbol, had to be placed 'on top of the green cross and the red background to symbolise the supremacy of God over the laws and the nation'.[32] Moreover, not only was the discourse deeply religious, so too was PNV's membership. Some of the most valuable members of the PNV came from the clergy: Engracio de Aranzadi (Kizkitza), Alberto Onaindía, and Policarpo de Larrañaga among others. Given these links, much of the Basque clergy supported Basque nationalism during the Civil War. In turn, when the nationalists gained autonomous power on 7 October 1936 they protected the Basque church and stopped the anti-clerical repression that characterised some Republican areas during the war.[33] It cannot be denied that Basque priests were killed and that some churches were destroyed, looted, and desecrated, but the level of violence in the Basque Autonomous Community was much lower than in the rest of Spain (Ruiz Rico 1977: 30). In the other half, dominated by Franco's troops, the Catholic Church actively supported Franco and legitimised his claims of fighting a religious crusade 'For God and Spain' (*Por Dios y por España*).[34]

4.4 CONCLUSION

In 1959, radical youths who were dissatisfied with the passivity of the Basque Nationalist Party founded ETA. The splinter group from EGI initially concentrated on printing and distributing propaganda and it took them almost a decade to resort to political violence. In 1968, the killing of Pardines and Etxebarrieta unleashed a vicious spiral of action-repression-action in which guerrilla actions of ETA were followed by indiscriminate state repression that, in turn, encouraged a larger revolutionary action starting the cycle all over again. The government was only too happy to comply and adopted disproportionately repressive measures against the Basque population, which increased the perceived legitimacy of ETA's struggle and confirmed the widespread view that these were young romantics. The organisation came to prominence during the Burgos trials (1970) when sixteen ETA members, among them two women and two priests, were brought before a military tribunal. Their trial sparked off an avalanche of national and international protest and turned an almost unknown armed group on the verge of disappearance into an internationally recognised insurgent group. ETA acquired a romantic aura of freedom fighters and the group's militancy grew spectacularly. The anti-Francoist credentials of ETA were consolidated when, in 1973, ETA assassinated the prime minister of the Spanish government and political heir of Franco, Admiral Luis Carrero Blanco.

ETA's ideology was a combination of traditional Basque nationalism and Marxism with influences from Third World revolutionary struggles. The generation of the serpent and the axe effectively fused the nationalism of the PNV's elders with socialism into the 'war of national liberation'. The two texts that most influenced ETA were Krutwig's *Vasconia* and Fanon's *The Wretched of the Earth*. The ideological corpus was gradually built up during ETA's assemblies, gatherings at which ETA adopted tactical, strategic, and ideological positions. In the Fifth Assembly, held between 1966 and 1967, ETA established the socialist and anti-colonial character of the group and based its nationalist struggle on four fronts: economic, cultural, political, and military. However, the revolutionary socialism of ETA was gradually abandoned in favour of nationalism and violence as core elements. The ETA trend that defended the central importance of the armed struggle kept control of the paramilitary organisation whereas the revolutionary leftist elements eventually left in 1966 (ETA-Berri), 1970, (ETA-VI), and 1974 (ETA-PM).

During Francoism, popular opposition coalesced behind an ETA which was widely perceived as a group of young idealists who were morally justified in using violent methods against an oppressive regime. ETA became a symbol of resistance against the excesses of the dictatorship and both Basques and the Spanish left-wing and liberal circles, particularly the communist party of Spain (PCE), were sympathetic to its struggle. By the mid-1960s, ETA had the mass support of many Basques who saw the armed separatist group as the only real alternative to the PNV. As the next chapter will explain, when the Spanish transition to democracy got under way after the death of General Franco in 1975 most observers hoped ETA would recognise the new political situation and would disband. On the contrary, radical Basque nationalists became fiercely opposed to the consolidation of the constitutional monarchy arguing that the only political change that had taken place in Spain was the 'democratisation of fascism.'

5 The Basque Movement of National Liberation (1975–1987)

Spain's political transition to democracy (1975–1978) has been the subject of much idealisation and has become a paradigmatic model of social and political change. The 'Spanish Pathway to Democracy' marked a historical landmark in political transitions, and many countries in Eastern Europe and Latin America explicitly declared that they had followed its pattern when making their own transitions. In this process, Spanish elites successfully negotiated the replacement of the Francoist state by a parliamentary democracy in only three years. The process was facilitated by the moderate political culture of a Spanish civil society which had gradually emerged since the 1960s and by the role played by the monarch. Carefully groomed by Franco as his successor, Juan Carlos was proclaimed heir to the throne in 1969 and became king after the dictator's death in 1975. In his first six months in power, many feared he would continue the political work of the Caudillo by imposing a totalitarian monarchy, but there was also hope that Juan Carlos could become the 'pilot of change'.[1] Political uncertainty diminished with the appointment of Adolfo Suárez, an unknown politician who persuaded the Francoist elites and the opposition forces to support his project of gradual democratic reform. The resulting 'politics of consensus' instituted a parliamentary monarchy based on a constitutional agreement which was endorsed by all political parties except the PNV. The Constitution of 1978 set in motion a process of devolution in order to meet historical demands for regional self-government. When, in 1979, the Basque Statute of Autonomy was approved, all the region's political parties supported it with the single exception of an anti-systemic party called Herri Batasuna (HB). Founded in 1978, HB was one of the constituent parts of the Basque Movement of National Liberation, a network of organisations led by ETA which insisted on the need to carry on with the 'armed struggle' until the Spanish democracy recognised the right to national self-determination. The continuing actions of Basque separatists convinced some anti-democratic military officers of the need to attempt a *coup d'état* in February 1981. The intervention of the monarch proved decisive. In his constitutional role as commander in chief of the armed forces, the King ordered the rebellious captain generals to remain loyal to the chain of command and to the incumbent government.

5.1 POLITICS IN POST-FRANCO SPAIN

After King Juan Carlos succeeded Franco as head of state there were several months of political ambiguity. The first two measures taken by the Royal Household after the disappearance of the *Generalísimo* had been to (1) reappoint Carlos Arias Navarro as Prime Minister; and (2) nominate a former mentor of his, Torcuato Fernández Miranda, as president of both the Parliament (*Cortes*) and the Council of Realm. Although there were domestic and international pressures to democratise swiftly, the King first surrounded himself with men he trusted and balanced the expected political changes against the internal sensitivities of the regime. These two appointments clearly illustrate the complex, even contradictory, nature of the Spanish process of transition. The re-assignment of Arias as premier was mainly aimed at reassuring the diehard Franco loyalists known as the 'Bunker' who were still in control of the state apparatus. Months after he was appointed, it became evident he was unable to lead a process of democratisation and Arias resigned in 1976 at the request of Juan Carlos.[2] The second decision the King and his aides took, to nominate his earlier professor of Constitutional Law to the presidencies of the Council of Realm and the Parliament, allowed Fernández Miranda to favour a 'legal' transition and speed up political reform. Fernández Miranda's first assignment was to work behind the scenes in the Council of Realm and to facilitate the appointment of a new head of government to replace Arias. The institution he chaired selected three names from which the King had to choose the new Prime Minister. In the final *terna* there were two well-known Franco ministers, Silva Muñoz and López Bravo, and an almost unknown 43-year-old moderate Falangist, Adolfo Suárez. The first two were the candidates preferred by the democratic opposition and were strongly opposed by the more staunch Francoists. The third candidate, Adolfo Suárez, did not have much support (or opposition) but he had already been chosen by the King to become his first Prime Minister (Vilallonga 1994).

5.1.1 Politics of consensus

Adolfo Suárez was a charismatic political figure with a natural gift for negotiation and compromise. As the chief architect of the transition, Suárez brought together the Francoist elites and the opposition parties in his 'politics of consensus'.[3] On the one hand, the democratic opposition, mainly the socialist party (PSOE) and the communist party (PCE), wanted an abrupt break (*ruptura democrática*) with the previous regime. On the other, the Francoists did not have a unified position and were divided between the reformists who wanted Spain to gradually become a liberal democracy through a *ruptura pactada* (Fraga, Areilza, Silva) and the more intransigent Francoists who wanted Franco's legacy to continue (the *camarilla*, Girón de Velasco, Rodríguez de Valcárcel). Suárez's responsibility was to reconcile the 'two Spains' which had fought the Civil War, while meeting the conflicting demands of Spain's political elites and balancing these concessions with pressures from the general public. Determined to avoid another fratricidal conflict, all political parties made significant concessions and decided to agree on an elite settlement which allowed the process to prosper (Gunther 1992). This disposition to compromise (*el consenso*) made the negotiated replacement of the authoritarian structures by the democratic ones not only possible but orderly and legal. In the words of Fernández Miranda, 'everything depends on the answer one gives to the question: was the transition undertaken by means of a *reforma* or a *ruptura*? As far as I am concerned, the transition to democracy [was] carried out within the law, by means of the law'.[4]

Prime Minister Suárez's intention was to dismantle the *Nuevo Estado* piece by piece. But first he needed the Francoist MPs to support his Law of Political Reform which effectively proposed the dissolution of the Francoist Cortes and the election of a new democratic parliament. After long negotiations behind the scenes, the government managed to convince the *procuradores* to commit political suicide by voting for the law on 18 November 1976. The reform bill was the most important legal measure of *La Transición* because, instead of modifying the legal system, it abolished the Francoist fundamental laws and opened the door to an entirely new situation without breaking with the immediate past.[5] After the *Ley para la Reforma Política* was ratified by referendum the government granted amnesties, legalised political parties and trade unions, and called the first free democratic elections since the 1930s Second Republic.

On 15 June 1977, 18 million Spaniards voted in the first democratic elections since February 1936. More than 200 parties were registered, giving birth to the expression 'taxi parties' as all the members of a party could be transported in a single taxi. The Communist Party (PCE) was unexpectedly legalised at Easter 1977, to the outrage of the more intransigent sections of the regime, and was able to participate in the elections. The party Suárez had created months earlier, the Unión de Centro Democrático (UCD), won a simple majority with 34.4 per cent of the total vote and was closely followed by González's socialist party, the PSOE, with 29.3 per cent of the vote (Figure 5.1). These two parties had been successful in finding a central political space from which they could stake a claim to initiatives of both reform and rupture. The edges of the political spectrum came next with the conservative Alianza Popular (AP) led by the ex-Francoist minister Manuel Fraga, which obtained 8.2 per cent of the vote, and the largest opposition group during Francoism, the Partido Comunista de España (PCE) less than 10 per cent of the votes. The electorate had decided

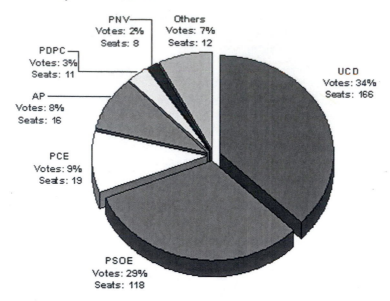

Figure 5.1 General elections, 15 June 1977. Others: *PSP-US (6), UDC/IDCC (2), EC/FED (1), EE (1), CAIC (1), and INDEP (1).*
Source: Ministerio del Interior (www.mir.es)

to support moderate compromise and penalised ideological intransigence. Suárez's conciliatory terms were rewarded and his mandate as architect of the transition was renewed and strengthened because the political space had been cleared of extravagant claims. The first democratic elections suggested that a restrained political culture was prevalent amongst the Spanish electorate and that any catch-all party willing to govern would have to fight for the political centre.

With a democratic system in place, the Spanish political elite faced two main challenges ahead of them: to stabilise the economic and social situation and approve a Constitution. The serious economic situation was tackled by an all-party agreement known as the Moncloa Pacts (1977) whereby the opposition parties and the trade unions agreed to cooperate with the government by keeping wage increases below the level of inflation in return for tax reform and an extension of the welfare state. Following the 1973 international oil crisis, unemployment had risen considerably, economic growth had declined, and the state had become highly indebted. Knowing that the economic crisis would only be solved by an austerity programme, Suárez asked all the political parties with parliamentary representation to support his measures. They all agreed and the Moncloa Pacts, designed by the economist Enrique Fuentes Quintana, were put in place to solve some of the short-term problems of the Spanish economy.[6] The task of drafting a new constitution was undertaken by a working committee of seven MPs representing the main political parties.[7] After eighteen months of debate the Constitution was finally approved in the Congress of Deputies on 31 October 1978. The Magna Carta officially returned parliamentary democracy to Spain after a forty-year dictatorship, proclaimed Spain as a constitutional monarchy, and established freedom of education, press, and expression and some social rights. The state had no official religion, though the 'role of the Catholic Church' was recognised. In addition, the Constitution established a 'state of autonomies' (*estado de las autonomías*) that combined the conception of Spain as a single political nation with the existence of limited self-government for all regions and nationalities. By 1983, seventeen statutes of autonomy had been drafted and approved in Parliament (Moreno 2001: 109–149).

5.1.2 The transition in the Basque Country

The processes of democratisation and decentralisation that followed the death of Franco meant that Spain could no longer be regarded as an exceptional case. The evolutionary convergence of norms and values with Western European standards, the consolidation of a well-functioning democracy, and the elimination of political uncertainty opened the door for Spain to join the European Community (Gunther, Montero, & Botella 2004: 21–78). Only one political anomaly remained: the existence of a Basque insurgent group with unwavering levels of social and political support. As already mentioned, radical Basque nationalists rejected the legitimacy of the new regime and supported ETA's continuing campaign of violence. In sharp contrast with the rest of Spain, the transition to democracy in the Basque Country was to be characterised by low support for the Constitutional settlement and high levels of political violence and social mobilisation (Edles 1998: 122–138).

The Suárez government was partly to blame for the lower level of support because his policy towards the Basque Country was largely reactive to pressures, events, and demonstrations (Gilmour 1985: 219). The lack of a coherent policy on Suárez part was seen in relation to the legalisation of the Basque flag, the *ikurriña*, and the amnesty of political prisoners. In Catalonia, the national flag (*senyera*) had been publicly displayed since 1975, but in the Basque Country, public display of the *ikurriña* was only permitted two years later, on 19 January 1977, after forty years of prohibition. The government's incomprehensible reluctance to legalise the Basque flag was best summarised by the Minister of Interior (*Ministro de Gobernación*), Manuel Fraga, who argued that the Basque flag would only be flown on public buildings if they trampled on his dead body (Carr & Fusi 1979: 219). The opportunism of the Suárez government could also be seen with regard to Basque political prisoners and ETA members. The pardons the government granted, in November 1975, July 1976, and March and October 1977, reduced the number of political prisoners in Spanish prisons by over 75 per cent.[8] However, many Basque prisoners did not benefit from the amnesty because they were directly responsible for crimes of blood (*delitos de sangre*). It was in the Basque Country where demonstrations for the freeing of prisoners (*presoak kalera*) were strongest and where feelings of frustration reached record levels. With both issues, the Basque flag and political prisoners, the government was slow to react and missed the opportunity to solve two key problems at a very low political cost. As in Catalonia, the flag could have been legalised and more flexible arrangements (based on repentance) could have been applied to ETA members.

The event which epitomised the lower Basque support for the process of democratisation was the 1978 constitutional referendum (Table 5.1). The results of the referendum illustrated the important differences between Spain as a whole, the Basque Country, and Navarre. A majority of Spaniards (67 per cent) participated in the referendum and of those 88 per cent voted yes. In the Basque Country, however, only 45 per cent of the electorate voted and of these, a slightly lower number, 70 per cent, approved the constitutional text. Within the Basque Country, the most nationalist provinces (Gipuzkoa and Biscay) showed higher levels of abstention (43 per cent and 42 per cent) than Araba (60 per cent). Generally speaking, the electoral behaviour of Navarre was in line with the Spanish average.

The PNV, which had not participated directly in the drafting of the Constitution, had recommended that its voters abstain in the referendum. The Basque nationalists' main objection to the Constitution was that it did not recognise the medieval *fueros* as a base for the autonomous government. The government, however, feared that basing a future Basque government on the *fueros* could be interpreted as an implicit recognition of the right to self-determination. Besides, the Suárez government was wary of the reaction further regional autonomy could provoke in the military and decided to risk a lower participation in the Basque Country. By recommending abstention, the PNV appropriated the 'natural abstention' of the Basque Country (around 35 per cent). However, the only way of knowing

Table 5.1 Constitutional referendum, 6 December 1978

	Electorate	Partici-pation (%)	Abstention (%)	'Yes' Vote (%)	'No' Vote (%)	Blank Votes (%)
All Spain	26.632.180	67.1	32.8	88.5	7.8	3.5
Navarre	361.243	66.6	33.3	76.4	17.1	6.4
Basque Country:	1.552.737	44.6	55.3	70.2	23.9	5.8
Araba	173.412	59.2	40.7	72.4	19.4	8.0
Bizkaia	874.936	42.4	57.5	73.0	21.4	5.5
Gipuzkoa	504.389	43.4	56.5	64.5	30.2	5.2

Source: Ministerio del Interior (http://www.mir.es)

how much opposition there was in the Basque Country to the Constitution would have been through the results for a 'no' vote accompanied by high participation levels (Benegas 1984: 88; Linz 1986: 226–257). In any case, the PNV concluded that the Constitutional arrangement had been rejected by a majority of the Basque people.

The position of the PNV during the process that led towards gaining home-rule status was radically different from that of the Constitution, and on that occasion, the opposition to regional autonomy came from radical Basque nationalists. A draft text was approved in December 1978 at the historic town of Gernika, and the Statute of Autonomy of the Basque Country was finally approved in the Madrid Parliament in December 1979. In the referendum, the PNV and all the Basque political forces enthusiastically recommended that their supporters vote in favour of it. Even Euzkadiko Ezkerra (EE), a party created by the splinter group ETA-PM and led by Juan María Bandrés and Mario Onandía supported the historic text. Only the radical nationalists of Herri Batasuna, a party which had been created a year earlier, recommended a 'no' vote (Pérez-Nievas 2002: 253–260). Their main objection to the project was that the statute, like the one drafted during the Second Republic, only had jurisdiction over the Basque Country and excluded Navarre. The text contemplated the possibility of the incorporation of Navarre if the latter approved it in its parliament, something that did not occur because Basque nationalism traditionally obtained poor electoral results in that area (Montero 1988: 111; Irvin 1999: 107; Granja, Beramendi, Anguera 2001: 227). Besides, in a previous consultation the population of Navarre had expressed their view that they did not want the statute to apply to their province and preferred a statute of their own. Eventually, 60 per cent of the Basque electorate voted in the referendum and, of those, 90 per cent voted 'yes' and only 5 per cent opposed the project. The Basque Statute of Autonomy, also known as the Statute of Gernika, created an autonomous police force (*Ertzaintza*), allowed the Basque government to collect taxes, take control of education and health care, own radio and television stations, and granted extensive responsibilities in the fields of public works, culture, agriculture, industry, and social welfare. Euskara was recognised as the official language of the Basque Country (together with Spanish) and a generous autonomy in financial matters was established. The economic agreement (*concierto económico*) allowed the autonomous Government to levy taxes in Araba, Biscay, and Gipuzkoa, a small share of which were to be delivered to the state, in what was considered to be one of the highest levels of regional self-government in the European Union (Mata 2005: 82).

The high levels of political violence and social mobilisation were, together with the low Basque support for the Constitution and, to a certain extent, the Statute of Autonomy, the elements that made the Basque transition so 'peculiar' (Aguilar 1998; Rivera 1998). The democratic process undoubtedly had other major challengers, the most important of which was the 'internal' threat of the army, but ETA's political violence pushed the Basque transition along a different path to that followed in the rest of Spain. Police forces continued to viciously suppress demonstrations and crowds with indiscriminate violence and individuals were often arrested, maltreated, and then released without being charged (Amnesty International Report 1977: 270). The most dramatic act of police brutality happened in Vitoria-Gasteiz, on 3 March 1976 when the police shot and killed five Basque workers who were demonstrating, along with 5,000 others, near a church. In this context, ETA could not be appeased by political compromise and continued to act as an agent provocateur. The virulence and intensity of the Basque paramilitaries during these years was unprecedented and contributed to an atmosphere of fear and uncertainty within both the state and civil society, neither of which were sure how best to deal with ETA.

The political transition was undermined by ETA and various other armed groups. The most important was the GRAPO (*Grupo Revolucionario Antifascista Primero de Octubre*), a Maoist armed group founded in 1975 which targeted members of the security forces, businessmen, and representatives of what they called 'the oligarchy' in an attempt to violently overthrow the Spanish government and establish a Marxist-Leninist state. There were also the extreme right-wing groups which targeted alleged leftist individuals and organisations in an attempt to cause unrest and interrupt the democratisation process. As can be seen in Table 5.2, the actions of ETA were most prominent, followed by those of GRAPO and the extreme right. In the years from 1975 to 1980, 378 people died. Of these, 284 had been killed by ETA accounting for 34 per cent of those killed between 1968 and 2006. That was an average of 44 deaths per year and almost one per week for seven years. In 1978 there were 65 deaths and in 1979 there were 80. The year 1980 was the bloodiest, with 96 deaths, half of them civilians.

Table 5.2 Killings by ETA, GRAPO, and the extreme right, 1975–1980

Year	ETA	GRAPO	Extreme Right
1975	15	5	0
1976	18	1	3
1977	10	7	8
1978	65	6	1
1979	80	31	6
1980	96	6	20
TOTAL	284	56	38

Source: Calleja & Sánchez-Cuenca (2006: 151); Laurenzano (2000: 122)

In sharp contrast, in the years from 1968 to 1974, only 29 people died as a result of ETA's actions (chapter 4).

The killings during these years were attributed to ETA and its various splinter groups which co-existed for several years: ETA-Militar (1959-to date), ETA político-militar (1975–1982), and the anti-capitalist Autonomous Commandos (Comandos Autónomos Anticapitalistas; CAA) which were active during the period from 1974 to 1984. During Francoism, when ETA had a clearly defined enemy and the room for strategic change was very small, several splits occurred. At a time when new possibilities for political participation were being opened up, the internal debate about how to proceed was ferocious. ETA came to be divided between those who held that 'revolutionary war' should be the only means of action and those who believed the political aspect should also be explored. The two positions evolved and produced a split in 1974 between ETA-PM, which advocated a combination of armed struggle and political action, and ETA-M, which proposed to engage in a war of attrition with the state. After the 1977 elections, a section within the political-military ETA obtained a government pardon, abandoned the armed struggle in 1982, and created the left-wing nationalist party Euskadiko Ezkerra (EE). As during Francoism, those organisations that split from ETA were accused of being pro-Spanish (*españolistas*) and, as in the case of Pertur, the leader of ETA-PM, some paid with their lives in an attempt to influence the military hardliners (Clark 1984: 92–93; Rincón 1985: 83; Gurruchaga 2001: 105). ETA-M continued its activities and established a hierarchical organisational form that would be maintained for the next two decades (Dominguez 2000: 283). As the Basque journalist Luciano Rincón argued when referring to the decision by some members to abandon the violent struggle and be re-integrate, 'ETA does not change; *etarras* do' (Rincón 1985: 13).

The question any scholar interested in transitology needs to ask is why did ETA increase their activities during the democratisation process? Why was it that, at a time when politics was becoming democratic, ETA stubbornly stuck to its methods? Why did it fight the pluralist regime even more ferociously than it had fought Francoism? The main reason for the increase in violence seemed to be the strategic need of ETA to remain a relevant force. During Francoism, ETA was the main reference group for Basque nationalism, but since 1979 a plethora of groups were able to accurately represent the existing multiplicity of views. By using violence, ETA made its presence visible and forced all political parties to take a stand with regard to nationalist violence. The argument put forward was that nothing had changed since Francoism and that the Spanish democracy was a mere façade for authoritarian rule. In order to demonstrate this optical illusion for what it was, ETA engaged in a bloody campaign that targeted military personnel. Between 1968 and 1977 not a single army officer had been killed but, between 1978 and 1983, thirty-seven people of rank died at the hands of ETA which hoped to provoke a reaction from the army and the security forces during the transition (Gilmour 1985: 225; Linz & Steppan 1996: 99; Peces-Barba 2000: 66; Powell 1996: 157–164; Aranzadi, Juaristi, & Unzueta 1994: 247).

The pressure from ETA did not remain unnoticed and in 1981 there was an attempt *coup d'etat*. Organised by several generals, the putsch wanted to create a military junta under the king's authority in order to slow down the pace of regional devolution and preserve the 'unity of Spain'. At 6:20 pm on 23 February, several Civil Guards armed with sub-machine guns stormed the *Cortes*, which was holding a plenary session to vote on the investiture of Leopoldo Calvo Sotelo as successor of Adolfo Suárez. Led by Lieutenant-Colonel Antonio Tejero, pistol in hand, the civil guards held the members of parliament hostage for ten hours. The attempted coup, to be known as 23F or *Tejerazo*, counted on the support of well-connected plotters such as General Armada, but only one of eleven captain-generals in charge of the military regions, General Milans del Bosch, took tanks onto the streets of Valencia 'to save the monarchy'. It was a long day and night for Spaniards who were unaware of the many telephone calls the head of state was making to the rest of the captain-generals to confirm their loyalty to the monarchy and the Constitution. With the whole government being held hostage in parliament, the only individual who could cut the Gordian knot was the King in his capacity as commander-in-chief of the armed forces. Later that night and dressed in uniform, Juan Carlos I appeared on TV at 1.23 am and reassured the public that he had personally ordered the civil and military authorities to defend the democracy. Knowing of the failure of their attempt, Milans del Bosch ordered the armoured vehicles to return to their garrisons and Tejero's civil guards surrendered. The event confirmed the king's leadership capabilities against the military's 'sword rattling' (*ruido de sables*). Regrettably, those who had urged a more cautious approach to regional devolution (including the armed forces) were rewarded with a legal initiative that slowed down the process of decentralisation and brought the route to autonomy under stricter control in accordance with the controversial *Ley Orgánica de Armonización del Proceso Autonómico* (LOAPA), approved in July 1981 (Agüero 1995: 161–180; Granja, Beramendi, & Anguera 2001: 203).

As has already been noted, radical nationalists encouraged their supporters to vote 'no' in the referendums for the Constitution, the Statute of Autonomy of the Basque Country, and that of Navarre, the *Ley de Amejoramiento Foral de Navarra*, by which the region was to have its own Parliament and autonomous institutions (Hausnarzten III, 13, 32). The main objection was that the regional political system was derived from the Spanish constitutional system where Basques could not participate freely. In fact, radical nationalists came to argue that the transition had never taken place in the Basque Country. In their eyes, ETA's violence was the symptom of a 'political problem' and the indicator that the Spanish democracy was no more than a cosmetic change from Francoism. Under the democratic façade, Spain retained the same authoritarian practices, and it was necessary for ETA to carry out its revolutionary war to unmask the true nature of the new democracy.

5.2 FROM ARMED GROUP TO SOCIAL MOVEMENT

After the death of Franco, radical nationalists maintained their pre-democratic ideology intact but adapted their organisational structures to the new political circumstances. From 1975 ETA created a network of organisations grouped in the Basque Movement of National Liberation (*Movimiento de Liberacion Nacional Vasco;* MLNV in its Spanish acronym) to complement ETA's war of psychological and physical attrition. This complex system was informally known as the nationalist or patriotic left (*izquierda abertzale*) and it was made up of a number of interconnected political organisations, social agents, and NGOs with interests in the fields of feminism, environmentalism, internationalism, Basque culture, youth, and students and prisoner's rights. During the 1980s the most important members were the trade union Langile Abertzaleen Batzordeak (LAB), the political party Herri Batasuna (later called Euskal Herritarrok and Batasuna), and the armed group Euskadi Ta Askatasuna (ETA), the undisputed leader of the movement. The key characteristic of the satellite organisations was their ideological and strategic dependency on ETA, which they followed as the vanguard of the movement to create an independent Basque socialist state (Hausnartzen II: 36–37).

The idea of opening up a political front to complement the military one came from an ETA-Militar (ETA-M) leader, José Miguel Beñaran Ordeñana (Argala). By the beginning of the transition, ETA had realised that the Spanish state could not be defeated by military force and decided to promote the creation of new political organisations in order to increase their pressure on Spain. In 1978, the strategy of splitting (*desdoblamiento*) complemented the 'revolutionary war' which had guided ETA actions since the Fifth Assembly (1966–1967) (Ibarra 1989: 99; Domínguez 2000: 292). The strategy was a combination of 'armed struggle and popular mobilisation through the social and political organisations which comprised the broader MLNV' (Llera, Mata, & Irvin 1993: 111). As laid down in the training notebooks Hausnartzen, the Basque Movement of National Liberation (MLNV), had a strategic goal which was to create a state for the Basque nation, and a tactical one, which consisted in securing all the contents of the Socialist Patriotic Coordinator (Koordinatzaile Abertzale Sozialista; KAS Alternative). The basis for the MLNV was the 'politics of aggregation of sectoral interests' (*política de acumulación de fuerzas*) by which a huge variety of political and social forces group together with a common goal: the independence of the Basque homeland (Hausnartzen I: 8).

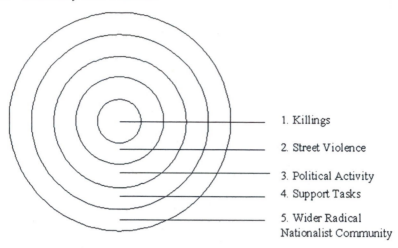

1. Killings

2. Street Violence

3. Political Activity

4. Support Tasks

5. Wider Radical
   Nationalist Community

Figure 5.2 Levels of involvement in radical Basque nationalism.

According to José Manuel Mata López, members of the MLNV showed different levels of involvement in the network (Mata 1993: 95–131). Direct involvement in ETA brought about higher risks (a clandestine life, imprisonment, and even death) than helping out in the electoral campaign of Herri Batasuna. ETA members were the most devoted because they were prepared to accept these high costs. According to this logic, one could graphically describe the levels of involvement in radical Basque nationalism as a series of concentric circles (Figure 5.2). In theory, the five circles were neat but organisations could change their degree of involvement and move from one level to another. This was even more so for individuals, whose tactical considerations evolved much more rapidly than those of organisations and, consequently, could change their location. The inner circle represented ETA, the 'vanguard' of the whole movement, and the reference point for all the organisations. The further away one moved from the centre the lower the risks and the less the influence. The second circle was represented by the building blocks of KAS which directed the violent strategy of the MLNV militancy under ETA's tutelage. The member organisations of KAS included ETA, the propaganda body ASK, the political party HASI, the trade union LAB, the youth organisation Jarrai, and the feminist NGO Egizan. The third circle represented the political party Herri Batasuna which was later known as Euskal Herritarrok and Batasuna. The fourth circle was for those organisations of the MLNV which have not been mentioned up to now. They were the ones that sympathised with ETA but were not directly involved in its activities (e.g., the newspaper *Egin*, the student union Ikasle Abertzaleak, the coordinator for Basque language teaching and literacy, AEK). Finally, the fifth circle represented the wider radical nationalist family. This included individuals who were occasional voters, might attend a demonstration, or might give their financial support or time through any of the organisations of the network (Mata 1993: 335–337; Dominguez 200: 278). The following pages will provide an analysis of the most important members of the MLNV. This analysis will be a brief detour from the general argument in order to illuminate the organisational complexities and variety of discourses within radical Basque nationalism.

5.2.1 KAS

The spiral of action-repression-action allowed ETA to create a significant level of support in Basque society by partially delegitimising the Francoist state. However, by 1977, ETA leaders had realised that a complete military victory was unattainable and that they had reached a stalemate with the state. In spite of the high costs for both sides, new *etarras* and security forces were replaced and the war of attrition was cyclically reproduced. In 1978, ETA adopted a strategy based on reaching an advantageous position for a future political negotiation in which violence would be used as a bargaining tool. ETA believed that a high number of deaths could push the state to the negotiation table (which would be accompanied by a ceasefire). Whereas during the previous period a high number of violent actions were necessary to eliminate the enemy, in the negotiation phase a selective use of violence was essential in order to maintain social support. By 1980 the Statute of Autonomy and the first Basque elections had already been held and there was a decline in the absolute number of killings. In parallel, ETA's extortion of entrepreneurs and businessmen increased and those who refused to pay the 'revolutionary tax' were sometimes kidnapped (e.g., Revilla, Aldaya, Delclaux, Iglesias Zamora,).

In the new phase, the Socialist Patriotic Coordinator Committee (KAS) managed the areas of culture, the masses, and politics and left the military strategy to ETA. Established in September 1975 to co-ordinate nationalist activities when faced with the court martial of two ETA members (Txiki and Otaegi) who were finally executed, the organisation evolved a year later to become the top decision-making organisation of the MLNV. Between 1976 and 1978, KAS defined the necessary political conditions needed for ETA to stop its violent action (Egaña 1996: 37; Jarrai 1984: 19). What came to be known as *Alternativa KAS* established five strategic goals which included: (1) an amnesty for all Basque political prisoners; (2) the legalisation of all political parties; (3) the withdrawal from the Basque Country of the Spanish Security Forces; (4) the improvement of social conditions for the workers and masses; and (5) the approval of a Statute of Autonomy that recognised the right to self-determination, established Euskara as the main language, gave the Basque government control of the Army, and allowed the Basque people to decide its own future.

The goals of KAS, renamed to *KAS Bloque Dirigente* in 1983, were the goals of ETA as they laid down the conditions necessary to stop the armed struggle (Zutabe no. 35: 2–14). The solution to the 'Basque conflict' needed the full adoption of the KAS Alternative, which would end in a political negotiation between ETA and the powers that be. The resulting situation, and the only one ETA would accept, would be one in which Spain withdrew all its security forces from Basque lands and guaranteed the right to self-determination, hence opening the door to an organised process of secession. For the Spanish state, this meant recognising a supposed illegitimacy in ruling the Basque lands and accepting the representative nature of ETA. For ETA, being recognised as a representative political force with which one had to negotiate was a pre-requisite to obtaining its goal of creating a Basque socialist state (Ibarra 1989: 103).

5.2.2 Herri Batasuna

Although not an integral part of the KAS coordinating committee, Herri Batasuna (Popular Unity) also supported the KAS Alternative as the only means to settle the problem of violence in the Basque Country. The tactical goal of the political coalition was to establish a political agreement between the Spanish Basque Country (*Hego Euskal Herria*) and Spain to confirm the political sovereignty of the Basques. Needless to say, from Herri Batasuna's perspective, the Basque problem was a struggle between Basques and Spaniards and political violence was an indicator of that ethno-territorial dispute (not the problem in itself). As one of the internal documents of Herri Batasuna stated:

> Euskal Herria was deprived of all its political rights by force, and being confronted by such dispossession, our nation has defended its rights and organised its self-defence, combining different forms of struggle, for the last 150 years. This constant clash with the Spanish state has generated a movement of resistance which has had a progressive evolution in terms of political consciousness and other internal and external factors. Hence, the methods of this struggle, its contents and its formulations have evolved. It is precisely in this last phase of the liberation process that ETA has become an essential reference. (HB-Urrats Berri 1992: 25)

The activity of Herri Batasuna was subordinated to the armed struggle from its genesis. The party's main priority was to 'add new forces around the MLNV in order to facilitate the agreement between ETA and the real powers' (Hausnartzen I: 7). HB was not born with concrete aims, other than to carry out the national liberation through political means. Established in 1978, Herri Batasuna became one of the fundamental organisations of the MLNV and, in spite of advocating independence and revolutionary change in the Basque lands, the more socialist elements of its programme remained largely unexplored (Rincón 1985: 98). Herri Batasuna's symbiotic relationship with ETA meant that HB got the votes of all those who supported ETA. However, when ETA committed indiscriminate killings, it was Herri Batasuna that suffered the loss of support. When, in July 1987, ETA bombed the Hipercor supermarket in Barcelona killing twenty-one people, two of them children, and injuring forty-two, it was Herri Batasuna that paid at the ballot box. Months before the attack, Herri Batasuna had obtained 210,430 votes in the European elections, thereby becoming the leading party in the region, but in the next European elections in 1989 HB had dropped to second position. The relevance of Herri Batasuna during the 1980s was crucial because its level of support was interpreted by the press, opinion-makers, and academics as support or sympathy for ETA (Llera, Mata, & Irvin 1993). In general, HB got an average of between 15 and 20 per cent of the vote of the Basque electorate, depending on the election. Since several of their candidates came from ETA and, in some instances there was dual membership of the two organisations, Herri Batasuna was widely regarded as the 'political arm' of ETA.[12] This close affiliation with ETA led to the banning of the party and the imprisonment of the twenty-three-member leadership (*mesa nacional*) by Judge Baltasar Garzón in December 1997.

The history of Herri Batasuna during the 1980s can be divided into two phases. The first covered its establishment as an electoral coalition in the years 1978 to 1981 whereas the second witnessed its consolidation as a movement of 'popular unity' from 1982 to 1987 (Hausnartzen III: 28; Herri Batasuna 1999: 6). The first phase began with the founding of Herri Batasuna as an electoral coalition on 27 April 1978 in the town of Alsasua, Navarre. The parties that made up HB were Herriko Alderdi Socialista Iraultzailea (HASI), Langile Abertzale Iraultzaileen Alderdia (LAIA), Euskal Sozialista Biltzarrea (ESB), Euskal Iraultzarako Alderdia (EIA), and Acción Nacionalista Vasca (ANV) which had been active during the 1930s. The coalition also had the support of a series of charismatic individuals of the 'abertzale left' such as Jon Idígoras, Txomin Zuloaga, Iñaki Aldekoa, Francisco Letamendía, Patxi Zabaleta, and Telésforo Monzón, former minister of the Basque Autonomous Government in 1937.[13] A noteworthy event during this first stage was the hostility of the *abertzales* to the King in 1981. The monarch attended the Casa de Juntas de Gernika on 4 February 1981 and the nineteen members of Herri Batasuna interrupted Juan Carlos's speech by singing the nationalist anthem, *Eusko Gudariak*, after which they were expelled from the chamber. The protest outraged both Basque and Spanish public opinion, which were shocked at Herri Batasuna's anti-system characteristics. The HB parliamentarians also showed their tactical intransigence after the 1979 general elections by refusing to occupy their seats in the Spanish and Basque Parliaments. The goal then became one of using the electoral process as a 'mechanism for demonstrating a high level of voter discontent in the Basque Provinces and to denounce the existing political system' (Irvin 1999: 120).

In a second phase (1982–1987), Herri Batasuna became the main political party of the 'patriotic left' (*izquierda abertzale*) and established a tactical alliance with working class organisations and other NGOs. According to Juan Linz, HB rejected the political order and advocated the creation of a Basque state, making it 'the most revolutionary political party of the Spanish political spectrum' (Linz 1986: 598). HB consolidated its social movement image with the adoption of a logo based on the Basque flag, the *ikurriña*, using the colours of the rainbow, each colour representing the different struggles in the Basque lands: red for the workers, purple for women, yellow for the antimilitarists, green for the environmentalists, and white for peace. The party also began opening its own bars, Herriko Tabernas, which proliferated into the hundreds (Herri Batasuna 1999). It was also during the second period of Herri Batasuna that some of its important successes came about. After a long debate on whether to participate in the Spanish political system, Herri Batasuna first participated in the General Elections of 1979 and obtained 149,685 votes and elected three deputies to the lower chamber of the Spanish Parliament. It was the fourth largest Basque political force, with 15 per cent of the electorate. In the following years it obtained similar results; during the 1980s it eventually became the third largest Basque political force. Its biggest success came in the 1989 European elections when it received 210,000 votes (20 per cent of the electorate), making it the largest political force in the Basque Country. However, Herri Batasuna's main successes came in the elections that were traditionally considered by the electorate as unimportant: the European elections and the elections to the provincial Parliament (Juntas Generales).

According to Cynthia L. Irvin, the Herri Batasuna voters were 'predominantly under forty-five, male, and working class' (Irvin 1999: 125). Among them there were a high percentage of the self-employed, workers, pensioners, housewives, and the unemployed (Núñez 1980: 114–117). Compared to the PNV voter who was much older, predominantly female, and with a higher socio-economic status, Herri Batasuna voters usually had lower incomes and a lower level of qualifications. As can be seen in Table 5.3, for the most part HB voters were male, in clear contrast to the PNV voters (40 per cent). Regarding age, the differences between the two parties were also considerable because the radical party attracted a much younger electorate. Of those aged between 18 and 24, up to 28 per cent supported Herri Batasuna whereas the PNV only managed to attract 5 per cent of this age group. Finally, the self-identification of social class also showed interesting differences between Herri Batasuna and the PNV. Whereas up to 59 per cent of PNV voters defined themselves as working class, for Herri Batasuna that number rose to 73 per cent.

Table 5.3 Social background of Basque nationalist voters: HB and PNV

Political parties Characteristics	HB (N=197) %	PNV (N=455) %
Gender		
Female	41	60
Male	59	40
Age		
18–24	28	5
25–34	27	14
35–44	17	23
45–54	14	23
55+	14	35
Social class		
Upper, upper middle class	6	9
Middle class–lower middle class	20	27
Working class	73	59
Don't know	1	1

Note: The survey was carried out by Juan José Linz and his team in the early 1980s
Source: Linz (1986: 575–576)

5.2.3 LAB and Jarrai

The trade union LAB and the youth organisation Jarrai were core organisations of the MLNV network during the 1980s. Each of these organisations represented a particular social cluster of society and allowed the radical movement to claim some degree of legitimacy and representativeness. LAB and ETA joined forces in arguing that the last protagonist of the long-term struggle against its neighbours was the Basque Working People (*Pueblo Trabajador Vasco*).

The Patriotic Workers Committee (*Langile Abertaleen Batzordea; LAB*) was a separatist, anti-bourgeois, and anti-Spanish trade union which aimed to reconcile the workers' struggle with the national one (Mojuelo 2000: 48). For LAB, the socio-economic problems of the Basque working class could not be separated from 'the political reality outside the factory' (Mojuelo 2000: 61). Most of its affiliates came from the province of Gipuzkoa and, to a lesser extent, from Biscay, Araba, and Navarre and, due to its involvement in the MLNV, LAB kept its distance from other trade unions. LAB accused CCOO and UGT, which were present all over Spain, of being accomplices of the Spanish repression and the Basque nationalist ELA of having close ties with the Basque bourgeoisie through its historical links with the PNV. LAB's great moment arrived in the late 1970s when the full impact of the Moncloa Pacts and the government's rationalisation of Spanish industry (*reconversión industrial*) was felt in the northern provinces. The confrontational tactics LAB defended became popular at a time when heavy industry, the motor of the Basque economy, was rapidly disappearing. The restructuring affected the main Spanish industrial sectors (shipbuilding, iron and steel, automobile manufacture, mining, and textiles) in preparation for the country's accession to the competitive European single market. The *reconversión industrial* mainly affected the province of Biscay where hundreds of companies filed statements of financial difficulties, hoping to cut down on the workforce and fixed costs. In 1977, 648 Basque companies filed statements, a number which rose to 1,353 in 1978, 2,195 in 1979, and 2,175 in 1980. The following year, the number of statements began to decline (1,823) but 1981 was the year when two of the most emblematic Basque companies, Altos Hornos de Vizcaya and the shipyard Astilleros Euskalduna, presented their statements, finally disappearing in 1984 (Mojuelo 2000: 100–105). It was estimated that between 1973 and 1985 up to 170,000 jobs were lost in the Basque industrial sector and per capita income declined. Social conflict and rising unemployment favoured LAB, which remained the fourth largest trade union in the Basque lands for most of the 1980s (Unanue 2002: 84). By 2000, LAB was the third largest Basque trade union with 27,000 members, 15 per cent of the Basque workforce (Majuelo 2000: 8).

Jarrai was the youth organisation of the MLNV and often provided the training ground for many future leaders of the movement. Its importance increased in the 1990s when Jarrai was the main actor in what came to be known as the street fight (*kale borroka*) and provided the MLNV with new recruits. Established in 1979 in Leioa (Biscay), Jarrai defined itself as,

> a youth political organisation which considers that the Basque youth, on top of the problems it already has as such, belong to an oppressed and occupied nation, Euskal Herria; and we are also part of the popular sections of society which, led by the Basque working class, are called to change the current situation until we eliminate this oppression. (Jarrai 1986: 5)

During the early 1980s the radical organisation debated issues which affected young Basques, such as the refusal to do military service (*insumisión*), unemployment, drugs, the squatter movement (*movimiento okupa*), and what came to be known as Basque radical rock (*rock radical vasco*). As elsewhere in Europe, during the 1980s single issues such as the environment, same-sex couples' rights, or anti-militarism became mobilising issues for an allegedly depoliticised and post-materialist youth. Of all these, the most important was Spain's controversial membership of NATO which was opposed by Jarrai and many other organisations. Spain had joined NATO in 1981 under a UCD government and the socialist party, then in opposition, carried on a very strong anti-NATO campaign. Felipe González promised a referendum on the matter once they reached power but, once in office, he changed his mind and argued that Spain should remain in the North Atlantic Alliance as a stepping-stone towards entry into the EEC. The PSOE won the 1986 referendum by a very small margin in spite of widespread opposition and anti-Americanism. Another issue in which Jarrai was very active was environmentalism, in particular the protest actions against the construction of the nuclear power station at Lemóniz (Biscay) (Barcena, Ibarra, & Zubiaga 1997). The plant was being built by the energy company Iberduero with the consent of the state's Ministry of Energy and Industry. The 1980s campaign against Lemóniz included popular demonstrations, rallies, and refusals to pay electricity bills. ETA sabotaged the building works in 246 separate actions, killing five people. The most dramatic action took place on February 1981, when ETA kidnapped and killed the chief engineer of the Lemóniz plant José María Ryan. The following year, ETA killed Angel Pascual, the Lemóniz project manager. Given the high financial costs of the sabotage (almost €12.5 million) and the intimidation by ETA of the plant workers, the government decided to drop the project in 1982 (Domínguez 2000: 307–308). Another environmentalist campaign in which the MLNV and Jarrai were very active was the construction of the Leizarán highway. The acts of sabotage numbered 158 but the human costs were not so striking. Under pressure from the MLNV, the project was redrawn in order to minimise the environmental impact. Both Lemóniz and Leizarán came to be remembered as great victories for the MLNV and for ETA.

5.3 A DISCOURSE ANALYSIS OF THE RADICAL NATIONALIST COMMUNITY

The following section will analyse the way in which ETA domesticated the past in order to justify its use of political violence. The argument will be divided between: (1) identifying the structure of radical Basque nationalist discourse; and (2) explaining how violence was integrated and legitimised in this discourse. If we were to follow the explanation of one of the ideologues of Herri Batasuna, Telesforo Monzón, the logic of violence would be simple: 'It is not ETA that has bred violence. It is violence that has bred ETA' (Egin 1997: 25). According to this nationalist mythology, it was the occupation and oppression of the Basque nation by Spaniards which triggered a legitimate defence movement. ETA would be the continuation of a long line of Basque patriots who gave their lives for the independence of the Basque Country (Muro 2005).

The discourse of radical Basque nationalism during the 1980s and much of the 1990s was made up of three myths which constituted a 'nationalist triad': (1) a myth of the Golden Age; (2) a myth of decline; and (3) a myth of regeneration or salvation. What is important to point out is that the thread that unites the three constituent myths is violence. As in medieval chronicles, tales of sacrifice, heroism, and defeat are all linked by violence. The ancestors, and more importantly, the heroic dead are essential in maintaining group cohesion. The martyrdom of one individual can do more to unite a nation than a hundred victories because social groups often come together in grief. That is because suffering and the process of mourning effectively unite individuals. It is not accidental that Jews remember the destruction of the Temple (and the Holocaust), Greeks the fall of Constantinople, Serbs the military defeat in Kosovo, Irish the Great Famine, or Armenians the genocide. In the same way, radical Basque nationalism remembers the traumatic defeats they suffered in the past. The structure of radical Basque nationalism is not unusual and, as Levinger and Franklin Lytle (2001) have consistently argued, elements of 'the triadic structure of nationalist rhetoric' can be found in several nationalisms such as the Italian, Bulgarian, Algerian, French, Croatian, and German. Furthermore, the structure could have been taken by all these nationalisms from the Judaeo-Christian scriptures which establish the origins and destiny of humanity—paradise, fall from grace, and redemption.

5.3.1.1 The Basque Golden Age

The use of the past by nationalist movements is of interest to most scholars of nationalism. The dispute lies in whether that past is a complete fabrication or whether it is based on pre-existing traditions, written sources, legends, and beliefs. Nevertheless, there is an overall agreement in the field that nationalism can be described as a 'Janus-faced' phenomenon; meaning that, like the Roman god, it looks both at the past and to the future (Nairn 1977). In the Basque Country, the myth of the Golden Age remains one of the most powerful mobilised by nationalists. As described in chapter 1, the Basque Golden Age was a period in time when Basques were citizens of an independent nation with their own political, religious, and social characteristics and who proudly defended their boundaries from invaders. This defensive attitude of the ancestor and the historical images of Basque warfare were glorified by Sabino Arana and other nationalists. For the supporters of ETA, the fighting character of the Basques was an integral part of the Golden Age. As Telesforo Monzón, one of the ideologues of Herri Batasuna, pointed out: 'the war has arrived. A long war which has not ended and that I call the war of the 150 years: the time of Zumalakarregi and the first war; of Santa Cruz and the second [war]; the time of Agirre and the Basque Government. And the time of ETA with Txikia and Argala (Herri Batasuna 1999: 426).

For radical Basque nationalists, the Golden Age has two components, which are intrinsically linked. In their lost past, the Basque nation had been defended by its members and, as a consequence, it had been eternally independent. In Jarrai's 1984 Training Notebook, the youth organisation explained how the Basque Country was an independent entity in the Middle Ages (Jarrai 1984: 18). Two years later, in 1986, Jarrai argued that the 'Basques are also an ancient people who have fought since the sixth century' (Jarrai 1986: 8). This emphasis on the national past and the importance of remembering the perennial fighting spirit of Basques also found its expression in events with massive attendances. In 1976 the *abertzale* city council of Bergara (Gipuzkoa) organised an act to commemorate the hundredth anniversary of the approval of the *Ley de abolición de los Fueros* of 21 July 1876 by which the Basque *fueros* were abolished. The act was attended by sixty-nine representatives of other city councils and representatives of the more moderate nationalism such as Carlos Garaikoetxea, the leader of the PNV, Xabier Arzalluz, and the widow of the *Lehendakari* Jose Antonio Aguirre, Mari Zabala. Two years later, on 15 August of 1978 the *Arbasoen Eguna* (Day of the Ancestors) was held in Orreaga to commemorate the 1200th anniversary of the Battle of Roncesvalles where Charlemagne was defeated by 'Basque' forces. According to an observer, the rally was mainly attended by young people and the event had been organised by the *abertzale* left (Zubillaga 1978: 81). Finally, after the elections to the Basque parliament in 1980, the members of Herri Batasuna who won electoral representation swore on the unity of the Basque nation (Euskal Herria), in Leire (Navarre), where the 'Basque Kings' (*Reyes de Vasconia*) were buried. For nationalists, the Kingdom of Navarre was the first Basque state and they constantly refer to it. For example, the clubs of Herri Batasuna, the Herriko Tabernas, have as their logo the Black Eagle (*Arrano Beltza*), symbol of this 'Basque Kingdom' (Herri Batasuna 1999: 59; Bilbao & Munarriz 1997: 26).

Given the capacity of radical nationalists to remember, or imagine in the Andersonian way, the national past, it does not come as a surprise that Jarrai also interpreted the dynastic disputes of the nineteenth century, the Carlist Wars, as wars of national liberation, thus following the trend initiated by Joseph Agustín Chaho. What is more surprising is that the Spanish Civil War was not understood as a fratricidal conflict but as a Third Carlist War (Jarrai 1986: 12). The Basque autonomous government during the civil war was also remembered as another example of the Basque's will to be independent. As the Herri Batasuna leader, Telesforo Monzón put it, 'in 1936 there was a Basque sovereign state that lasted nine months' (Herri Batasuna 1999: 426). Regardless of Monzón's assertions, the Basque autonomous community of the 1930s was an internally divided territory within a rapidly disintegrating Republican state. His lament for a 'Basque state' which no longer existed was indicative of the radical nationalists' attitude towards what they no longer possessed. The idealisation of the Basque statute of autonomy also showed two important features. First, it showed that for radical nationalists, the wholeness of the past could not be compared to the ruins of the present. Second, the very same remembrance of that virtuous 'Basque state' made the act of remembrance essentially nostalgic. Basque nationalists did not yearn for a specific autonomous institution but for an idealised Basque polity that was forever lost.

Of all the 'historical truths' the patriotic left used, the most important was the Basque resistance of ETA against Francoism. During Francoism ETA was a 'symbolic army' because many sections of Basque and even Spanish society supported its actions against the dictatorship. The anti-fascist and anti-authoritarian rhetoric gave ETA much support and legitimacy. In the democratic period, it continued to emphasise the popular and symbolic element of its fight against authoritarianism in what has been described as a nostalgic memory of Francoism (Rincón 1985: 189).

5.3.1.2 Myth of decline

ETA built a discourse based on revealing the 'national character' of Spain and condemning the treatment of their radical nationalist community. However, this radical community was not described as such, but rather as 'Basque', thus trying to revive the Aranist dichotomy between Spain and the Basque Country. The crucial point was to denounce Spain's posturing as a proper democracy. At least three elements can be identified here. First, radical nationalists argued that the Parliamentary Monarchy was not democratic. The argument put forward here was that the monarch was not equal to other citizens and that Juan Carlos I was the heir of Francoism. The nomination of the king by Franco and the fact that the transition was made by consensus, highlighted the dialogue and the secret pact with the previous regime. The political system that resulted from the Constitution was also non-democratic because it was 'rejected' by Basques in the constitutional referendum. The second element was that democracy was a continuation of Francoism. Since the Basques were not free under Francoism and did not have their own state under the democracy, there was nothing to distinguish between the two regimes. As an ETA member declared in an interview with *Le Monde*, the Spanish regime had changed after Franco in its 'form' but not in its 'real nature'.[14] In the eyes of radical nationalists, Franco was dead but Francoism was still very much alive after 1975. Since both systems were ready to defend the unity of Spain by military force, radical nationalists often use inverted commas to refer to Spain as a 'democracy' or a 'parliamentarian democracy'.[15] Moreover, the fact that some ETA prisoners were still ill-treated while in police custody reaffirmed the idea of continuity with the pre-constitutional regime (Bilbao & Munarriz 1997: 32). Third, the radicals' discourse often elaborated on the anti-Basque character of Spain. Amongst the individuals and groups who were not interested in recognition of the rights of Basques were the 'real powers' or the 'powers that be', among them the Church, the Army, and the more reactionary sections of the Spanish state. The mass media were also included in this group because journalists manipulated and tortured Basques both 'psychologically' and 'politically'.[16]

5.3.1.3 Political project

The political analyses of ETA was influenced by the writings of Sabino Arana and, in consequence, the proposed remedies do not differ from those of the founding father of Basque nationalism. The Basque lands continued to be occupied by foreign forces and the Basques needed to free themselves. The state of autonomies and the statute given to the Basques were clearly insufficient and a new political arrangement was required. The first concern here was the fact that the Basque Country and Navarre should be reunited. In a second stage, the reunification of the Basques would have to incorporate the French Basque Country, also known as Iparralde. And what was needed to realise that political project? Then, as always, the Basques needed to fight for their rights, if necessary using violent means. As one of Herri Batasuna's campaigns during the 1980s described it, Euskadi needed to be cheerful and combative (*Euskadi Alegre y Combativa*). In short, ETA's historical mission was to redeem the Basques from their present decline by all necessary means.

5.3.2 The issue of resonance

Uncovering the historical accuracy of a particular nationalist narrative is important for politicians, opinion-makers, and those who have to negotiate concessions, but it does not take scholars any closer to understanding why some people are willing to make sacrifices for the nation. In the Basque case, there is a long list of authors, including Aranzadi, Azurmendi, Caro Baroja, Corcuera, Elorza, and Juaristi, who have analysed the mobilising myths of Basque nationalism as historical forgeries. Given the diversity of interests, needs, and goals of members of any nation, it should not come as a surprise that nationalist claims are rarely based on a dispassionate and objective reconstruction of the historical past. The past is as much a zone of conflict as the present and we should not expect to find a single understanding of the communal past but two or more versions competing against each other. Moreover, if history is diverse and contested, this implies that a continuous process of reinterpretation of national messages has to be performed by new groups if the national heritage is to endure (Smith 1999: 16–17).

As has already been mentioned, one of the central elements of the radical discourse was the depiction of Spanish democracy as an authoritarian system devoid of legitimacy. In order for this message to be handed down, new generations had to be able to interpret their daily experiences within this nationalist framework. During the 1980s, two elements helped reinforce the idea that Spain had not changed since Francoism: the first one was the accusations of torture; the second was the dirty war against ETA by the paramilitaries of GAL. Under Franco, torture was standard practice in police stations. During the transition period suspects and political demonstrators were occasionally maltreated by the police and by 1978 Amnesty International recognised that torture was not used systematically (Amnesty International Report 1978: 232). In 1978 and 1979 the Spanish government introduced anti-terrorist legislation by which a detainee could be held in a police station, completely incommunicado and without access to family or a lawyer, for a period of seventy-two hours. Under the order of a magistrate of the National Court (*Audiencia Nacional*), the period could be extended by a further seven days. Most torture and ill-treatment of Basque detainees in police stations happened during this ten-day period. According to Amnesty International, several ETA members and supporters were tortured, some of whom died whilst in custody. The first measure the Spanish government took to avoid these allegations was the incorporation of *habeas corpus* in the 1984 anti-terrorist legislation; that is, the right to object before a judge regarding the legality of one's imprisonment. The legislation was substantially modified in 1988 when the maximum period of detention was reduced to 72 hours. However, allegations of ill-treatment of people held under anti-terrorist laws during the 1980s continued. Many of these cases of torture were denied or simply ignored by the Spanish authorities, who often argued that ETA members injured themselves while in custody. Although this might have been true in a few cases, the lack of transparency and investigations into serious allegations of torture showed the state's failure to confront the issue. One of the best-known cases was that of Mikel Zabalza Gárate, a 32-year-old Basque accused of being an *etarra*. The case of Zabalza exemplified both the lack of determination of Spanish authorities in tackling the problem of torture and the difficulty in ascertaining the truth in cases of torture. Zabalza was arrested on 26 November 1985 and his handcuffed body was found on 15 December, floating face-downwards in the Bidasoa River. The Civil Guards reported that he had escaped on the same day of his arrest and the autopsies concluded that the cause of death was asphyxiation by immersion and that there were no signs of ill-treatment.

Another well-known case of 'disappearance' was that of ETA members José Antonio Lasa and José Ignacio Zabala. Although they had disappeared in Bayonne in 1983, their bodies were found in the province of Alicante two years later and were finally identified in March 1995. The corpses had been buried in caustic lime and showed signs of extensive beatings and torture, including loss of finger and toenails, and each body had bullet holes in the back of the skull (Amnesty 1996: 279). These two cases helped to reveal something much more serious than the practice of torture in police stations. The cases of Lasa and Zabala uncovered the direct involvement of the Socialist governments in a series of shootings, bombings, and kidnappings in the French Basque Country between 1983 and 1987. Investigations at the highest judicial level proved that the Spanish state had secretly funded the organisation *Grupos Antiterroristas de Liberación* (Anti-Terrorist Liberation Groups; GAL), with the intention of changing the French government's attitude towards ETA. The clandestine organisation was composed of security officers and contract gunmen who had links with senior government officials, including the former Minister of Interior, José Barrionuevo, and the former Secretary of State Security, Rafael Vera. As a result of the Lasa and Zabala trial, the former General Enrique Rodríguez Galindo and the former civil governor of Biscay, Julen Elgorriaga, were sentenced to seventy-one years in prison. The 'dirty war' against ETA claimed twenty-seven deaths, including those of nine people with unclear connections to ETA, and became the darkest page in the history of the PSOE governments led by Felipe González (1982–1996), who was accused by the opposition of having masterminded the whole operation. Most of the incidents occurred in cities of the French Pays Basque such as Bayonne, Biarritz, Hendaye, and St-Jean-de-Luz. However, GAL also used their terror tactics in Spain. In 1984 GAL killed a well-known Herri Batasuna leader and paediatrician, Santiago Brouard, in his surgery. GAL's state terrorism accomplished its main objective, which was to end the 'French sanctuary' for ETA members and force the French government to cooperate with Spain in anti-terrorism operations, assistance that was provided from 1984 onwards. However, the 'dirty war' also backfired because it discredited the Spanish government and security forces while renewing ETA's support among Basque radical youth (Woodworth 2001, 2005).

5.4 CONCLUSION

After Franco's death in 1975, Spain witnessed a remarkable process of democratic transition led by Adolfo Suárez. A succession of gradual democratic reforms legally dismantled the Francoist state and secured a constitutional monarchy in only three years. The process had the overwhelming support of Spanish civil society and its political elites, who agreed to negotiate the main issues. The politics of consensus characterised the period of transition (1975–1978) whereas the consolidation of democracy (1978–1982) was marked by dissent. The vulnerability of the pluralist regime was shown by an attempted *coup d'état* in 1981 in which the intervention of King Juan Carlos I proved decisive. To a large extent, the military had reacted to the approval of home rule for regions and nationalities which eroded the pre-democratic centralist organisation of the state. The armed forces, who up to that point had been more concerned with the repression of the internal enemy than the defence of Spain's borders, saw the coup as an opportunity to respond to the numerous ETA killings of army officers and slow down the unfolding of the state of autonomies.

Radical Basque nationalists did not support the process of democratisation and argued that the political transition was nothing more than a cosmetic change and that the authoritarian nature of Spain remained intact. Lower support for the process of transition could also be detected in a semi-loyal PNV which recommended abstention in the constitutional referendum. In contrast to the situation of the Second Republic when Catalan nationalism had been a difficult force to accommodate, in the 1970s Basque nationalism and ETA's violence was the main peripheral challenge to the state. Although the right to national self-determination was not recognised and Navarre was given a separate statute of autonomy, the devolution of powers to the Basque Country helped stabilise the political situation. After the approval of the Statute of Autonomy in 1979, the PNV became the hegemonic governing party in every legislature and controlled the institutions of self-government which had powers over public order, tax collection, health system, education, culture, and mass media.

Political violence has been the most extreme form of expressing Basque dissent. When, in 1968, ETA made the first unpremeditated use of violence, there was no chance for participation in the existing political structures and their demands reflected concrete grievances which were shared by a significant proportion of the Basque population. State repression created a secretive and clandestine atmosphere in which underground action thrived. The success of ETA's violent campaign also depended on crucial timing, the existence of a skilful leadership and the use of repressive force by the Francoist state. Without an authoritarian response from the government, the spiral of action-repression-action could not fulfil its full potential. After Spain's radical transformation, the democratic system provided multiple opportunities to influence the decision-making process but sections of the police continued to display non-democratic attitudes and methods. The state funded activities of the GAL paramilitaries between 1983 and 1987 did nothing to reduce social sympathy for ETA and confirmed the widely held idea that the Basque conflict was a war between extremes. The authoritarian tendencies of the police and security services reinforced their image as 'occupation forces' and made it easier for ETA supporters to persuade new generations that little or nothing had changed in the Basque Country since the death of Franco. ETA's challenge to the sovereign authority inevitably attracted many radical youths in search of adventure. Whether they joined for patriotism, social mobility, or to prove their manliness, their courageous sacrifice was interpreted in the same way. Between 1968 and 2005, the ritual death of '160 gudaris' was inserted in a grand narrative whereby the nation was energised and the hero-martyr was to be forever remembered for fulfilling his duty (Casquete 2006: 195–196).

Refusing to introduce any ideological change to their strategic and tactical corpus, ETA responded to the new political system by taking up new organisational strategies. From the 1970s onward, radical Basque nationalism expanded from an underground violent organisation to an anti-systemic network of political and social organisations covering youth, student and trade unions, ecology, feminism, foreign affairs, education, media, prisoners, and so on. The principal organisation of the group was ETA which acted as the symbolic leader and source of inspiration for all tactical and strategic actions. The greatest achievement of the Basque Movement of National Liberation (MLNV) was the creation of a self-contained 'nationalist community' with its own myths, symbols, narratives, and spaces for socialisation where members could carry out their ordinary life without the interference of outside discourses and propaganda. This self-sufficient micro-society provided the necessary conditions for the social reproduction of their radical messages, discourses, and war memories.

6   The Polarisation of
Identities (1987–1997)

Spain's accession to the European Community on 1 January 1986 was celebrated as the end of the country's 'exceptionalism'. Integration into the EC (EU since 1992) had important domestic consequences such as the modernisation of the political and economic system and gradual convergence with European standards of living thanks to the redistributive effects of the Structural and Cohesion funds.[1] The multiple benefits of Europeanisation turned Spain into a staunch supporter of 'widening' and 'deepening' the integration project and its political elites came to equate national interests with European interests. As Carlos Closa and Paul Heywood (2004) have argued, the prospect of membership of the European club had been a key catalyst for democratisation and its final accession completed the 'national project' of political and economic modernisation which had begun after the death of Franco. When, in 1986, the accession treaty and the Single European Act (SEA) came into force the state-funded 'dirty war' was still ongoing. The following year the GAL disbanded and the first anti-ETA pact was signed in the Spanish parliament. With the end of the death squads the authoritarian methods disappeared and a new counter-terrorist strategy was launched.

The Spanish government's policies for dealing with ETA's politically motivated violence from 1987 were a comprehensive mixture of police action and peace negotiations. The new policy was based on having the support of the majority of elected political parties and on using all the available tools in accordance with the rule of law (*estado de derecho*). At the domestic level, the Spanish government promoted anti-ETA pacts in the Spanish, Basque, and Navarrese parliaments and established a semi-permanent line of communication with the insurgents. In the late 1980s, these contacts took the form of negotiations in Algiers which did not lead to a successful outcome (Clark 1990a). At the international level, and partly as a result of Spain's entry into both NATO and the EC, France began cooperating in an exchange of intelligence and expelled hundreds of ETA suspects to Spain. Moreover, the ambition to create a single market and eliminate all internal borders among signatory states resulted in the Schengen Agreements which established provisions for dealing with issues such as cross-border surveillance and 'hot pursuit' which allowed police forces to enter a few kilometres into the territory of another member state. The idea of France as a place of asylum finally collapsed in 1992 when the leadership of ETA was arrested in the French Basque town of Bidart.

The Franco-Spanish operation at Bidart forced ETA to change its leadership and direction. Its most violent operations were seriously undermined but the campaign of kidnappings and extortion of business leaders continued unaltered. The organisational predicament of the leading organisation of the MLNV also affected the rest of the operational network which launched a hasty counter-offensive known as the 'socialisation of pain'. The key idea was to compensate for ETA's weakness by regaining the street as a space of social struggle where the population would have a first-hand experience of the Basque conflict. The silent majority became threatened, or socialised, by minor acts of violence on public roads and those who dared to oppose radical Basque nationalism publicly risked becoming a target.

6.1 THE SPANISH STATE'S POLICIES TO ISOLATE ETA

According to Robert P. Clark, most violent insurgencies tend to end in one of two ways. One way is for the government's police and armed forces to lose their taste for combat or their confidence in the political system, and for the executive itself to lose its popular legitimacy.[2] This ensuing insurgent victory either sweeps away the existing regime or leads to territorial separation from the core state. The second way is for the government in power to combine a vigorous policy of repression with a judicious programme of reforms to isolate the insurgents from their base of popular support and ultimately defeat them militarily, ideologically, and politically. The end result of this defeat may be a negotiated truce and cease-fire which leads to a formal settlement with provisions for a general amnesty and facilities for the members of the insurgent group to integrate into civil politics (Clark 1990b: 1–5). The latter model fits impeccably the strategy followed by the Spanish government from 1987 to 1997 to resolve the violent conflict. As it will be seen in the next section, the various parliamentary pacts of the late 1980s were promoted by policy-makers with a double objective: (1) to deny the armed group any legitimacy to represent Basque grievances; and (2) to establish a situation whereby none of their uncompromising political demands could be negotiated outside the democratic channels. Although the state representatives' public discourse was that the only point worth negotiating was a process on how the group would disband ('first truce, then talks'), the Spanish executive secretly maintained intermittent contacts with ETA in order to facilitate a permanent cessation of hostilities.

6.1.1 The anti-ETA pacts

By the mid-1980s, the Spanish authorities understood that in order to win over ETA they also had to fight its support network. Thus, three political pacts were signed to unify the democratically elected forces and ostracise ETA and its most influential political organisation, Herri Batasuna. The first pact affected the whole of Spain, the second the Basque Autonomous Community (BAC), and the third the Foral Community of Navarre. The pacts encapsulated the social desire for peace and presented a consensual view that violence could not interfere in the normal functioning of democratic institutions.

First, the Madrid Agreement on Terrorism also known as the Pact of Madrid was signed on 5 November 1987 in the Spanish Parliament. The five-point Agreement was supported by all political parties with seats in the Congress of Deputies and the Senate except Eusko Alkartasuna and Herri Batasuna.[3] The first point of the agreement denounced 'the lack of legitimacy of ETA to express the will of the Basque people' and rejected ETA's 'pretension to negotiate the political problems of the Basque people', which was only to be done between 'the political parties with parliamentary representation, the Basque government and the Spanish government'. The rest of the text was devoted to issues such as the rehabilitation of ETA members if they abandoned the armed struggle, the abolition of the antiterrorist law which allowed the authorities to retain a suspected ETA member up to ten days incommunicado, the increasing cooperation with France and the rest of the European Community member states, and the establishment of information exchange mechanisms between the different institutions and parties involved. The pact was a political success for the socialist government led by Felipe González, which had managed to put together parliamentary support for the first ever pact against terrorism. It was also the beginning of an era in which the ruling party and the opposition would usually agree on security policy as a key issue (*tema de estado*) and the parliament would be used as backup for governmental policies against terrorism.

Second, two months later, the Pact for the Normalisation and Pacification of Euskadi, was signed by all Basque political forces with seats in the regional parliament except Herri Batasuna. This second anti-ETA agreement was the result of fifty intense hours of negotiation and came to be known as the Pact of Ajuria Enea, since it had been signed in the residence of the Basque president, the Palace of Ajuria Enea on 12 January 1988.[4] The accord was a longer document than the Pact of Madrid and its first goal was to denounce ETA's interference with Basque politics and emphasise the role of the autonomous Basque government in finding a solution to the problem of violence. The agreement was made up of seventeen points, and most of the Basque political forces agreed on the importance of reinforcing the legitimacy of politics in finding solutions to political problems and only one, Eusko Alkartasuna, had reservations on a minor point regarding police competency. After a lengthy preamble, point 1 of the text rejected 'the use of violence' while insisting that 'those who practice such violence are not legitimated to express the will of the Basque people' and emphasised that only political parties, the 'legitimate representatives of the people's will', could discuss 'political problems'. The text recognised the aspiration of large sectors of Basque society to strengthen links with Navarre but declared that 'the citizens of Navarre alone have the right to decide their own future'. The other points made reference to issues such as the role of the Basque executive and the *Lehendakari* in the 'eradication of terrorism', the importance of international collaboration, the role of the 'rule of law' in helping the victims of terrorism, and favouring the insurgents' reinsertion in society. Although the agreement saw a combination of the rule of law and police actions as a means to eliminate ETA's nationalist violence, it also opened the door to negotiations with the armed group if certain conditions were met. The text called for the support of other social and political institutions for the agreement in order to fight ETA. The text made references to Basque civil society and its political institutions but also to the Council of Europe and the Spanish, Navarrese, and European parliaments. By bringing on board all these actors, the pact aimed to isolate ETA and its anti-system political wing, Herri Batasuna, and redefine the 'Basque conflict'. The pact concluded that the Basque problem was not a historical conflict between the Basques and Spaniards but was due rather to the existence of a violent group which did not respect some of the most fundamental rights and freedoms (such as the right to life, liberty, and security of person). The promoter of the agreement, the *Lehendakari* José Antonio Ardanza, commented that up until 1988 the conflict had been seen in 'nationalist terms'; from that moment onwards it had to be seen in 'democratic terms' (Rivera 1998: 91). The Pact of Ajuria Enea established a clear cleavage that divided an overwhelming majority which was in favour of party politics and democracy from an intransigent minority that was ready to use all available means, including violence, in order to achieve its political objectives.

Third, an Agreement for Peace and Tolerance was signed in Pamplona (Navarre) in October 1988.[5] This last text was much shorter than that of Ajuria Enea but used similar language. The two regional agreements, that of the Basque Autonomous Community (BAC) and that of Navarre, emphasised democracy and parliamentary politics and rejected ETA's violent interference in their autonomous politics. They both agreed that ETA had no right to speak for the Basque or Navarrese people and repeated that the establishment of closer links between the BAC and Navarre was a decision for the population of Navarre. The Navarrese pact had, however, two main differences: first, it emphasised that the existing institutions, defined by the Constitution and the Statutes of the BAC and Navarre, were the legitimate and democratic means of making political changes happen in the Basque Country and Navarre; and second, its language was less nationalistic than that of Ajuria Enea. Whereas the Basque pact talked about the 'Spanish state', not just the state, and the role of the *Lehendakari* and his government in leading the fight against terrorism, the Navarrese pact relied on 'police action' and 'international collaboration among governments' in order to prevent new attacks. Navarre, a region where the PNV had traditionally obtained poor results, relied heavily on Spanish institutions and resources to solve the problem of violence.

The three multi-party agreements became a high point for democratic politics and complemented the security-led institutional responses. They helped reinforce the widely held view that political problems should be solved through the autonomic institutions, and put pressure on Herri Batasuna to enter a process of negotiation that could bring an end to the violent stalemate. At the same time, it sent a clear signal to ETA that the armed group was not a legitimate representative of the popular will and could never be directly involved in the negotiation of political issues. The three agreements were not designed to reduce ETA's activity and, in this respect, they contributed very little to the decline of the radical Basque nationalists. However, in the aftermath of the bloody bombing campaign of 1987 which claimed a total of fifty-two lives, the pacts signed in Vitoria-Gasteiz and Pamplona were seen as symbolic gestures against the increasing brutality and terrorist acts of ETA. Besides, the numerous preparatory meetings that led to these pacts and the meetings that followed their signatures became trust building exercises that brought together the leaders of all political parties with parliamentary representation. The newly-found unity of Basque parties, who had often quarrelled over the meaning and causes of violence, was particularly significant because it contributed to shift the main cleavage of division from Basque nationalists vs. non-nationalists to a division between democrats and supporters of violence.

In short, the three pacts galvanised a cross-party consensus regarding the strength of democratic institutions, the illegitimate use of violence to reach political aims and the urgent need for ETA to disband if certain conditions were given. Establishing what these conditions should be was the crux of the matter as representatives of ETA and the Spanish government found out in secret preparatory meetings in North Africa. For Spain's delegates, a permanent ceasefire was an essential requirement to start any sort of negotiations but, for ETA, the complete cessation of the group's violent activities was the end of the process, not a prerequisite. The linkage between the cessation of violence and the conduct of negotiations was a Gordian knot that needed decisive action in order for the insurgency to be appeased. The idea was to repeat the 1970s success of the governing party, the UCD, in negotiating the disbandment of the 'polimilis' of ETA-Político Militar in October 1982.

6.1.2 The Algiers negotiations

On the majority of occasions, contacts and negotiations between the Spanish government and ETA had been kept secret and were not very successful because they were used primarily to 'take the temperature' of the adversary (Javier 2002: 207). However, in the late 1980s, the PSOE government needed a stable security situation for the fast approaching festivities of 1992 and pushed for a round of negotiations in Algiers.[6] In 1992, the country was host to four major international events: the World Fair in Seville, Madrid as the cultural capital of Europe, the Barcelona Olympic Games, and the 500th anniversary of Columbus's discovery of America. Besides, the need to negotiate with ETA had also been one of the central issues of the 1986 Basque regional election. In 1986 the Basque Government had published the Rose Report in which a commission of experts recommended policies that would contribute to the elimination of violence.[7] One of the main recommendations of the report was the establishment of negotiations with ETA. In the following months, contacts between Ardanza, who became *Lehendakari* in 1985, and Prime Minster González prepared the ground for the negotiations of Algiers (Pozas 1992: 21).

From ETA's perspective, the goal since the death of General Franco had been to enter into political negotiations with Spain in order to solve what they saw as a long-term political conflict. The Spanish state was seen as a powerful entity that could not be defeated by military means but that could still be cornered into peace negotiations. With this goal in mind, the violent strategy intensified in 1985 when ETA increased the use of car bombs, which had a much more destructive and lethal effect than previous efforts and was aimed to apply pressure on the government. The unwavering strength of the two opposing parties convinced some ETA leaders that a negotiated settlement with the state was inevitable. According to Clark, by 1986 Iturbe asserted that, 'if we don't negotiate now, within a year the French will have dismantled everything, they will have decimated us, seized our weapons and money, and we will not have anything to negotiate' (Clark 1990: 168). Moreover, ETA had trouble recruiting new members and controlling internal discrepancies. One of the most dramatic examples of ETA's need for discipline was that of María Dolores González Catараín (Yoyes) who was killed in 1986. Yoyes had been in prison in the 1970s and had been living in exile in Mexico when she decided to publicly repent and benefit from the state's rehabilitation measures. After she was freed, she returned to her home-town Villafranca de Orditzia, in Gipuzkoa, where she was assassinated by a fellow ETA member in retaliation for her 'treason'. The case of Yoyes was significant because she had been one of the few women to hold a position of responsibility within the armed group but also because it showed the practical difficulties of *etarras* taking 'early retirement'.[8]

The Algiers negotiations had three rounds.[9] A first round of secret negotiations took place during 1986–1987, a second public round during 1987–1988 and, finally, a third one, also public, in 1989. For the 1986–1987 round, the government managed to secretly transfer the ETA spokesperson, Txomin Iturbe, from France, through Gabon and Angola to Algiers, where he met the rest of the ETA leaders. Contact between the two negotiating parties happened from November 1986 until February 1987 when they were suddenly interrupted by the death of Iturbe. According to the Algerian authorities, the person who was driving Iturbe and two more ETA members lost control of the car and hit a tree on 27 February 1987. Both the driver and Iturbe were killed immediately. The death of ETA's main representative was widely reported in the Spanish press and, since the public then became aware of the negotiations, they were immediately suspended.

The incident that triggered renewed interest in a second round of political negotiations was the explosion in June 1987 of a bomb in an Hipercor supermarket in a workers' district of Barcelona. The bomb had been placed in the underground car park and killed twenty-one civilians and wounded forty-five, thus becoming ETA's bloodiest attack ever mounted. A person claiming to speak on behalf of ETA warned of the existence of the bomb a few minutes before the explosion but the police did not have enough time to clear the area. The attack outraged the people of Catalonia, where Herri Batasuna had obtained its second highest results after the Basque Country, and harsh criticisms of ETA were made on all sides. Both Herri Batasuna and ETA recognised the error it had made in Barcelona but blamed the police for their 'slowness' in evacuating the area.[10] After the bombing of Hipercor, a new ETA leader, Eugenio Etxebeste, also known as Antxon, was transferred from Ecuador to Algiers in July 1987 for the second stage of negotiations. In August that year the Spanish government acknowledged for the first time that it was in contact with ETA. In the words of Javier Solana, at the time official spokesman of the PSOE government who then became High Representative for Common Foreign and Security Policy (CFSP), 'there have been, there are and there will be' contacts with ETA. During the following year there was an exchange of offers between ETA and the PSOE Government for truces but none of them were successful.[11] The main obstacle was that ETA wanted to discuss political matters such as the right to self-determination and the status of Navarre. The government, on the other hand, wanted to stop the violence immediately and argued that political questions should be discussed by elected political parties in the representative institutions which were accountable to the electorate. The solution was the establishment of a 'two-track approach'. The methodology suggested that only a party that represented a part of the electorate (referring to HB) could discuss political questions. The potential for success of the two-track approach lay in the separation of the negotiations into two venues, two agendas and two negotiating bodies. Such a division made it possible for parties in conflict to negotiate with one another without actually appearing to do so. Although the theoretical distinction was appropriate, the two-track formula was never applied because in December 1987, a car bomb was detonated in a Civil Guards living quarters killing eleven people, including five children, in the city of Zaragoza. In 1987, ETA killed fifty people, the highest number during the late 1980s, and the government had little option but to break off negotiations.

The third round of negotiations took place between January and April 1989. In January that year ETA declared a two-week ceasefire to coincide with the beginning of the Algiers negotiations. On 23 January the ceasefire was extended by two more months to allow negotiators to proceed. The final round of negotiations in Algiers was carried out by two representatives of the Spanish Government: Rafael Vera, Secretary of State for Security, and Juan Manuel Eguiagaray, Government delegate in Murcia. On the other side of the table, they faced the ETA members Eugenio Etxebeste (Antxon), Belén González and Iñaki Arakama. The main leader of the ETA representatives was Antxon, who had to report back on the state of the negotiations to the ETA leadership in France. He also had the support of a political committee of advisors made up of members of the trade union LAB, Herri Batasuna, and several lawyers.[12] The negotiations collapsed on 4 April 1989 as a result of the secrecy, leaks to the press, and mutual distrust on the part of the two delegations.[13]

A month after the negotiations collapsed, the government responded by putting in place the 'dispersion policy' by which imprisoned ETA members were scattered in prisons around Spain. Up until May 1989, *etarras* had been concentrated in the maximum security prisons of Carabanchel, Alcalá-Meco (both in Madrid), and in the Andalusian Herrera de la Mancha, almost 1,000 km from the Basque Country. The controversial measure was implemented by two Basque ministers, those of the Interior, Javier Corcuera, and Justice, Enrique Múgica, in order to break the internal unity of the inmates. This was problematic because after dying at the hands of the police, spending time in prison was seen by ETA supporters as the ultimate sacrifice. It was in prison where, after months or years of clandestine activity, everyone—family, friends, the police, the justice system, the media, and public opinion—finally recognised the convict as a 'member of ETA'. Whether arrested or killed in action, 'fallen gudaris' were not forgotten. Their sacrifice as frontline martyrs was remembered in rituals and ceremonies in order to imbue younger generations with their heroic example (Sáez 2002: 222). As Carrie Hamilton has persuasively argued, the prisoner took privileged centre stage in the *abertzale* iconography because during the time in prison he or she was living alongside the enemy, in the 'final front of struggle' (Hamilton 1999: 237). Given their moral weight and influence, ETA convicts kept a high level of group cohesion and exercised powerful control mechanisms over each other, hence making it difficult for individuals to repent and take up the benefits of rehabilitation which the authorities were offering.

There were no neutral observers in the Algiers negotiations and, as a result, there were contending views on why the negotiations failed.[14] According to Herri Batasuna (1999: 204) the leadership of ETA was contemptuous of the fact that it had been recognised as a valid participant in the Basque conflict and that the Spanish government had acknowledged that ETA could not be dealt with exclusively by police means. Herri Batasuna's view was shared by other MLNV organisations, such as ASK, which proudly asserted in an editorial of *JoTaKe* the 'political character of the official negotiators, ETA representing the Basque side and the PSOE representing the state'. The editorial also stated the 'political nature' of the negotiations and how it showed there were two kinds of violence: the one that denied the rights of the Basque people, therefore 'offensive' and the other, a 'defensive response' which defended those rights.[15] At this point, holding negotiations was already a success for ETA. According to Clark, the collapse of the Algerian negotiations can be explained by the unwillingness of the Spanish government to discuss political issues and accept 'the Basques' right of self-determination'.[16] This point is probably accurate and, given the anti-ETA pacts signed years earlier, it is not difficult to understand why the government was reluctant to accept the terms of a formal political negotiation with ETA beyond disarmament and prisoner issues.

6.1.3 The end of the 'French sanctuary'

The failure of the Algiers negotiations ended the aura of 'freedom fighters' that ETA members had in both Algeria and France. The Algerian authorities had hosted the negotiations and had involved personnel and resources in supporting the negotiations but, after the collapse of the contacts, they expelled all ETA members from Algerian territory. In France too, sympathy for the Basque paramilitaries ended and closer collaboration was established between the French and Spanish police. That partnership was the result of both years of diplomatic effort by the Spanish authorities and of the gradual establishment of the single market and common policies to regulate freedom of movement. Since Francoism, the Pays Basque had been a safe haven for ETA members because France had long prided itself on being a *terre d'asile* according to which they granted ETA members the status of political refugees up to 1979. In the Basque case, this traditional beneficence towards the exiled was reinforced by two other considerations: (1) ETA's struggle was regarded by many in France as being akin to the fight of the French Resistance in World War II; and (2) the Burgos trial was still a vivid memory in the minds of French citizens (Dominguez 2000: 290).

During the transition and consolidation of democracy in Spain (1975–1982), the French authorities continued to deny that the Pays Basque was used as a base by ETA cells after an action (*ekintza*). Accusations that Southern France was an ETA 'sanctuary' were categorically denied and it was argued that Basque political violence was an exclusively Spanish problem. ETA was conscious of the importance of keeping on good terms with France and, unable to fight a low-intensity war against two neighbouring states simultaneously kept a low profile in terms of its claims over the French Basque territories. As a 1983 *Zutabe* explained, 'Our struggle and our political goals are limited to what constitutes the Spanish state, more specifically, the Basque Country within the Spanish state.'[17]

Despite ETA's efforts to maintain France as its haven, three events during the 1980s facilitated a closer cooperation between the French and Spanish authorities regarding ETA. First, for most of the 1980s southern France would be the setting for most of the killings perpetrated by GAL against ETA members. The relatively distant 'Basque problem' became impossible to ignore because people were being killed in the streets and bars of Bayonne and Biarritz. Second, Spain had joined the EEC in 1986 and was deeply committed to the creation of an 'ever closer union', particularly in the area of justice and home affairs and any other areas that might help her terminate the Basque problem. Third, both countries had socialist leaders in power, François Mitterrand (1981–1995) and Felipe Gonzalez (1982–1996), who liked and understood each other. In 1986, following a conservative victory at the polls, Jacques Chirac became Prime Minister and, in spite of the period of cohabitation with the socialist presidency, the collaboration with France was not interrupted. In fact, one of the first measures taken by the conservative government led by Chirac was to extradite ETA residents to Spain through an expedited administrative procedure. The Chirac Government, faced with its own problems of terrorism, and a 'law and order' administration, had responded willingly to Spanish requests for extraditions.

The high point of the Franco-Spanish collaboration took place on 29 March 1992 when French police burst into a house in Bidart and arrested three ETA commanders: Francisco Mugica Garmendia (Pakito), Jose Luis Alvarez Sancristina (Txelis), and Jose Arregui Erostarbe (Fiti). The French national police seized large numbers of documents and several ETA members immediately fled, for the most part to Mexico and Cuba. The documentation found in Bidart, together with that found in the Sokoa Cooperative in 1986, helped the Spanish authorities understand the complex network of funding and money-laundering organisations that bankrolled ETA.[18] Ultimately, the action weakened ETA one month before the opening ceremony of the Seville Expo and four months before the Olympic Games in Barcelona and, on 11 July 1992, four months after the arrests, the Basque organisation proposed a two-month ceasefire. The offer was not taken up by the Spanish authorities, who mistrusted ETA's good will and understood the truce as a sign of weakness and an attempt to reorganise.

6.2 NEW SPACES OF STRUGGLE AND THE RETURN OF BASQUE CIVIL SOCIETY

ETA entered a period of military decline after 1992 as a result of the anti-ETA pacts, the failed Algiers negotiations, the increasing Spanish–French cooperation, and the crucial arrest of its leadership in Bidart. Their apprehension severely weakened the organisation and gave way to a period of internal deliberation and introspection within the MLNV network. After the 1992 arrests in Bidart, Herri Batasuna concluded that its dependency on ETA was a negative feature. The HB leaders began to argue that the secession of the Basque nation could not be achieved solely by the actions of the military vanguard and it was necessary for the whole of society to be involved. It was necessary for Basque society to take sides in favour of or against the nationalist project and not just remain an observer of the clashes between the security forces and ETA. However, instead of promoting a political programme to incorporate new social sectors, HB confirmed the supremacy of violent direct action as the leading 'voice' of the movement by approving a discussion document called *Oldartzen* and by endorsing ETA's 1995 Democratic Alternative. The MLNV's strategy was to make Basque society participate in the conflict through the 'socialisation of pain' in 'new spaces of struggle' such as street violence (*kale borroka*) and a controversial new selection of targets (Mansvelt Beck 2005: 179–180).

6.2.1 The 'socialisation of pain'

Before the 'socialisation of pain' was endorsed, Herri Batasuna reacted to the Bidart arrests by launching a process of debate known as Urrats Berri (New Step), which took place during 1993. This debate was a failed attempt on the part of the HB leadership to become an effective force and regain its prestige of being the only truly political organisation of the radical movement. Contrary to the case of the Sinn Fein-IRA, HB had never been in command of the MLNV and could request little else other than political autonomy from its more militarist counterparts. In other words, it was not a dispute about whether to abandon the violent insurgency in favour of more peaceful forms of revolutionary nationalist politics but an attempt to distinguish the different decision-making structures, goals, and strategies of ETA and Herri Batasuna. In the end, the document approved did not bring substantial changes to the party's long-term strategy. One of the few changes was Herri Batasuna's new self-definition: it changed its name from 'an alliance of workers and popular sectors' to a 'union of patriots (*abertzales*) and leftists'. The final document lacked original ideas and epitomised the crisis in which the *abertzale* left was immersed. The strategic goal of the nationalist left continued to be: 'the search of a political agreement between Hego Euskal Herria [Spanish Basque Country] and the Spanish state which could establish the basis for our political sovereignty'.

Naturally, the exercise of national sovereignty required recognition of the 'right to self-determination' (Urrats Berri II 1992: 16–18).

The only aspect of the text worth pointing out was the self-criticism of Herri Batasuna on its 'internal dynamic of work' and the party's dependence and expectation of the actions of ETA. As read in *Urrats Berri*, this 'dependency had become more noticeable, especially regarding the attitude of expecting what ETA could do next: be it the declaration of a truce or the carrying out of another armed action'.[19] In criticising Herri Batasuna's dependency on the military hard line, the party membership was claiming the right to be part of a political debate, independent of ETA's activities. Unless this was done, they warned, the *abertzale* left would only be active if ETA was active and vice-versa. At the same time, a tactical error by ETA, such as that of Hipercor, could seriously damage the whole of the MLNV network, which was experiencing a decline in its aggregate membership. In the end, *Urrats Berri* did not solve the organisational and tactical problems of the nationalist left and confirmed the supremacy of military activism over political action.

Three years later, in 1995, ETA updated the KAS Alternative with the Democratic Alternative which gave a minor political role to HB in a hypothetical peace process. The old KAS Alternative had been approved in 1976 and laid out the five objectives the government had to grant in order for ETA to enter political negotiations directly with state representatives: (1) an amnesty for all ETA prisoners; (2) the legalisation of all political parties; (3) expulsion from the Basque Country of the Spanish security forces; (4) improvement in the conditions of the working class; and (5) national sovereignty. The new Democratic Alternative of 1995 also addressed the negotiated end to the 'armed conflict' between ETA and the Spanish state but added a call for a 'democratic process' which could lead to the recognition of the 'territorial unity' of the seven Basque Provinces, the establishment of the Basque right to self-determination, and the eventual independence of Euskal Herria. The two-track programme had already been used in Algeria where the interests of ETA had been represented in the political negotiations through HB. This meant that ETA continued to demand active participation in all negotiations which would not be left to the political parties with an electoral mandate. Significantly, the Democratic Alternative was launched in April 1995, shortly after ETA nearly succeeded in assassinating José María Aznar, then leader of the opposition and a future prime minister. The document was enthusiastically embraced by HB because it introduced the need for all Basque citizens (*l@s ciudadan@s vasc@s*) to make nation-building a day-by-day task. ETA summoned their sympathisers to be involved in core organisations such as Jarrai or Herri Batasuna in order to obtain recognition of the right to self-determination. At the discursive level, the language underwent a minor change. Whereas the main goal of the armed group, independence, had been the driving force of the organisation, the other pillar, socialism, was abandoned and only one mention was made in the document of the need for 'social justice'. Following the collapse of the USSR, the tendency to rely on nationalism and violence as unifying factors was further consolidated with the complete abandonment of socialist goals (Mees 2003: 75–76).

The second and more important document approved in 1995 was the debate known as Oldartzen (Tackling). According to Oldartzen, from Bidart until 1995 Herri Batasuna had been too focused on a strategy of 'resistance' (*resisitir es vencer*) and the time had arrived to replace it with a pro-active strategy of 'nation building'.[20] In Oldartzen, the radical nationalists theorised that the network of organisations had to gain 'new social spaces' where they could develop an 'offensive phase, giving priority to the practical realisation of objectives'.[21] This radical construction of nationhood was going to be done from below and, literally, from the street. The leading agents in implementing this strategy were not the party that had approved it but the social movements which were seen to have spontaneous social support and legitimacy. As presented in Oldartzen: 'The street must be our main space of struggle, but the street understood as a range of different agents: the factories, the neighbourhood, the association or society, the study centre, the shop, the health clinic, the *cuadrilla*, the family, the cooperative, the *fiestas*, etc.'[22]

Oldartzen followed the line established in the Democratic Alternative that any nationalist initiative had to be subordinated to the violent insurgency. Herri Batasuna lost all autonomy in deciding the overall strategy of the *abertzale* left and, although its political destiny was directly affected by ETA, refused to influence the armed group. While the new strategy incorporated old elements, the radical nation-building went beyond 'the limits of conventional politics.'[23] The new MLNV strategy was to 'accumulate forces around the nation-building and social transformation programme [...] create social tension and pressure through mobilisations to show, on a daily basis, the imposition and limits of the current political framework' (Oiarzabal 2002: 40). As selective violence had done during Francoism, the street violence aimed at uncovering the structural violence of the Spanish institutions in which the Basque nation was integrated. As Joseba Álvarez, a leader of Herri Batasuna and son of an ETA-founder, pointed out, 'in the last few years, the problem of prisoners and many others were seen as problems of the nationalist left. What is the solution? Socialise the consequences of the struggle' (Rekondo 1998: 55). Although the style in which Oldartzen was written made it practically incomprehensible, the consequences of the 'socialisation of pain' would be very real on the streets of many Basque cities. One of the first consequences was the intensification of street violence (*kale borroka*), a Basque adaptation of the Palestinian Intifada through which a new generation of Basque youth was involved in the reproduction of Basque discontent.

Carried out by young radical nationalists, often members of the youth organisation Jarrai, the *kale borroka* involved acts of violence such as riots and confrontations directed against the Basque police, attacks on the property of rival political parties, the burning of buses, rubbish skips, and phone boxes, and even public beatings.[24] The *kale borroka* was prominent during the years 1994 to 2001 and was organised and perpetrated by organised groups called X, Y, or Z. The street violence was part of the overall strategy of the socialisation of pain and involved disciplining the 'passive' population in the 'political conflict' between 'Spain' and 'Euskal Herria'. By experiencing the forceful clash between nationalist youth and the security forces first hand, citizens were forced to take sides on the dynamics of the national struggle. By 2001, the street violence had become so disruptive to the lives of ordinary Basque citizens that the state designed special legislation, such as the minors' law (*Ley del Menor*), to tackle the problem. In the words of Prime Minister Aznar, a terrorist was always a terrorist, 'even if they are under age' (*Un terrorista es siempre un terrorista, aunque sea un menor*).[25] The analysis of commentators and policy-makers was that the members of the *Grupos Y* were the 'pups of ETA' (*cachorros de ETA*) and terrorists-in-training (Oiarzabal 2002: 45). This presumption was partly confirmed by the arrest of ETA members during these years who had started their radical activity in street violence.

ETA had a leading role in the 'socialisation of pain' by widening its choice of targets. The insurgent group had traditionally chosen targets that symbolised the state and the powers that be: police, military, police informers, and senior politicians. In the new situation, however, it included new people as potential targets: journalists, judges, prosecutors, civil servants, low-profile politicians, businessmen, academics, and so on (Gurruchaga and San Sebastian 2000: 183; Sánchez-Cuenca 2001: 73; Tremlett 2006: 308). In many cases they were threatened or kidnapped but also killed. In an internal ETA document, *Barne Buletina*, the organisation argued why it was necessary to target *españolistas* from the PSOE or the PP regardless of their importance. The state had already accepted the relatively low levels of violence caused by ETA and the loss of life that it produced in the police and security forces. Hence, it was necessary to target those influential groups, such as politicians, who had not been affected until then and could have a decisive influence on the government's policies:

> when a guy from the PSOE, PP, or PNV goes to the funeral of a *txakurra* [dog, referring to the police], he has lots of words of condemnation and crocodile tears. That's because he does not see himself in danger.[...] But if they have to go to a funeral of a party member, by the time they go back home they might start thinking that it is time to find solutions or they might be the next ones (i.e. feet first in a pine coffin). (Gurruchaga & San Sebastián 2000: 183; Sánchez Cuenca 2001: 99)

As a result of the increasing threat, the Spanish government provided armed bodyguards for those who appeared on ETA lists. The police forces were unable to cope with the new security needs, so private guards were hired to protect hundreds of Basque citizens. Those who were not provided with protection or refused to change their daily lives risked being killed at any moment. One of the first victims of this new kind of vendetta was Gregorio Ordóñez Fenollar. A member of the Popular Party and deputy mayor of San Sebastian, Ordóñez was anything but an influential politician. ETA shot him in the back on 23 January 1995 while he was having lunch with colleagues and justified its action by arguing that politicians were unequivocally responsible for not changing social reality. From the killing of Gregorio Ordóñez in 1995 until May 2003, twenty-three PSOE and PP politicians were killed in the Basque Country (Calle & Sánchez-Cuenca 2004: 64). However, it was the widely reported kidnapping of a prison official, José Antonio Ortega Lara, which captured the imagination of Basque society.[26] Ortega was not a businessman or a politician, but a prison official in the province of Burgos. Traditionally, ETA had kidnapped people who could pay a ransom and who could serve as an example to all those who did not pay the extortion money known as the 'revolutionary tax'. However, in this case, ETA kidnapped a civil servant of minor importance who could not have paid any significant sum. Ortega was seized on 17 January 1996 and was held for 532 days in deplorable conditions. The kidnapping was ended on 1 July 1997 when the Civil Guards stormed a factory in Mondragón (Gipuzkoa) and found a hidden chamber (*zulo*) where he had been left to starve for more than seventeen months. The television pictures of a skeletal, disoriented, and bearded Ortega who could barely stand on his own shocked public opinion.

As was usually the case when the police forces made an advance in the 'fight against terrorism', ETA responded with a spectacular action to show its continuing strength. This time ETA killed a 29-year-old Basque town councillor called Miguel Angel Blanco Garrido. As with Ortega, Blanco captured the popular imagination of many Basques and Spaniards for his low political significance and his status as an ordinary citizen. The town councillor worked in Ermua, a small town in Biscay, and belonged to the conservative Partido Popular (PP). ETA kidnapped him on 10 July 1997 and threatened to execute him if the government did not end its 'dispersion policy' and the 460 convicted members of ETA were not transferred to Basque Country prisons within forty-eight hours. Even if the Spanish Government had wanted to meet the organisation's demands forty-eight hours was too brief a time for anything to be done. The death sentence led thousands of emotional citizens to demonstrate in major cities hoping to save the town councillor's life. In a snowball effect, Blanco became a symbol of anti-ETA feeling and helped break what has been described as 'the spiral of silence' (Funes 1998). In the capital of Biscay, Prime Minster Aznar led a demonstration of over half a million anxious people, half the number of the million that inhabit Greater Bilbao. The televised forty-eight-hour kidnapping came to a sudden end on 12 July when ETA shot Blanco in the back of the head in the outskirts of Lasarte (Gipuzkoa). At the eleventh hour, the numerous pleas were ignored and a moved population, who had hoped their voices would be eventually heard, collectively experienced what being a victim could be like. According to *The Economist*, in the following days almost six million Spaniards spontaneously demonstrated against ETA's grave error, including one and a half million in Madrid and a million in Barcelona.[27]

6.2.2 Breaking the 'spiral of silence'

One of the most significant sociological developments after the killing of Blanco was the popular reaction against ETA. After 1997, a new group of Basque NGOs and intellectuals led a movement of protest that facilitated the return of a pro-active civil society. These individuals and organisations publicly rejected the 'socialisation of pain' which targeted politicians, journalists, judges, and lecturers and demanded an immediate cessation of hostilities. The main consequences of these mobilisations were (1) the renewed legitimacy of non-Basque nationalists' opinions and (2) the boosting of existing peace organisations in the Basque Provinces. A few of these peace organisations denounced the links between moderate and radical Basque nationalists and the 'ethnic cleansing' ETA was carrying out against those who were not Basque nationalists. They also propounded the 1978 Constitution and the 1979 statute of autonomy as an appropriate framework via which the national aspirations of Basques could be channelled. Among those organisations, it is worth emphasising the pioneering role played by the Foro de Ermua in its initial stages. This organisation had taken the name of the town where Blanco lived and was created a few months after his assassination. The aims of the forum were to defend the victims of what they considered to be 'ETA's fascism' and to oppose any negotiation with the insurgents. Other groups that followed the example of the Foro Ermua were COVITE, born in November 1998, and ¡Basta Ya! in 1999 which fostered empathy with the victims and mobilised public opinion against terrorism. In the latter, the philosopher Fernando Savater had a prominent role in denouncing the state of fear radical nationalists were creating in the street and claimed to be Spanish and Basque, not just Basque. The social mobilisation of civil society boosted the profile of well-established organisations such as the Madrid-based Asociación de Victimas del Terrorismo (AVT) and two Basque organisations worth noticing: Gesto por la Paz (Gesture for peace) and Elkarri (Among all of us) founded in 1986 and 1992 respectively, which had been promoting the conditions that could lead to a peaceful resolution of the conflict: absence of violence, dialogue, and the participation of all groups in negotiations (Mansvelt Beck 2005: 213–219).

All these organisations were important in breaking what the expert on public opinion, Elisabeth Noelle-Neumann, has called the 'spiral of silence'. According to Noelle-Neumann, the views that become prevalent first depend on who talks and who keeps quiet, not on what people think. Opinions are publicly expressed when they are perceived as 'acceptable' or, one might say, dominant. People sense the prevailing public opinion, even with no access to polls, and remain silent if they feel their views are not those of the majority. They do so because they believe holding minority views will lead to isolation or ridicule. Hence, it is the fear of isolation that 'seems to be the force that sets the spiral of silence in motion' (Noelle-Neuman 1980: 6). Participation or non-participation in the 'spiral of silence' is not a single decision, but one redefined over and over again by the members of a community who have identified the opinions and behaviour that make them more likely to be isolated. However, the spiral is not an endless process and it can be broken. People will voice their views when their personal opinion spreads and is taken up by others. It is the disappearance of the fear of isolation and of being ridiculed that sets in motion the change from a minority to a majority view. Applying Noelle-Neumann's model to the Basque case, one could argue that these organisations were pioneers in 'breaking the spiral of silence', allowing those who silenced Basques to speak up and show their legitimate anger in mass demonstrations. As Edurne Uriarte has pointed out, 'those who went onto the streets were non-nationalists, who started to realise that in the street, the social legitimacy and the force of their claims were as strong as those of the nationalists' (Uriarte 2001: 79).

The multiple civil demonstrations against ETA's terror generated a political debate over how to achieve a peaceful settlement. At a more fundamental level, all the organisations mentioned above helped place the victim at the centre of any negotiated end to violence. Any future de-escalation of the Basque conflict would have to comprise short-term political measures but also long-term processes of appeasement and reconciliation which would have to be sensitive to the victims' families. In this respect, some organisations agreed to equate the victims of ETA with the victims of GAL as casualties of terrorism. Other organisations with closer links to radical Basque nationalism followed their own agenda and aimed at equating the victims of ETA with the lawfully imprisoned insurgents. This view was rejected by the majority of organisations and demonstrated the growing gap between the MLNV and Basque public opinion.

6.2.3 Support for ETA

Civic organisations such as Elkarri, Gesto por la Paz, and ¡Basta Ya! increased their support because of an overall change of social attitudes towards ETA's violence. First, years of violence produced disenchantment amongst citizens with Basque politicians as actors who did not represent their collective desire for peace. Second, although the majority of Basque voters remained nationalist and aspired to increasing autonomy, or even

independence, they recognised that the indiscriminate killings were counterproductive for the separatist cause. Even some within the *abertzale* left
started to see ETA as an impediment for the ideological and programmatic
evolution of radical Basque nationalism which found it difficult to establish
political alliances in local, provincial, and autonomous institutions.

According to the statistical survey *Euskobarómetro*, there was a clear
evolution of Basque public opinion against ETA. As can be seen in Figure
6.1 the proportion of those who 'totally rejected' ETA grew from 23 per
cent in 1981 to 61 per cent in 2006. At the same time, those who gave occasional support to ETA also increased from 15 per cent to around 30 per
cent. An interesting point of the longitudinal study was how Basque civil
society had become politicised since the consolidation of democracy. In
1981, when asked directly about their views almost 50 per cent of Basques
did not have an opinion or gave no response to their support to ETA. By
2006, the figure was only 2 per cent as Basque people had acquired an
opinion on the topic that perhaps they did not have in 1981. It could also
be argued that Basque people were less afraid of expressing their views on
such a sensitive issue as violence. Another interesting and crucial element
of the poll was the decline in the number of those who gave total support
to ETA. In the early 1980s between 6 and 8 per cent of the respondents
were completely committed to ETA's goals and tactics. In the late 1980s
the trend started to decline and since the 1990s it has stayed at a minimum
of 1 or 2 per cent.

The Basque barometer also conducted panel studies to learn the citizens' opinions about the insurgents. The results of their cross-section inter-
views at regular intervals showed that Basque public opinion about ETA
had clearly evolved since the first polls were conducted. In 1978 up to 35
per cent of Basques believed the ETA members were idealists, while only 7

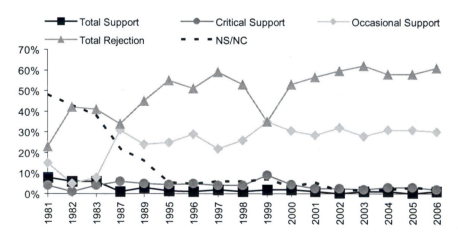

Figure 6.1 Support to ETA in the Basque Autonomous Community, 1981–2006.
Source: Euskobarómetro (www.ehu.es/cpvweb/)

per cent described them as criminals or assassins. Those numbers changed in the late 1990s, when 16 per cent of the population considered the paramilitaries romantic dreamers and the number of those who saw them as criminals had risen to 32 per cent. In the words of Michel Wieviorka, the evolution of Basque public opinion towards ETA was an 'inversion process' (Wieviorka 1993). The opposition to ETA's nationalist violence was due to the tactical shift in the selective use of violence to indiscriminate violence, henceforth terrorism. Among the milestones on that gradual development towards creating fear were the bombing of the Cafeteria Ronaldo in 1974 and the Hipercor supermarket in 1987. The targeting of civilians unconnected to the conflict (non-combatants) was further expanded in the 1990s to include PNV sympathisers. After the assassination in August 2000 of José María Korta, a well-known businessman who refused to pay extortion money, every nationalist who did not support ETA's uneven warfare became a potential target of the organisation.

Since the emergence of ETA, Basque society was divided between those who supported the radical nationalist agenda and those who opposed it. The purpose of violence was first to eliminate the 'representatives of the state' but it then became an instrument to reinforce Basque ethnicity and maintain the internal cohesion of the armed group. To date, ETA's campaign to nationalise the masses has not achieved the desired outcome as the Basques' self-identification remains stable. In the BAC, most people have fluid identities, what some authors call dual patriotism, and identify themselves with more than one country or nation. As Figure 6.2 shows, in the Basque case around 60 per cent of the population do not see their identity as a zero-sum game and feel both Spanish and Basque. This high

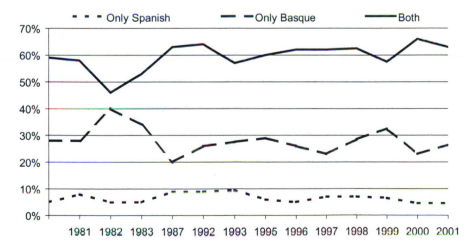

Figure 6.2 National self-identification of Basque citizens, 1981–2006.
Source: Euskobarómetro (www.ehu.es/cpvweb/)

level of attachment to both sources of identity is not unusual in Spain and can be explained by the consolidation of both the autonomous state and the devolved self-government institutions (Herranz de Rafael 1998). However, the percentage of those who identify themselves as only Basque has also remained relatively stable at around 30 per cent, the highest in all the autonomous communities, whereas those who identify themselves as only Spanish is a minority of less than 10 per cent.

In an another opinion poll conducted by the Centro de Investigaciones Sociológicas (CIS), the national consciousness of the Basques seemed to have grown between 1990, when 30 per cent of the population defined the Basque Country as a nation, and 1996, when up to 40 per cent of the population believed they lived in a Basque nation (Moral 1998: 25). Overall, the extent of the separatist sentiment has remained relatively stable (Figure 6.3). The number of Basques who have some desire (both strong and weak) to see an independent Basque nation has remained the same: from 63 per cent in 1979 to 62 per cent in 2006. The number of people who have no desire for independence has remained between 20 and 30 per cent, whereas those who are indifferent account for less than 10 per cent.

One should be reasonably sceptical when interpreting these results. On such a sensitive issue as support for the independence of the region from Spain, the results change depending on how the question is phrased. For example, when the style of the question is direct, people tend to answer in a much more conservative way. In the already mentioned 1998 CIS opinion poll by Félix del Moral, the question put to Basque citizens was: 'Would you be in favour or against the Basque Country being independent?' The results showed that 44 per cent of Basques were in favour of an indepen-

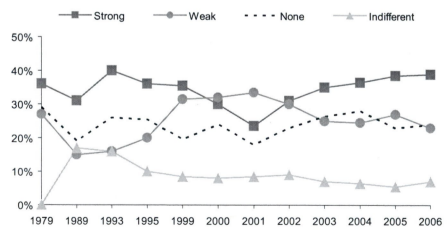

Figure 6.3 Support for independence in the Basque Autonomous Community, 1979–2006.
Source: Euskobarómetro (www.ehu.es/cpvweb/)

dent Basque Country, while 32 per cent opposed it and 24 per cent had no opinion in the matter. The results differ from the ones presented by the longitudinal surveys of the *Euskobarómetro* and are a good indicator of the plurality of views within Basque society. The disagreement between the two polls might be explained by the lack of information about what the questions really mean. This latter point was highlighted by Moral himself who stated that when talking about independence for the homeland, the respondents did not know what the geographical extent of the Basque nation was (BAC, BAC plus Navarre, or the seven Basque Provinces?). Also, what is meant by independence? Having sovereign armed forces, currency, and borders? What is the meaning of political independence in an interdependent European economy where most member states no longer have these competences? (Moral 1998: 60)

6.3 CONCLUSION

By the late 1980s, it made little sense to refer to the Franco dictatorship or post-Francoism to explain the dynamics and functioning of Spanish politics. With regards to Basque violence, much had been learned and new tools of counterinsurgency were being tested to deprive ETA of its social support. By 1987, GAL had disbanded, systematic ill treatment of ETA prisoners had ceased, and Herri Batasuna was ostracised by the political spectrum for its uninhibited support to ETA. Of all the anti-ETA initiatives, the most significant was the pact signed in 1988 at the Palace of Ajuria Enea by all Basque political parties except HB. The pact was the public expression of the Basques' desire to end violence and made it increasingly difficult for radical nationalists to use the Franco dictatorship or Spain's 'authoritarian practices' as pretexts for violence. Tougher antiterrorist measures, such as the dispersion policy, and a considerable increase in international police coordination, particularly with France, led to arrests of major ETA figures. It also had the effect of leading Basque nationalists to feel that the actions of ETA were counterproductive for the aspirations of those who wanted to go beyond regional home rule.

The chapter also examined the historical period from the end of the GAL campaign in 1987 to the killing of Miguel Angel Blanco in 1997. ETA's insistence on discussing political issues did not bring the meeting in Algiers to a successful conclusion and violence was resumed. Shortly before the World Fair in Seville and the Olympic Games in Barcelona, the French and Spanish police arrested the ETA leadership in March 1992. The arrests of the top three commanders in Bidart resulted in an organisational crisis for the armed group and in a three-year period of internal reflection for the political wing of ETA. Three years later, in 1995, radical Basque nationalists approved two key documents: ETA's Democratic Alternative which established the recognition of the right to self-determination as an essential condition for the cessation of violence, and Herri Batasuna's Old-artzen, which launched a campaign of 'socialisation of pain'. The street violence or *kale borroka* involved minor acts of violence and intimidation carried out by members of the youth organisation Jarrai and became the training ground for a new generation of violent activists. The aim of the 'socialisation of pain' was to deter any public opposition to ETA, and make those who, up until that point, had been bystanders into participants of the conflict. ETA decided to expand the range of legitimate targets beyond the traditional 'representatives of the state' (police, army officers, high rank politicians, etc.) to include judges, journalists, lecturers, businessmen, and, crucially, local politicians who needed bodyguards to continue working. Two of the most dramatic results of this radical nation building were the lengthy kidnapping of the prison official José Ortega Lara and the 'tele-vised' assassination of the young PP town councillor of Ermua, Miguel Angel Blanco, which captured the public's imagination.

ETA's decision to expand the range of 'legitimate targets' provoked renewed activity in Basque civil society leading to an institutional campaign to ostracise HB. Several civic movements, which had the sympathy of the mass media, emerged in response to broad social cleavages and discontents and voiced their opposition to ETA and Basque nationalism in general. The 'end of silence' was both a mobilisation to regain the public space to express dissent and a deliberative process about the legitimacy of unconventional warfare. In the eyes of radical nationalists, ETA's violent acts continued to *appear* as selective, disciplined, and fully under control. Peace and victims' organisations took centre stage in arguing that, on the contrary, violence was random, indiscriminate, and lacking any sort of logic and purpose. They further argued that violence was a broad and imprecise concept for a criminal campaign of murder against those, the majority, who did not sympathise with ETA's anti-system goals or actions. For the NGOs, the purpose of violence was to eliminate dissent by terrorising the Basque pop-ulation. The debate was much more than a dialectical confrontation but a crucial battle in determining who would lead an increasingly divided pub-lic opinion. The self-identification of Basques did not change during these years but the categories 'nationalist' and 'non-nationalist' became neat cat-egories which were widely used in the public sphere. The polarisation of identities and the rejection of 'nationalist demands' for as long as violence existed had the encouraging result of isolating the MLNV but also had the negative effect of alienating the more restrained expressions of nationhood of the PNV and EA. Both moderate and radical nationalists felt they were under siege and agreed to discuss strategies that could stop their declining popular support. As the next chapter will explain, this is how the 'national-ist front' between ETA and the nationalist parties was born.

7 Radical Nation-Building in Decline (1997–2006)

The killing of town councillor Blanco in July 1998 was one of the most controversial actions ever committed by ETA. The death of Blanco divided radical nationalists over the effectiveness of a war of attrition, eroded ETA's support base, and revolted the supporters of the two catch-all Spanish parties, the PP and the PSOE, who were forced to reconcile their views on security policies. The polarisation of Basque society between sympathisers and opponents of Basque nationalism went hand in hand with the emergence of a series of peace and victims' organisations characterised by their vocal opposition to both the *abertzale* left and the PNV. The consequences of ETA's 'socialisation of pain' had been disastrous for an organisation which had not fully recovered from the Bidart arrests of 1992. It had been aimed at targeting the 'occupation forces', their civilian leaders, but also new social groups such as judges, journalists, and local politicians. Both radical and moderate Basque nationalism looked for a way out in 1998, when they adopted the strategy of the 'nationalist front' which resulted in ETA declaring a unilateral and indefinite cease-fire a year after the killing of Blanco. The fourteen-month truce came to a sudden end in November 1999 when the armed group issued an unexpected communiqué stating that it was resuming its violent actions. According to the Basque paramilitaries, the political agreement it had signed with the PNV and EA in favour of a more separatist agenda had been ruined by the cowardice of the latter.

The 'nationalist front' was an attempt by ETA to regain the political initiative by suggesting that it was considering pursuing its strategic goals through the existing institutional structures. The leadership of the nationalist parties believed that backing ETA's long term goals would provide a soft landing for the Basque paramilitaries who were willing to disband. However, as became painfully clear to the PNV, backing the radical's secessionist agenda in exchange for a cease-fire did little else but confirm the usefulness of terror as a bargaining tool. Since its birth, ETA had consistently refused to give up its violent struggle and the 'nationalist front' was merely a tactical change in its recent history.

Before the 'nationalist front', ETA had tried three different aggression models to accomplish its secessionist project. First, during Francoism, it was believed that a spiral of action-repression-action would bring about a revolutionary war in which the Basque people would have a decisive victory over the Spanish. Second, in 1978 ETA adopted the war of attrition as a strategic concept that would bring the Spanish state to the point of collapse by continuous losses in personnel and matériel. According to the ETA leader José Miguel Beñarán (Argala), the Spanish government and ETA were in a virtual stalemate which could only be solved by discussing the 1970s KAS alternative in political negotiations. Radical nationalists remained convinced that Spanish public opinion would support the independence of the Basque nation if enough pressure was exercised. Third, after the transition period, ETA abandoned indiscriminate revolutionary war in favour of an urban mode of warfare based on a selective use of violence which would wear down the enemy's will to fight. ETA believed that a campaign of selective killings would demoralise the Spanish authorities and push them to discuss complete withdrawal from the Basque Country (Domínguez 1998; Ibarra 1987; Sánchez-Cuenca 2001; Sánchez-Cuenca 2004).

7.1 THE 1998–1999 PEACE PROCESS

The aftermath of the kidnapping and killing of Blanco in 1997 provoked a realignment of Basque political parties in their views of the Basque Movement of National Liberation. On the one hand, the PP government received the full support of the opposition party, the PSOE, and launched a relentless campaign of 'law and order' against radical organisations, many of which were dismantled by the police while their members were taken to court. Both these parties defended the legal status quo and came to be known as constitutionalists (*constitucionalistas*) and they received the support from the spontaneous movement called 'spirit of Ermua', a popular force generated by the killing of Blanco which publicly demonstrated against the actions of ETA. On the other hand, the PNV and EA saw this as an opportunity to achieve the disbandment of ETA and they approached the *abertzale* left by radicalising their rhetoric and short-term goals, which would lead to the signature of the pan-nationalist Pact of Lizarra and the short-lived peace process of 1998–1999.

7.1.1 Terrorism as a state problem

In March 1996, the Spanish electorate voted the socialist Felipe González out of office. In power since 1982, his governments had improved public finances, consolidated the welfare state, and implemented a series of economic reforms that included the privatisation, liberalisation, and deregulation of the Spanish economy in order to secure membership in the EEC. In the final years of his mandate a poor economic record, high unemployment, corruption scandals, and allegations implicating González himself in government collusion with GAL's 'dirty war' eroded the public's support for the PSOE. As the new Prime Minister, José María Aznar pledged to continue the free market reforms initiated by the socialists and implemented a vigorous programme of macro-economic policies to make the country eligible to join the first wave of the Economic and Monetary Union (EMU).

The economic continuities were in contrast to the political discontinuities, especially in relation to ETA. During the two legislatures during which Aznar was in power (1996–2000; 2000–2004) his security policies differed greatly from those of the socialists, who had adopted a softer approach to the Basque problem (Jaime 2002: 34). During the governments of Felipe González, ETA members would see their sentences cut if they renounced the organisation. The conservative leader, on the other hand, firmly kept in place the dispersion policy, by which Basque prisoners were scattered throughout Spanish territory, and insisted that they serve full sentences. Aznar's tougher approach included an understanding that ETA was an internal security matter and that, in principle, no negotiations would be established with its leadership. Another difference between González and Aznar was that for the conservative leader the problem was not only ETA, but Basque nationalism as a whole. The leader of the PP pursued a strategy of no concessions to the PNV which allegedly had an ambivalent relationship with ETA. In a widely quoted expression from Xabier Arzalluz, president of the PNV from 1980 to 2004: 'some [ETA] shake the tree, without breaking it, so the walnuts fall, and others [the PNV] pick them up in order to share them out' (*Unos sacuden el árbol, pero sin romperlo, para que caigan las nueces, y otros las recogen para repartirlas*) (San Sebastián & Gurruchaga 2000: 65).

Aznar's two terms in office greatly differed from one another. In 1996, Aznar won a qualified majority and formed a minority government supported by Catalan, Basque, and Canarian moderate nationalists. This state of affairs lasted until the March 2000 general election, in which the PP won an absolute majority and no longer needed the support of the CiU, PNV, and CC. During his second term, he decided to adopt a more confrontational agenda against his former political allies and decided to challenge both moderate and radical Basque nationalists. It became clear that his view of ETA's violence was that 'terrorism' was a state problem and that the armed group needed to be fought by all legal means necessary. In a pluralist democracy, he argued, there was no place for a violent organisation dedicated to extortion, blackmail, and assassination. Politics should be organised by democratically elected members of parliament, not by a self-elected armed group that claimed to speak on behalf of the Basque nation. By defining ETA's violent actions as 'terrorism' the state effectively transformed people's perceptions and government policies and further alienated MLNV sympathisers. Aznar's views about 'Basque terror' received further legitimacy with the events of 11 September 2001. After the collapse of the twin towers, he found it easier to equate radical Basque nationalists with Islamic militants and pushed European governments to do more to fight the threat. The European Union responded to his numerous requests by officially listing ETA and Batasuna as terrorist organisations in December 2001 and June 2003, respectively.

Two pivotal events had emboldened Aznar to take on Basque national-ism. First, he believed the 1978 Constitution had solved Spain's historical and institutional problem and that Basque nationalists, led by ETA, were threatening a stable constitutional arrangement that had the support of over 40 million Spaniards. Aznar personally helped to recuperate and popularise the term 'constitutional patriotism' as a way of boosting Spanish national identity.[1] Second, his personal animosity towards radical nationalists was also due to the fact that since the killing of Gregorio Ordoñez in 1995, ETA had targeted numerous PP and PSOE politicians in the Basque Country. A year later, in 1996, ETA tried to kill him in Madrid months before the general elections, when he was the leader of the opposition and had a clear chance of winning. The car-bomb was detonated early in the morning on 19 April on the route Aznar took to work. The explosion destroyed much of Aznar's armour-plated car but he escaped with cuts.

The consolidation of ETA's 'terrorism' as a state problem went hand in hand with the adoption of an unambiguous position by the government. This increasingly belligerent attitude led the PSOE and the PP to sign the Antiterrorist Pact (*Acuerdo por las libertades y contra el terrorismo*) in December 2000 which they hoped would stop the relentless killing of their local politicians in the Basque Country.[2] Another consequence of the newly acquired mindset were the judiciary's initiatives, particularly those of the Audiencia Nacional and the Supreme Court, which were pursuing the criminalisation of organisations that 'collaborated with the armed group' ETA. The long list of criminalisations started in December 1997 with the imprisonment of the twenty-three-person leadership (*mesa nacional*) of Herri Batasuna following the projection of videos of ETA during their 1997 electoral campaign. The removal of the Herri Batasuna leadership was followed by the criminalisation of the prisoners' association, Gestoras pro-Amnistía, and the youth organisation Jarrai. The latter proved to be highly resistant to the initiatives of Judge Baltasar Garzón, and radical youth changed its name to Haika and Segi to continue operating. The core of the radical nationalist world, KAS, was also cornered in 1998, only to be re-founded a year later with the name of EKIN (Sánchez-Cuenca 2001: 50). The press did not escape the legal initiatives and two newspapers were closed down by the police: *Egin* in July 1998 (which was replaced by *Gara* in January 1999) and *Egunkaria* in 2002. In the meantime, all the Basque nationalist parties and various other civil society organisations met in the Navarrese town of Lizarra (or Estella) to forge a common front against this new wave of Spanish nationalism (Douglass & Ibarra 2004: 147).

7.1.2 The Pact of Lizarra

The indefinite cease-fire declared by ETA in 1998 was preceded by the signing of the Pact of Lizarra on 12 September 1998 by the Partido Nacionalista Vasco, Eusko Alkartasuna, Herri Batasuna, Ezker Batua, and other organisations. The signature of the political agreement by the main Basque nationalist parties and trade unions had been preceded by manoeuvres from the PNV cadres who were determined to regain some of the lost terrain by facilitating the disbandment of ETA. Failing to disassociate itself from the goals and methods of the *abertzale* left, the leaders of the PNV were confident they could maintain their electoral hegemony if they were seen to take decisive steps towards a de-escalation of the conflict. Besides, the Basque paramilitaries had been gravely affected by the police and judicial offensive and needed some time to rebuild their funding, recruitment and propaganda mechanisms. Finding themselves in the same boat, the PNV and ETA established a series of discreet contacts which materialised, in August 1998, in a secret agreement by which the PNV took as its own the final goal of ETA (an independent Basque state) and committed itself to declaring the 1979 Statute of Autonomy as a dead end for their people (Roca 2002: 25). In return, ETA pledged to work for a negotiated end to the conflict (*salida negociada al conflicto*). In the words of ETA, 'the signatories assumed the commitment to take decisive steps in favour of a unique sovereign institution which could embrace the whole of Euskal Herria' while 'breaking relations with the pro-Spanish forces'.[3]

The main goal of the Lizarra Agreement was to solve what the signatories saw as the constituent problems of the Basque conflict: violence (or terrorism) and further autonomy (or independence). The PNV was keen on having the longest possible period with no violence, but ETA was more interested in using that time to push for the development of political institutions that covered the seven provinces. The agreement designed a new way of making politics based on the 'nationalist front' and presented Basque society with a lighter version of what had been decided between ETA and the PNV behind closed doors. However, the confidential agreement was never made public and it allowed the PNV to delay any radical political initiatives that could alienate its conservative constituency and its electoral alliance with Aznar in the Madrid parliament and with the socialists in the autonomous parliament of Vitoria-Gasteiz.

Four days after the Lizarra declaration was signed, ETA declared a unilateral and indefinite cease-fire on 16 September 1998. Inspired by the Northern Ireland Good Friday Agreement of April 1998, the unlimited truce began a time of hope for Basque society which allowed Basque nationalism, particularly the radical wing, to regain much of its political credibility. The Irish-inspired agreement signed at the Navarrese town of Lizarra facilitated a parliamentary collaboration between the Basque government, led by Juan José Ibarretxe, and Euskal Herritarrok (EH) which had taken over the electoral space formerly held by Herri Batasuna. In the European Parliament elections of 1999, held during the cease-fire, the Basque electorate rewarded EH for the truce and the coalition obtained a remarkable 20 per cent of the vote. The initiative for creating an assembly of Basque municipalities with 1,778 representatives from the seven Basque Provinces, called Udalbiltza, was launched by radical nationalists with the support of the other nationalist forces. It was the first time an institution covered the geographical area of what nationalists consider to be the Basque homeland.

Contrary to the 'Irish model', ETA was not content with the level of confrontation between the Basque nationalist parties and the 'pro-Spanish forces' and officially ended the fourteen-month cease-fire on 3 December 1999. According to the communiqué, the compromise had been broken by the moderate nationalists of the PNV and EA who had not done enough in uniting all Basque patriots in favour of independence. A month later, on 21 January 2000, ETA resumed violence by exploding a car bomb in Madrid which killed an army lieutenant colonel. Florencio Domínguez has argued that ETA decided to break the cease-fire in July 1999 after the PNV and EA had refused to hold elections for a 'parliament of Euskal Herria' in Euskadi, Navarre, and the French Basque Country ignoring the French and Spanish legal systems (Domínguez 2006: 37).

During the cease-fire, the Spanish government and ETA met only once, in Switzerland, where their antagonistic positions were underlined. In the Zurich negotiations of 19 May 1999 ETA was represented by Mikel Albisu (Antza), Vicente Goikoetxea, and Belén González (Carmen), whereas Prime Minister Aznar had sent a delegation made up of the Secretary of State Security, Ricardo Martí Fluxá, the Secretary of Presidency, Javier Zarzalejos, and his personal advisor, Pedro Arriola. As had happened in Algiers, the two parties could not find common grounds, and since they were not willing to discuss political issues, found no reason to meet again. However, the conservative government decided to amend the 'dispersion policy' and moved a substantial number of ETA inmates to prisons closer to the Basque Country. The armed group broke all contacts with the government on 25 August 1999 and the PP argued that the truce had been a trick by the nationalist left to regain lost political space and reorganise itself. The Basque paramilitaries' demands were also seen by the conservative government as unacceptable. From Aznar's perspective, Spain could not recognise the 'right to self-determination' and could not commit itself to the result of a hypothetical referendum on the future of the Basque Country, presumably one on independence.[4] That would not only mean accepting ETA's authority to discuss the institutional distribution of power, while bypassing the Basque parliament, but it would also entail amending the constitutional system agreed during the transition.

When one looks at the 1998–1999 Basque peace process in retrospect, neither the Spanish government nor ETA believed that a ceasefire could come about. The Lizarra Pact and the resulting truce had been promoted by nationalist parties for political and strategic reasons and the government had not played any role in facilitating the cease-fire. Significantly, the ETA truce was declared while Aznar was on an official trip to Peru. On top of being left out, the government did not believe the unilateral and unlimited ceasefire was sincere and argued that the truce was being sought by ETA as an opportunity to re-arm. In accordance with the government's thesis, young radical nationalists continued to participate in intimidatory acts of street violence such as arson attacks and threats against non-nationalists (Mees 2003: 60; Oiarzabal 2002: 34).

The end of the peace process confirmed the 'polarised pluralism' of the Basque political landscape, reinforced the social cleavage between Basque nationalists and non-Basque nationalists, and brought a deep sense of disaffection to the radical rank and file who were under siege by police and judicial initiatives. In the 1998 Basque elections, the ruling party, the PNV, managed to increase by 46,000 the number of votes they had obtained in previous autonomous elections (1994) and roughly maintained its percentage of the votes cast. The radical Basque nationalist party, Euskal Herritarrok, obtained an extra 58,000 votes and maintained its position as the third electoral force. The conservative Popular Party (PP), which emphasised the 'rule of law' and the 'union of the constitutionalists' against the 'fascist' and 'totalitarian' acts of ETA, increased its number of votes and moved from being the fourth political force to second place. Arguably, the underdogs of the elections were the PSOE and IU, which lost votes to the parties which had held more aggressive positions: namely the Popular Party and Euskal Herritarrok. Although there was not much change in the composition of the chamber, the high level of participation in the elections could be interpreted as civil society's increased interest in ending the conflict. In the previous 1994 elections, 60 per cent of the electorate had voted but in 1998 the turnout rose to 70 per cent.

The failure of the peace process of 1998–1999 deepened the security stalemate and ensured the continuation of the violent conflict for another decade. From the government's perspective, the nationalist front had been an attempt to initiate an 'ethnic cleansing' of non-Basque nationalists by ETA with the unforgivable help of the PNV and EA. The failure of moderate nationalists in securing a stable truce backfired, damaging their reputation, and proving that the end of violence could only be achieved through a disciplined multi-party agreement. From the radical nationalists' perspective, it was business as usual as the Spanish government continued a long tradition of authoritarian measures by criminalising some of their organisations. The most polemical of these initiatives was the banning of the antisystemic party Batasuna.

7.1.3   The banning of Batasuna

Most democratic political systems do not have to confront the idea of banning a political party. A strong and widespread political culture or a 'first past the post' electoral system often prevents the emergence of small extremist parties. If elected, these parties face an 'adaptation dilemma' by which they need to become relatively mainstream in order to prevent state repression while keeping a radical extra-parliamentary support base (Eatwell & Mudde 2004). However, there are occasions in which an extremist party is overtly anti-democratic and challenges the ethos of the political system. In the case of the MLNV, the radical network had traditionally combined democratic participation in the electoral game with the construction of an ample social network of affiliated organisations, enabling it to put down firm roots in many social sectors. Seeking to tread a path between the desire to appear 'respectable' and the need for a non-institutional strategy, whose aim was to proclaim Basque independence, Batasuna had found it difficult to remain in the mainstream. Its organisational and ideological links with ETA convinced the PP government of the need to balance the right to freedom of speech with protecting the rights of both individuals and groups.

The first steps towards a greater crackdown on Batasuna were taken in the summer of 2002. The conservative government argued that the activities of the radical nationalist party went beyond conventional forms of political participation (e.g., voting, community projects, and contacting public officials) and that it was an integral part of ETA. The Spanish authorities argued that there were good reasons to criminalise the party because it was regarded as the mouthpiece for ETA and its activities went beyond the limits of the normative procedures which defined the democratic political process. For example, members of Batasuna did not condemn ETA killings, some of their militants were also members of the armed group, and on several occasions, black-hooded men had appeared on stage at the end of Batasuna's political rallies to shout 'Long live ETA!' (*Gora ETA*). The central legal argument focused on the 'procedures' and not so much on the 'issues' the extremists raised. ETA's political wing gave active support for 'unconventional' methods such as inflammatory language, various forms of disruption, civil disobedience, and violent activities, and this was an indicator of its low regard for the prevailing ideological and organisational structures. In order for modern democracies to function, the prosecutors argued, conflict needed to be regulated and opposing interests had to be reconciled through negotiation and not just through a compulsory adherence to administrative procedures. Basque extremists, on the other hand, did not regard compromise as a virtue and saw in the functioning of a pluralistic society a manipulation of interests that led to an endless series of ideological surrenders.

Two parallel processes pursued the banning of Batasuna before the municipal elections of May 2003. One was in Parliament, where there was enough support for the Spanish executive to approve the Organic Law of Political Parties (June 2002), which was designed to outlaw parties that did not accept the legitimacy of the political order and actively engaged in undermining it. The law was approved on 27 June 2002 by 87 per cent of the lower chamber (304 MPs out of 349) and faced the opposition of those parties (IU, BNG, PNV, and EA) that did not see the need to criminalise political parties that condoned or glorified anti-democratic activities.[5] By approving the Law of Political Parties, the government was determined to follow the 'German model' of dealing with extremist challenges. According to the scholarly literature, one can find two ideal styles of dealing with extremism: the American and the German model. Cas Mudde (2004) has argued that the 'American model' implies that the state provides for as much freedom as possible and allows all ideas, democratic or not, to be bought and sold in the 'marketplace of ideas'. On the other hand, in the 'German model', which is formally known as *streitbare* or *wehrhafte Demokratie* (translated as 'militant democracy'), the state prohibits actions and ideas that oppose the 'fundamental principles of the free democratic order'.

First, after approving the new Law of Political Parties, the Spanish Parliament asked the Supreme Court (Spain's second highest tribunal) to dissolve Batasuna pursuant the amended law.[6] In March 2003, the Supreme Court's sixteen-member panel unanimously approved the government's request for a permanent suspension. The ban refused Batasuna members the right to be representatives in further elections, suspended their right to hold rallies and public demonstrations, and froze their assets. Batasuna appealed the Supreme Court's decision to the Constitutional Court (Spain's highest tribunal), which unanimously upheld the indefinite ban, citing the group's 'ideologies associated with terrorism and violence'.

Second, a process carried out by Baltasar Garzón, a judge sitting in the Spanish National Court (Audiencia Nacional), accused Batasuna of close links with ETA, including the funding of the armed group through a complex network of companies called the Udaletxe Project.[7] Garzón suspended the activities of Batasuna for three years and closed down the headquarters of Batasuna in Pamplona, Vitoria, Bilbao, and San Sebastián in August 2002. The banning was seen as the culmination of a tough and comprehensive policy to isolate ETA, which had proved extremely popular amongst the public. According to a 2002 opinion poll from the Centro de Investigaciones Sociológicas (CIS), 65.4 per cent of Spaniards supported the criminalisation of Batasuna.[8] Later on, Garzón closed down the radical social clubs known as *herriko tabernas*. The argument of the Audiencia Nacional was that many of the organisations of the *izquierda abertzale* had organisational links to ETA. In his report, Garzón first linked ETA to KAS but later included organisations such as the newspaper Egin, the radio station Egin Irratia, the NGOs Xaki and Fundación Zumalabe, the youth organisations

Haika and Segi, and the prisoners' associations Gestoras pro Amnistía and Askatasuna (Anuario Gara 2002: 119). His decision was supported by the Supreme Court on 28 March 2003 which confirmed Batasuna's suspension in all its forms (including Herri Batasuna and Euskal Herritarrok). Shortly after the banning, the Batasuna MPs formed a pro-independence parliamentary coalition called Sozialista Abertzaleak (Socialist Nationalists) and promoted the legalisation of parties which could participate in the forthcoming local elections. The platform Autodeterminaziorako Bilgunea (AuB) attempted to register over 200 local parties, but their applications were systematically rejected by the Supreme Court as the candidates of the new parties had previously appeared in electoral lists of HB and/or EH. The absence of the nationalist left from the elections of 25 May 2003 meant that its votes were lost or transferred to other political options, mainly the nationalists of the PNV and the left-wing Izquierda Unida (IU). During the summer of 2003, other building blocks of the Basque national liberation movement were criminalised (see Figure 7.1). However, the gaps left by these organisations were filled by others with different degrees of success.

7.2 THE ZAPATERO GOVERNMENT

The policies of Aznar towards the Basque Country were severely criticised at the time by the PNV-led autonomous government. Maintaining tense relations with moderate nationalists and criminalising Batasuna were seen by Aznar's political adversaries as measures that corroborated his anti-democratic and authoritarian temperament. However, he could be credited with severely weakening the legitimacy, strength, and visibility of the MLNV network. It could be argued that his initiatives did not, and could not, resolve the Basque problem but they facilitated a new stage in which peace negotiations were seen as the only feasible 'landing strip' for Basque paramilitaries.

During the two legislatures he was in office, Aznar (who did not run for a third term) achieved an outstanding economic record and also made some serious mistakes. On the one hand, unemployment levels decreased to a historical low and the Popular Party oversaw Spain's adoption of the European Union's single currency while fulfilling the conditions of the EU Growth and Stability Pact (Balfour 2005: 146). On the other hand, the darkest pages of the PP governments were the sinking of the oil-tanker *Prestige* (and the resulting ecological disaster in 2002), the death of sixty-two soldiers returning from Afghanistan in a cheaply rented Russian aircraft (Yak-42), and, more importantly, the participation of Spanish armed forces in the U.S.-led invasion of Iraq without parliamentary approval. In spite of these blunders, most of the opinion polls published a few days before the 2004 Spanish general election predicted the Popular Party would renew its

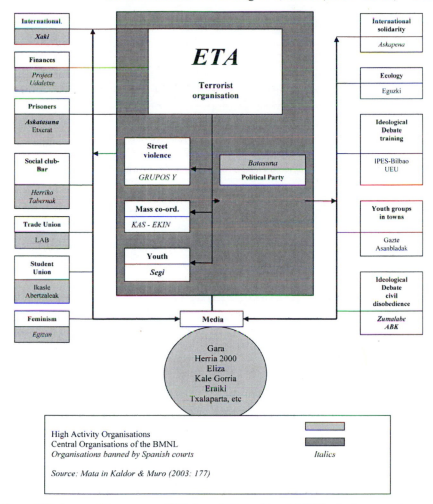

Figure 7.1 Basque Movement of National Liberation (BMNL)

absolute majority and that Aznar's designated successor, former Minister of Interior and Deputy Prime Minister Mariano Rajoy, would become head of government. Unexpectedly, on 11 March 2004, just three days before the elections, Madrid witnessed one of the deadliest terrorist attacks that Europe had seen in decades and the incumbent government was accused of exploiting the attack for electoral expediency. On 14 March, and against all predictions, the PP was swept out of office and the Socialist José Luis Rodriguez Zapatero became Spain's new prime minister.

7.2.1 March 11

The details of the attacks in March 2004 are well-known. Ten synchronised bombs exploded early in the morning of the 11th March, at 7:40 am, in trains that were loaded with commuters on their way to work, killing 191 people and injuring another 1,755. The bombs were set off in three stations—Atocha, Santa Eugenia, and El Pozo del Tío Raimundo—in a coordinated attack that had been possible due to the use of mobile phone technology. The first reaction of the authorities was to put responsibility for the massacre on the Basque insurgents. *Lehendakari* Juan José Ibarretxe was the first to tell the press that 'ETA was writing its own end' (*ETA está escribiendo su final*). Given the history of the armed group, political elites and much of public opinion were convinced that ETA was responsible for the attack. According to the Interior Minister Angel Acebes, a month earlier, on 29 February 2004, the Civil Guards had intercepted a van driven by ETA members and loaded with over 500 kg of titadyne and chlorate-based explosives heading to Madrid, and four months earlier, on 21 December 2003, ETA had left rucksacks full of explosives in a train which was also on its way to Madrid. Since ETA had last killed fourteen months earlier, in May 2003, many feared a spectacular action in the Spanish capital to reassert its presence.

The following day, 12 March, police and intelligence services were on an alternative trail to the Basque one. The police had found a van with detonators and verses from the Koran near one of the stations where one of the terrorists had travelled from, and Acebes notified the public that the involvement of Islamic militants was under investigation. The leader of Batasuna, Arnaldo Otegi, confirmed that ETA was not responsible for the acts and that the evidence pointed at the 'Arab resistance'. Later that day, a person claiming to speak on behalf of ETA called the Basque television Euskal Telebista (ETB) and the newspaper *Gara* to announce that the group was not responsible for the blasts. As judicial investigations confirmed much later, Islamic extremists were behind the attacks which were inspired, but not directed by, Osama bin Laden, leader of al-Qaeda. In spite of the growing evidence, the government decided to play the ETA card and it did so up to the eve of the elections.

The leaders of all political parties simultaneously and independently announced the suspension of their campaigns. In the meantime, large sectors of the electorate concluded that the PP government was being manipulative and that it was covering up the Al-Qaeda connection while insisting on a link to ETA in an attempt to capitalise gains for the general elections. A considerable number of Spaniards felt misled and started to see the attack as a consequence of Spain's involvement in the invasion of Iraq, which did not bring any immediate benefits but only the deaths of several members of the armed forces and intelligence services and the antipathy of Al Qaeda, which seemed to be the main reason why the Islamic network had targeted

Madrid (Pacheco 2004: 15). The popular dissatisfaction with the government's information policy grew when, on Saturday 13th March, the police arrested five alleged terrorists: three Moroccans and two Indians. On that day, peaceful demonstrations against the massacre saw millions taking to the streets in Spain, while mourning turned into anger and questions from both opposition parties and citizens, demanding transparency in the investigation and more answers from the PP government before the 14 March election. Popular disaffection was effectively mobilised by the main opposition force and an alleged PSOE-originated sms message was sent to thousands of mobiles calling on people to participate in demonstrations in front of the PP headquarters.

The following day, the 14 March 2004, Spaniards went to the polls. As can be seen in Table 7.1, the PSOE won 164 seats in the 350-seat chamber and 10.9 million votes, up from 125 seats and 7.9 million votes in the 2000 elections. The PP dropped from 183 to 148 seats after losing 700,000 votes. An important feature of the elections was that they were perceived as highly important by the electorate and abstention was very low (24 per cent) raising the Socialists' share of the total vote from 34 per cent to 42.6 per cent while the PP's declined from 44.5 per cent to 37.6 per cent.

The Madrid blasts did not achieve 'regime change'. The change in the vote was not the result of an apprehensive electorate desperate to withdraw troops from any involvement in the Middle East as a way of avoiding another terrorist attack. Rather, the high turnout, which had traditionally benefited the Spanish Left, was the result of popular anger at the government's poor handling of the situation. According to Raj S. Chari, the vote of 'abstainers', 'first-time voters', 'communist voters', and 'disgruntled

Table 7.1 General elections, 2004 and 2000

	2004		2000	
	Seats	*% of Votes*	*Seats*	*% of Votes*
Partido Socialista Obrero Español (PSOE)	164	42.6	125	34.1
Partido Popular (PP)	148	37.6	183	44.5
Convergència i Unió (CiU)	10	3.2	15	4.2
Esquerra Republicana de Catalunya (ERC)	8	2.5	1	0.8
Partido Nacionalista Vasco-Eusko Alderdi Jeltzalea (PNV-EAJ)	7	1.6	7	1.5
Izquierda Unida (IU)	5	4.9	9	5.9
Other Parties	8	3.2	10	4.9

Note: Census: 34,571,831; Turnout: 77.21% (2004) and 69.98% (2000)

Source: Ministerio del Interior (http://www.mir.es)

Christian democrats' punished a government that had played down the mounting evidence pointing to a Moroccan group tied to Al-Qaeda (Chari 2004: 960). As the year-long parliamentary commission that investigated the rail bombings argued, the centre-right PP government had manipulated and twisted information in order to further its electoral interests.

José Luis Rodriguez Zapatero, popularly known as ZP, became Prime Minister on 15 April 2004. One of his first initiatives as premier was to pull out 1,300 peacekeeping troops from Iraq (out of a total multinational force of 154,000) which had been deployed by his predecessor without parliament's backing. The initiative had been a central pledge of Zapatero's election campaign and was designed to completely reverse the Atlanticist policy of the Aznar governments and return to a more Europe-oriented foreign policy (which emphasised Germany and France as its traditional allies). The abrupt withdrawal was received with anger by the Bush administration even though the Spanish troops accounted for less than 1 per cent of the U.S.-led forces in Iraq. In a conciliatory diplomatic gesture, Spain deployed a Spanish mission to Afghanistan in order to release U.S. troops, but the departure of the Spanish troops was a blow to Washington's efforts to maintain a united allied front at time when the situation in Iraq was rapidly deteriorating.

The Socialist government closed the chapter on its military involvement in Iraq and opened a new page in its relations with the autonomous communities. First, the Socialists' kicked off an old debate about reforming the Senate and converting it into a body representing Spain's seventeen autonomous regions. Second, PM Zapatero showed he was prepared to be more flexible than Aznar in reforming the statutes of autonomy provided there was broad parliamentary support for the adjustment and that they did not violate the basic tenets of the constitution. This meant greater autonomy for Catalonia and the possibility for the Basque government to discuss and negotiate the controversial plan of its regional premier. The Ibarretxe Plan sought to reform the 1979 Autonomy Statute and substantially increase its autonomy by gradually disassociating the Basque Country from the rest of Spain and, possibly, calling for a possible referendum on becoming a 'free state associated with Spain'. The initiative suggested that the constitutional framework based on symmetrical federalism (*café para todos*) should be abandoned in favour of a more flexible confederate system.

7.2.2 The Ibarretxe plan

The plan to give the Basque Country the political status of 'free association' with Spain was first publicly mentioned by the Basque president Juan José Ibarretxe on 27 September 2002. Two years later, at the end of 2004, and after numerous debates in the Basque chamber, the proposal was approved in the autonomous parliament by the narrowest of margins after it received the unexpected support of three ex-Batasuna deputies. The status of 'free association' would introduce an independent judiciary, a penal system, devolved responsibility for social security, and provided the power to sign international treaties. Only defence, customs, and foreign affairs would remain exclusive competences of the central government. In effect, the proposal was a unilateral attempt to change the political nature of the Basque Autonomous Community. The bill had an ambitious and clearly secessionist preamble but the rest of the articles were technical and resembled a statute of autonomy. The project was the unofficial electoral manifesto with which the PNV wanted to attend the 2005 regional elections and incorporated a pseudo-separatist agenda (*giro soberanista*) with the idea of de-escalating the conflict once again. The inspiration for the project, a sort of Lizarra without ETA, was to allow Basques to decide their own future and leave the armed group with no justification for its existence. The Socialist and Popular Parties were vehemently opposed to the PNV government's plan to hold a referendum over changing the political status of the region and argued that the Basque Country enjoyed a much greater degree of autonomy (especially with regard to taxation) than any other region in Europe.

The *Lehendakari*'s ambitious programme had a dubious future from the moment it was conceived. First, the positions of Ibarretxe and virtually all of Spain's other political parties were far apart and it was difficult to see how there could be any compromise on either side or what more Madrid could cede in the way of self-government. Mariano Rajoy, the PP leader, called the plan 'the biggest challenge to national unity since 1978' whereas Prime Minister Zapatero said it was secessionist, unconstitutional, and incompatible with Europe.[9] Second, support for the Ibarretxe Plan within the Basque chamber was fragmented. His government was in a minority (by one seat) and the *Lehendakari* could hardly claim he was legitimately representing the will of Basques on such a decisive issue. In other words, the project did not have the necessary majority to reform the statute of autonomy in such a radical way. Third, Ibarretxe adopted a confrontational attitude towards the Spanish authorities which did not help achieve parliamentary approval of the bill. On top of the lack of popular backing, the project needed to be reformed in accordance with legal and political mechanisms, meaning that the Basque parliament had to approve a document that would then be negotiated with the state authorities. Nevertheless, Ibarretxe provocatively claimed that if there was no agreement and the 'will of the Basque people' was not respected he would proceed to unilaterally call a referendum to ratify the text. The referendum would have been illegal and could have led to the dissolution of the regional government (invoking article 155 of the constitution) and the beginning of legal action against the Basque president.

The Ibarretxe Plan was finally voted in the Congress of Deputies on 1 February 2005. After eight hours of debate, the plan was eventually rejected by 313 to 29 votes, with two abstentions. The ruling Socialists and the centre-right Popular Party, the main opposition, joined forces and rejected the plan because of its 'unconstitutional' content. PM Zapatero offered talks on improving the degree of Basque sovereignty (within the framework of the constitution), but Ibarretxe rejected the suggestion and vowed to put his plan to a referendum in the Basque Country (not in the rest of Spain). The main reason for the rejection in the Congress of Deputies, argued the premier, was that such an ambitious plan could not be approved by the nationalist half of the Basque population and that a new consensual, revised plan had to be agreed. Shortly afterwards, Zapatero promised to incorporate a new Basque statute into the Spanish constitutional system as long as it had been approved by two-thirds of the Vitoria parliament. In the end, the Congress of Deputies' rejection of the controversial plan prompted the Basque regional government to bring forward the date of the autonomy elections by several weeks.

The Basque autonomy election of 17 April 2005 presented several issues. On the one hand, it was a test for the PNV which had seen the Ibarretxe Plan defeated in Madrid. There was also the question of where the Batasuna votes would go, the party having been banned two years earlier. On the other hand, there were questions about how the 'constitutionalist side' made up of the PSOE and PP would do in the elections after resoundingly rejecting the *Lehendekaritza* plan. As can be seen in Table 7.2, the Basque Nationalist Party (PNV), which had ruled the autonomous community since 1980, obtained disappointing results. The party lost 144, 000 votes (in a country of less than 2 million voters) and won twenty-nine seats in the seventy-five-seat chamber. The Socialist Party of Euskadi (PSE) obtained their best electoral results in years, gaining five seats to achieve a total of eighteen seats, thereby becoming the second political force in the Basque Parliament, a position previously held by the conservative Popular Party (PP). The Basque branch of the Popular Party (PP), which took an even

Table 7.2 Basque autonomous elections, 2005 and 2001

Parties	2005			2001		
	Seats	Votes	%	Seats	Votes	%
PNV-EA	29	463,873	38.6	33	604,222	42.7
PSE-EE	18	272,429	22.7	13	253,195	17.9
PP	15	208,795	17.4	19	326,933	23.1
EB-IU	3	64,931	5.4	3	78,862	5.6
EHAK	9	150,188	12.5			
Aralar	1	28,001	2.3			
EH				7	143,139	10.1

Note: Census: 1.799.500; Turnout: 69% (2005) and 80% (2001)

Source: Eusko Jaurlaritza—Gobierno Vasco (http://www.euskadi.net/elecciones/)

stronger line than the Socialists against greater autonomy for the Basque Country, lost four seats.

The most surprising outcome of the vote was the emergence of the unknown Communist Party of the Basque Lands (EHAK-PCTV), which acted as a proxy for Batasuna. Since the *Lehendakari* had called for new elections in February 2005, the leaders of the banned radical party had tried to register a new party to which they could transfer their support. After failing to legalise the party Aukera Guztiak (All the Options) one week before the elections, Batasuna decided to bring back to life EHAK, a party registered in 2001 that aimed at bringing about 'the dictatorship of the proletariat', while telling supporters to vote for the communist party. The fact that EHAK increased by two seats the results Batasuna had won in the 2001 elections raised serious questions about the effectiveness of the Law of Political Parties and the resilience and internal cohesion of radical Basque nationalists. The results were also a blow to the aspirations of the PNV for an associated free state with Spain and strengthened the hand of the Socialist central government.

7.3.2 Catalan statute of autonomy

The unforeseen victory of the PSOE in the 2004 general elections raised great expectation in Catalonia where a three-party left-wing coalition led by the socialist Pasqual Maragall had been working on a new regional charter since November 2003 when they took control of the regional executive of the Generalitat. Many Catalan politicians had long complained that the region contributed too much to the Spanish economy (around 18.5 per cent of GDP) and did not receive enough in return. On 16 April 2004, Zapatero was invested with office and he responded to those claims by promising 'a more sympathetic approach to Catalan demands for greater devolution including a new Statute of Autonomy and a better financial arrangement' (Guibernau 2006: 218). In the following months, the debate over the Catalan charter was observed with worries from Madrid as the Catalan region, with a population of 7 million and one fifth of Spain's GDP, demanded higher levels of autonomy. The two most controverial issues were the dispute about the region's revenues and the definition of Catalonia as a nation. First, the Catalan government was pushing for the right to levy its own taxes through a Catalan Tax Agency and set its own limits on the contribution to the Spanish exchequer. Second, the preamble of the charter called Catalonia a 'nation' and not a 'nationality', which was the term used in the 1978 Constitution. The terminology was not just a question of contentious semantics as many Spaniards feared that becoming a 'nation' could open the door to exercising the right to self-determination.

The *Nou Estatut* was approved in the Catalan parliament by an overwhelming majority of deputies (120 out of 135) on 30 September 2005. All political parties with seats in parliament voted in favor of the legal text

except the Catalan branch of the Popular Party. In spite of the initial jubila-
tion, experienced politicians observed that the toughest was yet to come as
the text had to go through the Spanish parliament. In spite of Prime Minister Zapatero's promise to support anything that came out of the autonomous parliament, Catalan parties expected the charter to be watered down
in the problematic areas of funding and national definition. Indeed, once
it got to Madrid the two areas were amended by the Parliament's Constitutional Commission in order to fit into the 'constitutional framework'.
In the final draft, the statute did not call Catalonia a 'nation' but the preamble recognised its desire to be called so. In this respect, the new statute
was still circumscribed by the 1979 Catalan Statute of Autonomy (which
recognised Catalonia as a nationality), pursuant to the 1978 Spanish constitution (which defined Spain as a nation). With regards to funding, the
Nou Estatut gave Catalonia a greater share of the taxes raised in its region
but not the control over them that was sought nor the right to decide what
proportion should be transferred to Madrid. The region did not get its own
Tax Agency but it was to receive 50 per cent of the personal income tax
collected, up from 33 per cent, and also 50 per cent of VAT (formerly 35
per cent). It was also agreed that the model could be extended to all Spain's
other regions in order to appease those who complained Catalonia was
receiving privileged treatment.[10]

After the text was revised, the Spanish Congress of Deputies approved
the statute by 189 votes to 154. Not surprisingly, the conservative Popular Party (PP) voted against it, as did the much smaller secessionist party,
Republican Left of Catalonia (Esquerra Republicana de Catalunya-ERC).
The charter was later approved swiftly by the Senate and by the Catalan parliament before being put to the vote in a referendum in the region
on 18 June 2006. Catalans voted overwhelmingly in favour of the new
charter with the 'yes' vote (73.9 per cent) backed by the Socialists and the
conservative and nationalist Convergència i Unió (CiU) whereas the 'no'
vote, pursued vociferously by the Popular Party of Catalonia (PP), gained
20.7 per cent. The pro-independence ERC expressed its discontent with the
substantially watered down version of the original text, approved by the
Catalan parliament, by casting blank votes (5.3 per cent).

The debate about the Catalan statute inflamed passions right across the
political spectrum, ruffled some feathers in the armed forces,[11] pitted the
Catalan Socialists against the socialist-run national government, and led
to the collapse of the coalition government in Catalonia that sponsored the
charter. The *Nou Estatut* also produced the ousting of Pasqual Maragall,
the region's socialist premier who was replaced by the also socialist José
Montilla in the Catalan elections of November 2006. More importantly,
the approval of the Catalan charter paved the way for autonomous communities such as Andalusia, Galicia, Aragon, the Balearic Islands, Valencia, or
the Canary Islands to seek greater autonomy. In a way, Pasqual Maragall
had accomplished the dream of his grandfather, the post-1898 and regen-

erationist poet Joan Maragall, of finding accommodation for Catalonia in Spain while at the same time leading to the regeneration of the latter. Maragall's idea had been to end with the nationalist image of a 'tortured Catalonia' and an 'unfinished Spain' (Gabancho 2006: 23–36).

The deliberation, approval, and ratification of the Catalan reform were watched with interest from the Basque Country. First, during the time the text was negotiated nothing else could be done by expectant Basque nationalists but hope for a window of opportunity to launch a similar reform of their regional charter. After all, the Spanish government headed by Zapatero was not willing to open another damaging negotiation which could endanger its project of a multinational Spain (*España plural*) while giving the Popular Party additional ammunition to grumble over the 'disintegration of Spain'.[12] The Basque nationalists had little option but to enjoy a short period of tranquility as, for a few months, the media's attention and TV airtime did not concentrate on Basque politics but on the newly discovered Catalan bête noire. Second, because the approval of a much improved statute was to become a positive example of what consensual politics could achieve. The Catalan charter was received much more cordially than the Basque plan for an 'associated free state' with the rest of Spain, which was rejected as soon as it was presented to the national parliament in early 2005. This paradigmatic case was very important if ETA was ever to give up its arms and have its political wing negotiate political issues. The government gave a clear indication to the whole spectrum of Basque political elites that through political negotiation much was possible but that, under the shadow of violence, very little could be achieved.

7.3 THE 2006 BASQUE PEACE PROCESS

During the Basque elections of April 2005, the Socialist Party of Euskadi (PSE) benefited from the 'ZP effect'. During the campaign, the Prime Minister argued that political change was possible and that he was personally committed to ending violence. Along the same lines, the government was adamant that ETA had to lay down its arms and, in return, the executive would be prepared to reform the Basque country's autonomy statute provided the changes were approved by ample majorities in the Basque and Spanish parliaments. By May 2005, Zapatero argued that ETA had been weakened by numerous arrests and had not killed since May 2003, making it a good moment to work towards peace.[13] Politically speaking, the moment was appropriate for a PSOE that was willing to resolve the Basque problem once and for all. The Socialists were in a unique position as they controlled the government in Madrid and their regional branches had advanced greatly in the Basque Country (2005) and had ousted the conservative parties in Catalonia (2003) and Galicia (2005). In terms of public opinion, almost two-thirds of Spaniards were in favour of negotiating with

ETA. Besides, Zapatero felt he needed to respond positively to a series of letters and overtures for peace made from the radical camp. One of these calls took the form of a leaked letter from ETA's former leader Francisco Múgica (Pakito) and other imprisoned veterans addressed to the leadership of the armed group in August 2004. The authors analysed the poor results of the violent strategy, complained about the grim prospects for ETA prisoners, and suggested pursuing the 'institutional fight of the masses'. Three months after Pakito's letter was leaked, on 14 November 2004, Batasuna proposed to solve the 'Basque conflict' by 'political and democratic means'. At a rally in the San Sebastián Anoeta velodrome, the leader of the banned political party, Arnaldo Otegi, who had referred to PM Zapatero as the 'Spanish Tony Blair', suggested that Batasuna could participate in a political negotiation in order to reform the Basque statute of autonomy.[14] The suggested roadmap asked the Spanish government to initiate negotiations with ETA to discuss the cessation of hostilities and the issue of prisoners and indicated that Batasuna would join a working commission in the Basque parliament to find a political solution to the conflict.

On May 2005, the Spanish Congress of Deputies voted in favour of allowing the government to hold talks with ETA if it first abandoned its arms and renounced violence. This was the first time a government had sought and received approval to start a dialogue with ETA and the initiative was fiercely opposed by associations representing victims, notably the Asociación de Victimas del Terrorismo (AVT), but also by the opposition party, the Popular Party, which accused Zapatero of 'betraying the dead' and 'surrendering parliament'. Between July 2005 and February 2006, delegations from the Spanish government and ETA held three discreet meetings in Geneva and Oslo to facilitate a scenario where peace negotiations could be fruitful. The government's delegation was led by Jesús Eguiguren whereas ETA's chief negotiator was Josu Urrutikoetxea (Ternera), a former ETA leader and Batasuna MP. These contacts were kept secret by a Socialist government that was not willing to make public their efforts until the issue of the Catalan statute of autonomy was resolved. The turning point for the debate on the Catalan charter was a meeting on 21 January 2006 between PM Zapatero and the leader of the Catalan nationalists, Artur Mas, when an agreement on the funding system was reached. The key support of Convergència i Unió (CiU) paved the way for the parliamentary approval of the legal reform and secured a victory for the 'yes' camp in the Catalan referendum of 18 June 2006. As both public and media interest in the Catalan statute waned, events in the Basque Country unfolded rapidly and the Northern provinces became, once again, the focus of much reporting and speculation. In February 2006, rumours of a third contact between the government and ETA at the Geneva-based Centre for Humanitarian Dialogue intensified and the print media reminded its readers that ETA had not killed anyone for over 1,000 days.

Illustration 4 ETA announces a 'permanent ceasefire', 22 March 2006

On 22 March 2006 ETA released a statement in which it unilaterally declared a 'permanent cease-fire'. The communiqué proclaimed that ETA wanted to end the conflict and 'promote a democratic process in the Basque Country' in which Basque 'rights were recognised.' ETA's statement, which was read out by a woman in a mask wearing a black Basque beret did not explicitly speak of the right of self-determination. PM Zapatero welcomed the communiqué and argued that the end of violence would require a 'long, tough and difficult' process. At the beginning of the summer, in June 2006, the government officially announced that it would begin talks with ETA. In spite of the adequate conditions, the PSOE government was forced to go it alone because the opposition leader, Mariano Rajoy, argued the PP would not be prepared to back the peace initiative as no 'political price' should be paid for defeating terrorism. The two parties, which had been bitterly opposed on almost every issue since the 2004 general elections, were also divided on how to bring to an end the forty-year campaign of violence. The attitude of the conservative opposition contrasted with the role played by the PSOE during the 1998–1999 peace process when it supported Aznar's difficult decision to move ETA prisoners closer to the Basque lands.

The newly appointed Interior Minister, Alfredo Pérez Rubalcaba, who oversaw the talks with ETA, confirmed that negotiations with the radical nationalists would take place on two levels. On the one hand, the government would negotiate directly with ETA an exchange of 'peace' for 'prisoners'. At the time of the cease-fire, there were 544 ETA members in Spanish jails (163 in French ones) and there was hope that these would benefit from a change in penal policy. The prisoner's organisation Askatasuna hoped that ETA inmates could benefit from the end of the 'dispersion policy', early release, or some form of amnesty. On the other hand, there would be negotiations in an all-party roundtable (*mesa de partidos*) which would be able to discuss political questions. In order for Batasuna to regain its status as a political party and be present at the *mesa de partidos*, its leaders had to condemn ETA's violence or present new statutes in accordance with the Law of Political Parties.

The pressure mounted on ETA's political wing to follow the path of legalisation, and its leadership complained that the expectations on the *abertzale* left were too high. Batasuna first wanted reassurance that the judicial pressure on them would be completely lifted if they rejected violence. Its leaders also wanted the Zapatero government to provide some trust-building concession such as the gradual concentration of ETA inmates, the release of prisoners with health issues, or the abolition of the Law of Political Parties. Publicly, the government was adamant that no concessions would be made until the leaders of the banned party put some distance between themselves and ETA. By September 2006, the all-party roundtable had not been constituted and there was a widespread feeling of crisis on the political front. The government and ETA met another twice in Geneva (October) and then in Ankara (December) before the cease-fire was unexpectedly broken.

On 30 December 2006 ETA exploded a van loaded with over 200 kilograms of explosives in the four-storey car-park of Madrid's Barajas international airport. The huge bomb destroyed much of section D of the parking lot of the airport's newly built Terminal 4. It was estimated that the cost of reconstruction of the car park would be €30 million, with another €5 million spent on compensating the owners of the 1,500 cars damaged in the blast. An anonymous person claiming to represent ETA made three warning calls of the forthcoming explosion and the police were able to evacuate the terminal. However, two Ecuadoran citizens who were sleeping in their cars (Carlos Alonso Palate and Diego Armando Estacio) were killed, and twenty-six people were injured. It took five days for the rescue services to reach the two buried bodies among the 40,000 tons of rubble of what came to be known as 'ground zero'. The deaths of the two Ecuadoran men were the first fatalities caused by ETA in three and a half years (Figure 7.2).[15]

The PP argued that the ETA cease-fire had not been genuine and that the cessation of violence had never been completely verified. During the nine months and eight days of the cease-fire, the Ministry of the Interior recorded over a hundred acts of street violence (*kale borroka*) in support

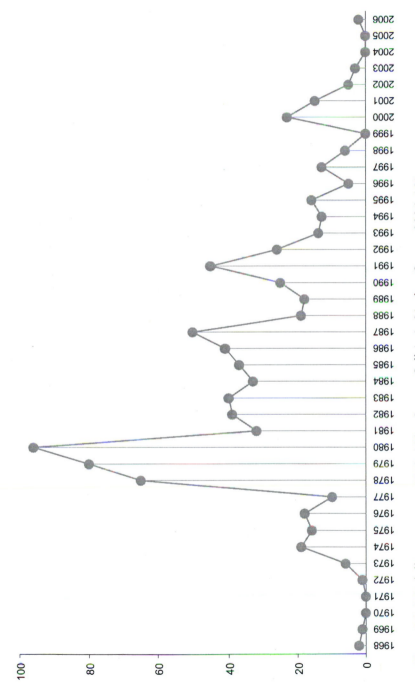

Figure 7.2 ETA killings per year, 1968–2006. *Source:* Calleja & Sánchez-Cuenca 2006: 151.

of ETA's cause which included threats against Basque non-nationalists and arson attacks against shops, banks, and public buses as had happened in 1998–1999 (Mees 2003: 87; Mansvelt Beck 2005: 223). There was not a single killing by ETA but the insurgents continued to send extortion letters to Basque businessmen claiming 'revolutionary tax' payments. They also engaged in car theft (as many as sixty in France during 2006) and arms; the most serious offence took place on 24 October, when an alleged ETA commando stole 300 revolvers and fifty pistols from a factory in Vauvert, France.

Zapatero's confidence about the prospects of peace talks proved to be misplaced and many accused the national-security agencies of negligence for the inadequate information the Prime Minister was receiving. As late as 23 December, the director-general of the national police and the civil guard, Joan Mesquida, argued that he had no intelligence pointing at a possible ETA rearmament or immediate preparation to launch attacks. Zapatero further embarrassed himself one day before the blast when he told the press that the peace process would be in a much better state in a year's time. To be fair to the PM, it was the first time that ETA had broken a truce without previously releasing a statement (as it did on 28 November 1999). The breakdown of the cease-fire was precipitated by frustration in the radical movement at the lack of political progress since the truce started. This last hypothesis was supported by ETA's closest political ally, Batasuna, who argued that that the Spanish executive had not made any gestures to reward ETA for its 1,310 days without fatal actions. An increasingly ostracised ETA felt the need to respond to the government's refusal to end the dispersion policy, halt the arrests and trials of radical members and sympathisers, and release on compassionate grounds the ETA convict Iñaki de Juana Chaos who had commenced a hunger strike a month earlier.[16] ETA finally claimed responsibility for the attack on 9 January 2007 in a letter to Gara and insisted that the March 2006 cease-fire was still in place despite the bombing. The communiqué argued that the objective of the attack was not to cause victims and blamed the government for the two dead and for the slow progress of the peace process.

Some scholars argued that ETA was sending a signal to the government to speed up the peace process and compared the bombing of Barajas airport to the IRA bombing of Canary Wharf in February 1996 which ended a seventeen-month cease-fire. On that occasion, the Sinn Féin leader Gerry Adams spoke of the need to continue the peace process, and John Major's government decided to break off the negotiations with the Irish republicans while maintaining a line of communication—a decision that benefited Tony Blair when the Labour Party won the May 1997 general election by a landslide. The Irish republican group's second cease-fire in July 1997 was followed by the Good Friday Agreement of April 1998. ETA sympathisers had often compared their 'national struggle' to that of the IRA, and looked to this sequence of events for a measure of guidance and inspiration.

Gerry Adams was a regular visitor to the Basque region, and in 2006, the Catholic priest Alec Reid—who had played a crucial mediating role in the Northern Ireland process—was also in evidence there. However, it was not clear that Arnaldo Otegi had the influence over its military wing that Gerry Adams or Martin McGuinness had over the Provisional IRA.

The Basque insurgents called off their cease-fire because of their dissatisfaction with the state of negotiations and miscalculated the tight constraints under which an elected government operates. In pluralist democracies, national executives have little opportunity to exercise their discretion in matters related to national security. The PSOE government felt under siege by some key victims' associations and the conservative opposition and Zapatero was forced to apologise in parliament for the 'clear mistake' of being too optimistic about the peace process. The airport attack left the Socialists little option but to halt the strategy of negotiating with a group that had evidently refused to give up its violent struggle.

7.4 CONCLUSION

The chapter traced the decline of ETA and the social movement it has led through Batasuna. By late 2006, the MLNV network had lost its public presence little by little as its income sources were endangered and many of its organisations were banned. Among those with open cases in Spanish courts there were the leaders of Batasuna who risked imprisonment. On top of the judicial initiatives, the police had been successful in arresting a considerable number of ETA members. Although it remained technically capable of killing, ETA's support dwindled as its activities were increasingly compared to the universal jihad of Al Qaeda. In the aftermath of September 11 and March 11, public perceptions of political violence and terrorism were transformed. The Madrid blasts were perpetrated by a home-grown cell of Islamic militants exactly 911 days after September 11, 2001 and came to be known as 11M. The Al Qaeda inspired cell had no links to ETA but their attack created an adverse atmosphere for the radicals' demands which entered a terminal phase. With the intrusion of Al Qaeda's superterrorism, ETA's ethno-territorial claims and low intensity warfare seemed more anachronistic than ever before.

There can be no doubt that peace processes are a long series of actions of extreme complexity. People representing rival parties need to build mechanisms of trust, which can be easily wrecked. Quite often, insurgent groups or governments do not agree on the methodology that would allow them to launch peace negotiations and, even when it has agreed, the established method might not be followed along the way leading one of the parts to break off negotiations. After the cease-fire of 1998, the government met the Basque paramilitaries only once due to their insistence on having a say about 'political issues'. In 2006, it was decided that the two dimensions of the Basque conflict would be tackled by different actors in two different settings (government-ETA negotiations and an all-party roundtable). Still, ETA's determination to discuss political matters and its frustration with the slow pace of negotiations during the nine-month process led the armed group to explode a van-bomb at Madrid's international airport on 30 December 2006.

The crux of the Basque problem seems to be the refusal of radical nationalists to abandon their violent subculture and embrace democratic institutions, which they see as a block to the realisation of their aspirations. Their core strategy is to bypass what they consider to be snail-like and ineffective bodies and continue to mobilise an increasingly divided movement on fronts beyond the political one. Even so, the Irish example shows that future negotiations between the Spanish authorities and ETA will only be successful if political elites have the courage to recognise that the measures that led to the weakness of the armed group might not lead automatically to its final disappearance. Leaders of all political parties will need to behave responsibly and move outside their comfort zones in order to balance their electoral concerns, agendas, and priorities with the inclusive measures needed to facilitate successful negotiations with the anti-system movement.

Conclusion

The emergence of nationalism in Europe is inextricably linked to revolutionary upheavals, inter-state wars, and organised violence. Some of the modern processes that helped spread the idea of nationalism include the emergence of 'mass armies', the formation of the territorial state, the extension of citizenship rights, and the uneven development of industrial capitalism (Giddens 1985; Mann 1986). However, it was the experience of modern warfare that turned the masses into increasingly literate soldiers who willingly sacrificed for their nations. Since the Napoleonic wars large citizen armies began replacing mercenary troops and warfare affected people from all social backgrounds. The nationalisation of the masses and the perception of the nation as a community of sacrifice intensified as the century progressed and culminated in the total wars of the twentieth century (Mosse 1975, 1990). Whereas the consequences of state mobilisation have been examined by a variety of scholars, the relationship between nationalism and violent outbursts by non-state actors still remains a complex and elusive one. Identifying the conditions or precipitants of violence in different historical and societal contexts is sometimes possible but creating a scientific, universal theory is unfeasible. Social reality is intricate and there is no single theory that can predict the unfolding of nationalist violence in a rich variety of historical sequences.

The wide diversity of theories that offer prevailing explanations on the emergence of politically motivated violence can be classified into two broad groups. On the one hand, there are a large number of theories that focus on structural factors to explain the emergence of violence. The most likely scenario in which violence emerges is a disadvantageous economic system or rigid political institutions in which moderate demands cannot be articulated (Hechter 1975, 1995, 2000). The lack of political liberties and opportunities for non-violent political participation generates frustration and discontent, which become necessary, but not sufficient, conditions for the emergence of social support for nationalist motivated violence. The development of discontent is the first step in the causal sequence leading to political violence, the second being the politicisation of that discontent, and the third one the instrumentalisation against other actors (Gurr

1970; Schwartz 1972). Other theories refuse to accept that violence can be mechanically determined by given social structures and prefer to focus on human beings as self-interested agents who interact with other individuals and groups (Bandura 1972). In order to understand human action (instead of human designs) it is necessary to study the relational setting in which agents take decisions but also the political, social, and moral concepts that form their ideology (Crenshaw 1990). Since not all discontented individuals are revolutionaries, it becomes necessary to study their system of beliefs and how ideology determines the selection of goals and the repertoire of actions available to pursue such objectives. In short, the first set of theories emphasises the importance of 'structure' whereas the second set prefers to focus on 'agency' as the prime factor of their all-encompassing explanation.

At first sight, structural approaches seem to be better suited to explain the Basque conflict. The political circumstances in which ETA emerged, the Franco dictatorship, seem to support the cause–effect approach defended by theories of social discontent. In conditions that precluded moderate political participation and the ascendancy of nationalists to any form of government, the strategic use of violence became a 'voice' strategy used by a handful of Basques (Hirschman 1970). It could be argued that, between 1939 and 1975, 'structural violence' created a legitimate cause for frustration and discontent which explains why the early ETA had the support of a wide majority of Basques and anti-Francoist opposition forces (Galtung 1969). There can be no doubt that the absence of open access to the political arena, lack of freedom, and relentless persecution of cultures other than those that were Castilian-centred, provided a fertile ground for the emergence of antagonistic ethnic identities and an armed group. From this pluralist perspective, it could be argued that political violence was an indicator of a larger conflict or measure of grievance which reflected in however distorted form, the beliefs and aspirations of a larger social group (Gurr 1990: 86). Similarly, Charles Tilly has argued that violence can be 'one of the best signs we have [to know] what is going on in a country's political life' (Tilly 1972: 342). After the death of the dictator, the political conditions that created the grievances (and ignored them) gradually disappeared in favour of a full-fledged democracy. Yet, radical nationalists continued to galvanise significant support for their violent efforts to shape political behaviour. With the transition to democracy (1975–1978), Basque political violence could not solely be explained by resorting to economic inequality, political grievances, or dysfunctional structures of some kind (Laitin 1995). The resilience of ETA, the resonance of its separatist message, and the considerable support it enjoyed after the restoration of democracy could only be explained by incorporating an account of the historical goals and ideals of radical Basque nationalists (Irvin 1999: 25).

The limitations of structural theories and models require the examination of the peaceful mechanisms that precede acts of violence. The most important factor in determining the sequence of events and decisions that led to the insurgency was radical Basque nationalism, a social movement led by ETA which aims to establish an independent socialist state for the Basque homeland, separate from Spain and France. This radical trend has its origins in the nineteenth century when it was articulated within the PNV. Radical Basque nationalism stood for different things during its history and evolved from being an ethnicist, to a separatist, and, finally, violent movement. Radical nationalism was a marginal force until the 1960s when the violent actions of ETA became the symbolic voice of all anti-Francoist Basques. The ideological roots of the movement are found in the figure of Sabino Arana who first outlined an ethnic and secessionist programme for the Basque nation. From the moment of his death, in 1903, the PNV began to oscillate in a patriotic pendulum between moderate and radical positions and still does so today (Pablo, Mees, & Rodríguez 1999, 2001). The next generation of radicals, the *aberrianos*, re-elaborated Arana's doctrine and began to introduce novel elements like socialism. The idea of violence as a legitimate means was considered by radical nationalists in the 1920s and 1930s, but it was only firmly established with the birth of ETA. At the organisational level, there is no continuity between the different groups but the members of ETA took note of the successes and weaknesses of the more intransigent elements of the PNV, the *aberrianos*, and the 1930s Acción Nacionalista Vasca (ANV). These examples of radicalism stood as important precedents in the cultural void of Francoism. The existence of a radical lineage of patriots that preceded ETA by at least sixty years facilitated the task of creating a vigorous alternative to the alleged passivity of the PNV. With these origins in mind, a new nationalist ideology which incorporated socialism and revolutionary violence was not built from scratch but with the bricks of a long-standing radical tradition. This connection to the past was one of the factors that explained the resilience and resonance of ETA's political message during both dictatorship and democracy. Another factor was the ability of radical nationalists to appropriate and use the defining features of the Basque *ethnie*, their self-portrayal as members of a defensive Basque army, and their ability to persuade people to join and act in its name.

The first references to a Basque ethnic consciousness were found in the pre-modern writings of Martínez Zaldivia, Garibay, Poza, and Larramendi. These authors elaborated an 'ethnohistory' which connected Basques to Tubal, Noah's grandson, and idealised the *fueros* as symbols of political autonomy while emphasising Basque race superiority, universal nobility, and a special covenant with God (Smith 2003: 169). This collection of myths and memories transmitted a belief in a common ancestry and a shared historical past and created the cultural reservoir of the Golden Age. The age of gold constituted, together with Carlism and foralism, one of the building blocks of Basque nationalism, a Catholic, ethnicist, separatist, and profoundly anti-Spanish movement born in Biscay at the end of the nineteenth century. The birthplace of Basque nationalism was Bilbao, a city which doubled its size in less than two decades as a result of rapid industrialisation driven by the mining, iron, and steel industries. For the most part, the newly arrived immigrants were poor and were seen by Arana as a disease that could contaminate the Basques' traditional customs, race, and unique language. The influx of immigrants, which he saw as a 'Spanish invasion', together with the Carlist defeat and the abolition of the *fueros* in 1876 ended the traditional world Arana remembered. His nationalism was an act of protest against the alleged Spanish historical affronts and the rapid disappearance of the Basque rural Arcadia. The rank and file of the PNV initially came from Carlists, foralist, and urban lower middle classes who yearned for a paradise lost but, from 1898 onwards, some tradesmen, bureaucrats, and even sectors of the upper bourgeoisie who had successfully adapted to the industrial world joined the party. Led by the shipping magnate Ramón de la Sota, they were not inspired by millenarian projects of building a nationalist heaven on earth and preferred to set up the necessary political structures for the Basque Country to develop economically. During the first half of the twentieth century, the two PNV factions maintained their ideological corpus—radical fundamentalism and moderate autonomy—and fought for control of a party that was gradually becoming hegemonic in the Basque Country. The Franco dictatorship interrupted the expansion of the PNV and radical youths took control of nation-building with the creation of an armed group called ETA. In spite of its socialist rhetoric, ETA politicised ethnic ties and sentiments and incorporated them into its nationalism. The point was that ETA based its message on ethnicity to forge emotional bonds through myths and symbols and, in return, secured the loyal participation of the members of the ethnic group. They referred to a primeval dividing boundary between Basques and Spaniards, although many of its members did not speak Euskara and did not have Basque parents. As a result of the process of economic modernisation in the 1960s, the Basque social structure changed dramatically with the arrival of immigrants and ETA was forced to redefine its appeals to ethnicity as members of the group met outsiders in a continuous sequence of collective self-definition.

Under normal circumstances, groups decide to cooperate for a combination of shared interests and loyalty to social norms. However, in the heat of the battle, it is emotion (rather than instrumental well-being) that explains why people sacrifice for their nations. To understand people's willingness to risk their own lives, one needs to examine the emotional bonds that tie together a community and how these sentiments overcome other group identities such as gender or class (Stern 1995). According to Max Weber, members of an ethnic group 'entertain a subjective belief in their common descent because of similarities of physical type or of customs or both, or because of memories of colonisation and migration' (Weber 1978: 385–398). The group's certainty about its common origins might not be historically verifiable but this should not be a problem as long as the shared heritage is perceived by the designated members of the group to be a truthful representation of social reality. Radical nationalists have often appealed to a sense of kinship, group solidarity, and common culture to elicit loyalty and mobilise resources for violent collective action against the Spanish and the French. Appeals for a glorious Basque past have convinced many young Basques of their moral obligation to help other members of the group by contributing to the national effort. Some authors have argued that Basque nationalism's propensity to use ethnicity rather than culture as a mobilising factor is due to the weakness of Basque language and culture (Conversi 1996). However, since the late 1970s, belonging to the radical community has not depended on genes, blood types, or surnames but on ritual participation in the national struggle. As Jeremy MacClancy has correctly pointed out, membership of the groups is not a status 'defined by birth but by performance: an abertzale is one who actively participates in the political struggle for an independent Basque nation with its own distinctive culture' (MacClancy 1997: 114). Hence, a Basque patriot is someone who actively participates in one of the member organisations of the Basque Movement for National Liberation (MLNV), a self-named network of organisations founded in 1974. This complex grouping is also known as the 'patriotic left' (*izquierda abertzale*) and it is made up of a number of interconnected political organisations, social agents, and NGOs with interests in the fields of feminism, environmentalism, internationalism, Basque culture, youth, students and prisoner's rights. The most important members are the trade union Langile Abertzaleen Batzordeak (LAB), the political party Batasuna (previously called Euskal Herritarrok and Herri Batasuna), and the violent organisation Euskadi Ta Askatasuna (ETA), the undisputed leader of the movement.

The survival of ethnic and national ties depends on the continuous reproduction and reinterpretation of myths, symbols, memories, and traditions. The functional importance of these cultural attributes is to convey norms, values, and a sense of solidarity to new generations. Among the devices used by nationalists to foster the development of emotional ties one can count emblems, flags, anthems, ceremonies of remembrance, and so on. State nationalists have more resources at their disposal and, on top of those already mentioned, they are able to provide 'hard evidence' for their shared heritage in the form of public festivals, national holidays, parades, museums, monuments, etc. In the Basque Country, the Golden Age became a key cultural resource to mark ethnic boundaries and define collective identity (Aranzadi 1979, 1994, 2000). A mixture of history and legend, the golden past does not have a fixed essence or meaning and it is best described as a constantly evolving myth (or even memory). In this distant episode of history, nationalists tend to find the distinct characteristics that helped made the nation great still intact. As it is the case with other nationalisms, the lost past soon becomes a self-evident example of virtue and great prosperity. This national splendour may take different forms; from literary merit, economic prosperity or religious asceticism, to military victories and political achievements. For nationalists, the political cult of the utopian age serves a clear canonical purpose: to inspire the co-nationals and impel them to regain the ancient days of national glory. Acting as a guiding light, the functional importance of the Golden Age is to cyclically 'awaken' the dormant masses to emulate the achievements of their ancestral nation in a project of national renewal (Smith 1997, 2003).

David Lowenthal (1985) once argued that no one would yearn for a past if it merely replicated the present. The need to emulate the past, and the kind of community it represented, often emerges in a historical period where there is a perceived sense of decline and need for retribution. The contrast between an 'invented tradition' of a healthy and happy world and the bewildering present gives rise to a sentimental yearning for fixed reference points. Although nostalgia, together with melancholy, is usually associated with images of passivity and depression, this image could not be more misguiding to describe nationalist movements that regularly resort to nostalgic images of the past as a mobilising factor. Furthermore, the kind of mobilisation that results is not an act of protest reacting to specific grievances, such as the bread riots of the French Revolution, but one preoccupied with national destiny. An issue for further research would be to conceptualise how, when, and why this nostalgia for the past embeds itself in individuals and groups as it does and how it is later mobilised into actions. In the Basque case, Arana relied on nostalgia for the *fueros* to develop his nationalist movement and ideology. Radical nationalists, on the other hand, have yearned for a lost time when Basques were a 'nation in arms' against the fighting invader: from the times of Charlemagne through the Carlist Wars, the Spanish Civil War, Francoism, and finally, during democratic times (Muro 2005).

Ethnicity and violence are intricately entwined in the historical formation of radical Basque nationalism. The effect of violence on the maintenance and reproduction of identity politics has been thoroughly studied by anthropologists, psychologists, sociologists, and political scientists. In a nutshell, violent conflicts are emotional bonding experiences that create socio-psychological borders between groups, delineate sharp contrasts between 'us' and 'them', and reinforce the cohesion of the community by eliminating internal dissent. A wartime social environment usually formulates a stereotyped perception of the 'self' and the 'other', which is just as decisive for the embedding of collective sentiments in individuals and groups as processes of identification, socialisation, and nationalist mobilisation. In the long run, violent confrontation increases group cohesion and creates committed activists with a deeper sense of duty. The conflict environment creates a sense of camaraderie, joint effort, and group loyalty that unites the national community in its darkest hour. Personal sacrifice inspires a sense of belonging in the members of the nation who willingly take up arms to reproduce an intoxicating cycle of violence. Indeed, once the spiral of violence has started there are great obstacles for the membership of any organisation to reconsider the use of violence. Police actions, judicial initiatives, or the issue of GAL have been perceived by radical nationalists as yet another sign of Spanish oppression. With such a cycle in motion, abandoning selective violence would be seen as a betrayal of the sacrifice of friends, colleagues, and relatives because violence is a self-reproducing phenomenon and an agent in itself. Although this may seem a self-defeating argument or, at best, a tautology, most scholars of Basque violence agree that, once set in motion, insurgent violence was no longer controlled by those who initiated it. Violence seems to take on a life of its own, and in order to explain the use of violence, it becomes necessary to refer to a previous history of violence (Clark 1984: 278; Mees 2003: 28).

To recapitulate, the reproduction of the Basque conflict depends on the continuing strength of radical Basque nationalism, the self-referential history of violence (both real and symbolic) and the recourse to ethnicity as a mobilising factor (such as the Golden Age). The mechanisms by which particular myths and symbols are remembered are essential in explaining why a particular message is effective. It is important to point out that nationalist elites cannot establish meaningful symbolic universes on their own. If it is to be successful, a 'top-down' initiative to create a nationalist ideological project needs to be matched by a 'bottom-up' legitimating process. In other words, a successful nation's narrative, to borrow Bhaba's phrase, needs to allow for the personal desires, projects, and aspirations of the individual to be read and understood into a wider communal discourse. When there is a continuous disagreement between the individual and the collective, the national message fails to be effective and needs to be revisited or abandoned. At the moment, the radical nationalist message continues to outlive individual participants in history and mechanically influences the way new generations look at their past and act in the present. The current cycle of ETA violence is seen by radical nationalists as the latest stage in a long conflict between Basques and Spaniards. This understanding of history and the need to glorify past sacrifices makes the use of political violence a tactic, strategic and a moral need. From the point of view of a radical nationalist there is a lineage of *gudaris* that have always fought the invader for centuries. Paraphrasing Renan, one could argue that radical Basque nationalism will continue to base its claims to statehood on the possession of a rich legacy of ethnic memories, a common desire to live together, and the will to preserve the unity of the Basque heritage by all means necessary.

In recent years, a combination of factors contributed to diminish considerably the threat of ETA. Once considered a sophisticated and dangerous violent organisation—presenting a major threat to politicians, journalists, judges, and other public figures through its campaign of urban violence, extortion, kidnapping, and assassinations—ETA was severely weakened by concerted counter-terrorist actions by French and Spanish authorities. In the aftermath of the Al Qaeda attacks of 11 September 2001 and 11 March 2004, there was also a growing consensus that indiscriminate violence or terrorism was becoming anachronistic in resolving an essentially territorial dispute. Since the mid-1990s, Basque public opinion has become more vocal in rejecting ETA and the organisational universe that surrounded it, arguing that the 'socialisation of pain' had been counterproductive. With little room to manoeuvre and in a political and security environment increasingly conducive to resolving the Basque region's grievances through political channels, ETA released a statement on 22 March 2006 in which it unilaterally declared a permanent cease-fire which lasted nine months. With the bombing of Madrid's international airport of Barajas on 30 December 2006, ETA killed two people, wrecked the hopes of many citizens, and shattered a nascent peace process. The cease-fire announcement came ten months after the lower chamber of the Spanish parliament authorised the government to launch a process of dialogue if ETA abandoned violence. Whether these political initiatives triggered a sequence of events that will eventually lead to a peaceful multiparty settlement remains to be seen.

If political violence is ultimately abandoned in favor of democratic political methods, a lengthy and complex peace process can be expected. The two-level nature of the Basque conflict brings into confrontation on the one hand, the state and ETA and, on the other, the non-nationalist and nationalist social and political sectors, and proposals for the de-escalation of the conflict are also likely to come in a two-level form. First, agreeing on a multi-party political settlement that satisfies both the Basque population and its political representatives while observing the legal status quo is likely to prove a challenge. Finding a permanent accommodation for Basque ethno-nationalist aspirations in the current State of Autonomies has traditionally proven a thorny issue. Renewed demands for increasing the level of self-government beyond autonomy will tighten even further an already stressed centre-periphery cleavage and will bring deep-rooted divisions to the surface. Second, the opposition between ETA and the state is likely to be resolved in the form of discussions about decommissioning of weapons, the release of convicted ETA members, and the end of the Spanish government's dispersion of prisoners policy. Mutual distrust and lack of confidence have traditionally characterised these 'technical' negotiations which could benefit from the presence of skilled intermediaries. Finally, the social wounds the conflict has created will take much longer to heal. As the South African and Irish processes have shown, a wider reconciliation process may have to include the establishment of commissions of truth, demands that all the perpetrators of violence acknowledge the suffering they have caused, establishing the condition of 'victim', reaching a collective memory of the recent past, and establishing joint ceremonies of commemoration. In the aftermath of nationalist violence, these will be some of the hardest conundrums to solve.

Notes

INTRODUCTION

1. According to Francisco J. Llera Ramo. there are a series of indicators and dimensions that justify defining the Basque party system as 'polarised pluralism': 'a mean of seven principal parties, two majority parties that do not reach 49 per cent of the valid vote, a parliamentary fractionalisation index of 0.81 per cent, important ideological tensions and an anti-system party (HB) with more than 15 per cent of the votes' (Llera 1993: 11; Linz 1986: 317; Gunther, Sani, and Shabad 1986: 312).
2. I follow Julio Aróstegui in describing political violence as 'all actions perpetrated by an individual or collective actors, which are not predicted by rules and aim to control the functioning of any political system or precipitate decisions within that system' (Aróstegui 1994: 44).
3. Theories of violence seem to be in agreement on the 'rationality' of violence (however misguided that can be) but there is little agreement on the causes of violence (Azzi 1998; Hardin 1995; Stern 1995). For a comprehensive discussion of rational actions see the work of Michael Allingham. Each of the volumes of his Rational Choice Theory is dedicated to a different combination of opportunities and preferences: (1) pure choice; (2) choice under uncertainty; (3) strategic choice; (4) social choice; and (5) bounded rationality (Allingham 2006).
4. A major challenge to his view, however, was provided by the publication in 1965 of Mancur Olson's The Logic of Collective Action. In the first pages of this political science classic, Olson argued that

   'it is not in fact true that the idea that groups will act in their self-interest follows logically from the premise of rational and self-interested behavior. It does not follow, because all the individuals in a group would gain if they achieved their group objective, even if they were all rational and self-interested. Indeed unless the number of individuals in a group is quite small, or unless there is coercion or some other special device to make individuals act in their common interest, rational, self-interested individuals will not act to achieve their common or group interest' (Olson 1965: 2).

5. José Manuel Pagoaga (Peixoto) cited in Unzueta (1988: 74).
6. *El Libro Blanco*, in *Documentos Y* (1979–1981: 240).
7. See Amigo (1978), Bruni (1987), Clark (1983, 1984, 1987a, 1990a, 1990b), Domínguez (1998, 2000, 2002), Elorza et al. (2000), Garmendia (1996), Giacopucci (1992), Ibarra (1989), Jáuregui (1981, 2000), Laurenzano (2000),

Letamendia (1994), Rincón (1985), Sanchez-Cuenca (2001), and Sullivan (1988).
8. Other definitions of the patriotic left or MLNV can be found in Mata (1993: 105), Sáez (2002: 30), Casquete (2003: 20) and Ibarra (2005: 167–168).

CHAPTER 1

1. The ethno-symbolist school of nationalism is mostly concerned with the role of ethnic pasts in shaping modern nations. This interest can be seen in the work of Anthony D. Smith (1986) and John Armstrong (1982) for whom the 'core' of ethnicity is constituted by a complex of 'myths, memories, values and symbols' (or 'myth-symbol complex'). This 'core' appears in early times, usually before the nation emerges, and plays a vital role in unifying populations and inspiring collective action. Armstrong considers a range of factors, such as nostalgia for past lifestyles, religious civilisations and organisations, imperial mythomoteurs, and language fissures, in creating shifting ethnic identities. Smith examines some of the causes of ethno-genesis, distinguishes between 'horizontal' (aristocratic) and 'vertical' (demotic) ethnies, and traces the patterns by which they give rise to modern nations. He also emphasises the cultural content of myths, memories, and symbols, notably myths of origin and ethnic election, and memories of the golden age.
2. Alternative explanations for the 'decline' of Spain include that of Spain's lack of natural resources (Braudel 1993), the financial exhaustion of Castile (Domínguez Ortiz 1971), or the fact that 'Spain never rose' (Kamen 1978).
3. An analysis of the role of the Spanish *arbitristas* (proposers of *arbítrios* or expedients) is provided by Henry Kamen in his book *The Later Seventeenth Century, 1665–1700* (1980: 68–70).
4. The authors who elaborated the Basque Golden Age had many sources that proved the long ethnic history of the Basques. The earliest evidence about Basques living in Northern Spain and Southern France comes from the records of several classical historians and geographers such as Livy, Pomponius Mela, Strabo, Ptolemy, and Pliny. According to all of them, the Basque territories, or *saltus Vasconum*, were occupied by different peoples. From the eighth century onwards, the largest ethnic group, the Vascons, constituted a focus of resistance against the Muslims and Charlemagne's Franks who were defeated at Roncesvalles in 788. The first 'Basque' political organisation was the Kingdom of Navarre, which was formed during the ninth century. Navarre had its maximum splendour under Sancho III the Great (992–1035). Then began a decline of his dynasty which ended with Sancho VII (1234) who left no heir. This provoked the introduction of French dynasties into Navarre. During a war between Spain and France, the Spanish king invaded Navarre and incorporated it into the Crown of Castile in 1512. The following year, the first *fueros* were signed between the Kingdom of Spain and Navarre. The *fueros* were agreements between the two kingdoms by which each would keep its own institutions and laws. See, for example, Julio Caro Baroja's *Los Vascos* (1958).
5. Historically, the idea of the chosen people has had a profound and lasting effect on the Jews, because it imparted a special significance to their relationship with God. This sacred belief implied a covenant between God and the people of Israel whereby the latter were to be faithful to God and obey his commandments, and God in turn was to protect and bless his faithful people. According to Anthony D Smith, 'any backsliding, any infringement

of God's ordinances, incurred divine displeasure and punishment, and the possible loss of elect status. That was indeed, the classical interpretation of the destruction of the temple at the hands of the Babylonians in 586 BC, and then again by the Romans in 70 AD' (Smith 1999: 335).

6. In Monreal (1985: 29). According to Mikel Azurmendi (2000: 39) Esteban de Garibay had read the books of Martínez de Zaldivia, hence the similarities between the two authors. For a detailed analysis of Garibay see Julio Caro Baroja's *Los Vascos y la historia a través de Garibay* (2002).

7. Andrés de Poza had written *De la Antigua Lengua de las Españas* (1587) where he argued that the Basque language was first spoken by Tubal. See Juaristi (1992: 57–58).

8. Juan García first wrote *De Hispaniorum Nobilitate Exemptione* which provoked an official Basque response, *De Nobilitate in Proprietate*, penned by Andres de Poza. In this treatise, Poza dated the pure ascendancy of Basques back to Tubal but also the Battle of Arrigorriaga which is analysed in detail by Jon Juaristi (1994).

9. Gregorio Monreal has pointed out that Andrés de Poza's theory of nobility was faithfully reproduced by other legal experts such as Juan Gutiérrez, Juan de Azebedo, and García de las Landeras Puente (Monreal 1985: 26).

10. Larramendi was trying to emphasise the 'narcissistic minor differences' between Basques and Spaniards. The expression is from Michael Ignatieff who describes nationalism as a movement that emphasises minor differences and transforms them into major differences. [...] Nationalism is a distorting mirror in which believers see their simple ethnic, religious, or territorial attributes transformed into glorious attributes and qualities. Though Freud does not explain exactly how this happens, the systematic overvaluation of the self results in systematic devaluation of strangers and outsiders. In this way narcissistic self-regard depends upon and in turn exacerbates intolerance (Ignatieff 1997: 51–52).

11. This view was not unusual at the time. On the contrary the view that Basques' racial purity was based on the notion of 'universal nobility' was prevalent among eighteenth century Basques (Caro Baroja 1998: 91).

12. The use Larramendi is making of the word 'nation' denotes evolution from the traditional medieval meaning to a more modern one. The word 'natio' comes from Latin, and it was first used in medieval universities to designate the sector of the country from whence the students were coming. Larramendi's use of the word is of a medieval character with modern overtones. He wants to overcome the traditional meaning of natio in the eighteenth century as a territory with unique characteristics, and transform it into an ethnic concept that allows everyone to recognise the immemorial distinct character of the Basques.

CHAPTER 2

1. For example, in the early 1990s two renowned historians, Juan Pablo Fusi and Borja de Riquer, debated their views in the pages of *Historia Social* on this very same issue. A first article, by Fusi, argued that it was the failure of the Spanish nationalist project to incorporate the peripheral nationalist elites that produced the birth and development of nationalism in various regions in Spain (mainly Catalonia, the Basque Country, and Galicia). An opposing view, held by the Catalan historian de Riquer argued that the reason why the Spanish nationalist project did not succeed was that it did not take in

account other pre-existing forms of identity (Fusi 1990; and the response by de Riquer 1990).

2. And yet, Eugene Weber has demonstrated that the majority of the population of France did not become 'Frenchmen' until the First World War after they had been subject to state education (Weber 1979).

3. Ethnies have been defined by A.D. Smith as 'named human populations with shared ancestry myths, histories, and cultures, having an association with a specific territory, and a sense of solidarity' (Smith 1986: 32).

4. The Basque case seems to contradict Marxist approaches to nationalism. Theories of uneven development argue that nationalism is a reaction to the uneven spread of capitalism and tend to associate 'periphery' with 'backwardness'. In the words of Tom Nairn, capitalism 'generates and requires the exploitation of peripheries whose deprived elites have no alternative but to turn to the masses and engage them in the nationalist project' (Nairn 1977: 339). Paradoxically, Basque nationalism was born in one of the most advanced and industrialised regions of Spain.

5. By the 1830s the process of disentailing the Church lands that would gradually strip the Church of its property had begun, creating many problems for the Church and much political resentment. Between 1836 and 1895 some 615,000 properties covering about 10 million hectares, about a quarter of the surface area of Spain, changed hands. The expropriation was originally implemented in order to alter the structure of land ownership and improve the worsening agrarian situation by redistributing the land in a more economically efficient manner, and more importantly, as a way of relieving Spain's chronic debt crisis. However, the policy was extremely unpopular and led to defenders of the Church forming the largest support base for the Carlist movement (Schubert 2003: 60).

6. In 1835, Bilbao was the scene of an event that decided the course of the war. Conscious of its need for liquidity to fund the war, the Carlist side asked international creditors for loans. The latter made one condition: a large city had to be taken. The decision would prove to be disastrous and Bilbao became the grave both of the Carlist forces and of their leader, General Zumalacárregui.

7. Article 1 of the Law of 25 October 1839 on the *fueros* (De Pablo, De la Granja, and Mees 1998: 23).

8. Some scholars consider the Guerra dels Matiners as the Second Carlist War (Clemente 1990; 2000).

9. For a glimpse of the disastrous Carlist siege of Bilbao during the Second Carlist War, see Miguel de Unamuno's historical novel, *Paz en la Guerra*. Unamuno invested ten years in writing this novel where he described the events he had witnessed as a child. The novel aims at describing and assembling the triggers of 'internal history', what he called the 'intrahistory'. Unamuno clearly distinguished between the noisy 'external history' made by renowned citizens and the silent 'intrahistory' made by ordinary people, the real subject of history. Hence, in the preface to the second edition of Paz en la Guerra, Unamuno dedicates his work to the nation and describes the real nature of the book: 'This is not a novel; it is a people' (Unamuno 1999; Extramiana 1983).

10. Jon Juaristi (1987b: 93) uses the term 'historico-legendary literature' and has dated the beginning of this movement to Juan Antonio Moguel's Peru Abarca, written in 1802 (Juaristi 1987a: 69). The book can be seen as a defence of the disappearing rural society in which the author sees the seeds of regeneration for the Basque people. Written as a 'pedagogical dialogue' between a Basque

doctor and a barber, Peru Abarca highlights the urban–rural tension of the time.

11. The glorification of the *fueros* was also made by non-Basques. For example, two years after the abolition of the *fueros*, the Catalan Juan Mañé y Flaquer published a book about his trips to 'Euskal-Herria' and described it as a 'true oasis' inhabited by 'a noble people' and contemplated how an 'exotic rationalism' covered all its territory. Mañé y Flaquer was, of course, talking about the abolition of the *fueros* (Mañé y Flaquer 1878: prologue).

12. See 'Errores catalanistas', in Arana (1980: 405).

13. Bizkai-Buru-Batzar (BBB), which can be translated as Supreme Council of Biscay, was the board that made the executive decisions of the Basque nationalists at that time (although still confined to Biscay). Today's PNV structure has, at the top of the pyramid, the Euskadi-Buru-Batzar (EBB) and is the directive organ of the party. The EBB is made up of the following *burukides*: the president of the PNV, top officials and representatives from all the Basque territories including Navarre and Southern France.

14. The Disastre of 1898 was a second phase of the loss of overseas territories. Between 1810 and 1825 Spain lost thirteen immense territories: Argentina, Chile, Peru, Ecuador, Bolivia, Venezuela, Mexico, Colombia, Central America, Paraguay, Uruguay, Santo Domingo, and Florida. One of the chief causes for the independence movements was the impact of liberal ideas of democracy and self-determination on the Creoles, who had an inferior status in relation to the Peninsulars. In fact all the great leaders of the South American independence movements were of Creole origin. These include Simón Bolívar, José de San Martín, and Agustín de Iturbide.

15. José Ortega y Gasset named the turn of the century artists and writers 'the generation of 1898', a group who responded to *El Desastre* by seeking to analyse the character and essence of a newly diminished Spain and identify the solutions to regain its original greatness. The generation of '98 was divided between the proponents of Europeanisation and *casticismo* (a recovery of traditionally Spanish essences), both of them solutions for Spain to regain its original greatness. The Basque philosopher Miguel de Unamuno believed Spain had to return to the roots of Castile and should not Europeanise itself. Ramón María del Valle Inclán felt that Spain should be more Catholic, the way it used to be, and should therefore not look to the rest of Europe as an example. And Vicente Blasco Ibáñez, a Valencian novelist, felt Spain should become a Republic again (Balfour 1997).

16. Arana's constitutive elements of a nation can be found in his article '¿Qué somos?' published in *Bizkaitarra* (16 June 1895); see Arana (1980: 606). He elaborated on the notion of the Basque race in the following articles: 'Del orígen de la raza euskeriana', 'La pureza de raza', and 'Del orígen de nuestra raza' (Arana 1980: 71; 545; 1340).

17. See, for example, 'Los invasores', 'La invasión maketa', 'Efectos de la invasión', and 'Extranjerización' (Arana 1980: 197,261, 1326, 1761).

18. 'Nuestros moros' in Arana (1980: 196).

19. Ironically, after Arana died in 1903, Nicolasa went against her husband's views and married a Spanish policeman. Arana's quote about the rural origins of Basques has been taken from Elorza (2001: 182).

20. See Conversi (1997: 60) and Douglass (2002: 107).

21. 'Efectos de la invasión' Arana (1980: 1326).

22. 'Errores catalanistas', Arana (1980: 403).

23. 'Errores catalanistas', Arana (1980: 403).

24. The Basque philosopher Miguel de Unamuno argued that agglutinating languages like Basque were not capable of articulating sophisticated ideas. Euskara has a rich vocabulary but a limited number of abstractions. In an agglutinative language like Euskara, argues Mark Kurlansky, new concepts are formed by adding more and more suffices: 'etxea' being the word for house or home is the origin of other words like 'etxean' (at home), 'etxera' (to the house) or 'etxetik' (from home). That is the reason why Basque only has 200,000 words compared to 60 million words compiled in the Oxford English Dictionary (OED) (Kurlansky 1999: 22, 164).

25. See Arana (1980: 1734). Arana wrote two articles where he praised the excellence of the Jesuit organisation: 'Apuntes sobre la Compañía de Jesús' and 'La Fundación de la Compañía' (Arana 1980: 1734–1738; 328–338).

26. Arana (1980: 1328). He also wrote two articles about the idea of regeneration: 'Regeneración' in El Correo Vasco (11 June 1899), 'Camino de la Regeneración' in *El Correo Vasco* (20 June 1899), and 'Degeneración y Regeneración' in *El Correo Vasco* (28 July 1899).

27. '¿Somos Españoles?' *Bizkaitarra* (17 December 1893; Arana 1980: 181).

28. See 'La Historia' in *Baserritarra* (6 June 1897); see Arana (1980: 1295).

CHAPTER 3

1. Nowadays, the Euzkadi Buru Batzar (EBB) also includes a delegate from the Ipar Buru Batzar, the organisation that represents the Pays Basque. See http://www.eaj-pnv.com.

2. It might surprise the reader that the weekly from Gipuzkoa was started in 1907 and preceded by two years the birth of *Bizkaitarra*. However, the Biscayan newspaper had not really been founded in 1909 because it was only a rebranding of *Aberri* (Pablo, Mees, & Rodríguez 1999: 96).

3. In the Basque Country, all political parties own bars which are clearly distinguishable by their names. The PNV has Batzokis, the socialist party PSE has Casas del Pueblo-Herriko Etxeak, the Basque nationalists of EA have Gaztetxes, and the political wing of ETA, Batasuna, has Herriko Tabernas.

4. The quote is from José Antonio Aguirre, Basque *Lehendakari* during the Spanish Civil War. Cited in Elorza (2001: 259).

5. The article was titled 'Grave y trascendental' and was published on the 22 June 1902 in the weekly *La Patria*, official organ of the PNV. The article was followed by a one-year debate in the pages of *La Patria* and other newspapers. See Arana (1980: 2173–2186). For a complete account of the 'evolution' see Corcuera (2001: 585–614), Payne (1975: 79–82), Pablo, Mees, and Rodríguez (1999: 51–57) and Pablo, Mees, and Granja (1998: 51–57).

6. Interview with Arana in *La Gaceta del Norte*. Cited in Jemein y Lambarri (1935: 299).

7. On 2 May 1902 the Basque Centre was attacked and the suspects were not prosecuted. On 30 May that year, Arana was imprisoned for his letter to Roosevelt and, in the following month, some PNV councillors were suspended from their activities (Corcuera 2001: 573–585).

8. Eli Gallastegi, 'Las grandes inquietudes de los pueblos. La Marcha Heroica de Mahatma Gandhi' in *Patria Vasca*, no. 5, April 1930 (Gallastegi 1993: 22–23).

9. Emakume-Abertzale Batza was constituted on 7 May 1922. The idea for the association had come after a Sinn Fein member, Ambrose V. Martin O'Daly, had given a conference in Bilbao and it represented a breakthrough in Basque

politics. Women had been traditionally seen as keeping the culture alive in the Basque home, and now they could enter politics on equal terms with men. The move was significant if we take into account that women were granted the suffrage almost twenty years later. Gallastegi proposed Ireland as a model, particularly Sinn Fein. As Eric Hobsbawm has pointed out, the Irish showed the young Basques the real meaning of 'revolutionary nationalism' (Hobsbawm 1990: 139).

10. The party was known as Comunidad Nacionalista from 1913 but the name was only officially changed in 1916 when the new statute was approved (Pablo, Mees, & Rodriguez 1999: 102).

11. The article was published in *Aberri* in December 1917 and was signed by the editor-in-chief, Jesús de Gaztaña (Elorza 2001: 329).

12. The expression 'iron surgeon' was coined after the 1898 Disaster by Joaquin Costa, a member of the regenerationist movement and author of Oligarquía y Caciquismo, a book which criticised the corrupt political system of the Restoration Monarchy. The *regeneracionistas* wanted to cure the structural maladies of the Spaniards and their country, develop its economy, educate its people, and reform its government: in short, 'restor[e] Spain's pulse' (Ben Ami 1983: 117). The expression 'revolution from above' was a concept that derived from the conservative politician Antonio Maura and the phrase 'saviour of the Fatherland' was coined by Manuel Jover.

13. 'La rebelión militar de Barcelona, *Aberri*, 14 September 1923.

14. La rebelión militar de Barcelona, *Aberri*, 14 September 1923.

15. Y nosotros los vascos, ¿con qué fe vamos a morir por una Patria que el corazón rechaza?. ¿El ejército contra el pueblo?, *Aberri*, 14 September 1923.

16. 'El separatismo: he aquí el enemigo', *Aberri*, 18 September 1923.

17. After the approval of the Constitution on 9 December 1931 Alcalá-Zamora became President of the Second Republic until 1936 when he was replaced by Manuel Azaña.

18. See Tellagorri (1957) *Comentarios a la Doctrina de ANV*. Arxiu Pavello Rebublica, Box 78, File 52.

19. Mainly in the newspaper of the ANV, *Tierra Vasca*, and the ones owned by the PNV, *Euzkadi* and *Bizkaitarra* (Granja 1986: 55).

20. Elcano, 'Sólo JEL no basta' *Tierra Vasca*, 24 November 1933: 1.

21. J. Olivares Larrondo, 'Los políticos y los trabajadores', *Tierra Vasca*, 9 November 1933: 1; and Juan de Zuazo, 'Hacia la formación de un nacionalismo izquierdista', *Tierra Vasca*, 7 December 1933: 1.

22. J. Olivares Larrondo, 'Solidaridad de Trabajadores Vascos', *Tierra Vasca*, 10 November 1933: 1. A summary of the ideological principles of the party can be found in Tellagorri (1957) Comentarios a la Doctrina de ANV. Arxiu Pavello Rebublica, Box 78, File 52.

23. The Statute of Autonomy of the Basque Country was approved in the Cortes in October 1936. The Basque Socialist leader Indalecio Prieto, who had a crucial input in the negotiations, later complained that Basque nationalists had only intervened in the war to defend the statute, not the Second Republic (Granja 1990: 185).

24. See Southworth (1977) and Tuñón de Lara (1987).

25. The negotiations with the Italians had taken two months and it was agreed that all Basque soldiers who surrendered would be Italian prisoners of war and would be protected from reprisals, while nationalist leaders would be allowed to leave by sea (Payne 1975: 217). At the same time, Franco's troops arrived in Santander and replaced the Italian contingent. After assuring the Italians that the terms of the capitulation would be respected, the Basque

prisoners were handed over to Franco's forces. Summary trials began immediately and hundreds of death sentences were passed. The Italians, says Preston, 'were appalled by Franco's duplicity and cruelty' (Preston 1994: 285). Franco distanced himself from the promises his subordinates had made and ignored the complaints from the Italian officer who had arranged the surrender. By doing so, he had the Basques surrendering at little cost, seriously weakened the Republican position in the north of Spain, and kept the Biscayan industries intact.

CHAPTER 4

1. However, it needs to be pointed out that in the post-war era the Basque Provinces were not the areas that were most heavily punished by Franco, as has often been argued by Basque nationalists. According to Paloma Aguilar, the average number of deaths for the whole of Spain due to repression in the post-war period was 2.45 per 1000 inhabitants. In Araba this number falls to 1.45 as it also does in Gipuzkoa (1.10) and Biscay (0.70). Only in Navarre (2.74) is the number of deaths superior to the Spanish average (Aguilar 1998: 15). For more information on the loss of life as a result of the war see Salas Larrazábal (1977).
2. The Decree-Law of 23 June 1937 was modified in 1968 when the most offensive sections were removed. However, the decree was only revoked in 1976 by the first Suárez Government.
3. The 'New State' was based on the conservative sectors of Spanish society: the Army, the Catholic Church, the Spanish industrial and financial bourgeoisie, big landowners, and various right-wing organisations. The *Nuevo Estado* was also a personal instrument of Franco, who liked to think of Spain as a military garrison. He was head of the government and of the state and, at the same time, supreme head of the armed forces, *generalísimo* of the army, navy, and air forces, national head of the one party, the Falange Española Tradicionalista de las JONS (also known as the Movement or Movimiento Nacional), and 'Caudillo of Spain by God's Grace, responsible for his actions to God and history' (Molinero and Ysàs 1994: 12). Franco's regime was based on the ideological and political control of the Spanish population through the state. Political parties and the trade unions were banned and were replaced by the one-party system and a single trade union. The state trade union was the Central Nacional Sindicalista (CNS). The mass media were also controlled by the State, which used them to propagate the state ideology: national-catholicism. According to the historian Juan Pablo Fusi, national-catholicism was based on (1) the army as the symbol and backbone of national unity; (2) Catholicism as the essence of nationhood; and (3) a centralist and authoritarian state as the instrument for national regeneration (Fusi 2000: 256). The ideology of the regime was summarised in the nationalist motto 'Spain one, great and free' which appeared in all the official symbols of the State.
4. See Beltza (1977: 41) and Jáuregui (1981: 54). The British Foreign Office, for example, refused to take any action against Franco and argued that it was 'a matter for the Spanish people to decide which kind of State they want[ed]'. See FO 371/60420 (1946).
5. Jose Antonio Aguirre in the Christmas Message of 1952. Reproduced as an appendix in Beltza (1977: 132–133).
6. And not just metaphorically. American foreign policy had shifted from having Nazism as its ultimate nemesis to opposing communism. This was most

acutely seen in Central and South America, where the United States would support anti-communist dictatorships in the years to come. In the Dominican Republic, for example, the FBI and the CIA killed one of its own Basque agents and member of the Servicios, Jesús Galíndez, a Columbia University professor, in order to preserve a good relationship with the dictator Leónidas Trujillo. Agent Galíndez, a delegate of the Basque Government in the United States, was kidnapped in New York in March 1956 and flown to the Dominican Republic where he was tortured and executed. He had been previously warned by the FBI that if he continued to criticise Trujillo's regime 'they could no longer protect him'. See José Luis Barbería, 'Las últimas verdades sobre el agente Galíndez' in El País, 22 September 2002. For a fictional account of the disappearance of the Basque agent see Vazquez Montalbán's novel, *Galíndez*.

7. José Luis Emparanza, a.k.a. Txillardegi, in *Documentos Y* (1979–1981: 9).
8. In Bilbao they were José María Benito del Valle, Julen Madariaga, Iñaki Gainzarain, Alfonso Irigoyen, José Manuel Aguirre, and Gurutz Ansola. In San Sebastián, Rafael Albisu, José Álvarez Emparanza (Txillardegi) ,and Iñaki (Larramendi Herrera, & Durán 2002: 546).
9. Ekin was founded in 1952. Four of the eight members had already participated in an short-lived student movement, Eusko Ikasle Alkartasuna (EIA). The organisation had been disbanded by the police two years earlier, in 1950, but while it existed it had shown the Ekin members the nature of a clandestine organisation and what security measures were needed to preserve it. Jose Luis Alvarez Emparanza (Txillardegi) in Ibarzabal (1978: 362–365).
10. The name ETA was proposed by José Luis Álvarez Enparanza, a.k.a. Txillardegi. However, as he recalls, the first suggestion was ATA, an acronym for Aberri Ta Askatasuna (Homeland and Liberty), but it was soon dropped because in the Biscayan dialect 'ata' means 'duck' (Txillardegi 1978: 370).
11. In 1979–1981, the largest compilation of ETA documents was published in an eighteen-volume set titled *Documentos Y*. The compilers decided to translate 'eta' as a conjunction, therefore remaining 'y'. (Aita Agirre [Lazkao], personal observation).
12. Detailed analysis of the ideological struggles within ETA can be found in Clark (1984: ch. 2), Garmendia (1996: ch. 2), Jáuregui (2000: ch. 6), Sánchez-Cuenca (2001: ch. 2), Zirakzadeh (1991: ch. 7), and Unzueta (1988: ch. 2).
13. Zutik!, April 1962, reproduced in *Documentos Y* (1979–1981: 418).
14. The influence of Arana on ETA can be spotted right from the very beginning. ETA was founded on 31 July 1959, the day of San Ignatius, when Sabino Arana had his 'revelation' and turned, in 1882, to nationalism. Thirteen years later and on the same day, he founded the Basque Nationalist Party. Both organisations, ETA and the PNV, adopted the Society of Jesus as an organisational model (Garmendia 2000: 77).
15. For the distinction between *ius solis* and *ius sanguinis* see Hastings (1997) and Brubaker (1996)
16. The 'Ideological Principles' are reprinted in Beltza (1977: 96–99) and in Jáuregui (1981: 137).
17. According to Ignacio Sánchez-Cuenca, there is a difference between insurgency and terrorism. An insurgent force tends to control a rural territory and in some ways resembles a small army. It can penetrate the enemy zone and attempt to break the government's grip on the zone through acts of sabotage and military operations against the security forces and civilians who do not cooperate with the insurgency. Terrorism, however, does not require liberated territory and is a mainly urban phenomenon. The only feasible strategy

for terrorist organisations is to hurt the enemy by means of specific attacks against the security forces or civilians. Terrorist organisations are much weaker than insurgencies in terms of armaments and militant personnel. At the same time, the distinction between the two terms is blurred in cases such as the Colombian FARC, the Peruvian Shining Path, or the Tamils of LTTE (Sánchez-Cuenca 2004: 5).

18. Moreover, Etxebarrieta became the first ETA martyr and inspired many generations of nationalists. A young Yoyes, who was to become the only female leader of ETA in the late 1970s, analysed in 1971 whether the independence of the Basque nation was worth the death of Etxebarrieta. She concluded: 'is the problem so serious? It must be, when there are so many people...who are prepared to die for it' (Yoyes 1987: 28–29).

19. FCO 9/1450.

20. The prosecutor accused the following ETA members: Josu Abrisketa Korta, Itziar Aizpurúa Egaña, Víctor Arana Bilbao, Julen Kalzada Ugalde, Antón Carrera Aguirrebarrena, José María Dorronsoro Ceberio, Jone Dorronsoro Ceberio, Juan Etxave Garitacelaya, Jokin Gorostidi Artola, Enrique Venancio Guesalaga Larreta, Javier Izko de la Iglesia, Francisco Javier Larena Martínez, Gregorio Vicente López Irasuegui, Mario Onaindía Nachiondo, Eduardo Uriarte Romero, and María Asunción Arruti. The Tribunal was set up in accordance with the Penal Code and the Decree on Military Rebellion, Banditry and Terrorism of 21 September 1960. On the history of the 1960 Decree and for a detailed account of the Burgos trial (Indictment number 31/69) see Salaberri (1971). For a brief historical account see Vilar (1984: 406–410).

21. FCO 9/1450.

22. Ibid.

23. The action was called Operation Ogre and was later recounted in detail in a book (Forest 1974) and in the film directed by Gillo Pontecorvo in 1979.

24. TVE (1993) *La Transición Española*, video 1.

25. The importance of violence as a unifying factor is not peculiar to radical Basque nationalism and can be found in many case-studies from pre-modern to modern times; see the work of Giddens (1985), Mann (1995), Tilly (1975), and Smith (1981).

26. Xabier Arzalluz quoted by Juaristi (2002: 146).

27. For an account of actions where the clergy worked closely with ETA see Herrera and Durán (2002: 299–336). The links between the church and the nationalists are also mentioned in Unzueta (1988: 237) and Jáuregui (2000: 201).

28. The only copy of Dechapare's *Linguae Vasconum primitiae* (1545) can be found at the National Library in Paris. For an analysis of the social origin of Basque and French authors during the sixteenth and eighteenth centuries see Gurruchaga (1985: 338) and Perez-Agote (1984: 101).

29. The division was first conceived by Paulo Iztueta in *Sociología del fenómeno contestatario del clero vasco: 1940–1975* (1981) and was followed by Mikel Barreda (1995: 15), Perez-Agote (1984: 103), and Unzueta (1988: 237).

30. In the collective letter, the priests asked the bishops of Vitoria, San Sebastian, Bilbao, and Pamplona to intervene in order to restore the Basques' 'lost peace'. They denounced the extensive practice of torture by the police and the civil guards and briefly mentioned the 'rights of the Basque people'. The letter was also submitted on 30 May 1960 to all the Spanish Bishops and the Vatican. Reproduced in *Documentos Y* (1979–1981: 127–135).

31. 'Efectos de la Invasión' in Arana (1980: 1331–1333).

32. See Unzueta (1987: 237) and Merry del Val (1939: 24).
33. According to Mikel Barreda (1995: 15) the post-war repression affected around 750 Basque clergyman. In Spain, more than 6,300 priests and members of various religious orders were killed during the war. Linz quoted by Boyd (1997: 232).
34. That is the way Franco (and the State) liked to remember the Spanish Civil War. Hence, the official version of the conflict was titled *Historia de la Cruzada Española*. The eight-volume work was written between 1939 and 1944 by Joaquín Arrarás, Ciriaco Pérez Bustamante, and the State Delegate Carlos Sáenz de Tejada. A bibliography of titles on 'the crusade' can be found in Perrino (1954) and Southworth (1963).

CHAPTER 5

1. The following historical account is based on the work of the following historians and political scientists: Carr and Fusi (1981), Cotarelo (1992), Gilmour (1985), Gunther, Montero, and Botella (2004), Heywood (1995), Linz and Stepan (1996), Magone (2004), Maravall (1982), Powell (2001), Preston (1996), and Tezanos, Cotarelo, and de Blas (1989).
2. *Newsweek*, 'Juan Carlos Looks Ahead', 26 April 1976: 14.
3. Consensus, which became one of the distinct features of the Spanish transition together with the role of the King, has no equivalent in other transitions (Linz 1992: 432).
4. *El País*, 2 November 1977 cited in Powell (1996: 144).
5. Adolfo Suárez presented the *Ley para la Reforma Política* as an expression of the King's wishes and hammered home the idea that to disobey the King was tantamount to disobeying Franco's will (as expressed in his political testament). Using a mixture of persuasion and political pressure the government convinced 425 of the 497 members of parliament to vote 'yes'. Suárez would ironically call these MPs 'procuradores de Hara-kiri', as they had effectively dissolved the Francoist assembly and many of them would not have any role to play in the new democratic scenario. The results of the referendum on the bill a month later were a success for the Suárez government. Almost 80 per cent of the electorate voted (76.4 per cent), and of these 94.2 per cent voted 'yes'; 2.6 per cent voted 'no'.
6. The *Pactos de la Moncloa* (1977) were signed by the leaders of all political forces: Adolfo Suárez González, Felipe González Márquez, Joan Reventós Carner, Joseph María Triginer Fernández, Manuel Fraga Iribarne, Enrique Tierno Galván, Juan Ajuriaguerra Ochandiano, Miquel Roca i Junyent, Leopoldo Calvo-Sotelo y Bustelo, and Santiago Carrillo Solares. The text of the Pact is reproduced in Cotarelo (1992: 473–487) and a personal account is provided by Fuentes Quintana (1990).
7. The governing UCD had three representatives on the *ponencia constitucional*, with one representative each for the PSOE, the AP, the PCE, and the Catalan nationalist PDC. The members of this *ponencia* were: Miguel Herrero de Miñón (UCD), Landelino Lavilla (UCD), José Pedro Pérez-Llorca (UCD), Gabriel Cisneros (UCD), Gregorio Peces-Barba (PSOE), Jordi Solé Tura (PCE), Manuel Fraga (AP), and Miguel Roca Junyent (Basque-Catalan representative).
8. The first pardon was granted shortly after the death of Franco in 1975. The second on 30 July 1976, the third on 9 December 1977, and the fourth in

October 1977. See Amnesty International Report (1977: 269, 272; 1978: 230).

9. The PNV proposed constitutional amendments regarding three issues: (1) the competences of each of the future autonomous communities; (2) the procedure to approve the statute of autonomy; and (3) the level of cooperation between the different autonomous communities and the potential federation (PNV 1978: 20). The third point was important for the PNV as it could open the door for a reunification between the Basque Country and the province of Navarre. The official position of the PNV in the constitutional debate can be found in a book published in 1978 titled *El Partido Nacionalista Vasco ante la Constitución*. For an opposing view see the personal account of Gregorio Peces-Barba, one of the 'fathers' of the Constitution. Peces-Barba accused the PNV of being 'a sniper on the outside' without 'any commitment to the common goal' (Peces-Barba 2000: 65).

10. The referendum on the statute was held in 1977 when there were negotiations between the Spanish government and the Basque parties. The outcome of the referendum meant that Navarre was not part of the Basque General Council which later discussed the Statute of Autonomy (Carr and Fusi 1979: 235).

11. Results of the Referendum for the Statute of Autonomy (1979). Electorate: 1,464,541. Participation: 921,436. Abstention: 644,105. 'Yes' Vote: 94.6 per cent 'No' Vote: 5.4 per cent. See http://www.euskadi.net.

12. Herri Batasuna chose candidates who were still in prison. In the 1979, 1982, 1986, and 1989 Cortes elections, HB included ETA members in its list. In the 1980 Basque elections, it included another two ETA members who were in prison and in 1986 the HB candidate for the Basque presidency (*lehendakaritza*) was the ETA member Juan Carlos Yoldi, at the time imprisoned in the prison of Herrera de la Mancha (Sumario 35/02 Y 26-8-2002).

13. The Junta de Apoyo was made up of twelve individuals who represented each of the Basque Provinces under Spanish sovereignty. Their names were Xabier Añua, Xabier Palacios, Xabier Sanchez Erauskin (Araba); Jon Idigoras, Jose Anjel Iribar and Francisco Letamendía 'Ortzi' (Biscay); José Luis Elkoro, Jokin Gorostidi, and Telesforo Monzón (Gipuzkoa), and José María Aguado, Josu Goya and Patxi Zabaleta (Navarre). HB, 20 años de lucha: 64. Information on Telesforo Monzón in Herri Batasuna (1999: 129–132).

14. In *Zutabe* (1983, no. 33, p. 58).

15. Hausnartzen III: 6; LAB. Resoluciones del III Congreso. p. 11.

16. *Zutabe* no. 22, p. 5; LAB. Resoluciones del III Congreso. p. 10; ETA, *Zuzen*, 1980, no. 2, p. 8.

17. Cited in Amodia (1977: 233).

CHAPTER 6

1. According to *El Pais*, from 1986 to 2005, Spain received €174 billions. If one deduces the €97 billions Spain has contributed to the European budget a net balance of €78,000 remains. El País, Domingo 12 June 2005: 3.

2. In spite of the high economic costs generated by a conflict situation, economic factors do not seem to override a state's political decision to withdraw, or not, from a given territory. For the Basque case, it has been estimated that the cost of violence amounts to some 10 per cent of the region's GDP (Abadie and Gardeazabal 2003).

3. The signatory parties of the Pact of Madrid were the PSOE, AP, CDS, CiU, PNV, PDP, PL, PCE and EE.

4. The following Basque leaders signed the agreement: Xabier Arzalluz (PNV), Txiki Benegas (PSE-PSOE), Inaxio Oliveri (EA), Kepa Aulestia (EE), A. Marco Tabar (CDS), Julen Guimón (AP), and the *lehendakari* José Antonio Ardanza.

5. The Pact of Navarre was signed on 7 October 1988 by the Navarrese President, Gabriel Urralburu Tanta and the following political parties: EE, AP, PL, DC, CDS, UPN, and PSN-PSOE.

6. For a complete account of the Algiers Negotiations see Clark (1999), Fonseca (1996), Pozas (1992), and Egaña and Giacopuzzi (1992).

7. The full name of the report was *Informe de la Comisión Internacional sobre la Violencia en el País Vasco*, and was presented by the Basque government in 1986. The report had been written by five experts on terrorism and had taken the name of the head of the working group, Clive Rose. The other authors were Franco Ferracuti, Hans Horchem, Peter Janke, and Jacques Leaute.

8. Yoyes resigned from ETA in 1979 and went into exile in Mexico a year later where she unwillingly remained a reference point for radical nationalists. Up until that point, ETA members who retired were often ostracised, but Yoyes was a charismatic former member and her example could have seriously damaged the organisation. Among the many papers found after her death, Yoyes wrote, referring to the obstacles she had faced in abandoning the armed struggle, that it was: 'unacceptable for an organisation that calls itself revolutionary to use fascist or Stalinist tactics (whatever one prefers) with former members'. Yoyes (1987: 185).

9. Sánchez-Cuenca points out that before these three rounds there was a preliminary and almost unknown stage of contacts between representatives of the State and ETA during July 1984 and November 1985 (Sánchez-Cuenca 2001: 123).

10. Interview with ETA leaders in the Catalan newspaper *L'Avui*, 25 May 1988; see also Alcedo (1996: 129–130).

11. The first one was offered by ETA in January 1988, the second by the government in February, and the third by ETA in October. See 'Trick or Truce?' in *The Economist*, 6 February 1988: 46.

12. These were the lawyer Iñigo Iruin, the leader of LAB Rafa Díez, the journalist and sociologist Luís Nuñez, and the leaders of Herri Batasuna Iñaki Aldekoa, Txema Montero, and Tasio Erkizia (Herri Batasuna 1999: 200; Egaña & Giacopucci 1992: 167).

13. For a more detailed account of the negotiations see Domínguez (2000: 335–381) or Egaña & Giacopucci (1992: 153–195).

14. Using rational choice theory, Ignacio Sánchez-Cuenca provides an explanation of what ETA and the State gained from the 'political negotiations' (Sánchez-Cuenca 2001: 109–142). The ETA perspective is well represented in Egaña and Giacopuzzi (1992) and the Minister of Interio's view in Pozas (1992).

15. Jotake (1989), *Martxoa*, 14 *Zenbakia.*

16. Robert P. Clark, 'Basque Terrorism', *The Economist* 1988.

17. *Zutabe* 33, 1983: 57.

18. The Sokoa operation was a joint effort of the Spanish security and intelligence services, the French police, and the CIA. Using a tracking device in two Sam 7 missiles, on 18 November 1986 the Spanish authorities discovered a secret chamber (*zulo*) in the Cooperativa Sokoa furniture company where ETA kept important documentation. The documents the police gathered made clear how ETA's funding system worked (Moran 1997: 246; Pozas 1992: 49–53).

19. Oldartzen. 1er Documento Definitivo(1995): 36–37.

20. Oldartzen, 2° Documento Definitivo: 6.
21. Oldartzen, 1er Documento Definitivo: 50.
22. Oldartzen, 2° Documento Definitivo: 7
23. Oldartzen, 1er Documento Definitivo: 50.
24. However, the 'street violence' did not come out of the blue and had a precedent in the Basque Country. In the late 1980s and early 1990s ETA had attempted to lead the protest against construction of the Leitzaran highway. The highway was strongly opposed by environmentalists and nationalists and ETA contributed to the acts of protest with 158 acts of sabotage worth €6 million (Gurruchaga 2001: 28–292). In the end, the plan was changed and the work became much more costly one, and ETA was able to capitalise on the gains resulting from the action. The actions against the Leitzaran highway also helped to mobilise and politicise a high number of radical nationalists hence making ETA stronger. After this short precedent, street violence really took off after 1992.
25. Carmen Remirez de Ganuza (2002) 'El Juzgado Central de Menores celebro solo dos juicios en un ano', *El Mundo*, 20 January.
26. Between January 1995 when Ordoñez was killed, to February 2003 when Batasuna was prohibited, thirty politicians, most of them members of the PP and PSOE, were killed by ETA (Patxo Unzueta, 'La buena conciencia' *El País*: 8 June 2006.
27. 'A murder too far', *The Economist*, 19 July 1997: 38–40. Also 'Millones de Españoles se unen a la rebelion de los vascos contra ETA y HB' *El País*, 15 July 1997: 1.

CHAPTER 7

1. See *The Economist*, 'Charlemagne José Maria Aznar', 15 September 2001: 48. On the Basque problem see Aznar's prologue to Jaime de Burgo's book, *Soñando con la paz* (1994).
2. The Anti-terrorist Pact, or Acuerdo por las libertades y contra el terrorismo, was signed in Madrid on 8 December 2000 by the general secretaries of the Popular Party, Javier Arenas, and the PSOE, José Luis Rodríguez Zapatero.
3. Declaración de Euskadi Ta Askatasuna al Pueblo Vasco, 3 December 1999. The secret agreement between the two forces was leaked two years later by an unhappy ETA, which believed the PNV was not confrontational enough with the Spanish state. The ETA communiqué was published in the newspaper Gara on 30 April 2000.
4. *The Economist*, 'A Period of Calm and Turbulence', 6 November 1999: 59.
5. The *Ley Orgánica 6/2002 de Partidos Políticos* was published in the *Boletín Oficial de las Cortes Generales* on 4 June 2002 and came into effect on 27 June 2002. The parties that opposed the law were Izquierda Unida (IU), the Galician nationalist party, the BNG, and the Basque nationalist parties PNV and EA. For an analysis of the Ley Orgánica de Partidos Políticos (LOPP) see Turano (2003).
6. The law was approved by 304 votes (PP, PSOE, CiU, CC and PA) and received 16 opposing votes (IU, PNV, EA and BNG).
7. Audiencia Nacional. Juzgado Central de Instrucción no. 5, Sumario 35/02 Y, 26 August 2002.
8. The poll number 2466 from the Centro de Investigaciones Sociológicas of September 2002 had a sample of 2484 people. Question 9 of the poll was 'Are you in favour, very much in favour, against or very much against the

illegalisation of Batasuna?' The results were: very much in favour 28.4 per cent; in favour 37.0 per cent; against 11.6 per cent; very much against 3.1 per cent; indifferent 6.2 per cent; don't know 10.8 per cent; and no answer 2.8 per cent. See http://www.cis.es.

9. *The Economist*, 'Spain and the Basques. Ibarretxe and Bust?', 15 January 2005: 36.
10. William Chislett, *Inside Spain*, no 21, Real Instituto Elcano. See: http://www. realinstitutoelcano.org.
11. Notably the one belonging to General José Mena Aguado who publicly exhorted his fellow officers to defend Spain's unity against the prospect of the government giving 'too much' autonomy to the Catalans. See *The Economist*, 'Spain and Catalonia. Bad Echoes from the Past', 14 January 2006: 40.
12. The project of the *España plural* as a nation of nations was launched by the PSOE in Santillana del Mar (Cantabria) on 30 August 2003. The socialist blueprint to consolidate Spain as a decentralised state included the reform of the Senate into a territorial chamber, the incorporation of the autonomous communities into EU councils and the parliamentary reforms of the statutes of autonomy.
13. *The Economist*, 'Spain and ETA. Peace Talk', 21 May 2005: 44.
14. *The Economist*, 'Spain and the Basques. Independence Days', 12 February 2005: 35.
15. If we exclude the two Ecuadorian men killed in December 2006, ETA had killed a total of 832 people. Of those, 93 per cent were men and 7 per cent women. The military and the police were the main target, accounting for 58 per cent of deaths; the other 42 per cent were civilians. Most of the killings took place in the Basque Country (67.5 per cent) followed by Madrid (14.5 per cent) and Catalonia (6.5 per cent) (Calleja and Sánchez-Cuenca 2005: 147–167).
16. De Juana Chaos was a renowned hardliner who should have been released in October 2004 after serving his sentence in full and having spent eighteen years in jail for the murder of twenty-five people. He went on hunger strike on 7 November 2006 in protest at the additional sentence of twelve years and seven months he had been given for alleged 'terrorist threats' in two opinion articles he had published in the newspaper *Gara* on 1 and 30 December 2004. The ETA prisoner was not charged with the offence when the articles were originally published.

Bibliography

Abadie, Alberto and Gardeazabal, Javier (2003) 'The Economic Costs of Conflict: A Case Study of the Basque Country', *American Economic Review*, Vol. 93, No. 1, pp. 113–132.

Agirreazkuenaga, Joseba (1992) 'La tradición historiográfica vasca: su desarrollo en el marco de las ciencias sociales', *Historia Contemporánea*, No. 7, pp. 257–281.

Agüero, Felipe (1995) *Soldiers, Civilians, and Democracy. Post-Franco Spain in Comparative Perspective*. Baltimore & London: Johns Hopkins University Press.

Aguilar Fernández, Paloma (1998) 'The Memory of the Civil War in the Transition to Democracy: The Peculiarity of the Basque Case', *West European Politics*, No. 21, pp. 5–25.

Aguirre y Lecube, José Antonio (1935) *Entre la libertad y la revolución, 1930–1935*. Bilbao: Talleres Gráficos E. Verdes Achirica.

Aguirre y Lecube, José Antonio (1991) *Escape via Berlin. Eluding Franco in Hitler's Europe*. Reno: University of Nevada Press.

Alcedo Moneo, Miren (1996) *Militar en ETA: historias de vida y muerte*. San Sebastián: Haranburu Editor.

Allingham, Michael (ed.) (2006) *Rational Choice Theory. Critical Concepts*. London: Routledge. 5 vols.

Alonso, Gregorio (2000) 'La mirada de la izquierda. Las guerras coloniales de 1898 desde la prensa socialista y federal', Sánchez, Rafael (ed.) *En torno al 98*, Huelva: Universidad de Huelva, Vol. 2, pp. 261–269.

Álvarez Emparantza, José Luis (Txillardegi) (1978) 'Cincuenta años de nacionalismo vasco: 1928–1978', Ibarzábal, Eugenio (ed.) *50 años de nacionalismo vasco 1928–1978 a través de sus protagonistas*. San Sebastián: Ediciones Vascas/Argitaletxea, pp. 359–372.

Álvarez Junco, José (1996) 'The Nation-Building Process in Nineteenth-Century Spain', Mar-Molinero, Clare & Smith, Angel (eds.) *Nationalism and the Nation in the Iberian Peninsula*, Washington & Oxford: Berg, pp. 89–107.

Álvarez Junco, José (2001a) 'El nacionalismo español: las insuficiencias en la acción estatal', *Historia Social*, No. 40, pp. 29–51.

Álvarez Junco, José (2001b) *Mater Dolorosa. La idea de España en el siglo XIX*. Madrid: Taurus.

Amigo, Angel (1978) *Pertur. ETA 71–76*. Donostia: Hordago.

Amodia, José (1977) *Franco's Political Legacy: From Dictatorship to Façade Democracy*. London: Penguin.

Anasagasti, Iñaki and San Sebastián, Koldo (1985) *Los años oscuros. El Gobierno vasco—El exilio (1937–1941)*. San Sebastián: Editorial Txertoa.

Anasagasti, Iñaki and San Sebastián, Koldo (1998) 'El PNV y la crisis de la República', *Historia 16*, No. 150, pp. 39–48.

Anderson, Benedict (1991) *Imagined Communities. Reflections on the Origin and Spread of Nationalism*. London: Verso.

Apter, David E. (1997) 'Political Violence in Analytical Perspective', Apter, David E. (ed.) *The Legitimization of Violence*. Basingstoke: Macmillan/UNRISD, pp. 1–32.

Arana Goiri, Sabino (1980) *Obras completas de Sabino Arana Goiri*. Donostia: Sendoa Argitaldaria. 3 vols.

Arantzadi y Etxeberria, Engracio de (Kizkitza) (1980) *Ereintza: siembra de nacionalismo vasco, 1894–1912*. Zarauz: Editorial Auñamendi.

Aranzadi, Juan (1979) 'El mito de la edad de oro vasca', *Tiempo de Historia*, Vol. 5, No. 59, pp. 4–21.

Aranzadi, Juan (1994) 'Violencia etarra y etnicidad', Aróstegui, Julio (ed.) *Violencia política en España, Revista Ayer*, No. 13, pp. 189–209.

Aranzadi, Juan (2000) *Milenarismo Vasco. Edad de Oro, etnia y nativismo*. Madrid: Taurus.

Aranzadi, Juan, Juaristi, Jon, and Unzueta, Patxo (eds.) (1994) *Auto de Terminación*. Madrid: El País-Aguilar.

Arendt, Hannah (1970) *On Violence*. London: Allen Lane, Penguin Press.

Aretxaga, Begoña (1988) *Los funerales en el nacionalismo radical vasco: ensayo antropológico*. San Sebastián: Editorial La Primitiva Casa Baroja S.A.

Armstrong, John A. (1982) *Nations before Nationalism*. Chapel Hill: University of North Carolina Press.

Aróstegui, Julio (1994) 'Violencia, sociedad y política: la definición de la violencia', Aróstegui, Julio (ed.) *Violencia política en España, Revista Ayer*, No. 13, pp. 17–55.

Arteaga, Federico de (1971) *ETA y el proceso de Burgos*. Madrid: Editorial E. Aguado.

Arzalluz Antia, Xabier (1992) 'Las ideas políticas de Larramendi', Tellechea Idígoras, J. Ignacio (ed.) *M. Larramendi. Hirugarren Mendeurrena*. Andoain, pp. 65–75.

Aulestia, Kepa (1998) *HB: crónica de un delirio*. Madrid: Temas de Hoy.

Azcona, Jesús (1989) 'On Time: Notes Regarding the Anthropology of Julio Caro Baroja', Douglass, William A. (ed.) *Essays in Basque Social Anthropology and History*, Reno: Basque Studies Program, pp. 9–41.

Azurmendi, Mikel (1994) 'Etnicidad y violencia en el suelo vasco', *Claves de Razón Práctica*, No. 43, pp. 28–41.

Azurmendi, Mikel (2000) *Y se limpie aquella tierra. Limpieza étnica y de sangre en el País Vasco (siglos XVI–XVIII)*. Madrid: Taurus.

Azzi, Assaad E. (1998) 'From Competitive Interests, Perceived Injustice, and Identity Needs to Collective Action: Psychological Mechanisms in Ethnic Nationalism', Dandeker, Christopher (ed.) *Nationalism and Violence*. New Brunswick, NJ: Transaction Publishers, pp. 73–138.

Balfour, Sebastian (1997) *The End of the Spanish Empire, 1898–1923*. Oxford: Clarendon Press.

Balfour, Sebastian (ed.) (2005) *The Politics of Contemporary Spain*. Abingdon: Routledge.

Bandura, Albert (1972), *Aggression. A Social Learning Analysis*, Englewood Cliffs, N.J.: Prentice-Hall.

Barash, David P. (2001) *Understanding Violence*. Boston: Allyn & Bacon.

Barbería, José Luis and Unzueta, Patxo (2003) *Cómo hemos llegado a esto. La crisis vasca*. Madrid: Taurus.

Barcena, Iñaki, Ibarra, Pedro and Zubiaga, Mario (1997) 'The Evolution of the Relationship between Ecologism and Nationalism', Redcliff, Michael and Woodgate, Graham (eds.) *The International Handbook of Environmental Sociology*. Cheltenham: Edward Elgar, pp. 300–315.

Barreda, Mikel (1995) 'L'Església Basca i ETA', *L'Avenç*, No. 191, pp. 14–18.

Batista, Antoni (2001) 'Sobre els inicis d'ETA. Entrevista a Iulen de Madariaga', *L'Avenç*, No. 258, pp. 38–41.

Ben-Ami, Shlomo (1983) *Fascism from Above: the Dictatorship of Primo de Rivera in Spain 1923–1930*. Oxford: Clarendon.

Ben-Ami, Shlomo (1991) 'Basque Nationalism between Archaism and Modernity', *Journal of Contemporary History*, Vol. 26, No. 3, pp. 493–521.

Benegas, Txiki (1984) *Euskadi: sin la paz nada es posible*. Barcelona: Argos Vergara.

Beramendi, Justo G. and Máiz, Ramón (eds.) (1991) *Los nacionalismos en la España de la II República*. Madrid: Siglo XXI.

Bilbao, Karmele and Munarriz, Fermín (1997) *Egin. Euskal Herria eginez. Dos décadas en imágenes y palabras*. Bilbao: Orain, D.L.

Billig, Michael (1995) *Banal Nationalism*. London: Sage.

Blasco, Rogelio (1987) 'Nuevo Rock Vasco: un fenómeno sociológico', *Cuadernos de Alzate*, No. 6, pp. 12–30.

Blinkhorn, Martin (1975) *Carlism and Crisis in Spain, 1931–45*. Cambridge: Cambridge University Press.

Blinkhorn, Martin (1984) 'War On Two Fronts: Politics and Society in Navarre 1931–6', Preston, Paul (ed.) *Revolution and War in Spain, 1931–1939*. London: Methuen, pp. 59–84.

Boyd, Carolyn P. (1997) *Historia Patria. Politics, History, and National Identity in Spain, 1875–1975*. Princeton, NJ: Princeton University Press.

Boyd, Carolyn P. (2000) 'The Military and Politics', Alvarez Junco, José and Shubert, Adrian (eds.) *Spanish History Since 1808*. London: Arnold, pp. 64–78.

Braudel, Fernand (1993) *A History of Civilizations*. New York: Penguin Books.

Brenan, Gerald (1943) *The Spanish Labyrinth. An Account of the Social and Political Background of the Civil War*. Cambridge: Cambridge University Press.

Breuilly, John (1993) *Nationalism and the State*. Manchester: Manchester University Press.

Brubaker, Rogers (1996) *Nationalism Reframed: Nationhood and the National Question in the New Europe*. Cambridge: Cambridge University Press.

Bruni, Luigi (1982) 'Nationalist Violence and Terror in the Spanish Border Provinces: ETA', Mommsen, Wolfgang J. and Hirschfeld, Gerhard (eds.) *Social Protest, Violence and Terror in Nineteenth and Twentieth century Europe*. New York: St. Martin's Press, pp. 112–136.

Bruni, Luigi (1987) *ETA. Historia política de una lucha armada*. Bilbao: Txalaparta.

Burdiel, Isabel (2000) 'The Liberal Revolution, 1808–1843', Alvarez Junco, José and Shubert, Adrian (eds.) *Spanish History Since 1808*. London: Arnold, pp. 17–32.

Burgo, Jaime Ignacio del (1994) *Soñando con la paz: violencia terrorista y nacionalismo vasco*. Madrid: Temas de Hoy.

Calle, Luis de la and Sánchez-Cuenca, Ignacio (2004) 'La selección de víctimas en ETA', *Revista Española de Ciencia Política*, No. 10, pp. 53–79.

Calleja José María Calleja and Sánchez-Cuenca, Ignacio (2006) *La derrota de ETA. De la primera a la última víctima*. Madrid: Adhara Publicaciones.

Camino, Iñigo and Guezala, Luis (1991) *Juventud y nacionalismo vasco: Bilbao (1901–1937)*. Bilbao: Fundación Sabino Arana.

Caro Baroja, Julio (1958) *Los Vascos*. Madrid: Ediciones Istmo.

Caro Baroja, Julio (1998) *Ser o no ser vasco*. Madrid: Espasa Calpe, S.A.

Caro Baroja, Julio (2002) *Los vascos en la historia a través de Garibay*. Madrid. Caro Raggio.

Carr, Raymond (1992) *España, 1808–1975*. Barcelona: Editorial Ariel, S.A.

Carr, Raymond and Fusi, Juan Pablo (1979) *Spain: Dictatorship to Democracy*. London: Allen & Unwin.

Casquete, Jesús (2003) 'From Imagination to Visualization: Protest Rituals in the Basque Country', Working Paper, Discussion Paper SP IV 2003-401, Wissenchaftszentrum Berlin für Sozialforschung (WZB). http://skylla.wz-berlin. de/pdf/2003/iv03-401.pdf. (accessed 15 December 2006)

Casquete, Jesús (2006) 'Música y funerales en el nacionalismo vasco radical', *Historia y Política*, Vol. 15, No. 1, pp. 191–215.

Chari, Raj S. (2004) 'The 2004 Spanish Election: Terrorism as a Catalyst for Change?', *West European Politics*, Vol. 27, No. 5, pp. 954–963.

Cioran, Emile M. (1998) *History and Utopia*. Chicago: Chicago University Press.

Cirujano Marín, Paloma, Elgorriaga Planes, Teresa, and Pérez-Garzón, Juan Sisinio (1985) *Historiografía y nacionalismo español (1834–1868)*. Madrid: CEH-CSIC.

Clark, Robert P. (1979) *The Basques, the Franco Years and Beyond*. Reno: University of Nevada Press.

Clark, Robert P. (1983) 'Patterns in the Lives of ETA Members', *Terrorism. An International Journal*, Vol.6, No. 3, pp. 423–454.

Clark, Robert P. (1984) *The Basque Insurgents: ETA, 1952–1980*. Madison: University of Wisconsin Press.

Clark, Robert P. (1987a) 'The Legitimacy of Political Violence? The Case of Western Europe', University of Massachusetts Series, No. 5.

Clark, Robert P. (1987b) 'Rejectionist Voting as an Indicator of Ethnic Nationalism: The Case of Spain's Basque Provinces', *Ethnic and Racial Studies*, Vol. 10, No. 4, pp. 427–447.

Clark, Robert P. (1990a) 'Negotiating with Insurgents. Obstacles to Peace in the Basque Country', *Terrorism and Political Violence*, Vol. 2, No. 4, pp. 489–507.

Clark, Robert P. (1990b) *Negotiating with ETA: Obstacles to Peace in the Basque Country, 1975–1988*. Reno: University of Nevada.

Clemente, Josep Carles (1990) *El Carlismo. Historia de una disidencia social (1833–1976)*. Barcelona: Ariel.

Clemente, Josep Carles (2000) *Breviario de Historia del Carlismo*. Sevilla: Muñoz Moya Editores.

Closa, David and Heywood, Paul (2004) *Spain and the European Union*. Houndmills, UK & New York: Palgrave Macmillan.

Cohn, Norman (1970) *The Pursuit of the Millennium. Revolutionary Millenarians and Mystical Anarchists of the Middle Ages*. New York: Oxford University Press.

Connor, Walker (1992) 'A Nation Is a Nation, Is a State, Is an Ethnic Group, Is a...', *Ethnic and Racial Studies*, Vol. 1, No. 4, pp. 378–400.

Connor, Walker (1994) *Ethnonationalism: The Quest for Understanding*. Princeton, NJ: Princeton University Press.

Conversi, Daniele (1990) 'Language or Race?: The Choice of Core Values in the Development of Catalan and Basque Nationalisms', *Ethnic and Racial Studies*, Vol. 13, No. 1, pp. 50–70.

Conversi, Daniele (1997) *The Basques, the Catalans and Spain. Alternative Routes to Nationalist Mobilisation*. London: Hurst.

Corcuera Atienza, Javier (1979) *Orígenes, ideología y organización del nacionalismo vasco (1876–1904)*. Madrid: Siglo XXI.

Corcuera Atienza, Javier (1984) 'La difícil definición del "problema vasco"', Reinares, Fernando (ed.) *Violencia y política en Euskadi*. Bilbao: Editorial Desclée de Brouwer, S.A., pp. 37–53.

Corcuera Atienza, Javier (2001) *La patria de los vascos*. Madrid: Taurus.

Corcuera Atienza, Javier, Oribe, Yolanda and Saenz de Gorbea, Xabier (eds.) (1991) *Historia del nacionalismo vasco en sus documentos*. Bilbao: Eguzki. 4 vols.

Coser, Lewis A. (1956) *The Functions of Social Conflict*. Glencoe: Free Press.

Cotarelo, Ramón (ed.) (1992) *Transición política y consolidación democrática: España (1975–1986)*. Madrid: Centro de Investigaciones Sociológicas.

Coverdale, John F. (1984) *The Basque Phase of Spain's First Carlist War*. Princeton, NJ: Princeton University Press.

Crenshaw, Martha (1990) 'The Logic of Terrorism: Terrorist Behaviour as a Product of Strategic Choice', Reich, Walter (ed.) *Origins of Terrorism*. Cambridge: Cambridge University Press, pp. 7–24.

Cruise O'Brien, Conor (1978) *Hesiod: Reflections on Political Violence*. London: Hutchinson.

Cueva Alonso, Justo de la (1988) *La escisión del PNV: EA, HB, ETA*. Bilbao: Txalaparta Agitaldaria.

De Pablo, Santiago, De la Granja, José Luis, and Mees, Ludger (eds.) (1998) *Documentos para la historia del nacionalismo vasco. De los Fueros a nuestros días*. Barcelona: Editorial Ariel, S.A.

De Pablo, Santiago, Mees, Ludger and Rodríguez Ranz, José Antonio (1999) *El Péndulo Patriótico. Historia del Partido Nacionalista Vasco: 1895–1936*. Barcelona: Crítica.

De Pablo, Santiago, Mees, Ludger and Rodríguez Ranz, José Antonio (2001) *El Péndulo Patriótico. Historia del Partido Nacionalista Vasco II: 1936–1979*. Barcelona: Crítica.

Díaz-Andreu, Margarita and Champion, Timothy (eds.) (1996) *Nationalism and Archaeology in Europe*. London: UCL Press.

Díaz-Andreu, Margarita and Keay, Simon (1997) *The Archaeology of Iberia. The Dynamics of Change*. London: Routledge.

Díaz Herrera, José and Durán, Isabel (2002) *ETA. El Saqueo de Euzkadi*. Barcelona: Planeta.

Díez Medrano, Juan (1995) *Divided Nations: Class, Politics, and Nationalism in the Basque Country and Catalonia*. Ithaca, NY: Cornell University Press.

Documentos Y (1979–1981). San Sebastián: Hordago. 18 vols.

Domínguez Iribarren, Florencio (1998) *ETA: Estrategia Organizativa y Actuaciones 1978–1992*. Bilbao: Universidad País Vasco. Servicio Editorial.

Domínguez Iribarren, Florencio (2000) 'El enfrentamiento de ETA con la democracia', Elorza, Antonio (ed.) *Historia de ETA*. Madrid: Temas de Hoy, pp. 277–420.

Domínguez Iribarren, Florencio (2002) *Dentro de ETA: la vida diaria de los terroristas*. Madrid: Aguilar.

Domínguez Iribarren, Florencio (2006) 'Las treguas de ETA', *Claves de Razón Práctica*, No. 162, pp. 34–40.

Domínguez Ortiz, Antonio (1971) *The Golden Age of Spain 1516–1659*. London: Weidenfeld and Nicolson.

Douglass, William (2002) 'Sabino's Sin. Racism and the Founding of Basque Nationalism', Conversi, Daniele (ed.) *Ethnonationalism in the Contemporary World: Walker Connor and the Study of Nationalism*. London: Routledge, pp. 95–112.

Douglass, William and Zulaika, Joseba (1990) 'On the Interpretation of Terrorist Violence: ETA and the Basque Political Process', *Comparative Studies in Society and History*, Vol. 32, No. 2, pp. 238–257.

Douglass, William and Ibarra, Pedro (2004) 'A Basque Referendum: Resolution or Political Conflict or the Promised Land of Error', Aretxaga, Begoña, Dworkin, Dennos, Gabilondo, Joseba and Zulaika, Josefa, *Empire & Terror: Nationalism/Postnationalism in the New Millennium*. Reno: Centre for Basque Studies, pp. 137–162.

Druckman, Daniel (1995) 'Social-Psychological Aspects of Nationalism', Comaroff, John L. and Stern, Paul C. (eds.) *Perspectives on Nationalism and War*. Amsterdam: Gordon and Breach Publishers, pp. 47–98.

Eatwell, Roger and Mudde, Cas (2004) *Western Democracies and the New Extreme Right Challenge*. London and New York: Routledge.

Edles, Laura Desfor (1998) *Symbol and Ritual in the New Spain: The Transition to Democracy after Franco*. Cambridge: Cambridge University Press.

Egaña, Iñaki (1996) *Diccionario histórico-político de Euskal Herria*. Tafalla: Txalaparta.

Egaña, Iñaki and Giacopucci, Giovanni (1992) *Los días de Argel: crónica de las conversaciones ETA-gobierno Español*. Tafalla: Txalaparta.

Eliade, Mircea (1955) *The Myth of the Eternal Return*. London: Routledge & Kegan Paul.

Elkarri (2002) *Claves para hacer las paces. El libro de la Conferencia de Paz*. Donostia: Elkarri.

Elliott, John H. (1963) *The Revolt of the Catalans. A Study in the Decline of Spain, 1598–1640*. Cambridge: Cambridge University Press.

Elliott, John H. (1969) *Imperial Spain, 1469–1716*. London: Edward Arnold.

Elorza, Antonio (1976) 'El tema rural en los orígenes literarios del nacionalismo vasco', Tuñón de Lara, Manuel et al. *La Cuestión Agraria en la España Contemporánea*. Madrid: Editorial Cuadernos para el Diálogo, pp. 457–521.

Elorza, Antonio (1992) 'El protonacionalismo de Larramendi', Tellechea Idígoras, J. Ignacio (ed.) *M. Larramendi. Hirugarren Mendeurrena*. Andoain: 1992, pp. 137–149.

Elorza, Antonio (ed.) (2000) *La historia de ETA*. Madrid: Temas de Hoy.

Elorza, Antonio (2001) *Un pueblo escogido. Génesis, definición y desarrollo del nacionalismo vasco*. Barcelona: Crítica.

Elorza, Antonio (2003) 'Sabino Arana, el sentido de la violencia', *Claves de Razón Práctica*, No. 130, pp. 46–54.

Elster, Jon (1989) *Nuts and Bolts for the Social Sciences*. Cambridge: Cambridge University Press.

Escudero, Manu (1978) *Euskadi: dos comunidades*. San Sebastián: L. Haranburu.

Estévez, Xosé (1991) *De la triple alianza al pacto de San Sebastián (1923–1930): antecedentes del Galeuzca*. San Sebastián: Cuadernos Universitarios.

Estornés Zubizarreta, Idoia (1990) *La Construcción de una nacionalidad vasca. El Autonomismo de Eusko-Ikaskuntza (1918–1931)*. San Sebastián: Editorial Eusko Ikaskuntza, S.A.

Extramiana, José (1983) *La guerra de los vascos en la narrativa del 98. Unamuno, Valle-Inclán, Baroja*. San Sebastián: Aramburu.

Fanon, Frantz (1986) *The Wretched of the Earth*. New York: Grove Press.

Fernández Albaladejo, Pablo (1977) 'Manuel de Larramendi: la particular historia de Guipúzcoa', *Saioak*, No. 1, pp. 148–156.

Fernández Albaladejo, Pablo (1992) 'Imposible vencido, imposible vencida: la provincia invencible de Manuel de Larramendi', Tellechea Idígoras, J. Ignacio (ed.) *M. Larramendi. Hirugarren Mendeurrena*. Andoain, pp. 77–89.

Fernández Pardo, Francisco (1990) *La independencia vasca. La disputa de los fueros*. Madrid: Editorial Nerea.

Fernández Sebastián, Javier (1991) *La génesis del fuerismo. Prensa e ideas políticas en la crisis del Antiguo Régimen (País Vasco, 1750–1840)*. Madrid: Siglo XXI.

Fonseca, Carlos (1996) *Negociar con ETA. De Argel al Gobierno del PP: crónica de un diálogo siempre negado*. Barcelona: Temas de Hoy.

Forest, Genoveva (Eva) (1994) *Operación Ogro (Cómo y por qué ejecutamos a Carrero Blanco)*. Hondarribia: Argitaletxe HIRU, S.L.

Foucault, Michel (1972) *The Archaeology of Knowledge*. London: Tavistock.

Foucault, Michel (1991) *Discipline and Punish: The Birth of the Prison*. Harmondsworth, UK: Penguin.

Friedman, Thomas (1999) *The Lexus and the Olive Tree*. London: HarperCollins.

Fuente Langas, José Maria (1998) *La dictadura de Primo de Rivera en Navarra*. Pamplona: Gobierno de Navarra.

Fuentes Quintana, Enrique (1990) 'De los Pactos de la Moncloa a la Constitución (julio 1977—diciembre 1978)', Garcia Delgado, José Luis (ed.), *Economía Española de la Transición y la Democracia 1973–1986*. Madrid: Centro de Investigaciones Sociológicas, pp. 23–34.

Funes, Maria J. (1998) 'Social Responses to Political Violence in the Basque Country', *Journal of Conflict Resolution*, Vol. 42, No. 4, pp. 493–510.

Fusi Aizpurúa, Juan Pablo (1975) *Política obrera en el País Vasco, 1880–1923*. Madrid: Turner.

Fusi Aizpurúa, Juan Pablo (1984) 'The Basque Question, 1931–37', Paul Preston (ed.) *Revolution and War in Spain, 1931–1939*. London: Methuen, pp. 182–201.

Fusi Aizpurúa, Juan Pablo (1987) 'La Guerra Civil en el País Vasco: una perspectiva general', Garitaonandía, Carmelo and Granja, José Luis de la (eds.) *La guerra civil en el País Vasco 50 años después*. Leioa: Servicio Editorial Universidad del País Vasco, pp. 43–50.

Fusi Aizpurúa, Juan Pablo (1990) 'Revisionismo crítico e historia nacionalista (A propósito de un artículo de Borja de Riquer)', *Historia Social*, No. 7, pp. 127–134.

Fusi Aizpurúa, Juan Pablo (2000) *España: la evolución de la identidad nacional*. Madrid: Temas de Hoy.

Gabancho, Patricia (2006) *La batalla de l'Estatut*. Barcelona: Editorial Empúries.

Gallastegi, Eli (Gudari) (1993) *Por la Libertad vasca*. Tafalla: Txalaparta.

Galtung, Johan (1969) 'Violence, Peace and Peace Research', *Journal of Peace Research*, 3, pp. 167–192.

García Venero, Maximiano (1969) *Historia del nacionalismo vasco 1793–1936*. Madrid: Editora nacional.

Garmendia, José María (1995) 'El PNV, de Aguirre a Arzalluz', *Historia 16*, No. 235, pp. 65–74.

Garmendia, José María (1996) *Historia de ETA*. San Sebastián: Huranburu.

Garmendia, José María (2000) 'ETA: nacimiento, desarrollo y crisis (1959–1978)', Elorza, Antonio (ed.) *La historia de ETA*. Madrid: Temas de Hoy, pp. 77–168.

Garmendia, Vicente (1985a) 'Carlism and Basque Nationalism', Douglass, William A. (ed.) *Basque Politics: A Case Study in Ethnic Nationalism*. Reno: Basque Studies Program Occasional Papers Series, No. 2, pp. 137–154.

Garmendia, Vicente (1985b) *La ideología carlista en los orígenes del nacionalismo vasco (1868–1876)*. Zarautz: Itxaropena, S.A.

Gellner, Ernest (1983) *Nations and Nationalism*. Oxford: Blackwell.

Giacopuggi, Giovanni (1992) *ETA. Historia política de una lucha armada*. Navarra: Txalaparta.

Giddens, Anthony (1985) *A Contemporary Critique of Historical Materialism. Vol. 2, The Nation-State and Violence*. Cambridge: Polity Press.

Gillis, John R. (1994) *Commemorations. The Politics of National Identity*. Princeton, NJ: Princeton University Press.

Gilmour, David (1985) *The Transformation of Spain. From Franco to the Constitutional Monarchy*. London: Quartet.

Gómez-Navarro, José Luis (1991) *El régimen de Primo de Rivera: reyes, dictaduras y dictadores*. Madrid: Cátedra.

González-Arnao, Mariano (1994) 'Los niños vascos refugiados en el Reino Unido (1937)', *Historia 16*, No. 223, pp. 20–27.

González Kantauri, María Dolores (Yoyes) (1987) *Yoyes, desde su ventana*. Iruña, 1987.

Graham, Helen (2005) *The Spanish Civil War: A Very Short Introduction*. Oxford: Oxford University Press.

Granja Sainz, José Luis de la (1984) 'La izquierda nacionalista vasca en la II República: ANV', *Nacionalismo y Socialismo en Euskadi. Revista del colectivo IPES*. Cuaderno de Formación, No. 4. Bilbao, pp. 123–134.

Granja Sainz, José Luis de la (1985) 'The Basque Nationalist Community during the Second Spanish Republic (1931–1936)', Douglass, William A. (ed.), *Basque Politics: A Case Study in Ethnic Nationalism*. Reno: Basque Studies Program Occasional Papers Series, No. 2, pp. 155–174.

Granja Sainz, José Luis de la (1986) *El nacionalismo y la II República en el País Vasco*. Madrid: Centro de Investigaciones Sociológicas.

Granja Sainz, José Luis de la (1987) 'El Gobierno Vasco', *Historia 16. La Guerra Civil*, Extra 12, pp. 70–77.

Granja Sainz, José Luis de la (1990) *República y Guerra Civil en Euskadi. Del Pacto de San Sebastián al de Santoña*. Oñate: IVAP.

Granja Sainz, José Luis de la (1992) 'El nacionalismo vasco: de la literatura histórica a la historiografía', *Historia Contemporánea*, No. 7, pp. 209–236.

Granja Sainz, José Luis de la (1995) *El nacionalismo vasco: un siglo de historia*. Bilbao: Tecnos.

Granja Sainz, José Luis de la, Beramendi, Justo, and Anguera, Pere (2001) *La España de los nacionalismos y las autonomías*. Madrid: Editorial Síntesis.

Guerin, Daniel and Pelletier, Rejean (2000), 'Cultural Nationalism and Political Tolerance in Advanced Industrial Societies: The Basque Country and Catalonia', *Nationalism & Ethnic Politics*, Vol. 6, No. 4, pp. 1–22

Guibernau, Montserrat (1999) *Nations without States: Political Communities in a Global Age*. Malden, MA: Blackwell.

Guibernau, Montserrat (2000), 'Nationalism and Intellectuals in Nations without States: The Catalan Case', *Political Studies*, Vol. 48, No. 5, pp. 989–1005.

Guibernau, Montserrat (2006) 'Nations without States in the EU: The Catalan Case', McGarry, John and Keating, Michael, *European Integration and the Nationalities Question*, Abingdon & New York: Routledge, pp. 216–224.

Guibernau, Monterrat and Hutchinson, John (eds.) (2001) *Understanding Nationalism*. Cambridge: Polity.

Gunther, Richard (1992) 'Spain, the Very Model of Modern Elite Settlement', Higley, John and Gunther, Richard (eds.), *Latin America and Southern Europe*. Cambridge: Cambridge University Press, pp. 38–80.

Gunther, Richard, Montero, José Ramón, and Joan Botella (2004) *Democracy in Modern Spain*. New Haven & London: Yale University Press.

Gurr, Ted Robert (1970) *Why Men Rebel?* Princeton, NJ: Princeton University Press.

Gurr, Ted R. (1976) 'Violent Nations, and Others', *Journal of Conflict Resolution*, Vol. 20, No. 1, pp. 79–110.

Gurr, Ted R. (1990) 'Terrorism in Democracies: Its Social and Political Bases', Reich, Walter (ed.) *Origins of Terrorism: Psychologies, Ideologies, Theologies, States of Mind*. Cambridge: Cambridge University Press, pp. 86–102.

Gurruchaga, Carmen (2001) *Los Jefes de ETA*. Madrid: La Esfera de los Libros.

Gurruchaga, Carmen and San Sebastián, Isabel (2000) *El árbol y las nueces. La relación secreta entre ETA y PNV*. Madrid: Ediciones Temas de Hoy, S.A.

Gurrutxaga, Ander (1985) *El código nacionalista vasco durante el franquismo*. Barcelona: Ed. Anthropos.

Gurrutxaga, Ander (1990) *La refundación del nacionalismo vasco*. Bilbao: Servico Editorial de la Universidad del País Vasco.

Gurrutxaga, Ander (1997) *Del PNV a ETA: la transformación del nacionalismo vasco*. Donostia: R&B Ediciones.

Hamilton, Carrie (1999) *The Gender Politics of ETA and Radical Basque Nationalism, 1959–1982*, unpublished thesis, University of London.

Hardin, Russell (1995) 'Self Interest, Group Identification', Comaroff, John L. and Stern, Paul C. (eds.) *Perspectives on Nationalism and War*. Amsterdam: Gordon and Breach, pp. 15–45.

Hastings, Adrian (1997) *The Construction of Nationhood*. Cambridge: Cambridge University Press.

Hayes, Carlton Joseph Huntley (1960) *Nationalism: A Religion*. New York: Macmillan.

Hechter, Michael (1975) *Internal Colonialism: The Celtic Fringe in British National Development, 1536–1966*. Berkeley, CA: University of California Press.

Hechter, Michael (1995) 'Explaining Nationalist Violence', *Nations and Nationalism*, Vol. 1, No. 1, pp. 53–68.

Hechter, Michael (2000) *Containing Nationalism*. New York: Oxford University Press.

Heiberg, Marianne (1975) 'Insiders/Outsiders: Basque Nationalism', *Archives Européenes de Sociologie*, No. 16, pp. 169–193.

Heiberg, Marianne (1989) *The Making of the Basque Nation*. Cambridge: Cambridge University Press.

Heiberg, Marianne and Escudero, Manu (1977) 'Sabino de Arana: la lógica del nacionalismo vasco', *Materiales*, pp. 87–133.

Herranz de Rafael, Gonzalo (1998) 'An Empirical Survey of Social Structure and Nationalistic Identification in Spain in the 1990s', *Nations and Nationalism*, Vol. 4, No.1, pp. 35–59.

Herri Batasuna (1999) *Herri Batasuna. 20 Años de lucha por la libertad, 1978–1988*. Donostia-San Sebastián: Herri Batasuna.

Hesiod (1996) *Works and Days*. Berkeley: University of California Press.

Heywood, Paul (1995) *The Government and Politics of Spain*. Basingstoke: Macmillan.

Hobsbawm, Eric J. (1990) *Nations and Nationalism since 1780*. Cambridge: Cambridge University Press.

Hobsbawm, Eric J. and Ranger, Terence (eds.) (1984) *The Invention of Tradition*. Cambridge: Past and Present.

Hroch, Miroslav (2000) *Social Preconditions of National Revival in Europe. A Comparative Analysis of the Social Composition of Patriotic Groups among the Smaller European Nations*. New York: Columbia University Press.

Ibarra Pedro (1989) *La evolución estratégica de ETA: de la guerra revolucionaria (1963), a la negociación (1987)*. Donostia: Kriselu.

Ibarra, Pedro (2005) *Nacionalismo: Razón y Pasión*. Barcelona: Ariel.

Ibarra, Pedro and Ahedo, Igor (2004) 'The Political Systems of the Basque Country: Is a Non-Polarized Scenario Possible in the Future', *Nationalism and Ethnic Politics*, Vol. 10, pp. 355–386.

Ignatieff, Michael (1997) *The Warrior's Honor. Ethnic War and the Modern Conscience*. New York: Metropolitan Books.

Irvin, Cynthia L. (1999) *Militant Nationalism: Between Movement and Party in Ireland and the Basque Country*. Minneapolis: University of Minnesota Press.

Iturralde, Juan de (1978) *La guerra de Franco, los vascos y la iglesia*. San Sebastián: Publicaciones Clero Vasco. 2 vols.

Iztueta, Paulo (1981) *Sociología del fenómeno contestatario del clero vasco: 1940–1975*. Zarautz: Elkar.

Jacobson, Stephen and Moreno Luzón, Javier (2000) 'The Political System of the Restoration, 1875–1914: Political and Social Elites', Alvarez Junco, José and Shubert, Adrian (eds.) *Spanish History Since 1808*. London: Arnold, pp. 94–109.

Jaime Jiménez, Oscar (2002) *Policía, terrorismo y cambio político en España, 1976–1996*. Valencia: Tirante Lo Blanch & Universidad de Burgos.

Jáuregui Bereciartu, Gurutz (1981) *Ideología y estrategia política de ETA. Análisis de su evolución entre 1959 y 1968*. Madrid: Siglo XXI.

Jáuregui Bereciartu, Gurutz (2000) 'ETA: Orígenes y Evolución Ideológica y Política', Elorza, Antonio (ed.) *La Historia de ETA*. Madrid: Temas de Hoy, pp. 171–274.

Jáuregui Bereciartu, Gurutz (2006) 'Basque Nationalism. Sovereignty, Independence and European Integration', McGarry, John and Keating, Michael, *European Integration and the Nationalities Question*, Abingdon & New York: Routledge, pp. 239–257.

Jemein y Lambarri, Ceferino de (1935) *Biografía de Arana-Goiri'tar Sabin*. Bilbao: Editorial Vasca.

Jiménez de Aberásturi, Juan Carlos (1999) *De la derrota a la esperanza: políticas vascas durante la segunda guerra mundial (1937–1947)*. Oñati: IVAP.

Jiménez de Aberasturi, Juan Carlos and San Sebastián, Koldo (1991) *La huelga general del 1º de mayo de 1947*. Donostia: Eusko Ikaskuntza.

Juaristi, Jon (1984–1985) 'Joseph-Augustín Chaho: las raíces antiliberales del nacionalismo vasco', *Cuadernos de Alzate*, No. 1, pp. 72–77.

Juaristi, Jon (1987) *El linaje de Aitor. La invención de la tradición vasca*. Madrid: Taurus.

Juaristi, Jon (1989) 'Las fuentes ocultas del romanticismo vasco', *Cuadernos de Alzate*, No. 7, pp. 86–103.

Juaristi, Jon (1992) *Vestigios de Babel. Para una arqueología de los nacionalismos españoles*. Madrid: Siglo Veintiuno Editores, S.A.

Juaristi, Jon. (1994) 'Los mitos de origen en la génesis de las identidades nacionales. La batalla de Arrigorriaga y el surgimiento del particularismo vasco (ss. XIV–XVI)', *Studia Historica-Historia Contemporánea*, Vol. 12, pp. 191–228.

Juaristi, Jon (1997) *El Bucle Melancólico*. Madrid: Espasa.

Juaristi, Jon (2002) *La Tribu Atribulada. El Nacionalismo Vasco Explicado a mi Padre*. Madrid: Espasa.

Kaldor, Mary (1999) *New and Old Wars: Organized Violence in a Global Era*. Cambridge: Polity Press.

Kaldor, Mary and Muro, Diego (2003) 'Religious and Nationalist Militant Groups' Anheier, Helmut, Glasius, Marlies and Kaldor, Mary (eds.) *Global Civil Society Yearbook 2003*. Oxford: Oxford University Press, pp. 151–184.

Kaldor, Mary and Vashee, Basker (eds.) (1997) *Restructuring the Global Military Sector. Volume1. New Wars*. London: Pinter.

Kamen, Henry (1978) 'The Decline of Spain—A Historical Myth?', *Past and Present*, Vol. 81, No. 1, pp. 24–81.

Kamen, Henry (1980) *Spain in the Later Seventeenth Century, 1665–1700*. London: Longman.

Kamen, Henry (1983) *Spain 1469–1714. A Society of Conflict*. London: Longman.

Kamen, Henry (2001) *Phillip V of Spain. The King who Reigned Twice*. New Haven & London: Yale University Press.

Keane, John (1996) *Reflections on Violence*. London: Verso.

Kedourie, Elie (1960) *Nationalism*. Oxford: Blackwell.

Kedourie, Elie (ed.) (1971) *Nationalism in Asia and Africa*. London: Weidenfeld and Nicolson.

Krutwig, Federico (1973) *Vasconia. Estudio Dialéctico de una Nacionalidad*. Buenos Aires: Ediciones Norbati. [Published under the pseudonym Fernando Sarrailh de Ilhartza].

Kunbeltz, K de (ed.) (1975) *Hacia una estrategia revolucionaria vasca*. Ciboure: Editions Hordago.

Kurlansky, Mark (1999) *The Basque History of the World*. London: Jonathan Cape.

Laitin, David D. (1995) 'National Revivals and Violence', *Archives Européenes de Sociologie*, No. 36, pp. 3–43.

Larramendi, Manuel de (1882) *Corografía o descripción general de la muy noble y muy leal provincia de Guipúzcoa*. Barcelona: Imprenta de la Viuda e Hijos de J. Subirana.

Larramendi, Manuel de (1983) *Sobre los Fueros de Guipúzcoa. Conferencias curiosas, políticas, legales y morales sobre los fueros de la M.N. y M.L. provincia de Guipuzcoa*. Donostia: Argitalpen eta Publikapenen Gipuzkoar Erakundea.

Laurenzano, Marco (2000) *ETA: il nazionalismo radicale basco, 1973–1980*. Roma: Semar.

Legarreta, Dorothy (1984) *The Guernica Generation: Basque Refugee Children of the Spanish Civil War*. Reno: University of Nevada.

Legarreta, Dorothy (1985) 'Basque Refugee Children as Expatriates: Political Catalysts in Europe and America', Douglass, William A. (ed.) *Basque Politics: A Case Study in Ethnic Nationalism*. Reno, Nevada: Associated Faculty Press and Basque Studies Program, pp. 175–200.

Letamendía Belzunce, Francisco (Ortzi) (1975) *Historia de Euskadi: el nacionalismo vasco y ETA*. París-Barcelona: Ruedo Ibérico.

Letamendía Belzunce, Francisco (Ortzi) (1994) *Historia del nacionalismo vasco y de ETA*. San Sebastián: R & B Ediciones. 3 vols.

Levin, Henry (1970) *The Myth of the Golden Age in the Renaissance*. London: Faber.

Levinger, Matthew and Franklin Lytle, Paula (2001) 'Myth and mobilization: the triadic structure of nationalist rhetoric', *Nations and Nationalism*, Vol. 7, No. 2, pp. 175–194.

Lewis, Bernard (1975) *History Remembered, Recovered, Invented*. Princeton, NJ: Princeton University Press.

Linz, Juan José (1973) 'Early State-Building and Late Peripheral Nationalisms against the State: The Case of Spain', Eisenstadt, Samuel N., and Rokkan, Stein (eds.) *Building States and Nations. Analyses by Region*. London: Sage, pp. 32–116.

Linz, Juan José (1986) *Conflicto en Euskadi*. Madrid: Editorial Espasa-Calpe, S.A.

Linz, Juan José (1992) 'La transición a la democracia en España en perspectiva comparada', Cotarelo, Ramón (ed.) *Transición Política y Consolidación Democrática. España* (1975–1986). Madrid: CIS, pp. 431–457.

Linz, Juan José and Stepan, Alfred (1996) *Problems of Democratic Transition and Consolidation: Southern Europe, South America, and Post-Communist Europe*. Baltimore: Johns Hopkins University Press.

Llera, Francisco and Shabad, Goldie (1995) 'Political Violence in a Democratic State: Basque Terrorism in Spain', Crenshaw, Martha C. (ed.) *Terrorism in Context: Comparative Case Studies*. University Park: Pennsylvania State University Press, pp. 410–472.

Llera Mata, Francisco, Mata, José M. and Irvin, Cynthia L. (1993) 'ETA: From Secret Army to Social Movement—The Post-Franco Schism of the Basque Nationalist Movement', *Terrorism and Political Violence,* Vol. 5, No. 3, pp. 106–134.

Llera Ramo, Francisco José (1985) *Postfranquismo y fuerzas políticas en Euskadi: sociología electoral del País Vasco*. Bilbao: Universidad del País Vasco.

Llera Ramo, Francisco José (1993) *The Construction of the Basque Polarized Pluralism*, Working Papers 64/93. Barcelona: ICPS.

Llobera, Josep R. (1994) *The God of Modernity: The Development of Nationalism in Western Europe*. Oxford: Providence.

Llobera, Josep R. (1996) *The Role of Historical Memory in (Ethno) Nation-Building*. London: Goldsmiths.

Lluch, Ernest (1995) 'Els orígens económics de la violència basca', *L'Avenç*, No. 191, pp. 30–55.

López Adán, Emilio (Beltza) (1977) *El nacionalismo vasco en el exilio 1937–1960*. San Sebastián: Editorial Txertoa.

López Adán, Emilio (Beltza) (1978) *Del carlismo al nacionalismo burgés*. San Sebastián: Editorial Txertoa.

Lorenzo Espinosa, José Maria (1988) *Rebelión en la Ría. Vizcaya 1947: obreros, empresarios y falangistas*. Bilbao: Universidad de Deusto.

Malinowski, Bronislaw (1963) *Sex, Culture, and Myth*. London: Rupert Hart-Davis.

MacClancy, Jeremy (1988) 'The Culture of Radical Basque Nationalism', *Anthropology Today*, Vol. 4, No. 5, pp. 17–19.

MacClancy, Jeremy (1993) 'Biological Basques, Sociologically Speaking', Chapman, Malcolm (ed.) *Social and Biological Aspects of Ethnicity*. Oxford: Oxford University Press, pp. 92–127.

MacClancy, Jeremy (1996) 'Nationalism at Play: The Basques of Vizcaya and Athletic Bilbao', MacClancy, Jeremy (ed.) *Sport, Identity and Ethnicity*. Oxford: Berg, pp. 181–199.

MacClancy, Jeremy (2000) *The Decline of Carlism*. Reno & Las Vegas: University of Nevada Press.

Machiavelli, Niccolò (1988) *The Prince*, ed. by Quentin Skinner and Russell Price. Cambridge: Cambridge University Press.

Magone, José M. (2004) *Contemporary Spanish Politics*. London: Routledge.

Majuelo, Emilio (2000) *Historia del sindicato LAB, Langile Abertzaleen Batzordeak 1975–2000*. Tafalla: Txalaparta.

Mañé y Flaquer, Juan (1878–1880) *El Oasis. Viaje al país de los fueros*. Barcelona: Imprenta de Jaime Jesús Roviralta (3 vol.).

Mann, Michael (1986) *The Sources of Social Power*. Cambridge: Cambridge University Press.

Mann, Michael (1995) 'A Political Theory of Nationalism and Its Excesses', Periwal, Sukumar (ed.) *Notions of Nationalism*. Budapest: Central European University Press, pp. 44–64.

Mansvelt Beck, Jan (2005) *Territory and Terror. Conflicting Nationalisms in the Basque Country*. Abingdon & New York: Routledge.

Maravall, José María (1982) *The Transition to Democracy in Spain*. London: Croom Hell Ltd.

Mata López, José Manuel (1993) *El Nacionalismo Vasco Radical. Discurso, organización y expresiones*. Bilbao: Servicio Editorial Universidad del País Vasco.

Mata López, José Manuel (2005) 'Terrorism and Nationalist Conflict. The Weakness of Democracy in the Basque Country', in Balfour, Sebastian (ed.) *The Politics of Contemporary Spain*. Abingdon: Routledge, pp. 81–105.

Mees, Ludger (2003) *Nationalism, Violence and Democracy. The Basque Clash of Identities*. Houndmills, UK: Palgrave Macmillan.

Merkl, Peter H. (1986) *Political Violence and Terror. Motifs and Motivations*. Berkeley: University of California Press.

Merry del Val, Alfonso (1939) *Spanish Basques and Separatism*. London: Burns, Oates & Washbourne.

Miralles, Ricardo (1992) 'Historiografía del movimiento obrero en el País Vasco: 1880–1936', *Historia Contemporánea*, No. 7, pp. 237–255.

Molina, Fernando (2005) *La Tierra del Martirio Español*. Madrid: Centro de Estudios Políticos y Constitucionales.

Molinero, Carme and Ysàs, Pere (1992) *El Règim Franquista. Feixisme, modernització i consens*. Vic: Eumo.

Monreal, Gregorio (1985) 'Annotations Regarding Basque Traditional Political Thought in the Sixteenth Century', Douglass, William A. (ed.) *Basque Politics: A Case Study in Ethnic Nationalism*. Basque Studies Program Occasional Papers Series, No. 2. Reno, NV: Basque Studies Program, pp. 19–49.

Montero, Manuel (1998) 'La transición y la autonomía vasca', Ugarte, Javier (ed.) *La transición en el País Vasco y España. Historia y Memoria*. Bilbao: Universidad del País Vasco, pp. 93–120.

Monzón Olaso, Telésforo (1995) *Últimos Artículos*. Egin: Biblioteca.

Moral, Félix (1998) *Identidad regional y nacionalismo en el estado de las autonomías: informe (resultado del estudio 2228)*. Madrid: Centro de Investigaciones Sociológicas.

Morán Blanco, Sagrario (1997) *ETA entre España y Francia*. Madrid: Editorial Complutense.

Moreno, Luis (2001) *The Federalization of Spain*. London: Frank Cass.

Mosse, George L. (1975) *The Nationalization of the Masses*. New York: Howard Fertig.

Mosse, George L. (1990) *Fallen Soldiers: Reshaping the Memory of the World Wars*. Oxford: Oxford University Press.

Mudde, Cas (2004) 'Conclusion: Defending Democracy and the Extreme Right', Eatwell, Roger and Mudde, Cas (eds.), *Western Democracies and the New Extreme Right Challenge*. London and New York: Routledge, pp. 193–212.

Muro, Diego (2002), 'The Logic of Violence', *Politics*, Vol. 22, No. 2, 109–117.

Muro, Diego (2005), 'Nationalism and Nostalgia: The Case of Radical Basque Nationalism', *Nations and Nationalism*, Vol. 11, No 4, pp. 571–589.

Muro, Diego and Quiroga, Alejandro (2004) 'Building the Spanish Nation: The Centre-Periphery Dialectic', *Studies in Ethnicity and Nationalism*, Vol. 4, No. 2, pp.18–37.

Muro, Diego and Quiroga, Alejandro (2005) 'Spanish Nationalism: Ethnic or Civic?, *Ethnicities*, Vol. 5, No. 1, pp. 9–29.

Nairn, Tom (1977) *The Break-up of Britain: Crisis and Neo-Nationalism*. London: New Left Books.

Newman, Saul and Piroth, Scott (1996) 'Terror and Tolerance: The Use of Ballots, Bombs and Bullets by Ethnoregional Movements in Advanced Industrial Democracies', *Nationalism and Ethnic Politics*, Vol. 2, No. 3, pp. 381–414.

Noelle-Neumann, Elisabeth (1980) *The Spiral of Silence. Public Opinion—Our Social Skin*. Chicago: University of Chicago Press.

Nuñez, Clara Eugenia (1992) *La fuente de la riqueza. Educación y desarrollo económico en la España contemporánea*. Madrid: Alianza.

Nuñez Astrain, Luis (1980) *Euskadi Sur Electoral*. San Sebastián: Ediciones Vascas.

Nuñez Astrain, Luis (1997) *The Basques. Their Struggle for Independence*. Caerdydd/Cardiff: Welsh Academic Press.

Núñez Seixas, Xose-Manoel (1992a) 'Historical Research on Regionalism and Peripheral Nationalism in Spain: A Reappraisal', *EUI Working Paper in European Cultural Studies*, No. 92/6.

Núñez Seixas, Xose-Manoel (1992b) 'El mito de Irlanda. La influencia del nacionalismo irlandés en los nacionalismos gallego y vasco (1880–1936)', *Historia 16*, Vol. 16, No. 199, pp. 32–44.

Núñez Seixas, Xose-Manoel (1992c) 'El mito del nacionalismo irlandés y su influencia en los nacionalismos gallego, vasco y catalan (1880–1936)', *Spagna Contemporánea*, No. 2, pp. 25–58.

Núñez Seixas, Xose-Manoel (1998) 'El espejo irlandés y sus reflejos ibéricos', *Cuadernos de Alzate*, No. 18, pp. 169–190.

Nuñez-Seixas, Xose-Manoel (2001) 'The Region as Essence of the Fatherland: Regionalist Variants of Spanish Nationalism (1840–1936)', *European History Quarterly*, Vol. 31, No. 4, pp. 483–518.

Nuñez-Seixas, Xose-Manoel (2005) 'Nations in Arms against the Invader: On Nationalist Discourses during the Spanish Civil War', Ealham, Chris and Richard, Michael (eds.) *The Splintering of Spain. Cultural History and the Spanish Civil War, 1936–1939*. Cambridge: Cambridge University Press, pp. 45–67.

Oiarzabal, Pedro (2002) 'Kale Borroka: Discursos de los Medios de Comunicación', *Hermes*, No. 7, pp. 34–46.

Olavarría Agra, Juan (1997) 'El Bucle Melancólico. Historias de Nacionalistas', *Cuadernos de Alzate*, No. 17, December, pp. 193–202.

Olson, Mancur (1965) *The Logic of Collective Action: Public Goods and the Theory of Groups*. Harvard: Harvard University Press.

Ortega y Gasset, José (1961) 'The Pride of the Basques', *The Atlantic Monthly*, Vol. 207, No. 1, pp. 113–116.

Ortega y Gasset, José (1999) *España Invertebrada. Bosquejos de Algunos Pensamientos Históricos*. Cáceres: Servicio de Publicaciones de la Universidad de Extremadura.

Özkirimli, Umut (2000) *Theories of Nationalism. A Critical Introduction*. Basingstoke: Palgrave.

Pablo, Santiago de (1985) *Álava y la autonomía vasca durante la Segunda República*. Vitoria: Diputación Foral de Alava, Departamento de Publicaciones.

Pacheco López, Iñigo (2004) *11-M. La respuesta*. Madrid: Record, S.A.

País, El. Equipo de Investigación (1983) *Golpe mortal: asesinato de Carrero y agonía del franquismo*. Madrid: Promotora de Informaciones.

Palomares, Cristina (2003) *The Quest for Survival after Franco. Moderate Francoism and the Slow Journey to the Polls, 1964–1977*. Brighton: Sussex Academic Press.

Parellada de Cardellac, Juan (1976) *El orígen de los vascos*. Madrid: Plaza y Janés.

Payne, Stanley G. (1975) *Basque Nationalism*. Reno: University of Nevada.

Payne, Stanley G. (1977) 'Carlism—'Basque' or 'Spanish' Traditionalism', Douglass, William A. (ed.) *Anglo-American Contributions to Basque Studies. Essays in Honor of Jon Bilbao*. Reno: University of Nevada Press, pp. 119–126.

Payne, Stanley G. (2000) 'Catalan and Basque Nationalism: Contrasting Patterns', Ben-Ami, Shlomo, Yoav Peled, and Spektorowski, Alberto (eds.) *Ethnic Challenges to the Modern Nation State*, New York: St. Martin's Press, pp. 95–107.

Peces-Barba Martínez, Gregorio (2000) 'The Constitutional Consensus and the Basque Challenge', Threlfall, Monica (ed.) *Consensus Politics in Spain. Insider Perspectives*. Oxford: Intellect, pp. 61–76.

Perales, Iosu (1998) 'Conocer HB', *El Viejo Topo*, No. 117, pp. 21–31.

Pérez-Agote, Alfonso (1984) *La reproducción del nacionalismo. El caso vasco*. Madrid: CIS-Siglo XXI.

Pérez-Agote, Alfonso (1987) *El nacionalismo vasco a la salida del franquismo*. Madrid: CIS-Siglo XXI.

Pérez-Agote, Alfonso (2006) *The Social Roots of Basque Nationalism*. Reno: University of Nevada Press.

Pérez-Nievas Montiel, Santiago (2002) *Modelo de partido y cambio político. El partido nacionalista vasco en el proceso de transición y consolidación democrática en el País Vasco*. Madrid: CEACS-Instituto Juan March de Estudios e Investigaciones.

Perkins, Mary Anne (1999) *Nation and Word, 1770–1850. Religious and Metaphysical Language in European National Consciousness*. Aldershot: Ashgate.

Perrino, Fidel (1954) *Bibliografía de la Cruzada Española (1936–39)*. Madrid: Servicio de Publicaciones del Ministerio de Educación Nacional.

Piñuel, José Luis (1986) *El terrorismo en la transición española (1972–1982)*. Madrid: Editorial Fundamentos.

PNV (1978) *El Partido Nacionalista Vasco ante la Constitución. Historia y alcance de unas negociaciones*. Zarauz: Itxaropena S.A.

Poliakov, Léon (1971) *Le Mythe Aryen. Essai sur les sources du racisme et des nationalismes*. Paris: Calmann-Lévy.

Popper, Karl R. (1963) 'Utopia and Violence', Popper, Karl R., *Conjectures and Refutations*. New York: Harper and Row, pp. 355–363.

Porter, Roy (ed.) (1988) *Romanticism in National Context*. Cambridge: Cambridge University Press.

Powell, Charles (1996) *Juan Carlos of Spain: Self-Made Monarch*. Basingstoke: Macmillan.

Powell, Charles (2001) *España en democracia, 1975–2000. Las claves de la profunda transformación de España*. Barcelona: Plaza & Janés Editores.

Pozas, Alberto (1992) *Las conversaciones secretas Gobierno-ETA*. Barcelona: Ediciones B.

Pradera, Javier (1997) 'Sobre el Bucle Melancólico de Jon Juaristi', *Cuadernos de Alzate*, No. 17, December, pp. 187–191.

Preston, Paul (1986) *The Triumph of Democracy in Spain*. London: Methuen.

Preston, Paul (1994) *Franco. A Biography*. London: Harper-Collins.

Preston, Paul (1996) *A Concise History of the Spanish Civil War*. London: Fontana.

Puelles Benítez, Manuel de (1991) *Educación e ideología en la España contemporánea*. Madrid: Editorial Labor, S.A.

Putnam, Robert D. (1988) 'Diplomacy and Domestic Politics: The Logic of Two-Level Games', *International Organization*, Vol. 42, No. 3, pp. 427–460.

Quiroga, Alejandro (2004) *Making Spaniards. National Catholicism and the Nationalisation of the Masses during the Dictatorship of Primo de Rivera (1923–1930)*. Unpublished thesis, London School of Economics and Political Science.

Raento, Paulina and Watson, Cameron J. (2000) 'Gernika, Guernica, Guernica? Contested Meanings of a Basque Place', *Political Geography*, No. 19, pp. 707–736.

Ramos, Cipriano (1985) 'El nacionalismo vasco durante la dictadura de Primo de Rivera', *Letras de Deusto*, No. 31, January–April, pp. 137–167.

Ramos, Cipriano (1988) *El nacionalismo vasco durante la dictadura de Primo de Rivera y la II Republica Española*. Universidad del País Vasco (UPV).

Real Cuesta, Javier (1991) *Partidos, elecciones y bloques de poder en el País Vasco, 1876–1923*. Bilbao: Universidad de Deusto.

Real Cuesta, Javier (1985) *El carlismo vasco, 1876–1900*. Madrid: Siglo XXI de España Editores.

Reboredo Olivenza, José Daniel (1995) *El primer nacionalismo vasco o la Arcadia feliz*. Vitoria-Gasteiz.

Reich, Walter (1990) *Origins of Terrorism: Psychologies, Ideologies, Theologies, States of Mind*. Cambridge: Cambridge University Press/Woodrow Wilson International Center for Scholars.

Reig Tapia, Alberto (1987) 'Guernica como Simbolo', Garitaonandia, Carmelo and Granja, José Luis de la (eds.) *La Guerra Civil en el País Vasco. 50 años después*. Leioa: Servicio Editorial Universidad del País Vasco, pp. 123–155.

Rekondo, José Antonio (1998) *Bietan jarrai. Guerra y paz en las calles de Euskadi*. Arañadle.

Renan, Ernest (1996) 'What Is a Nation?', Bhabha, Homi K. (ed.) *Nation and Narration*. London: Routledge, pp. 8av22.

Reynolds, Susan (1984) *Kingdoms and Communities in Western Europe, 900–1300*. Oxford: Clarendon Press.

Richards, Michael A. (1998) *A Time of Silence: Civil War and the Culture of Repression in Franco's Spain*. Cambridge: Cambridge University Press.

Rincón, Luciano (1985) *ETA (1974–1984)*. Barcelona: Plaza & Janés Editores, S.A.

Riquer i Permanyer, Borja de (1990) 'Sobre el lugar de los nacionalismos-regionalismos en la historia contemporánea española', *Historia Social*, No. 7, pp. 105–126.

Rivera, Antonio (1998) 'La transición en el País Vasco: un caso particular', Ugarte, Javier, *La transición en el País Vasco y España. Historia y Memoria.* Bilbao: Servicio Editorial de la Universidad del País Vasco, pp. 79–91.

Roca Junyent, Miquel (2000) 'To Reform or Not to Reform the Constitution? A Catalan View', Threlfall, Monica (ed.) *Consensus Politics in Spain. Insider Perspectives.* Oxford: Intellect, pp. 77–88.

Roca, José M. (2002) 'Un conflicto español y tres conflictos vascos', *El Viejo Topo*, No. 171, pp. 25–30.

Rodríguez Ranz, José Antonio (2001) 'El Péndulo Patriótico', *Hermes*, April, 1, pp. 136–141.

Romero Salvadó, Francisco J. (1996) 'The Failure of the Liberal Project of the Spanish Nation-State, 1909–1923', in Smith, Clare & Smith, Angel, *Nationalism and the Nation in the Iberian Peninsula*, Washington, D.C. & Oxford: Berg, pp. 119–132.

Romero Salvadó, Francisco J. (1999) *Twentieth-Century Spain. Politics and Society in Spain, 1898–1998.* Houndmills & New York: Palgrave.

Rubiralta i Casas, Fermí (1997) *El nuevo nacionalismo radical: los casos gallego, catalán y vasco (1959–1973).* Donostia: Tercera Prensa-Hirugarren Prentsa.

Ruiz Rico, Juan José (1977) *El papel político de la Iglesia Católica en la España de Franco.* Madrid: Editorial Tecnos.

Sáez de la Fuente Aldama, Izaskun (2002) *El Movimiento de Liberación Nacional Vasco, una religión de sustitución.* Bilbao: Editorial Desclée de Brouwer.

Salaberri, Kepa (1971) *El proceso de Euskadi en Burgos. El sumarísimo 31/69.* Paris: Ruedo ibérico.

Salas Larrazábal, Ramon (1977) *Pérdidas de la guerra.* Barcelona: Planeta.

Sánchez-Cuenca, Ignacio (2001) *ETA contra el Estado. Las estrategias del terrorismo.* Barcelona: Tusquets Editores.

Sánchez-Cuenca, Ignacio (2004) 'Terrorism as War of Attrition: ETA and the IRA', *Instituto Juan March Estudio/Working Paper*2004/204. http://www.march.es/ceacs/publicaciones/publicaciones.asp (accessed 15 December 2006).

Sánchez Erauskin, Javier (1994) *Por Dios hacia el imperio. Nacionalcatolicismo en las Vascongadas del primer Franquismo 1936-1945.* Donostia-San Sebastián: R&B Ediciones.

Santamaría, Antonio (2002) 'La estrategia de la tensión. Euskadi 1994–2002', *El Viejo Topo*, No. 172, pp. 35–50.

Sartori, Giovanni (1991) 'Comparing and Miscomparing', *Journal of Theoretical Politics*, Vol. 3, pp. 243–257.

Schubert, Adrian (2003) *A Social History of Modern Spain.* London: Routledge.

Schwartz, David C (1972) 'Political Alienation: The Psychology of Revolution's First Stage', Ivo K. Feierabend and R.L. Feirabend (eds.) *Anger, Violence and Politics.* Englewood Cliffs, NJ: Prentice-Hall, pp. 58–66.

Scott, James Cameron (1976) *The Moral Economy of the Peasant.* New Haven & London: Yale University Press.

Seton-Watson, Hugh (1977) *Nations and States.* London: Methuen.

Sironneau, Jean-Pierre (1982) *Sécularisation et religions politiques.* La Haye: Mouton.

Smith, Angel and Davila Cox, Emma (eds.) (1898) *The Crisis of 1898: Colonial Redistribution and Nationalist Mobilization.* New York: St. Martin's Press.

Smith, Anthony D. (1976) 'Neo-Classicist and Romantic Elements in the Emergence of Nationalist Conceptions', Smith, Anthony D. (ed.) *Nationalist Movements.* London: Macmillan, pp. 74–86.

Smith, Anthony D. (1981) 'War and Ethnicity: The Role of Warfare in the Formation, Self-Images, and Cohesion of Ethnic Communities', *Ethnic and Racial Studies*, Vol. 4, No. 4, pp. 375–397.

Smith, Anthony D. (1986) *The Ethnic Origin of Nations*. Oxford: Blackwell Publishers.

Smith, Anthony D. (1991) *National Identity*. Harmondsworth: Penguin.

Smith, Anthony D. (1997) 'The Golden Age and National Renewal', Hosking, Geoffrey and Schopflin, George (eds.) *Myths and Nationhood*. London: Macmillan, pp. 36–39.

Smith, Anthony D. (1998) *Nationalism and Modernism*. London & New York: Routledge.

Smith, Anthony D. (1999) *Myths and Memories of the Nation*. New York: Oxford University Press.

Smith, Anthony D. (2001a) 'The 'Sacred' Dimension of Nationalism', *Millennium*, Vol. 29, No. 3, pp. 791–814.

Smith, Anthony D. (2001b) *Nationalism*. Cambridge: Polity Press.

Smith, Anthony D. (2003) *Chosen Peoples: Sacred Sources of National Identity*. Oxford: Oxford University Press.

Solazábal, Juan José (1975) *El primer nacionalismo vasco. Industrialismo y conciencia nacional*. Madrid: Túcar Ediciones.

Southworth, Herbert Rutledge (1963) *El mito de la cruzada de Franco: crítica bibliográfica*. Paris: Ruedo Ibérico.

Southworth, Herbert Rutledge (1977) *Guernica! A Study of Journalism, Diplomacy, Propaganda, and History*. Berkeley: University of California.

Stern, Paul C. (1995) 'Why do People Sacrifice for Their Nations?' *Political Psychology*, Vol. 16, No. 2, June, pp. 217–235.

Sullivan, John (1988) *ETA and Basque Nationalism: The Struggle for Euskadi, 1890–1986*. London: Routledge.

Tellechea Idígoras, J. Ignacio (ed.) (1992) *M. Larramendi. Hirugarren Mendeurrena*. Andoain.

Tilly, Charles (1972) 'Collective Violence in European Perspective', Feierabend, Ivo K., Feierabend, Rosalind L, Gurr, Robert, Ted (eds.), *Anger, Violence and Politics: Theories and Research.*: Englewood Cliffs NJ: Prentice Hall.

Totoricagüena, Gloria (2004) *Identity, Culture, and Politics in the Basque Diaspora*. Reno, Las Vegas: University of Nevada Press.

Tremlett, Giles (2006) *Ghosts of Spain: Travels through a Country's Hidden Past*. London: Faber and Faber.

Tuñón de Lara, Manuel (1987) 'Guerra Civil española y guerra en el País vasco', Garitaonandia, Carmelo and Granja, José Luis de la (eds.) *La Guerra Civil en el País Vasco. 50 años después*. Leioa: Servicio Editorial Universidad del País Vasco, pp. 21–41.

Turano, Leslie (2003) 'Spain: Banning Political Parties as a Response to Basque Terrorism', *International Journal of Constitutional Law*, Vol. 1, No. 4, pp. 730–740.

Tusell, Javier, Martín, José-Luis, and Martínez Shaw, Carlos (1998) *Historia de España*. Madrid: Taurus.

Ugalde Solano, Mercedes (1993) *Mujeres y nacionalismo vasco. Génesis y desarrollo de Emakume Abertzale Batza (1906–1936)*. Bilbao: Servicio Editorial Universidad del País Vasco.

Ugarte, Javier (ed.) (1998) *La Transición en el País Vasco y España. Historia y Memoria*. Bilbao: Universidad del País Vasco.

Unanue Letamendi, José Miguel (2002) *La relaciones laborales en Euskal Herria. Apuntes históricos y análisis de su evolución desde la transición política*. Bilbao: Fundación Manu Robles-Aranguiz Institutua.

Unzueta, Patxo (1987) *Sociedad Vasca y Política Nacionalista*. Madrid: El País.

Unzueta, Patxo (1988) *Los Nietos de la Ira. Nacionalismo y violencia en el País Vasco*. Madrid: El País, S.A./Aguilar, S.A.

Unzueta, Patxo (1997) *El terrorismo de ETA y el problema vasco*. Barcelona: Destino.

Uriarte, Edurne (2001) 'La sociedad civil contra ETA', *Claves de Razón Práctica*, No. 111, pp. 77-82.

Vilallonga, José Luis de (1994) *The King: A Life of King Don Juan Carlos I of Spain*. London: Weidenfeld & Nicolson.

Vilar, Sergio (1984) *Historia del Anti-Franquismo, 1939–1975*. Barcelona: Plaza y Janés Editores, S.A., 1984.

Villa, Imanol (2004) *País Vasco: 1900*. Madrid: Sílex Ediciones.

Von Humboldt, Wilhelm (1998) *Los Vascos*. Donostia: Roger Editor.

Waldmann, Peter (1997) *Radicalismo Étnico. Análisis comparado de las causas y efectos en conflictos étnicos violentos*. Madrid: Akal.

Watson, Cameron James (1992) *Nationalism during the Dictatorship of Primo de Rivera, 1923—1930*. MA Dissertation. University of Nevada, Reno.

Watson, Cameron James (1996) *Sacred Earth, Symbolic Blood: A Cultural History of Basque Political Violence from Arana to ETA*. Unpublished thesis, University of Nevada, Reno.

Weber, Eugène (1979) *Peasants into Frenchmen: The Modernisation of Rural France, 1870-1914*. London: Chatto and Windus.

Weber, Max (1978) *Economy and Society: An Outline of Interpretative Sociology*. Berkeley: University of California Press. 2 vols.

Weber, Max (1991) *From Max Weber: Essays in Sociology*, ed. Gerth, H. H. and Wright Mills. London: Routledge.

Wieviorka, Michel (1993) *The Making of Terrorism*. Chicago: University of Chicago Press.

Wieviorka, Michel (1997) 'ETA and Basque Political Violence', Apter, David E. (ed.) *The Legitimization of Violence*. Basingstoke: Macmillan/UNRISD, pp. 292–349.

Woodworth, Paddy (2001) *Dirty War, Clean Hands. ETA, the GAL and Spanish Democracy*. Cork: Cork University Press.

Woodworth, Paddy (2005) 'Using Terror against Terrorists. The Spanish Experience', Balfour, Sebastian (ed.) *The Politics of Contemporary Spain*. Abingdon: Routledge, pp. 61–80.

Zabala, Angel (Kondaño) (1985) *Primeros años del nacionalismo*. Zarauz: Alderdi.

Zirakzadeh, Cyrus Ernesto (1991) *A Rebellious People: Basques, Protests and Politics*. Reno: University of Nevada Pres.

Zubillaga, Iñaki (1978) 'Notas sobre la actualidad del debate histórico en Euskadi', *Materiales Gaiak*, Sept.–Oct., No. 11, pp. 81–95.

Zulaika, Joseba (1988) *Basque Violence: Metaphor and Sacrament*. Reno: University of Nevada Press.

Zulaika, Joseba (1996) *Del Cromañon al Carnaval: Los vascos como museo antropológico*. Donostia: Erein.

NEWSPAPERS AND PERIODICALS

Aberri
L'Avui
The Economist
Egin
Euzkadi
Gara
Inside Spain (Real Instituto Elcano)
Jagi-Jagi
El Mundo
Newsweek
El País
Tierra Vasca

VIDEOS

BBC Correspondent (1998) *Coming in from the Cold.*
TVE (1993) *La Transición Española* (13 videos).

YEARBOOKS

Euskadi (Egin), 1987–1995.
Amnesty International Annual Report, 1961–2003.
Anuario El País, Madrid, 1982-2005.
Anuario Gara, 1999-2003

PRIMARY SOURCES

ASK

Manifiesto (1977)
Barne Agerkaria (1980)
Jo ta Ke (1981)
Jo ta ke. Estatutos de ASK (1984)

Audiencia Nacional

Audiencia Nacional. Juzgado Central de Instrucción no. 5, *Sumario 35/02 Y*, 26 August 2002.
Audiencia Nacional, Juzgado Central de Instrucción no. 5, *Sumario 33/2001-M Integración en organización terrorista*, 29-10-2002.

ETA

Zuzen, No. 1–43, 45–51, 62–64 and 66 (1980–1997)
Zutabe, No. 22, 31, 32, 35, 38, 40, 41, 42, 43, 45, 46, 47, 72 and 79 (1980–1999)
Barne Buletina, No. 1, 2, 7, 55, 56, 57 andy 59 (1990–1991)

Foreign and Commonwealth Office (FCO)

FCO 9/1450, *Activities and Trial of Basque nationalists*, Burgos, December 1970.

FO 371/60420, *Pleas by Basques and Catalans for Action against General Franco's Regime*, 1946.

HASI

Hertzale (up to 1979)
Barnekoa (up to 1978)
Eraiki (1980–1987)

Herri Batasuna

Euskal Herriko Batzarre Nazionala (1979)
Herri Batasuna, objetivos y reestructuración (1980)
Reestructuración (1981)
Herri Batasuna al Pueblo Vasco (1981)
Herri Batasuna al Pueblo Vasco (1983)
HB, Comité de Relaciones Exteriores: OTAN y penetración imperialista en Euskadi (1983)
Martxa eta Borroka (Euskadi alegre y combativa) (1985)
Bases para un Estatuto Nacional de Autonomía (1989)
Hausnartzen I. Cuadernos de Formación de Herri Batasuna: "La soberanía de Euskadi" (1988)
Hausnartzen II. Cuadernos de Formación de Herri Batasuna: "El Movimiento de Liberación Nacional Vasco 1959–1977" (1988)
Hausnartzen III. Cuadernos de Formación de Herri Batasuna: "Herri Batasuna en el contexto del MLNV 1977–1988" (1988)
Herri Batasuna (1988) Hausnartzen. Caracterización y Organización de Herri Batasuna,
Urrats Berri II. (Documento Definitivo). Hacia un proyecto común de los abertzales y de la izquierda (1992)
Oldartzen. 1er documento (definitivo) (1995)
Oldartzen. 2° documento (definitivo) (1995)
Eraikitzen, Euskal Herria, de Izquierdas y Abertzale, propuesta de acción política elaborada por Herri Batasuna con motivo de las elecciones al Parlamento Vasco en 1994.

Jarrai

Lehen Aldizkaria (1980)
Material sobre Premilitancia (1984)
Libros de Premilitancia (1986)
Libros de Premilitancia (1987)
Bases ideológicas de Ikasle Abertzeleak (1988)

KAS

Dossier KAS (1979)
KAS (1980)

KAS, propuesta para el debate (sobre HB) (1980)
Ponencia KAS Bloque Dirigente (1983)
Ponencias KAS Bloque Dirigente (1987)
Análisis de coyuntura (1987)
Análisis de coyuntura (1988)
KAS. Euskal Herria necesita la independencia. Enero 1994.
Alternativa Democratica (1995)

LAB

Tesis sobre LAB (1977)
I Congreso de LAB: Batasunerantz, Ponencias (1978)
II Congreso de LAB: Ponencias (1980)
III Congreso de LAB (1992)
IV Congreso del sindicato LAB (2000)
Revista Iraultzen (1977–1989)

Index